AF607847

BITTER LEGACY

In memory of those who died
in the Soviet Union
and in honor
of those who fought.

Bitter Legacy

Confronting the Holocaust in the USSR

Edited by Zvi Gitelman

INDIANA UNIVERSITY PRESS

Bloomington and Indianapolis

The paper used in this publication
meets the minimum requirements of American National Standard
for Information Sciences—Permanence of Paper
for Printed Library Materials,
ANSI Z39.48-1984.

Manufactured in the United States of America

Library of Congress Cataloging-in-Publication Data

Bitter legacy : confronting the Holocaust in the USSR / edited by Zvi Gitelman.
p. cm.
Includes index.
ISBN 0-253-33359-8 (cl : alk. paper)
1. Jews—Persecutions—Soviet Union. 2. Holocaust, Jewish (1939-1945)—Soviet Union. 3. Holocaust, Jewish (1939-1945)—Soviet Union—Historiography. 4. Jews—Soviet Union—History—1917- . 5. Soviet Union—History—German occupation, 1941-1945. 6. Soviet Union—Ethnic relations. 7. World War, 1939-1945—Collaborationists—Soviet Union. 8. Antisemitism—Soviet Union.
I. Gitelman, Zvi.
DS135.R92B54 1997
940.53'18'0947—dc21 97-25138

1 2 3 4 5 02 01 00 99 98 97

Contents

Preface

This volume describes and analyzes how the Holocaust was perpetrated in the USSR and how it was treated after the war in Soviet scholarly publications and popular literature. Political calculations determined the Soviet treatment of the Holocaust, though that treatment was by no means uniform. The Holocaust has not been fully and honestly confronted in many parts of the former Soviet Union because it raises painful unresolved issues. This book elucidates some of these issues, the consequences of the Holocaust, and how it has been represented in the USSR and in some of its successor states.

Among the highly sensitive and potentially explosive issues emanating from the Holocaust is the collaboration of local peoples with the Nazis in the murder of their Jewish neighbors. Spokesmen for those nations have not fully acknowledged the role of some of their countrymen in the systematic mass murders that constituted the Holocaust. Some spokesmen of those peoples continue to hold the Jews responsible for the Soviet conquest of their homelands and for the rise of a Communist state in the former Soviet Union. The killing of Jews in World War II is sometimes justified by the supposed betrayal of their homelands by local Jews who collaborated with the Soviet authorities. Thus, some believe that there are historical accountings that need to be made, and perhaps even scores to be settled, before relations between Jews and non-Jews in parts of the former USSR can be "normalized." It is hoped that this volume will make a modest contribution toward bringing the issues to wider attention and shedding the light of scholarship on one of the darkest episodes in modern history.

Some of the documents in this volume are reprinted from English translations, as indicated in references to the sources. Others have been translated from Russian and Ukrainian by me, Leonid Livak, Diahanna Lynch, and John Squier. Daniela Har-Paz translated part of Yosef Litvak's chapter from

Hebrew. Some of the articles have appeared previously elsewhere. These have been revised and updated with the consent of the authors and the original publishers. The project which produced this book was supported by the National Council for Soviet and East European Research; the Dean's Office, College of Literature, Science and Arts, The University of Michigan. The Department of Hebrew and Jewish Studies, University College London provided facilities for a workshop. Technical assistance was given by Carrie Bickner, Amy Hamermesh, and Michelle Newton, all of The University of Michigan. Dr. Janet Rabinowitch of Indiana University Press was very patient and understanding, and her wise judgment was invaluable in guiding the manuscript toward publication. To all of these people and institutions I am grateful. Of course, none is responsible for errors or opinions expressed in this book.

BITTER

LEGACY

ONE

Soviet Jewry before the Holocaust

Zvi Gitelman

The Nazis' systematic murder of Jews in the Soviet Union caused enormous numbers of personal tragedies as well as the devastation of what had been the world's largest Jewish community in the nineteenth century. Russian Jewry had created the most important modern ideologies and cultural movements of world Jewry, and by virtue of the emigration of millions of Russian Jews, it had made a great impact on the Jewish communities of Western Europe, North America, and Palestine. In 1897 there were more than five million Jews living in the Russian Empire, where they constituted the largest Jewish community in the world. They were never fully accepted by the tsarist authorities or by society.[1] Until 1772 they were legally barred from residing in the empire. When the tsars annexed eastern Poland in the late eighteenth century, they found themselves "burdened" by a large Jewish population that had lived in Poland for centuries. In order to prevent the Jews from "contaminating" the rest of the population, the government decreed that they could reside only in the fifteen western provinces newly annexed to the empire. These provinces include roughly present-day Lithuania, part of Latvia, Belarus, Ukraine, and Moldova. At the time of the first comprehensive census, in 1897, about 97 percent of the Jews lived in these areas, known as the Pale of Settlement.

Other restrictions were imposed on the Jews from time to time. Under Tsar Nicholas I (1825–55), young Jewish boys were drafted into the military for terms of twenty-five years, sometimes undergoing preinduction military training for years that were added to their term of service. The aim was not so much to beef up what was already the largest standing army in the world, but to remove Jewish youngsters from their families and communities and thus to wean them away from their faith and people.[2] It is estimated that about 50,000 Jewish teenagers were drafted in this way, and that about half of them were lost to the Jewish people. Moreover, since each community was assigned a quota of recruits it had to deliver to the authorities, and communal leaders generally selected the children of the poor and uninfluential for the draft, serious tensions were created within the Jewish communities. In the view of Marxist historians, this was the beginning of class conflict among the Jews of the empire, as the poor began to rebel against the coalition of the wealthy and learned, who manipulated the *rekruchina* to protect their own children.[3]

A *numerus clausus*, or quota system, was imposed on Jewish aspirants to higher education and the professions. It set very low limits on the numbers of Jews who could be accepted to institutions of higher education and allowed to practice in the professions. These limitations were imposed even though the great majority of the Russian population was illiterate even as late as 1914, and Russia had to import professors, engineers, agronomists, and architects from abroad to meet the modest needs of an overwhelmingly agrarian and still essentially feudal country. By 1865, nearly a thousand Jews were enrolled in Russian *gymnazii* and by 1880 there were more than seven thousand (12 percent of all students). By the 1880s there were more than 1,800 Jewish students in Russian universities, where they constituted almost 15 percent of the student population.[4] Nevertheless, at the end of the nineteenth century many Jews who sought higher education had to do so abroad. In 1888 there were fewer than sixty Russian Jews matriculating at German universities, but this number increased tenfold by the early 1900s. On the eve of World War I, between 2,500 and 3,000 Russian Jews were studying at German institutions of higher learning. Others were in France, Switzerland, England, and other West European countries.[5]

An even more serious liability was the denial to the Jews of the right to own land, the primary source of wealth in an agrarian economy. From time to time the government would permit some Jews to settle on land in Ukraine or in newly acquired territories, but these were exceptional episodes, so that the vast majority of Jews became traders, craftsmen, workers in small factories and workshops, storekeepers, or simply *luftmentshn*, people without any profession, "living off the air" and making their livelihood from chance opportunities. In many communities 40 percent of the population fell into the *luftmentsh* category. In 1898 nearly 20 percent of the Jews in the Pale applied for Passover relief. A report by a non-Jewish statistician observed that in the Grodno (Belarus) region, "In most cases a pound of bread, a herring, and a few onions represent the daily fare of an entire family."[6] In 1900 in Odessa, one of the wealthier cities in the empire, nearly two-thirds of the Jewish dead had to be buried at communal expense. At the turn of the century, about a third of the Jews were dependent on relief provided by Jewish institutions.

Finally, government antisemitism was complemented by popular anti-Jewish sentiment. In 1881, following the assassination of Tsar Alexander II, for which the Jews were held responsible, a wave of pogroms swept over Ukraine and Belarus and reached as far west as Warsaw. Anti-Jewish laws passed in May 1882 and pogroms in 1903 and 1905 impelled nearly two million Jews to flee the Russian Empire, most of them immigrating to Western Europe and North America, and smaller numbers going to Latin America and Palestine.[7] As late as 1911 the government accused a humble Ukrainian Jew, Mendel Beilis, of murdering a Christian child in order to use his blood in Judaic ritual. High officials conspired to suppress evidence that Beilis was in no way involved in the murder, which had actually been committed by a gang of thieves. Beilis sat in prison for two years while the authorities tried to make a case against him. He was brought to trial in September 1913, and though he was acquitted, the government was still appealing the verdict up to the eve of the 1917 revolution.[8] Thus, the tsarist government was committing its resources to sustaining a medieval canard right up to its own demise. This is eloquent testimony to tsarism's bankruptcy and to its obsessions.

Jewish Communal Life

Perhaps because society in general shunned and isolated them, Jews in the Russian Empire turned their energies and talents inward and developed a dynamic, vibrant communal and cultural life. Religious life was especially strong in the small towns (*shtetlakh*) and villages. In most of these, Jews constituted a majority of the population. This gave them a strong sense of community and solidarity, but it also induced conformity to powerful social pressures. Though the official community organization (*kahal*) had been abolished by the government in 1844, Jewish communities continued to regulate their internal affairs much as before.[9] They had their burial societies, charitable organizations, educational institutions, orphanages, old-age homes, infirmaries, and other welfare institutions. In a country where four-fifths of the population could not read nor write, almost all Jewish boys and girls learned to read and write Hebrew and Yiddish, and a substantial proportion could read Russian as well. The most famous *yeshivot*, or schools of higher rabbinic learning, were in the Russian Empire, often in small towns. By the twentieth century, there were substantial numbers of Jewish students in Russian schools, as well as in Yiddish and Hebrew secular schools.

One of the remarkable achievements of Russian Jewry was that it produced two major modern literatures, Yiddish and Hebrew. Perhaps even more remarkable is the fact that two of the three "classic" Yiddish writers, Mendele Mocher Sforim and Y. L. Peretz—the other was, of course, Sholem Aleichem—were also among the creators of modern Hebrew literature. Usage of Hebrew as a living language, propagated by the "Haskalah" or enlightenment movement of the mid-nineteenth century, became a plank in the platform of the Zionist movement, and Yiddish became the cornerstone of the secular culture advocated by some elements in the Jewish socialist movement. But these languages and literatures stood on their own as cultural forces that attracted their loyalists, creators, and publics. Yiddish theater emerged at the end of the nineteenth century, and the beginnings of the Hebrew theater were also in Russia. Jewish folk and cantorial music were well developed, and there were some Jewish composers and performers of classical music, though many of them had to convert to Christianity in order to be accepted. By the first decade of the twentieth century, serious study and production of Jewish music was undertaken by a society established for that purpose. In addition, a Historical-Ethnographic Society was established, and important research was carried out. Russian Jewish scholars made contributions in Semitics, history, sociology, ethnography, and demography.[10]

Efforts to Protect Jewish Rights

In the latter half of the nineteenth century, some Jews began to become politically active. Beginning in the 1860s and 1870s, some joined the radical youth who looked to the peasantry to rise against the tsarist autocracy and liberate the entire population, including the Jews, from political, social, and economic oppression.[11] The *narodniki* (Populists) who regarded the peasantry as the revolutionary class were disappointed in the social conservatism and political inertness of this class. Jewish *narodniki* were shocked by the pogroms perpetrated largely by the peasantry, but even more so by the reactions of their fellow revolutionaries, some of whom welcomed the pogroms as a sign that the peasants were at last being activated, even though they were venting their frustrations in the wrong way.[12] Disillusioned Jewish Populists generally tended either to emigrate, which meant that they had given up on Russia; or to become Marxists, which meant that they transferred their hopes from the peasantry to the proletariat; or to become Zionists, which signaled their despair of finding solutions to the "Jewish problem" anywhere in the Diaspora.[13] By 1897 Russian Jewry had seen the birth of both the Jewish Labor Bund, a Marxist, secular, anti-Zionist movement oriented toward Yiddish, as well as of Zionism, a movement with several streams (including socialist, religious, culturalist) all of which saw the future of the Jewish people in a state of their own. The Bund, which helped found the Russian Social-Democratic Labor Party out of which the Bolsheviks and Mensheviks emerged, advocated the overthrow of tsarism and the replacement of the feudal-capitalist system by socialism. This, they reasoned, would solve the Jewish problem, which needed no unique solution, as the Zionists argued, but would be part of the overall transformation of the world into a more just society in which ethnic and racial hatreds would be unknown.[14] The Zionists, on the other hand, felt that only a Jewish state or homeland could provide Jews with security and equal opportunity. However, they decided that as long as Jews remained in the Diaspora, their rights would have to be protected and fought for.[15] A group of generally wealthier, educated, and privileged Jews defended Jewish rights through legal channels and associated themselves with Russian constitutionalist movements and parties. They hoped that a constitutional democracy would be sufficient to guarantee civil rights to all and equal rights to Jews.[16] But the tsarist system was unyielding, and concessions made in the aftermath of the 1905 revolution were soon withdrawn. The last tsar, Nicholas II, retreated into reaction and policies even less enlightened than those of his predecessors.

It should be remembered that only a minority of Jews were active in any of the movements described. The need to eke out a living, isolation from the larger society, and the self-contained nature of Jewish society, which had a well-developed institutional infrastructure and which was spiritually self-sufficient, enabled most Jews to live their daily lives outside the political arena. Contrary to popular belief, Bolshevism enjoyed little support among Jews. A census of Bolshevik Party members taken in 1922 revealed that there were only 958 Jews who had joined before 1917; in the latter year, the Bund had more than 30,000 members. The myth that Bolshevism was a "Jewish conspiracy"[17] is based on the presence of a disproportionate number of people of Jewish origin—none of whom was a practicing or committed Jew—in the upper echelons of the Bolshevik Party in 1917 and for several years afterward. The myth gained credence in 1918–21 when many Jews joined the Party and became Soviet officials, largely because only the Bolsheviks did not pogromize the Jews, whereas their White opponents, Ukrainian nationalists, and others systematically attacked Jews; the new regime removed restrictions on their education and employment; and some former anti-Bolshevik socialists became convinced that the world revolution was at hand and that the Bolshevik analysis of the situation was correct. Thus, by 1922, when Jews comprised less than 2 percent of the population—there were about 2.4 million Jews in the country at the time—they were 5.2 percent of party members. That proportion declined to 3.8 percent by 1930.[18]

Open political activity by Jews became possible only with the fall of tsarism in February-March 1917 when the legal impediments to Jewish equality were removed. For the first time in the history of Russia, Jews became full-fledged citizens. They greeted the revolution with great enthusiasm and set about creating a comprehensive public Jewish life. Publications, cultural groups, and political parties flourished in 1917. The Zionists, given a boost by the Balfour Declaration of that year wherein the British government promised the Jews a homeland in Palestine, emerged as the most popular political force among Jews.

All the activity was brought to a halt by the Bolshevik seizure of power late in 1917. The Bolsheviks were militantly opposed to Zionism, which they saw as splitting off the Jewish workers from the rest of the proletariat and retarding the assimilation of the Jews, which they considered a progressive phenomenon to be emulated by all nationalities. Ex-Bundists and other socialists who eventually joined the Communist Party persuaded the leadership to mount campaigns against the Hebrew language, now considered the language of the class enemy, the bourgeoisie and the clericals, whereas Yiddish was the language of the "toiling masses." In the 1920s, the foundations of traditional Jewish life were undermined by Communist assaults on Judaism, Hebrew, and Zionism. The Jewish religion was attacked as part of the general campaign against religion, Zionism was declared a subversive ideology and movement, and Hebrew was banned as a language of study, discourse, and publication. Religious Jews, Zionists, and Hebraists were hounded, driven underground, forced to change their ways of life, imprisoned, or exiled.

Some Communists, active in the Jewish sections of the party (*Evsektsii*), tried to devise a secular, socialist, Soviet Yiddish culture as a replacement for traditional Jewish culture. They created Jewish schools, theaters, newspapers, journals, and research institutes that operated in Yiddish and reflected the Bolshevik ideology. By 1931 there were 1,100 Yiddish state-supported schools, 40 daily newspapers in Yiddish, and trade unions and even party cells operating in Yiddish. Moreover, they tried to solve Jewish economic problems by settling Jews on land and making them into farmers. The Communists planned to settle 100,000 Jewish families on lands in Belorussia, Crimea, the Ukraine, and Birobidzhan, an underpopulated area of the Soviet Far East.[19]

Neither the "Yiddishization" nor the agricultural settlement campaigns succeeded. Traditional Jews considered Soviet Yiddish culture ersatz and inimical to their values. They often preferred to send their children to non-Jewish schools, where Judaism and Zionism were not attacked as frequently or directly as they were in the Yiddish schools. On the other hand, most other Jews saw no reason for clinging to the shtetl culture and its language once the doors to a "higher" culture, Russian, were opened. The majority of younger Jews were quite content to trade the culture of their shtetl upbringing for the educational and vocational mobility offered by the drive to modernize and industrialize the Soviet Union. Millions of workers were needed to build the factories and plants that would propel a backward country into the modern industrial world. Therefore, thousands of Jews moved out of the *shtetlakh* of the former Pale areas, migrating to the larger cities of Ukraine and Belorussia, and to the cities of the Russian republic, especially Moscow and Leningrad, that had been off limits to almost all Jews before 1917. Now they were no longer *luftmentshn* but industrial workers, technicians, engineers, economists, and factory managers. They entered universities and technical institutes and took up governmental posts, reaching the highest echelons of the military, the state apparatus, the police, and the Party. Between 1926 and 1935, the number of Jewish wage and salary earners nearly tripled. At first, Jews became blue-collar workers, but very soon they moved into the white-collar ranks. By 1939 there were 364,000 Jewish white-collar employees. In 1934–35 Jews made up 18 percent of all graduate students. By the late 1930s, Jews were well established in the proletariat and in the managerial and professional strata.[20]

In achieving this mobility, they did what their relatives and ancestors who had crossed oceans had done: abandoned their traditions, changed their language to that of the majority, changed their clothes, cuisine, cultures, and social milieux. Jews were offered the opportunity to go as far as their talents and education would carry them, and they seized upon it eagerly. By the early 1930s it was clear that the high road to modernization was industry, not agriculture, and so most preferred to move to the cities rather than to the now-collectivized farms. Birobidzhan was too far away and too undeveloped to attract any but the most politically enthusiastic or economically desperate. A high proportion of the original pioneers made their ways back to where they had come from. Moreover, most Jews seemed to accept at face value the myth of "proletarian internationalism," which rendered ethnic identities and cultures meaningless. They were convinced that ethnicity was now irrelevant, as all peoples had overcome their mutual prejudices and were united in their commitment to "progressive" ideals. There was not much reason to settle on specifically Jewish farms or to cling to Jewish identity and culture in the urbane, cosmopolitan settings of Moscow, Leningrad, Kiev, and Odessa. Little wonder that rates of marriage between Jews and non-Jews rose precipitously in the 1930s. Acculturation—the adoption of another culture—was being followed by assimilation—the abandonment of one's original identity.

Antisemitism in the Soviet Union

Jews' belief that they had at last achieved equality with all others was buttressed by the explicit stand the government took against antisemitism. Lenin had denounced antisemitism in strong terms before and during the revolution. In the 1920s the government published several pamphlets directed at the working class which explained that antisemitism was a tool of the capitalist bosses for splintering the workers and diverting them from their true class interests. Lectures and even films were used to combat anti-Jewish feelings. Antisemitism was labeled a reactionary, anti-socialist phenomenon that had no place in socialist society. It became punishable by Soviet law. Yet, there were manifestations of Jew-hatred, and they seemed to grow with time. During the New Economic Policy (NEP) period (1921–28), when some private enterprise was allowed, some Jews went back to their prerevolutionary occupations and engaged in small-scale commerce. But "NEPmen" soon became objects of ridicule and condemnation, barely tolerated as marginal figures in Soviet society. The population was socialized to despise private trade, and some transferred this class-based animosity to an ethnic one, characterizing Jews in general as "exploiting elements." Ironically, other people held the Jews responsible for making the revolution and destroying the private economic sector, for had not Jews been prominent among those who had made the revolution? Some among those who opposed the revolution and its values—for example, religious people, those ideologically opposed to Bolshevism, and those economically ruined by socialism—associated the revolution with the Jews and blamed them for the troubles it had visited upon them.[21]

When efforts were made to settle Jews on land, there was resentment among some peasants who feared that their lands would be expropriated for Jewish settlement. Just as many non-Jews found it strange and "unnatural" that Jews should hold leading political and military positions in a country where they had been only recently barred from such positions, so, too, did some peasants look with a mixture of resentment and amusement at the spectacle of large numbers of urban types being made over into farmers. Some were convinced that there was a plot by the Jewish-dominated government to take away their land and hand it over to the Jews. Perhaps such attitudes could be expected in a sector of the population that had no enthusiasm for socialism and was considered politically and culturally backward by the Bolsheviks. But the Bolsheviks could not easily account for the antisemitism that cropped up in the ranks of the proletariat. Soviet newspapers reported instances of violent antisemitism among workers and condemned them. Apparently, the "New Soviet man" had not yet been created and "survivals of the past," including antisemitism, were visible in many strata of Soviet society.

Moreover, by the early 1930s reports of antisemitism among the "toiling masses" and condemnations of it no longer appeared. Where once the authorities had condemned "Great Power chauvinism" (Russian nationalism) as a more serious evil than "petit bourgeois nationalism" (nationalism among the non-Russians), in the 1930s the latter came to be identified as the greater evil. This was in line with Stalin's shift in emphasis from encouraging the nationalities to develop their cultures to promoting the interests of the Russians. After all, devoting energies to the development of Ukrainian theater, Jewish literature, Belarussian music, or the Uzbek language would detract from the common, single aim, the economic modernizaition of *all* Soviet peoples. "Socialist in content, national in form" became the catchphrase of nationality policy. Purges of cultural and political leaders among the non-Russians made it clear to everyone that "socialist content" took precedence over "national form." Thus, the problems of particular nationalities were not a matter of great concern. Antisemitism was talked about less and less, but this did not mean that it had disappeared. On the contrary, it may have been spreading in the 1930s because it was no longer as widely and consistently condemned as it had been in the previous decade.

Finally, Jews were prominent in the secret police. In the early days of the revolution, Jews had joined the police partly in order to protect and revenge themselves against the White enemies of Bolshevism who were pogromizing their people. Bolshevik leaders regarded Jews as especially trustworthy because they could not conceivably be sympathetic to a tsarist restoration. It may also be that, having been deprived of power for so long, some Jews found the lure of the secret police and its nearly unlimited powers irresistible. Then, too, as an urban, educated element, Jews were more likely than many others to be recruited for such functions. Nevertheless, the visible presence of Jews in the organs of repression could not but arouse antipathy to Jews generally. Although enormous numbers of Jews were themselves purged—not as Jews but as party members, military, governmental, and economic officials, and cultural leaders—the impression might well have been created that a disproportionate number of Jews were involved in repressing millions of Russians and members of other nationalities. These, then, were some of the proximate causes of anti-Jewish sentiments in the early Soviet period. Clearly, many of the prejudices and stereotypes of prerevolutionary days had survived as well, despite Bolshevik assertions that they were creating a wholly new society and that any ethnic hatreds that remained were mere "survivals of capitalism." Anti-Jewish feelings played an important role in deciding the fate of Jews who tried to hide from Nazi persecution after 1941.

Following Adolf Hitler's rise to power in Germany in 1933, the USSR attempted to become part of a broad international "popular front" against fascism. Soviet publications and media detailed the evils of German Nazism, among them antisemitism. Yet, in August 1939 the Soviets signed a treaty with the Nazis. Stalin took care to remove from his post his Jewish foreign minister, Maxim Litvinov, before signing the treaty. The Soviet line had changed and so had the domestic media's treatment of fascism, Nazism, and events in Germany. From 1939 until the German invasion of the USSR nearly two years later, little or nothing was said about the evils of antisemitism and what the Germans had been doing to Jews, first in Germany and then in the countries they had annexed or invaded. Thus, the Soviet population as a whole and Jews in particular ceased to hear about Nazi antisemitism or even to learn about the atrocities that were being perpetrated against the Jews. On the eve of the German invasion, therefore, the Soviet population was not sensitized to the problem of antisemitism generally nor to the specifics of Nazi policies toward Jews. Those Jews living in the western Soviet Union encountered Jewish refugees from Poland and learned something about Nazi treatment of Jews, but the Jewish population of the rest of the USSR, living as they were in a country where information was tightly controlled and where there was very little contact with foreigners, were even less prepared for the horrors soon to befall them.

On the Eve of War

Under secret agreements attached to the 1939 Soviet-German "Non-Aggression" pact, the two powers divided much of Eastern Europe between themselves. Thus, less than three weeks after Germany invaded Poland on September 1, 1939, Soviet troops moved into eastern Poland on the pretext of liberating Ukrainians and Belarussians living in that area from the oppressive rule of the Poles. Staged referenda, conducted under the watchful eyes of the Soviet army and police, "proved" that the local population wished to join the USSR, and provided the legal mask for the annexation of eastern Poland to the Soviet Union, which called the territories "West Belorussia" and "West Ukraine."[22] Then in 1940 Soviet troops occupied the Baltic republics, Estonia, Latvia, and Lithuania. The same charade followed, with the local populations "requesting" to be admitted to the Soviet Union as republics. Of course, the "request" was granted. In 1940 the USSR also acquired Northern Bukovina and Bessarabia from Romania in roughly the same way. Eventually, these formerly Romanian territories were divided between the Ukrainian republic and the newly created Moldavian republic. The full panoply of Soviet institutions was installed in all these areas. Schools and cultural institutions were Sovietized, the economies were nationalized, and the Communist Party was given a monopoly of power in the political arena. Thousands of people were identified by the authorities as "class enemies" and deported to the interior of the USSR or sent to prison and labor camps. These were usually non-Communists who had been politically active, religious functionaries, private entrepreneurs, including even shopkeepers, and others suspected of being potential enemies of the new regime. The Communist Party had been illegal in these areas before the coming of the Soviets, and Jews constituted substantial proportions of the underground parties. While these Communists were only a tiny fraction of the Jewish population as a whole, their proportions in the Communist parties were considerably larger than the proportion of Jews in the overall population. The reasons for this were that Jews were more urbanized and educated than the rest of the population; they had not been treated equitably by the ruling powers, and some of them sought to replace the prevailing systems with those that would not discriminate among different ethnic groups; and some Jews had been attracted to the secular Yiddish culture promoted by the Soviets. Again, as in 1918–21 in the USSR proper, the new regime relied on Jewish Communists to identify and arrest "class enemies" and "reactionary elements." Naturally, this did not endear the Jews generally to the local populations who had just lost their political independence, acquired only two decades earlier, to the Communists.

It should be noted, however, that all Jewish institutions in the newly acquired territories were also Sovietized. The same persecutions of Hebrew, Zionism, and religion that Soviet Jews had experienced earlier were now felt by Baltic, Polish, and Romanian Jews.[23] There is also some evidence that the Soviet occupiers soon realized how unpopular Jews were in the new areas and took care not to place Jews in visible positions of authority.[24] They even replaced some Jews who had been installed in such positions early in the Sovietization process. Some Jewish leftists in the new territories also soon realized that the purges of the 1930s had not singled out genuine enemies of the Soviet system alone and that many of their Communist colleagues across the border had been repressed unjustifiably. But by the time Jews in the new areas realized the full import of Sovietization, they were faced with the frightful dilemma of choosing between areas dominated by Romanian fascists, German Nazis, or Soviet Communists—if they could still make any choices at all.

The acquisition of the new territories added substantially to the Soviet Jewish population. According to the 1939 census, the results of which have only recently been declassified and which are today acknowledged by Russian scholars to have been substantially falsified and distorted, there were 3.1 million Jews in the USSR.[25] In 1939–40 about 1.9 million Jews lived in the territories annexed to the Soviet Union: 1.3 million in eastern Poland, 255,000 in the Baltic states, and about 330,000 in territories that had formerly belonged to Romania. Thus, when the Nazis invaded the USSR on June 22, 1941, there were about five million Jews in the country. They were concentrated heavily in the western parts of the country, closest to the invading forces. Some "lucky" Jews had been arrested by the Soviet occupiers of eastern Poland, the Baltic states, and former Romanian territory and had been deported to Central Asia and Siberia on the grounds that they were "bourgeois elements" (factory owners, bankers, even shopkeepers), political enemies (mainly Zionists and Bundists), ideological enemies (clergy, writers, and cultural leaders), or because they had tried to flee to Soviet territory from German-occupied lands. As it turned out, these people had a better chance of survival than those who fell into German hands, though they endured imprisonment, forced labor, social isolation, and political persecution. Jews living under German occupation and Jewish military personnel captured by the Nazis and their allies had a far lower probability of survival. All together, at least 1.5 million, and perhaps as many as two million Jews who were Soviet citizens in 1941, died at the hands of the Nazis and their collaborators.[26]

Notes

1. See John Klier, *Imperial Russia's Jewish Question, 1855–1881* (Cambridge: Cambridge University Press, 1995).
2. Michael Stanislawski, *Tsar Nicholas I and the Jews* (Philadelphia: Jewish Publications Society, 1983).
3. See, for example, O. Margolis, *Geshikhte fun yidn in rusland: etiudn un dokumentn* (Moscow-Kharkov-Minsk: Tsentraler felker farlag fun FSSR, 1930), 323–35.
4. Michael Stanislawski, "Russian Jewry, the Russian State, and the Dynamics of Jewish Emancipation," in Pierre Birnbaum and Ira Katznelson, eds., *Paths of Emancipation* (Princeton: Princeton University Press, 1995), 274–75.
5. See Jack Wertheimer, *Unwelcome Strangers* (New York: Oxford University Press, 1987), 63. One such student was Chaim Weizmann, later the first President of Israel. See his *Trial and Error* (New York: Harper, 1949), ch. 3.
6. Quoted in Salo Baron, *The Russian Jew under Tsars and Soviets* (New York: Macmillan, 1964), 113.
7. For tsarist policies, see Hans Rogger, *Jewish Policies and Right-Wing Politics in Imperial Russia* (Berkeley: University of California Press, 1986). On pogroms, see I. Michael Aronson, *Troubled Waters: The Origins of the 1881 Anti-Jewish Pogroms in Russia* (Pittsburgh: University of Pittsburgh Press, 1990); and John Klier and

Shlomo Lambroza, eds., *Pogroms: Anti-Jewish Violence in Modern Jewish History* (Cambridge: Cambridge University Press, 1992).

8. On the Beilis case, see Alexander Tager, *The Decay of Czarism* (Philadelphia: Jewish Publication Society, 1935).
9. On the *kahal*, see Isaac Levitats, *The Jewish Community in Russia, 1772–1844* (New York: Octagon, 1970). For critical observations on the *kahal* as an instrument of "bourgeois oppression," see Margolis, op. cit.
10. On the intellectual currents in Russian Jewry, see Lucy Dawidowicz, ed., *The Golden Tradition* (New York: Holt, Rinehart, and Winston, 1967).
11. See Erich Haberer, *Jews and Revolution in Nineteenth-Century Russia* (Cambridge: Cambridge University Press, 1995).
12. The Jewish question in the Russian revolutionary movements is treated in Yitzhak Maor, *She'elat hayehudim bat'nuah haliberalit vehamehapchanit berusiya* (Jerusalem: Mosad Bialik, 1964).
13. On the development of political life, see Eli Lederhandler, *The Road to Modern Jewish Politics* (Oxford: Oxford University Press, 1989).
14. See Henry J. Tobias, *The Jewish Bund in Russia* (Stanford: Stanford University Press, 1972).
15. A survey of the ideological streams in Zionism can be found in Arthur Hertzberg, *The Zionist Idea* (New York: Meridian, 1960). See also Walter Laqueur, *A History of Zionism* (New York: Schocken, 1976).
16. The memoirs of some of the leading figures of that movement include G. B. Sliozberg, *Dela minuvshikh dnei* (Paris, 1933); see also his *Ocherki i rechi* (New York, 1944). O. O. Gruzenberg, *Vchera* (Paris, 1938); English translation is *Yesterday* (Berkeley: University of California, 1981). See also Christoph Gassenschmidt, *Jewish Liberal Politics in Tsarist Russia, 1900–1914* (Houndmills: Macmillan, 1995).
17. On the myth of the *Zhydokomuna* (Jewish-Communist conspiracy), see Andre Gerrits, "Antisemitism and Anti-Communism: The Myth of 'Judeo-Communism' in Eastern Europe," *East European Jewish Affairs* 25, 1 (1995).
18. Zvi Gitelman, *Jewish Nationality and Soviet Politics* (Princeton: Princeton University Press, 1972), 105–16.
19. On Jewish agricultural settlement in Crimea, see Allan Kagedan, *Soviet Zion* (New York: St. Martin's, 1994). On Birobidzhan, see Yaacov Lvavi (Babitsky), *Hahityashvut hayehudit bebirobidzhan* (Jerusalem: Historical Society of Israel, 1965), and Robert Weinberg, "Jews into Peasants? Solving the Jewish Question in Birobidzhan," in Yaacov Ro'i, ed., *Jews and Jewish Life in Russia and the Soviet Union* (Essex: Frank Cass, 1995).
20. For a general history of Soviet Jewry, see Zvi Gitelman, *A Century of Ambivalence: The Jews of Russia and the Soviet Union, 1881 to the Present* (New York: Schocken, 1988).
21. See Solomon Schwarz, *The Jews in the Soviet Union* (Syracuse: Syracuse University Press, 1951), part two.
22. See Keith Sword, *Deportation and Exile: Poles in the Soviet Union, 1939–48* (New York: St. Martin's Press, 1994), and Jan Gross, *Revolution from Abroad: The So-*

viet Conquest of Poland's Western Ukraine and Western Belorussia (Princeton: Princeton University Press, 1988). On the Jews in these areas, see Norman Davies and Antony Polonsky, *Jews in Eastern Poland and the USSR, 1939–1946* (New York: St. Martin's Press, 1991).

23. See Dov Levin, *Baltic Jews under the Soviets, 1940–1946* (Jerusalem: Centre for Research and Documentation of East European Jewry, Hebrew University, 1994).

24. See Dov Levin, *The Lesser of Two Evils: Eastern European Jewry under Soviet Rule, 1939–1941* (Philadelphia: Jewish Publication Society, 1995), ch. 3.

25. The distribution of that population is presented in Mordechai Altshuler, ed., *Distribution of the Jewish Population of the USSR 1939* (Jerusalem: Centre for Research and Documentation of East European Jewry, 1993).

26. According to Yitzhak Arad, "Out of a total of 2,750,000–2,900,000 Jews . . . under German rule in the occupied territories of the Soviet Union . . . very few had survived. . . . To the victims of Soviet Jewry in World War Two we should add between 120,000 and 180,000 Jews who fell . . . while serving in the Soviet Army, as well as about 80,000–85,000 shot in POW camps. Together with other Soviet citizens, tens of thousands of Soviet Jews died due to hard living conditions, shellings and bombings. . . . " Yitzhak Arad, "The Holocaust of Soviet Jewry in the Occupied Territories of the Soviet Union," *Yad Vashem Studies XXI* (Jerusalem: Yad Vashem, 1991), 47.

TWO

Politics and the Historiography of the Holocaust in the Soviet Union

Zvi Gitelman

Between one-fourth and one-third of all the Jews killed in the Holocaust were under Soviet rule as of 1940. As noted in the previous chapter, according to most estimates, about 1.5 million Soviet Jewish citizens who lived in the pre-1939 borders of the USSR were murdered by the Nazis, and perhaps 200,000 more died in combat.[1] The rest of the victims, perhaps as many as 300,000 to 400,000, were Jews who came under Soviet rule in 1939–40. Yet, the Soviet treatment of the Holocaust has been very different from that in the West. William Korey writes of "the Kremlin's suppression of all reference to the holocaust until now."[2] This is somewhat exaggerated. While most Soviet writers either ignored the Holocaust or submerged it in more general accounts of the period, none denied it, and some did treat it not simply as German atrocities but as a uniquely Jewish fate. A survey of Soviet writings reveals that they vary significantly in the prominence and interpretations they give to the Holocaust. Most Soviet works either pass over it in silence or blur it by universalizing it. Western assertions to the contrary, there was no consistent Soviet "party line" on the Holocaust. Some works do acknowledge and describe the Holocaust, while others discuss only some aspects of it. We can only speculate regarding Soviet motivations, but we can point with greater certainty to some consequences, intended and unintended, of the general Soviet tendency to ignore or downplay the Holocaust. In any case, as the Soviet Union and its dominating party broke up, the treatment of the Holocaust began to change. Post-Soviet states such as Ukraine, Latvia, and Lithuania have dealt rather gingerly with the Holocaust because of the collaboration of some of the indigenous peoples with the Nazis in the mass murder of Jews. Moreover, some people in these states hold the Jews responsible for what they see as the catastrophes of Soviet rule. Thus, the Holocaust in the former Soviet Union (FSU) is not a subject of historical interest alone, but raises serious questions about the relations between the indigenous or titular nationalities and the Jews and about responsibility for the atrocities of the war period and for the evils of the Soviet system.

Soviet treatment of the Holocaust had profound, if subtle, effects on both Jews and non-Jews in the USSR. On the one hand, it denied Jews any particular sympathy on the part of non-Jews. Unlike in the West, Soviet non-Jews, for the most part, did not feel a need to "make up" to the Jews, as it were, for any of the wrongs done to them. Many still do not feel that way today. For example, when Prime Minister Slezivicius of Lithuania said on that country's television that "we should recognize that hundreds [*sic*] of Lithuanians took direct part in this genocide," considerable controversy ensued and many declared that Lithuanians had nothing for which to apologize.[3] On the other hand, Soviet treatment has aroused Jewish consciousness, as it has in the West. But it has also engendered first puzzlement and then bitterness when Jews, especially younger ones, realized that a vital part of their recent history is being denied them. Hence, they felt that their worth and importance have been denigrated, their particular history and culture dismissed, and their claims to being discriminated against rejected. Soviet treatment of the Holocaust—or lack of it—played a significant role in the reemergence of Jewish national consciousness in the former Soviet Union. It is interesting not only from an academic point of view, but from social and political perspectives, to see whether the current reexamination of Soviet history in the successor states will reopen the pages of the Holocaust and will permit this chapter to be written in full. In 1991 and 1992, indications were that this was beginning to occur. In Ukraine and Russia, articles began to appear in non-Jewish journals that described the Holocaust and raised some of the sensitive issues of complicity by local populations, Soviet suppression of discussion of the Holocaust, and the impact of the Holocaust on Jewish perceptions. Since then, the discussion of these issues seems to have abated somewhat. In Lithuania most of the discussion centered on official pardons by the newly independent Lithuanian government (1991) of several thousand Lithuanians convicted by the Soviets of collaboration. Criticism of the wholesale pardons by Jewish and Israeli bodies evoked countercharges of sympathy for Communism, and the issue remains unresolved and highly sensitive.

After briefly identifying the main outlines of how the Holocaust was perpetrated in the USSR, we shall discuss how it has been treated in Soviet writings, offer some suggestions as to why it was accorded such treatment, and examine the consequences of that treatment.

The War against Soviet Jewry

Around a quarter of a million of the Jews from the territories annexed in 1939–40 either fled to the interior beyond the Nazi grasp or were inadvertently saved by the Soviets from Nazi annihilation when the former deported them to Siberia and Central Asia.[4]

The Soviet occupation of the western territories brought with it a tragic, fateful divergence in the perceptions and interests of Jews and non-Jews. In all those territories antisemitic regimes in the 1930s had made life increasingly uncomfortable—even intolerable—for the Jews. America and Palestine were closed to immigration, and emigration was not a realistic option for most people. Jews in Poland, Romania, Latvia, and Lithuania had little hope of improving their lot. The entry of the Red Army, with its Jewish officers and men and its promises of national equality and social justice, gave hope to some of the younger and more radically inclined Jews. Despite misgivings about the Bolsheviks' militant atheism, their persecution of Zionism, and their nationalization of property, many Jews welcomed the Red Army as a liberator. A resident of eastern Poland recalled that when the Red Army came, "There was a holiday atmosphere. Things changed overnight . . . the Germans would not come in and that was the most important thing."[5] Others saw the Soviets as the lesser of two evils. Another survivor from the same area comments, "when the Russians came in we were a little afraid, but not as afraid as we were of the Germans in the Western part of Poland."[6]

By contrast, the Poles, Baltic peoples, and Romanians saw the Red Army as an invader, not a liberator, depriving them of their hard-won and all-too-brief political independence. Jews who welcomed the Red Army were seen as traitors, and all Jews were assumed to be Bolshevik sympathizers and betrayers of the lands of their birth. Little wonder, then, that when the Germans drove the Red Army out in 1941, many non-Jews greeted them as liberators from Soviet oppression and took the opportunity to wreak harsh vengeance on the traitorous Jews. In the first few days of the German occupation of Lithuania, for example, Lithuanian groups murdered between 4,000 and 5,000 Jews.

Three million German troops invaded the USSR from the west, quickly encircling the main centers of Jewish population. The Nazis had long been explicit about their consuming hatred for both Bolsheviks and Jews, whom they equated with each other. Adolf Hitler wrote in 1930, "The Nordic race has a right to rule the world. . . . Any cooperation with Russia is out of the question, for there on a Slavic-Tatar body is set a Jewish head."[7] German General Von Reichenau issued an order stating, "The most essential aim of war against the Jewish-Bolshevistic system is a complete destruction of their . . . power. . . . Therefore, the soldier must have full understanding for the necessity of severe but just revenge on subhuman Jewry." General Von Manstein wrote, "More strongly than in Europe, [Jewry] holds all the key positions in the political leadership and administration . . . the Jewish-Bolshevist system must be exterminated once and for all. The soldier must appreciate the necessity for harsh punishment of Jewry, the spiritual bearer of the Bolshevist terror."[8]

Though the Nazis could not have been more explicit about their intentions, the Soviet media had draped a blanket of silence over Nazi atrocities following the Nazi-Soviet pact of August 1939. Together with older people's memories of the Germans of World War I as "decent people," this left many Soviet Jews unprepared for the mass murder campaign conducted by four *Einsatzgruppen*, or mobile killing squads, who liquidated much of Soviet Jewry by machine gunning them in or near their home towns. Other Jews were placed in ghettos, most of which were liquidated, along with their inhabitants, by 1941–42. Within five months, the *Einsatzgruppen*, whose officers were largely intellectuals and professionals—as Raul Hilberg observes—had killed about half a million Jews. The *Einsatzgruppen* worked closely with the Wehrmacht, the regular German army, which, according to Hilberg, "went out of its way to turn over Jews to the Einsatzgruppen, to request actions against Jews, to participate in killing operations, and to shoot Jewish hostages in 'reprisal' for attacks on occupation forces."[9] The army's rationale was that the Jews were Bolsheviks who encouraged partisan warfare against the Germans, and so killing Jews was a prophylactic military measure.

The *Einsatzgruppen* numbered only about 3,000 men but were supplemented by Lithuanian, Latvian, Estonian, and Ukrainian collaborators. The mobile killing squads aimed to reach as many cities as quickly as possible and to kill local Jews before they could realize what fate Hitler had planned for them: "The Einsatzgruppen had moved with such speed behind the advancing army that several hundred thousand Jews could be killed like sleeping flies."[10] Needless to say, these killings were often preceded by extensive torture.[11] By war's end, perhaps two or three million Jewish civilians had been killed, singled out from the rest of the population for "special handling."

Soviet Historiography of the Holocaust

Some Western observers charge that it was Soviet policy to suppress any public discussion of the Holocaust. William Korey writes of "the Soviet attempt to obliterate the Holocaust in the memories of Jews as well as non-Jews."[12] Writing in 1970, Mordechai Altshuler asserted, "The wall of silence regarding the holocaust still stands in the Soviet Union, though here and there small cracks were observed . . . the paucity of publications on the Holocaust of Soviet Jewry . . . and the attacks on Yevtushenko's 'Babi Yar' . . . testify to a purposeful policy of the regime to suppress the Holocaust in the Soviet Union."[13] This policy is sometimes explained as a consequence of Soviet antisemitism and hostility toward Jewish history and culture. Korey's explanation is more sophisticated: "Expunging the Holocaust from the record of the past was hardly a simple matter, but unless it were done the profound anguish of the memory was certain to stir a throbbing national consciousness. Martyrdom, after all, is a powerful stimulus to a group's sense of its own identity."[14] In his study of Lithuanian Jewry's resistance to the Nazis, Dov Levin points out that Soviet writing on World War II generally downplayed the role of the Jews in the war, and did so regarding Lithuanian Jewry as well. He reasons that this was in order not to diminish the already marginal role of the Lithuanians in the resistance against the Nazis.[15]

Closer examination of Soviet writings on World War II reveals that if there was a policy of repressing the Holocaust, it was applied unevenly at best. Nevertheless, it remains true that the overall thrust of the Soviet literature was to assign the Holocaust far less significance than it has been given in the West. One cannot entirely dismiss the possibility that this is the consequence of having large, articulate, nationally conscious Jewish populations in the West where they are mostly free to explore Jewish history and draw whatever conclusions they wish, whereas conditions in the Soviet Union permitted neither such exploration nor such expression until the late 1980s. Moreover, no country in the West lost as many of its non-Jewish citizens in the war against Nazism as did the USSR, so that the fate of the Jews in France, Holland, Germany, or Belgium stands in sharper contrast to that of their co-nationals or co-religionists than it does in the East. On the other hand, in Yugoslavia and Poland, where civilian populations were decimated in no less a proportion than they were in the USSR, greater public attention has been paid to the specifically Jewish tragedy of the war period. Thus, the Soviet Union did treat the issue differently from the way it was treated in most other countries, whether socialist or not, though the Soviet treatment was not uniform.

In striking contrast to the way it has been treated in the West, in the USSR the Holocaust was not presented as a unique, separate phenomenon. It was not denied that six million Jews were killed, among them many Soviet ones, nor that Jews were singled out for annihilation. But the Holocaust was seen as an integral part of a larger phenomenon—the murder of civilians—whether Russians, Ukrainians, Belorussians, Gypsies, or other nationalities. It was said to be a natural consequence of racist fascism. The Holocaust, in other words, was but one of several reflexes of fascism, which was, in turn, the ultimate expression of capitalism. Thus, the roots of the Holocaust lay in capitalism, expressed in its most degenerate form. Armed with the theory of "scientific socialism," the Soviets were able to explain in a facile way how so many were murdered. For the Soviets there was no mystery about the Holocaust.

In the West there is a vast body of literature that seeks to understand how it happened. There are cultural explanations, psychological and sociological ones, and political and bureaucratic ones. There is an extensive theological literature that seeks to confront God with the Holocaust. I know of no book published in the USSR that sought to explain the Holocaust as *sui generis*. In fact, the term "Holocaust" is completely unknown in the Soviet literature.

In discussions of the destruction of the Jews, the terms "annihilation" (*unichtozhenie*) or "catastrophe" (*katastrofa*) have been used. It is only recently that "Holocaust," transliterated from English, has appeared.

The *Black Book* of Soviet Jewry, containing documentation gathered from all over the country by the writers Ilya Ehrenburg and Vassily Grossman and others, had 1,200 typescript pages and was printed in 1946. Recently uncovered documents from archives in the FSU show how sensitive Ehrenburg was to the political implications of the project. As early as 1944 he wrote that "It is extremely important to show the solidarity of the Soviet population, the rescue of individual Jews by Russians, Belorussians, Ukrainians and Poles. Such stories will help heal terrible wounds and raise the ideal of friendship among peoples even higher."[16] Grossman observed that "When I read the material . . . I was struck by the all too frequent use of the word 'Jew.' . . . If the book as a whole is about Jews, then we should avoid the use of the word 'Jew.' Otherwise this word will be repeated 6,000 times and will irritate the reader. We can write 'they assembled the people,' or 'people went to the square,' or 'five people fell,' without writing the word 'Jew.' "[17] Ehrenburg replied that use of "Jew" was unavoidable and that he had also not taken out the term "politsai." "By 'politsai' we understand not a German, but a traitor. Establishing just who exactly was a 'politsai' will be very difficult. I didn't take out the word 'Jew' but I did take out the word 'Ukrainian' and wrote 'politsai.' "[18] In 1945 a review commission concluded that "too much is recounted in the sketches about the vile activity of traitors among the Ukrainians, Lithuanians, et al."[19] Finally, in 1947, the head of the Party Secretariat's Agitprop department, G. Alexandrov, wrote to Andrei Zhdanov, regarded at the time as Stalin's heir apparent, that "in reading the book, especially the first section concerning . . . Ukraine, one gets a false picture of the true nature of fascism. . . . Running through the whole book is the idea that the Germans murdered and plundered Jews only. The reader unwittingly gets the impression that the Germans fought against the USSR for the sole purpose of destroying the Jews," whereas "Hitler's ruthless slaughters were carried out equally against Russians, Jews, Belorussians, Ukrainians, Latvians, Lithuanians and other peoples of the Soviet Union. . . . As a result of these considerations, the Propaganda Department considers the publication of 'The Black Book' in the USSR inadvisable." The decision was made on October 7, 1947, that since the book "contains grave political errors," it "may not be published."[20] All copies were sent to storage warehouses where they were destroyed in 1948, along with the type from which they were set. Thus, because it might mar the image of "friendship of peoples" in Soviet society and because it singled out Jewish suffering, the major work on the Soviet Holocaust has never been published in the USSR. Because manuscript copies had been sent abroad, Hebrew, English, and even Russian (published in Jerusalem) editions were published.[21] Finally, a Russian language edition was published in Vilnius, capital of the former Soviet republic of Lithuania in 1993, though not in the Commonwealth of Independent States itself.

The Holocaust was treated as regrettable, but merely one small part of the larger phenomenon that, according to the Soviets, resulted in the death of twenty million of their citizens. (In the early 1990s, in the post-Soviet media the figure of twenty-seven million war casualties came to be used.) If the Nazis gave the Jews "special treatment," the Soviets would not.

This premise translated into a policy of bypassing the Holocaust for most general audiences and addressing it in a highly ideological way for certain specialized ones. William Korey's survey has shown that Soviet elementary school history textbooks contain no reference to Jews at all, and a thirty-page chapter on World War II in one of them has not a single reference to either Jews or antisemitism. The same is true of secondary school texts and syllabi, except for a single reference to "terrible Jewish pogroms."[22]

The controversy over the construction of a monument at Babi Yar, the site in Kiev where more than thirty-three thousand of the city's Jews were shot in the course of two days, is well known. For years no monument was placed there, and the site was prepared for housing, a park, and other uses. In 1959 the writer Viktor Nekrasov protested plans to turn the site into a park and soccer stadium. Support began to mount for the construction of a memorial monument. The issue gained world attention when popular Soviet poet Yevgenyi Yevtushenko published a poem, "Babi Yar," whose first line is "Over Babi Yar there are no monuments." The poem was a sensation because it condemned antisemitism and made it clear that Soviet society was not free of that problem. When Dmitri Shostakovich included the poem in his thirteenth symphony, authorities banned public performances of the symphony for several years. Clearly, they were uncomfortable with the issue of antisemitism as well as with the memorialization of Jewish suffering in the war. But public pressure resulted in a memorial placed at Babi Yar. The memorial is a typically "socialist realist" monument on a heroic scale. The inscription reads, "Here in 1941–1943, the German fascist invaders executed more than 100,000 citizens of Kiev and prisoners of war." There is no reference to Jews. Somewhat ludicrously, in the late 1980s another plaque was added to the monument, this time in Yiddish. But in an obvious, if ridiculous, political compromise, the Yiddish text also does not mention Jews! Finally, in 1991, after Ukraine had become independent, a new monument in the shape of a menorah was erected some distance from the Soviet monument. The latest monument is inscribed in Hebrew and Yiddish and makes explicit reference to Jews. In the 1960s Yevtushenko was roundly criticized by conservative writers who charged that his poem slandered the "Russian crew-cut lads" who had fought the Nazis because it focused on Jews. The writer Dmitri Starikov asserted that "the antisemitism of the Fascists is only part of their misanthropic policy of genocide . . . the destruction of the 'lower races' including the Slavs."[23] When Shostakovich included "Babi Yar" in his symphony, Yevtushenko was forced to make two additions to the text. One line reads, "Here together with Russians and Ukrainians lie Jews," and the other is, "I am proud of Russia which stood in the path of the bandits."

Again, the point is not that others had suffered along with Jews, which no one would dispute, but that there was nothing unique about the quality and quantity of Jewish suffering, a far more dubious assertion. The same issue arose in regard to Anatoly Kuznetsov's novel, *Babi Yar*, published in 1966. Public controversy ensued over whether Jewish travails should have been singled out from among those of all others. Kuznetsov's novel and *Heavy Sand* (1978), by the Jewish writer Anatoly Rybakov, are among the very few Russian-language novels which acknowledge—even assert—a special fate for the Jews during the war.

The problem arose not only in regard to novels and monuments but also in connection with museum displays. For example, despite the testimony of her uncle and several others, the seventeen-year-old Jewish partisan Masha Bruskina, who was hanged by the Nazis in Minsk, was identified as an "unknown partisan" in the Minsk Museum of the History of the Great Patriotic War. Significantly, the authorities' refusal to identify her by name and nationality was seen by some Jews as a deliberate insult and a refusal to acknowledge Jewish heroism. A highly decorated war veteran, Lev Ovsishcher, commented, "This story explains why Jews who understand what is happening in this country feel the only correct decision is to leave." He subsequently emigrated and went to Israel, after a long struggle.[24]

Scrutiny of strictly historical treatments of the period 1941–45, whether popular or scholarly, reveals a more complex picture. The overall tendency was to downplay, even ignore, the Holocaust, but some striking contrasts appear. While some works that should logically discuss the Holocaust ignore it completely, others touch only on selected aspects of it, and still others present a relatively straightforward and well-rounded account. Even during the war (1944), the Soviet Extraordinary State Commission to Examine and Investigate German-Fascist Crimes was "instructed to avoid stating that the victims of the massacres had been Jews" and "to suppress the extent of Ukrainian collaboration with the Germans and particularly with the SS in the mass shootings of Jews."[25]

A fairly close examination of the six-volume official Soviet history of the war reveals not a single reference to Jews. Nor do the terms "antisemitism" or "Holocaust" appear in the index. In the third volume, the Nazi occupation of the USSR is referred to as "a regime of terror and occupation" and the *Einsatzgruppen* are mentioned, as is Babi Yar, but the word "Jew" does not appear in any of these connections.[26] A large history of Ukraine, published in 1982, does not mention Jews even once, not even in connection with the Holocaust, even though Jews have lived there for centuries, played a major role in its economy and culture, and died there in the hundreds of thousands during the Holocaust.[27] In striking—almost ludicrous—contrast is a study of wartime Estonia. In 1939 there were more than 1.5 million Jews living in the Soviet Ukraine and only 5,000 in "bourgeois" Estonia. Yet, while at least two histories of Ukraine passed over Jewish history and the Holocaust in silence, the study of Estonia presented a sympathetic account of Jewish suffering during the Holocaust and an undistorted account of Jewish participation in the armed struggle against the Nazis. The Germans' robbery of art and other treasures in private Jewish hands was referred to explicitly. German documents were quoted that report "the total liquidation of the Jews . . . at the present time there are no more Jews in Estonia." The editors commented, "Implementing their monstrous racial theories, the German fascists and their collaborators in Estonia exterminated each and every Jew and Gypsy."[28] Collaboration by Estonians with the Nazis in the murder of Jews is also discussed frankly.[29] The authors acknowledged that Estonian collaborators "boasted to their bosses that they had outdone the others in annihilating the Jews" and that the groundwork had been laid before the war by antisemites, one of whom is quoted as saying to an audience at the Estonian military academy, "We should be happy that we have few Jews among us. We took in a good number from Tsarist Russia, but we look down on the Jews."[30] Unlike other studies, this one prominently features Red Army men and partisans of obviously Jewish extraction.[31]

A documentary collection on Belarus included, among others, the order establishing the ghetto in Minsk; descriptions of Germans killing Jews wantonly, mass murders of Jews in the Brest-Litovsk area, and the extermination of the Jews in Pinsk; a German report on the resistance of one of the condemned men; and a photograph of Jews being herded into the Grodno ghetto. The historical origins of ghettos were explained, concluding with the observation that "the Hitlerites revived ghettos in territories occupied by them, turning them into camps for the mass annihilation of the Jewish population."[32] A pamphlet on the Ninth Fort in Lithuania, where thousands of Jews were killed, mentioned several Nazi *Aktionen* against the Jews. Here, however, a greater attempt was made to blur the specifically Jewish tragedy. It was said that *Einsatzgruppe* A entered Kaunas with "the special task of exterminating the local party and Soviet Aktiv, eliminating the resistance by Soviet patriots, and exterminating the Jews." The order in which the victims were listed here may be significant. Even clearer is the contrast between the reproduction of a German document reporting on the "special handling" of 4,000 *Jews* in the Ponary death camp and the Russian caption that says, "the Hitlerite security police report: another 4,000 *people* [emphasis added] have been killed."[33]

One of the most popular Soviet works on the war treated the Holocaust most curiously. S. S. Smirnov's three-volume work appeared in an edition of one hundred thousand, and Smirnov was a popular participant in media features on the war. In the work Smirnov referred several times to the suffering of the Jews, but seemed to go out of his way to avoid references to Jews as fighters and resisters.

> For the Hitlerites, all peoples, aside from the Germans, all nations aside from the Germanic ones, were inferior and superfluous inhabitants of this earth. . . .

> The first among these 'inferior' nations that would have to disappear were the Jews. The Germans left them no choice—this nation was to be completely exterminated. In all countries captured by the Hitlerite armies the extermination of the Jews was carried out on an unprecedented scale, with typical German planning and organization. Millions of people of Jewish nationality or with a tinge of Jewish blood became victims of mass shootings, were burned in crematoria or asphyxiated in the gas chambers and trucks. Whole neighborhoods were turned into Jewish ghettos and were burned to the ground with their thousands of inhabitants who wore the yellow six-pointed star, the compulsory badge for Jews in lands occupied by the Germans.

Smirnov went on to say that the people of Kiev "remember how, hour after hour, endless columns of Jews passed on the way to being shot at Babi Yar. Prisoners at Auschwitz, Maidanek, Treblinka remember how thousands of groups of Jews from Poland and Hungary, the Soviet Union and Czechoslovakia, from France and Holland, passed through the gas chambers in an endless convoy of death and how piles of bodies lay at the ovens of the crematoria." He wrote of "the terrible fate of those who lived behind the barbed wire of innumerable ghettos." His generalizations were exemplified in the story of Roman Levin: "The ten year old Roman, who until then had been simply a Soviet boy, a Pioneer and school boy, suddenly learned that he was a Jew, and because of that they could insult him with impunity, beat him or even kill him." Levin escaped the Brest ghetto and was hidden by a devout Polish Catholic woman who was later shot when the Gestapo discovered her ties to the partisans.[34]

In subsequent volumes, Smirnov discussed the persecution of Jews in Ukraine and Hungary. In Ukraine the Nazis "often . . . marched groups of people, condemned to being shot, along the streets . . . on their way out of town. At first they shot groups of communists, Soviet officials and people active in civic affairs. After that along the same route they began to take Jews, whole families, young and old. After that came columns of Gypsies who were also considered an inferior nation."[35] Smirnov reported that the Germans used a slogan: "Germans—*gut*; Jews—*kaput*; Russians—*tozhe* [also]; Ukrainians—*pozzhe* [later]." Smirnov also described the huge concentration of Jews in the Budapest ghetto and their deportation.[36] Yet, he assiduously avoided identifying fighters as Jews. Describing the defenders of the Brest fortress, he mentioned "the Russians Anatoly Vinogradov and Raisa Abakumova, the Armenian Samvel Matevosian, the Ukrainian Aleksandr Semenenko, the Belorussian Aleksandr Makhnach, . . . the Tatar Petr Gavrilov" and even "the German Viacheslav Meyer." The one hero whose nationality is not mentioned is Efim Moiseevich Fomin. Lest there be any doubt about his nationality, he is described as "short . . . dark haired with intelligent and mournful eyes," a political commissar from a small town in the Vitebsk area, the son of a smith and a seamstress. All these are stereotypical characteristics of the Jew. Yet, Fomin is identified only as "the renowned commissar of the Brest fortress, a hero and a true son of the Communist Party, one of the chief organizers and leaders of the legendary defense."[37] When referring to the other heroes, Smirnov pointed out their nationality (Gavrilov, the Kazan Tatar; Matevosian, "of a poor Armenian family"; and Kizhevator, "the son of a Mordvin peasant").[38] Smirnov followed the same pattern when describing Soviet partisans in Italy.[39] Why did Smirnov describe Jewish martyrdom in detail and assiduously ignore Jewish heroism? Was this in line with an official directive? Was it the compromise he reached with himself, or, more likely, with a censor? We cannot tell, of course, but the pattern is too consistent to be accidental.

Another book, published a year earlier, presents Jews in a heroic light as partisans. A character in the book, Sarah Khatskelevna Levin, and her Yiddish-speaking daughter meet "remarkable people who have not lost their courage and their human dignity," even in the Minsk ghetto. They "refused to give in without a struggle" and formed a fighting organization.[40] The sharp contrast between treatments of the Holocaust in Ukraine, Belarus, Lithuania, and Estonia raises several possibilities. The variance is explained either by the choices made by the writers themselves, or, less likely, by a republic-level policy that differed from one republic to another, or by the caprice of censors in different places. It should be noted that the Holocaust was treated most openly in the Estonian volume and avoided in Ukrainian literature. In Estonia there is no tradition of antisemitism, whereas in the Ukraine there is a substantial one. Whatever the reason for the different treatments of the Holocaust, they clearly show the absence of a uniform, universally applied party line on the issue, though there was an overall thrust toward downplaying it or generalizing it to include many peoples.

A Soviet study of Nazi propaganda mentioned Nazi views of Poles, Gypsies, and Jews as inferior races and the fact that the Nazis played up "the Jewish origins" of the leaders of the Russian revolution. The author referred to the Nazis' "pathological anti-Semitism" and their claim that in the Soviet Union those who could not show Jewish origins were considered class enemies. This foreshadowed the "fate that the German racists prepared for the Jews."[41] Further details were not given, and it should be noted that this is an academic monograph, published in a relatively small edition. A documentary history of the Soviet Union that devoted an entire chapter to World War II included no references to the Nazis' racial policy. The excerpt from the diary of Masha Rolnikaite, a Jewish girl in the Vilnius ghetto, does not mention the word "Jew."[42] The authoritative *Great Soviet Encyclopedia* admitted that antisemitism "found its most extreme expression in fascist Germany." It stated succinctly that "the Nazis carried out a policy of mass extermination of the Jews; about six million Jews were murdered in World War II."[43] Thus, Soviet audiences were generally not exposed to even the most elementary details of the Holocaust, though in the 1960s, a few volumes were published that did provide more information. Significantly, at least some were translations from other languages.[44]

It is all the more striking, therefore, that almost every issue of *Sovietish heymland,* the Soviet Yiddish monthly which appeared from 1961 to 1991 (originally with a circulation of twenty-five thousand, later reduced to seven thousand and less), contained material on the Holocaust—stories, poems, memoirs, factual information. Of course, this journal was published with the approval of the authorities—in fact, the initiative for publishing it probably came "from above," part of Khrushchev's campaign to refute Western charges of official Soviet antisemitism. Therefore, it is not surprising that the journal features consistently certain themes that serve a didactic political purpose. These are: 1) gentiles frequently saved Jews in occupied territories; 2) Jews who resisted did so for universal, not parochial, reasons; 3) there was much cooperation among all nationalities against the Nazis; 4) the only collaborators with the Nazis were fascists, and nearly all of them now live in the West. The first theme is illustrated by documents such as a letter from a woman, now living in New York, who describes how a Lithuanian couple named Ruzgis, a Polish doctor named Hrabowiecka, and a Russian family named Yakubovsky saved her daughter. Short stories present Russians, especially workers, saving Jews, and wealthy Jews serving on *Judenraten* (Jewish Councils).[45]

The second theme, *druzhba narodov* (friendship among peoples), is emphasized throughout. Even an account of the Warsaw Ghetto uprising praises Soviet Yiddish writing on it because, of course, the role of Communists in the uprising is emphasized, and there are fictional accounts of Red Army men sneaking into the ghetto to help the resisting Jews.[46] The uprising is described as "an important contribution of the Jewish masses to the international struggle of the progressive forces of all peoples, led by the Soviet Union, against fascism and international reaction."[47]

A description of how Bulgarians saved Jews concludes that "the struggle of the Bulgarian people to save the Jews, under the leadership of the Communists, can in no way be separated from the general struggle of the Bulgarian people against Fascism." The struggle against antisemitism can be successfully conducted "only in close alliance with the progressive and democratic forces of the world."[48] The other side of this coin is seen in the resistance of Soviet authorities to the publication of Peretz Markish's novel *Trot fun doires* (Footsteps of the Generations, 1966), on the grounds that its hero was a "Zionist." The portrayal of him dying wrapped in a prayer shawl was also objectionable. The objections to publishing the novel were overridden by special authorization of the Soviet Writers Union.[49] Thus, resistance to the Holocaust and to antisemitism had to be universalized. It was to be portrayed as part of larger progressive struggles, led by Communists.

The third theme is the cooperation of all nationalities in the struggle against the Nazis. "One of the main sources of the world-historical victory . . . was the friendship among the Soviet peoples. Against the . . . enemy, Russians, Ukrainians, Belorussians, Jews, Georgians, Armenians—the sons and daughters of all the peoples of the Soviet Union fought shoulder to shoulder."[50] A story about a Jewish Hero of the Soviet Union, Chaim Tevelevich Diskin, points out the heroism of his two Russian comrades,[51] and another relates how Russians in Taganrog saved Jews.[52] In discussing the proposal to build the Babi Yar monument in Kiev, it is stressed that "people of different nationalities—Russians, Ukrainians, Jews—were attracted by the idea of putting up a monument in Babi Yar."[53]

The well-known writer Boris Polevoi claimed that Gentiles "stubbornly opposed the murderers of the Jews, and Jewish families were hidden."[54] An editorial comment asserted that "in the days of the Great Patriotic War, friendship among peoples, among nations, was the most powerful weapon in the struggle with the fascists."[55] Writing about the sculptor Elmar Rivosh, whose entire family was killed in Riga, Misha Lev pointed out that Rivosh could not have saved himself without the assistance of his friends, "identified and anonymous Latvians and Russians, Jews and Poles." A Russian woman on the "Aryan side" fed him, a Russian doctor healed him, and a Latvian friend helped him find a hiding place.[56] This is the pattern emphasized throughout the literature, whether in Russian or Yiddish.

How then can one explain collaboration with the Nazis on the part of hundreds of thousands? The fourth theme provides the simple answer. The collaborators were all ideologically deformed. "Petty bourgeois are the same all over. Whoever has might, is right, they feel."[57] All the collaborators—whether Latvian, Polish, Ukrainian, or Russian—were "bourgeois nationalists" or marginal elements, "the refuse of the Latvian people," as one article put it.[58] Many of them, it was claimed, were leading anti-Soviet agitators in the West. The Soviets long denounced anti-Soviet emigres as collaborators with the Nazis, and there is no doubt that the label fits many. Sometimes it was acknowledged that these people participated in the annihilation of the Jewish population. By 1987, some were calling for a reassessment of Soviet emigres: "Our compatriots abroad—until just recently we pretended they didn't exist (and if there were some abroad, they were all former Vlasovites, traitors to the homeland one and all). And yet millions of our fellow countrymen—Russians, Ukrainians, Belorussians, Armenians, Jews—live far from their native land and many of them were scarcely burdened with inexpiable guilt."[59] But the more usual pattern was to omit the Jews: "It is precisely in the West . . . that traitors on whose hands the blood of Latvians, Lithuanians and Estonians will never dry have taken refuge."[60] Of course, these discussions avoided the fundamental problem of explaining how such large numbers of people could have been so infected with antisemitism and/or so hostile to the Soviet regime that they participated in the Nazis' work.[61]

The existence of antisemitism in the Red Army and among the partisan groups was another problem that was never mentioned.[62] Also, the existence of separate Jewish partisan groups was completely unacknowledged. The role of Jews in the armed struggle against the German invaders was generally downplayed, as we have seen in the work of S. S. Smirnov. Writing about Hero of the Soviet Union Chaim Tevelevich Diskin, Marshal V. Kazakov never mentions Diskin's very obvious Jewish nationality.[63] Even partisan leader Colonel Dmitri Medvedev, who accepted Jewish survivors, including women and children, into his group, never mentions the nationality of three Jewish heroes he describes, "although in his two books Medvedev rarely forgot to tell his readers whether his heroes were Russians, Ukrainians, Belorussians, Poles or Kazakhs."[64] He also does not mention how he saved 150 Jewish women, children, and old people. The assumption is that the censors or editors deliberately omitted these items. Jewish combatants were mentioned in general discussions of the armed forces,[65] and there are a few pamphlets or books published about Jewish war heroes, though the total number of biographies was very large.[66] Again, *Sovietish heymland* is different from the literature in Russian. In this Yiddish journal there is considerable fictional and non-fictional material about Jewish fighters. Jewish partisans were described in positive terms,[67] memoirs of Jewish generals and soldiers of lesser rank were often published,[68] and many Jewish soldiers, including those who gave their lives, were portrayed.[69] But the overwhelming majority of Soviet readers, even Jewish ones, had no access at all to this literature. The role of Jews as combatants was largely ignored, even more than as victims, in most cases, it would seem, deliberately. This may be one reason that in recent years a relatively large number of works on Jewish fighters have been published, almost all of them outside the FSU.[70] It is as if the veterans of the struggle and some of their children and grandchildren are trying to establish their place in history.

For many years it was assumed that anything published in the Soviet Union reflected policy at some level, since it had to pass official censorship. Examination of the literature on the Holocaust casts some doubt on this assumption. Nevertheless, the published literature remains almost the only source on reactions to the Holocaust, since to date there have been no other instruments for gauging public reaction to it. Thus far, there have been no surveys of people's reactions to the fate of the Jews during the war, nor are there any measures of their knowledge of the Holocaust. However, a survey conducted among nearly 400 Soviet Jewish immigrants in Detroit, within half a year of their arrival in 1989–91, reveals that few knew the approximate number of Soviet Jews killed in the Holocaust, though a majority cited the figure six million for the total number of Jews who died. When asked whether they had read about the Holocaust in the USSR, a majority of those over the age of thirty had read some literature on the subject. The most frequently cited works were Rybakov's novel *Heavy Sand*, Yevtushenko's poem "Babi Yar," and Kuznetsov's novel of the same name. The most frequently cited source of information on the Holocaust was discussion among family and friends. Thus, almost no nonfictional, historical sources of information were cited. One can presume that if Jews were not aware of any other sources of information on the Holocaust, non-Jews were even less aware.

The Holocaust and the Soviet Political Calculus

Why was the Holocaust generally glossed over, suppressed, or universalized in the Soviet literature on the subject? Several possible explanations present themselves. One is that this is simply the consequence of antisemitism. The Soviets were incapable of showing sympathy for the Jews and refused to acknowledge the national tragedy. This may be too simplistic. As we have seen, there was considerable variation in the treatment of the Holocaust in Soviet works on the subject. Another explanation sees the origins of this policy in Stalin's postwar antisemitism. A different kind of Holocaust was being prepared after the war, as foreshadowed by mass arrests in 1948, the "anti-cosmopolitan campaign," the execution of the Yiddish writers in 1952, the "doctors' plot," and the building of large barracks in Siberia. To admit that Jews had just been so terribly persecuted and to signal to the Soviet public that their suffering was a matter of concern might have impeded this policy.

A third explanation has to do with the shift in the Soviet "political formula." The basis of legitimation of the Soviet regime, the legitimating myth, shifted from the revolution to World War II.[71] After all, only a tiny minority of Soviet people remembered the revolution, but a far greater number could identify with the Great Patriotic War. Moreover, while the outcome of the revolution was not welcomed by all, no Soviet citizen could wish for a different outcome of World War II. For several decades there was a virtual cult of World War II in the Soviet Union in literature, movies, art, and television. To emphasize the Jewish role and fate would have diminished the all-Union effort and experience. It is bad enough, some would have argued, that the revolution was identified with the Jews. To "give the war to the Jews" would not only be a gross distortion of history but would also erode the legitimating power of the experience and would arouse great resentment by other nationalities. Of course, this does not explain why such strenuous efforts were made to diminish artificially the Jewish fate. After all, straightforward treatment would not in any way diminish the overall Soviet sacrifice or effort.

Soviet authorities no doubt were aware that knowledge of the Holocaust raises Jewish consciousness and can retard assimilation. It is no accident that Jewish educators in the United States emphasize the Holocaust in curricula for children and adults, especially for audiences that have less-than-intensive exposure to other Jewish experiences. The Holocaust is so recent, so devastating, that few can remain untouched or unmoved by it. Even the most assimilated Jew—whether in the United States or the FSU—must be in some way affected by it. The Soviets, who saw assimilation as the solution to "the Jewish question," were opposed to anything that "artificially" raised Jewish consciousness. Moreover, the Holocaust raises the troublesome question of what the non-Jews were doing during the mass murder of Jews. An "incorrect" understanding could lead one to draw equally "incorrect" conclusions about prospects for assimilation. Indeed, in the Detroit survey, most immigrants who were asked to describe the attitude of most non-Jews to the murder of Jews during the war thought they had been supportive of the killing or indifferent to it. The conclusion the respondents drew from that was that "there is no place for me in the Soviet Union," as many phrased it. Zionists have used the Holocaust to justify the "negation of the Diaspora," to argue that the world is inherently antisemitic and that, therefore, there is no solution to the Jewish problem other than a Jewish state and immigration to it. Since the Soviets opposed this conclusion, they were wary of even dealing with the premise as raised by the Holocaust. Finally, any discussion of the Holocaust brings up the troublesome issue of collaboration and betrayal by citizens of the USSR, a topic with which Soviet historiography was not comfortable and which continues to trouble the successor states. Already in 1944 members of a Soviet state commission to investigate Nazi crimes used the word "politsai" to conceal Ukrainian collaboration, just as Ehrenburg had hinted.[72] Indeed, the subject of collaboration has not been thoroughly investigated in the West and remains a major source of tension between Jewish and East European communities there.

Some Consequences of the Soviet Treatment of the Holocaust

The ultimate universalization of the Holocaust is the Soviet equation of fascism with Zionism and the charge of collaboration between the two. As one Soviet writer asserted, "Many facts have convincingly demonstrated the fascist nature of the ideology and policies of Zionism. Fascism is disgusting in any of its guises—its Zionist version is no better than its Hitlerite one."[73] Between 1975 and 1978 at least twenty-three articles in the Soviet press claimed that Zionists collaborated actively with the Nazis. A 1983 pamphlet outlined alleged Zionist collaboration with the Nazis as manifested in the presence of Zionists on *Judenraten*, in Zionist attempts to negotiate with Nazis in order to save Jews, and in the Zionists' defense of war criminals.[74] In another pamphlet Zionism was described as "a bourgeois-nationalistic ideology, suffused with the poison of racism and chauvinism, militarism and extremism, representing a threat to all of humanity"—precisely the characteristics generally attributed to Nazism.[75]

In the late 1980s some anti-Zionist works were criticized for their "inexact formulations and even incorrect assertions," including exaggerations of the linkages between Zionism and Nazism and the claim that Zionists attempted to form a "united anti-Soviet front of Hitlerism . . . [and] West European and American capitalism at the end of World War II." But there was no rejection of the Nazism-Zionism link, only an admonition to "evaluate properly the real dimensions of the cooperation among various elements in the course of historic events."[76] The legitimacy of associating Nazism and Zionism remained unchallenged. One can make such an assertion if one argues that ideology and class, not ethnicity, were what determined the behavior of the Nazis and the fate of the Jews. Nazis and Zionists were said to share class-based interests, strategies, tactics, and goals. One of the great ironies in this is that in 1947 Soviet diplomat Andrei Gromyko said at the United Nations that "during the last war, the Jewish people underwent exceptional sorrow and suffering . . . the time has come to help these people not by word but by deeds."[77] This was his explanation for the Soviet vote to partition Palestine and create a Jewish state.

Half a century ago, then, Zionism was a justified consequence of fascism. Later it became but a variant of it. The equation of Zionism with fascism may have made Zionism comprehensible to Soviet citizens—otherwise it would have been as abstract as Buddhism—but it was deeply insulting to Soviet Jews. In fact, even the universalization or suppression of the Holocaust deeply injured them, because a traumatic part of their recent history was denied. Not surprisingly, it led them to ask questions about a system that did such a thing, about their neighbors, about their own fate as Jews, as the Detroit study makes clear. Many came to precisely the Zionist conclusions the regime wished to avoid. In late 1989 and through 1991, when over 300,000 Soviet Jews emigrated, largely to Israel, the fear of social breakdown and "anarchy" were cited by many as the reason for their hasty departure. Not a few made specific reference to the Holocaust and said that they thought there was a realistic chance that it could be repeated, this time without a foreign invasion.

A less important, but not trivial, consequence of the Soviet downplaying of the Holocaust is that it was perceived in the West as further evidence of Soviet antisemitism. Moreover, the issue of collaboration by some Jews with the Bolsheviks, and by some Balts, Poles, and Ukrainians with the Nazis, remains extremely controversial and touchy in the relations between Jews and Eastern Europeans.

The dominant Soviet approach to the Holocaust, criticized by most Westerners who are aware of it, raises an interesting question. It is obviously a malicious distortion to pass over it in silence. It robs people of an important part of their history, desecrates the memory of millions, and signals that Jewish lives are not worth remarking on. But what about the other Soviet strategy, embedding the Holocaust in the larger "struggle against fascism"? Disregarding the question of historical accuracy for the moment and concentrating on the question of using the knowledge of the Holocaust to prevent future such occurrences, one wonders whether the latter aim is best served by emphasizing the Jewish catastrophe's uniqueness. Especially in a country with some antisemitic traditions, assigning the Holocaust to a marginal minority that was despised by some may allow many to dismiss it as either irrelevant to their concerns or something Jews might have "deserved." Perhaps the approach of some Soviet writers—discussing the Holocaust in the context of the overall Soviet struggle, but pointing out those features that set the Jews apart from others—might be most effective in the FSU and other Slavic countries in alerting readers to the dangers that face all people while not diminishing the Jewish tragedy. Since Western Gentiles did not suffer nearly as much as East Europeans from the Nazis, and American noncombatants suffered not at all, the Jewish tragedy stands out more starkly for them than for East Europeans who witnessed the Nazi occupation. In Eastern Europe and the FSU, the Holocaust must be embedded in a larger mosaic of palpable, immediate suffering, though its unique configurations should not be blurred in that mosaic, for even in the experience of those regions the unspeakable tragedy of the Jews remains unique.

By the late 1980s the time seemed to be at hand for Soviet reassessments of the war, and it was announced that a new ten-volume history of the Great Fatherland War was in preparation. The previous history "no longer meets the present-day requirements of our society, in which an expansion of openness and democracy is now under way."[78] As part of *glasnost'* and *perestroika*, there was a major reexamination of Soviet history in the Soviet Union. An article in *Izvestiia* explained, "The creation of an honest school course in USSR history is a task of paramount state importance."[79] Another article noted that "The public's growing interest in history is an indisputable fact. . . . Only by not concealing facts, but subjecting them to public scrutiny, thorough examination, objective analysis and impartial assessments can our historical scholarship restore its reputation."[80]

Not surprisingly, the new ten-volume history of the war that was supposed to be published in 1991, the fiftieth anniversary of the Nazi invasion, became embroiled in political controversy. The chief of a team of editors, the late Colonel-General Dmitry Volkogonov, was dismissed from that post and also left his post as director of the Military History Institute. He was attacked from two sides. In November 1990 three historians charged that the team was not properly trained, had not reviewed non-Soviet literature on the subject, and did not have access to the necessary documents.[81] Thus, the new work would be no improvement over its predecessor published from 1973 to 1982. The new edition, the critics said, was under the supervision of Marshall Yazov and others selected on the basis of their posts, not their abilities or knowledge, and so it was "doomed to be a repetition of its predecessors."

On the other hand, Marshall Sergei Akhromeyev accused Volkogonov of being "clever and glib" but having a "deep antipathy for socialism," though earlier he hypocritically espoused Communism. It was no wonder, he said, that the draft of the first volume "makes it seem that Stalinism was the dominant, distinguishing feature of the prewar decades" and it "relates almost nothing of the Soviet people's dedication and heroic efforts in building socialism during those years."[82] Even after the draft of the first volume had been reedited, Marshall Yazov accused Volkogonov of "giving a tendentious, anticommunist interpretation of the events preceding the start of the war." Volkogonov replied that his work in the archives made him realize that "a great deal that people ought to know is kept shrouded in secrecy." He observed that it might be possible to compile a true history of the war in twenty or thirty years after the last of the participants had died.[83]

In 1989–90 several articles on the Holocaust appeared in the Soviet press, particularly in Ukraine. The massacre at Babi Yar and its specifically Jewish aspects were commemorated in public ceremonies. A Kiev newspaper devoted an entire page to an excerpt from Ehrenburg and Grossman's *Black Book*, referring to an earlier article in a Moscow evening newspaper that had revealed to Soviet readers the existence and fate of that documentary study.[84] In September 1988 a large gathering in Moscow commemorated the slaughter at Babi Yar, and the event was marked publicly at Babi Yar itself. Not only did police not interfere, as they had in earlier years, but scenes from the meetings were shown on television. In Minsk, Lvov, and Vilnius memorial sculptures commemorating the Jewish Holocaust were commissioned or planned.[85] In 1989 an agreement was reached between Soviet archivists and the Yad Vashem Institute in Jerusalem permitting several researchers from Jerusalem to go through some Soviet archives and microfilm German and Soviet documents pertaining to the Holocaust; later, researchers from the United States Holocaust Memorial Museum and other foreign institutions were given access to Holocaust-related materials. At an April 1990 international congress of historians in Moscow, Dr. Yitzhak Arad, then director of Yad Vashem, and one or two others delivered papers on the Holocaust period. It is highly significant that groups of amateur historians in Moscow, St. Petersburg, Minsk, Odessa, and elsewhere have been studying the Holocaust, conducting taped interviews with survivors and with non-Jews who observed aspects of the mass murder of the Jews.[86] The great majority of these researchers appear to be people who were themselves born after the war. In the fall 1989 and in subsequent years several of them were invited to Israel to participate in a training seminar for Holocaust researchers. In Moscow, Dr. Ilya Altman has established a Holocaust Center which engages in both research and public education. In the spring of 1996, ground was to be broken for a synagogue on Moscow's Poklonnaya Gora, site of a huge memorial complex dedicated to World War II. The synagogue, which is supposed to house a Holocaust museum, will complement the church on the site and a mosque to be built there. In the war museum itself, there is no panel or display case devoted specifically to the Holocaust, but in one display, it is mentioned, *inter alia*, that "Of 9,600,000 Jews living in Germany and German-occupied Europe, 5,700,000 vanished [*ischezli*]; of them, 4,500,000 were physically annihilated." No explanation is given as to the fate of the 1.2 million others who "disappeared." In another case, a yellow star marked "Jude" is displayed, but no explanatory caption accompanies it. Several Jewish war heroes are mentioned and their pictures displayed.

The politicization of the Holocaust continued after the breakup of the USSR. In September 1991, the Lithuanian government, having just achieved Soviet recognition of its declaration of independence, pardoned about a thousand Lithuanians who had been convicted by Soviet tribunals of collaborating with the Nazis. Jewish and Israeli circles immediately protested. Clearly, the Lithuanian motivation was political: having achieved independence, they were inclined to say everything Soviet was bad. If a Soviet tribunal adjudged a man guilty, he must have been innocent. This was not only *prima facie* absurd, but also a foolish move politically. The Lithuanians modified their position, suspending the rehabilitations in October and considered setting up a Lithuanian-Israeli-American commission of experts to review rehabilitation requests.[87] Though the commission was established, it moved slowly. In February 1995 three Israeli members spent a week in Lithuanian archives examining records of those convicted of collaboration with the Nazis, but the issue does not seem to have been resolved. Dov Levin, a member of the commission, asserts that the Lithuanians insist on a " 'formula of symmetry' which equates Jewish and Lithuanian suffering during and after World War Two" and which serves to remove or mitigate Lithuanian responsibility for the murder of the Jews.[88]

These incidents point to: 1) the continued sensitivity of the collaboration issue; 2) the tendency to politicize the issue and give it contemporary significance; 3) the very different perceptions of Jews and other peoples. In Ukraine the issue is at least as sensitive as it is in the Baltic. Ukrainian images of Jews as Communists and Jewish images of Ukrainians as fascists survive long after the war. The trial and acquittal in 1993 of John Demjanjuk in Israel, where he had been extradited from the United States on charges that he was a notorious guard at Treblinka, highlighted the issue. It is impossible to establish with certainty how many Ukrainians collaborated with the Nazis and in what ways, and how many saved Jews, though there is no doubt that the former vastly outnumbered the latter. In Ukraine, collaboration with the Nazis took the form not only of individual acts, but of organized politics. Ukrainian collaboration took six general forms. The Organization of Ukrainian Nationalists, formed in Poland (West Ukraine) before the war, split into two factions in 1940. One faction, led by Stepan Bandera (after whom a major boulevard in Lviv [Lvov] has been renamed today), declared at its second congress in April 1941 that "The Jews . . . are the most faithful prop of the Bolshevik regime and the vanguard of Muscovite imperialism in Ukraine. . . . The Organization of Ukrainian Nationalists is engaged in a struggle against the Jews. . . . "[89] In July 1941, Yaroslav Stetsko, head of the Ukrainian government supported by Bandera, stated that "The principal enemy of the Ukraine is not Jewry but Moscow. . . . Yet the role of the Jews must not be underestimated. We are of the opinion that a struggle against the Jews of the Ukraine should be undertaken according to the German methods, and so I am firm in my view that the Jews must be annihilated completely, and the German methods for liquidating the Jews should be brought to the Ukraine."[90]

The second form of Ukrainian collaboration was the formation of Ukrainian armed units, which were attached to German military and police formations.

The Ukrainian units included the "Nachtigal" and "Roland" battalions, and the Waffen-SS division "Halychyna."[91] Third, leaders of at least two Ukrainian churches blessed the German army and called upon their followers "to cooperate with the Nazi regime."[92] Fourth, when the Germans occupied West Ukraine, a wave of pogroms broke out in the major cities of Lvov, Stanislavov, Kremenetz, and elsewhere. Fifth, "During the liquidation of the ghettos[s] in . . . 1942, the Ukrainian police was among the forces that participated in the action, and its men were responsible for shooting thousands of Jews who had been marched to sites of execution and thousands of others who tried to remain in hiding or to escape."[93] On the basis of his research in archives in the FSU, John Garrard concludes that in Berdichev "It was the Ukrainian *Polizei* who rounded up Jews and herded them into the ghetto; it was the *Polizei* who policed the ghetto and saw to it that Jews obeyed a whole series of draconian laws. . . . It is hard to see how the mass shooting of many thousands of Jews could have been accomplished had the *Polizei* not rounded them up and driven them to the massacre sites, then guarded the pits overnight and . . . made sure none of the victims managed to escape."[94] Finally, countless Jews were turned over to the authorities by Ukrainians who were motivated either by enmity or greed. The same was done by members of the Ukrainian Insurgent Army who encountered Jews who had fled the ghettos for the forests. In East Ukraine, which had been part of the USSR since 1918–21, there apparently were fewer pogroms, but there are many German reports of individuals fingering Jews. Thus, in one way or another, whatever their motivations, tens of thousands of Ukrainians assisted the Nazis in their attempt to annihilate the Jews. Whether this is "mass collaboration" or "isolated acts" is a matter for subjective judgment. One historian states that "The majority of Ukrainians did not participate in atrocities against Jews, but a minority did so on an individual basis." He also asserts that "Ukrainophobia still has a place in some Jewish communities, as does anti-Jewish sentiment in Ukrainian communities (but not necessarily anti-Semitism)" [?].[95]

Against this background, which was not much discussed in public, in September 1991 Ukrainian and Jewish groups, with the sponsorship of the Ukrainian government as well, organized a large-scale commemoration of the massacre at Babi Yar that had taken place half a century earlier. The main streets of Kiev were lined with photographs of Kievan Jews who had been murdered at Babi Yar. Several days of conferences, meetings, exhibitions, concerts, and speeches were devoted to the commemoration, and a *Book of Memory* was published in 75,000 copies. The media reported these events extensively, and the subject of the Holocaust generally achieved a prominence unknown in the Soviet period.

The collapse of the USSR means that its successor states will have to face the issue of the Holocaust individually. As they rewrite their histories, the Holocaust will again become a major issue between the Ukrainians, Latvians, Lithuanians, Belarussians, Moldavians, Russians, and others, on one hand, and the Jews, on the other. Revisions of history may be politicized and tendentious at first. One would hope that these would be only infantile disorders of newly won independence, though they might turn out to be symptoms of a more chronic illness of longer duration.

Notes

I am grateful to Dr. Yury Polsky and Scott Tarry for their assistance in research and to the Office of the Vice-President for Research at the University of Michigan for financial support.

1. Mark Kupovetsky estimates that 2,733,000 Soviet Jews died during the war, 10 percent of all Soviet deaths, at a time when Jews were only 2.5 percent of the population. This figure includes natural deaths and those due to the harsh conditions even in the unoccupied areas. Mark Kupovetskii, "Ludskie Poteri Evreiskogo naseleniia v poslevoennykh granitsakh v gody velikoi otechestvennoi voiny," *Vestnik Evreiskogo Universiteta v Moskve* 2 (9), 1995. An earlier version of this article is Mark Kupovetsky, "Estimation of Jewish losses in the USSR during World War II," *Jews in Eastern Europe* 2 (24), (summer 1994). Mordechai Altshuler asserts that "estimates of the number of Jewish Holocaust victims in the Soviet Union fluctuate between 2.5 million and 3.3 million." *Soviet Jewry since the Second World War* (New York: Greenwood Press, 1987), 4. A later assessment is Yitzhak Arad, "The Holocaust of Soviet Jewry in the Occupied Territories of the Soviet Union," *Yad Vashem Studies XXI* (Jerusalem: Yad Vashem, 1991). For the period 1939–1941, see Keith Sword, *Deportation and Exile: Poles in the Soviet Union, 1939–48* (New York: St. Martin's Press, 1994); Jan Gross, *Revolution from Abroad: The Soviet Conquest of Poland's Western Ukraine and Western Belorussia* (Princeton: Princeton University Press, 1988); Norman Davies and Antony Polonsky, eds., *Jews in Eastern Poland and the USSR, 1939–1946* (New York: St. Martin's Press, 1991), and S. Schwarz, *Evrei v Sovetskom Soiuze* (New York: American Jewish Labor Committee, 1966).
2. *Hadassah Magazine*, September 1991, 10. In another place he writes that "A veritable blackout was to engulf the Holocaust in Soviet Russia." William Korey, "Anti-Semitism and the Treatment of the Holocaust in the USSR/CIS," in Randolph Braham, ed., *Anti-Semitism and the Treatment of the Holocaust in Postcommunist Eastern Europe* (New York: Columbia University Press, 1994), 209.
3. Stephen Kinzer, "Lithuanian Asks Remorse for Crimes against Jews," *New York Times*, September 23, 1994.
4. On the movement of Jewish refugees eastward, see the article by Yosef Litvak in this volume and B. Z. Pinchuk, *Yehudai brit hamoetsot mool pnai hashoah* (Tel Aviv: Tel Aviv University, 1979); Mordechai Altshuler, "*Hapinui veham'nusah shel yehudim mibielorussiya hamizrakhit bitkufat hashoah* (Yuni-August 1941)," in *Yahadut Zmaneinu*, vol. 3 (Jerusalem: Hebrew University, 1986); Altshuler, "Escape and Evacuation of Soviet Jews at the Time of the Nazi Invasion," in Lucjan Dobroszycki and Jeffrey Gurock, eds., *The Holocaust in the Soviet Union* (Armonk, NY: M. E. Sharpe, 1993); and Solomon Schwarz, *Evrei v Sovetskom Soiuze.*

5. Z. Segalowicz, *Gebrente trit* (Buenos Aires, 1947), 96. See Jan Gross, "The Jewish Community in the Soviet-Annexed Territories on the Eve of the Holocaust"; and Andrzej Zbikowski, "Local Anti-Jewish Pogroms in the Occupied Territories of Eastern Poland, June-July, 1941" both in Dobroszycki and Gurock, op. cit.
6. Interview with Allen Small, Video Archive for Holocaust Testimonies at Yale University, interview no. T-833, December 14, 1986.
7. Quoted in Alexander Dallin, *German Rule in Soviet Russia, 1941–1945*, 2nd ed. (London: Macmillan, 1981), 9.
8. Von Reichenau and Manstein are quoted in Matthew Cooper, *The Phantom War* (London: Macdonald and James, 1979), 171–73.
9. Raul Hilberg, *The Destruction of the European Jews* (New York: Holmes and Meier, 1985), 301. On the relationship between the army and the *Einsatzgruppen*, see Hans-Heinrich Wilhelm, *Rassenpolitik und Kriegfuhrung* (Passau: Wissenschaftsverlag Richard Rote, 1991). Jurgen Foster points out that before the invasion of the USSR Wehrmacht soldiers were being prepared psychologically to murder Jewish civilians. The Wehrmacht, he says, was responsible for the holocaust in the USSR because it participated in or allowed the killings. "The majority rationalized that the war of destruction against the Soviet Union permitted such harshness. The deliberate mixing together of ideological goals with military needs, of preventive with punitive measures, paved the way for the army's joining the SS in striking a fatal blow against the phantom of Jewish Bolshevism." Jurgen Foster, "The Relation between Operation Barbarossa as an Ideological War of Extermination and the Final Solution," in David Cesarani, ed., *The Final Solution* (London: Routledge, 1994), 99. Omer Bartov adds that "It was by fighting a barbarous war in the east that the German soldier came to view the industrial murder of millions of men, women and children as a logical and unavoidable by-product of his own battle for survival rather than as a horrendous crime." "Operation Barbarossa and the Origins of the Final Solution," ibid., 120. Further evidence of the participation by ordinary soldiers in the murder of civilian Jews is contained in 15,000 documents recently given to the U.S. Holocaust Memorial Museum by the Russian government. Alessandra Stanley, "Russia to Give U.S. Museum Files Detailing Nazi Crimes," *New York Times*, October 29, 1996.
10. Hilberg, p. 295 and chap.7, esp. 288–89.
11. Many accounts of the tortures inflicted on the victims can be found in Ilya Ehrenburg and Vasily Grossman, *The Black Book* (New York: Holocaust Library, 1981); Raul Hilberg, *The Destruction of the European Jews* (New York: Holmes and Meier, 1985), ch. 7, esp. 288–89.
12. William Korey, "Down History's Memory Hole: Soviet Treatment of the Holocaust," *Present Tense*, vol. 10 (Winter, 1983), 53. A good survey of some Soviet publications on the Holocaust is to be found in Lukasz Hirszowicz, "The Holocaust in the Soviet Mirror," in Dobroszycki and Gurock, op. cit.
13. Mordechai Altshuler, "*Pirsumim russiyim bivrit hamoetsot al nos'im yehudiyim bashanim* 1917–1967," in Altshuler, ed., *Pirsumim russiyim bivrit hamoetsot al yehudim veyahadut* (Jerusalem: Society for Research on Jewish Communities and the Historical Society of Israel, 1970), lxvi. See also "Seventy years of Soviet Jewry," *Insight* (London), November 1987, 6.

14. William Korey, *The Soviet Cage* (New York: Viking, 1973), 90.
15. Dov Levin, *Fighting Back: Lithuanian Jewry's Armed Resistance to the Nazis, 1941–1945* (New York: Holmes and Meier, 1985), xii.
16. Document 123 in Shimon Redlich, ed., *War, Holocaust and Stalinism* (New York: Harwood Academic Publishers, 1995), 350.
17. From minutes of the *Black Book* literary commission, October 13, 1944, in ibid., 352–53.
18. Ibid., 353.
19. Ibid., 355. Further information on how the *Black Book* was put together, edited, and suppressed is found in Khaya Lifshitz, "Kak my gotovili k izdaniia 'chernuiu knigu,' " *Di yidishe gass* 5 (21), 1996, 40–45.
20. Ibid., 366, 368. Alexandrov was later Minister of Culture and was considered a protege of Georgii Malenkov, prime minister until 1955. See Robert Conquest, *Power and Policy in the U.S.S.R.* (London: Macmillan, 1961).
21. The English version is *The Black Book* (New York: Holocaust Library, 1981). More materials that were to have been in the Black Book have been published in Y. Arad and T. Pavlova, eds., *Neizvestnaia chernaia kniga* (Jerusalem and Moscow: Yad Vashem and State Archive of the Russian Federation, 1993). Additional materials relating to the war period which were in Ilya Ehrenburg's archives are found in Mordechai Altshuler, Yitzhak Arad and Shmuel Krakowski, eds., *Sovetskie evrei pishut Il'e Erenburgu, 1943–1966* (Jerusalem: Centre for Research and Documentation of East-European Jewry, Hebrew University, and Yad Vashem, 1993), 113–254.
22. Korey, "Down History's Memory Hole."
23. Quoted in Korey, *The Soviet Cage*, 109.
24. Bill Keller, "Echo of '41 in Minsk: Was the Heroine a Jew?" *New York Times* (September 15, 1987), A1, A8.
25. John Garrard, "The Nazi Holocaust in the Soviet Union: Interpreting Newly Opened Russian Archives," *East European Jewish Affairs* 25, 2 (1995), 8. For detailed evidence, see V. Shubinsky, "Sobytiia kholokosta v materialakh Gaisinskogo gorodskogo arkhiva," in V. A. Dymshitz, ed., *Istoriia Evreev na Ukraine i v Belorussii* (St. Petersburg: Peterburgskii Evreiskii Universitet, 1994).
26. *Istoriia velikoi otechestvennoi voiny Sovetskogo Soiuza, 1941–1945 gg*, 6 vols. (Moscow: Voenizdat, 1962–1965). See vol. 3 (1962), 438, 442, 443, 446.
27. Yu. Yu. Kondufor et al., *Istoriia Ukrainskoi SSR* (Kiev: Naukova dumka, 1982).
28. L. N. Lentzmann et al., *Estonskii narod v velikoi otechestvennoi voiny Sovetskogo Soiuza 1941–1945* (Tallin: Eesti Raamat, 1973), 437.
29. Ibid., 440, 449.
30. Ibid., 452.
31. See, for example, p. 330 and the pictures between pp. 448 and 449.
32. P. P. Lipilo and V. F. Romanovskii, eds., *Prestupleniia nemetsko-fashistskikh okkupantov v Belorussii 1941–1944* (Minsk: Belarus, 1965), 24–25, 28, 56–58, 231, 397.
33. O. Kaplanas, *Deviatyi fort obviniaet* (Vilnius: Mintis, 1964), 37–38, 40.

34. S. S. Smirnov, *Sobranie sochinenii: tom pervyi Brestkaia Krepost', krepost' nad Bugom*, 3 vols. (Moscow: Molodaia gvardiia, 1973), 331–32.
35. Ibid., vol. 3, *Stalingrad na Dnepre; Na poliakh Vengrii; Liudi, kotorykh ia videl'*, 23.
36. Ibid., 32, 274.
37. Ibid., vol. 1, 227, 187, 194.
38. Ibid., 157, 44, 235.
39. Ibid., vol. 2, *Rasskazy o neizvestnykh geroiakh*, 131, 214–15.
40. N. Matveev, *Parol'—'Brusnika'* (Moscow: Molodaia gvardiia, 1972). This book was published in an edition of one hundred thousand by a publishing house that has issued several books considered antisemitic by many. Yet, this volume favorably presents heroes of obvious Jewish nationality, such as Captain David Keimach (whose pseudonym was Dima Korneenko), a Red Army officer who worked behind the German lines, Rafael Monusovich Bromberg, and Sarah Levin. Thus, the portrayal of the Jews is not consistent.
41. Yu. Ya. Orlov, *Krakh nemetsko-fashistskoi propagandy v period voiny protiv SSR* (Moscow: Moscow State University, 1985), 95, 61.
42. V. I. Vinogradov, *Istoriia SSR v dokumentakh i illustratsiiakh* (Moscow: Prosveshcheniia, 1981).
43. *Great Soviet Encyclopedia* (Moscow, 1970. English trans., New York: Macmillan, 1975), vol. 9, 293. There is no "Holocaust" entry in the encyclopedia. On the way Holocaust materials were censored, see A. Blium, "Otnoshenie Sovetskoi tsenzury (1940–1946) k probleme kholokosta," *Vestnik Evreiskogo Universiteta v Moskve* 2 (9), 1995, 156–67.
44. For example, F. Kral's *Prestuplenie protiv Evropy* (1963) and *SS v deistvii* (1961).
45. See, for example, Henrikh Hoffman, "*Dos iz geshen in Taganrog*," *Sovietish heymland SH* no. 2 (1966); Hirsh Dobin, "*Der koiech fun lebn*," *SH* no. 3 (1966); and Yekhiel Falikman, "*Der shvartser vint*," *SH* no. 8 (1967).
46. Hersh Remenik, "*Der ufshtand in Varshever getto in der Yidisher Sovetisher literatur*," *SH* no. 2 (1963), 150.
47. Ibid., 153. In a poem by Shmuel Halkin, the Soviet Warrior Bereza comes to the ghetto to help the fighters. The Jewish fighter Ratnitsky says, "Let the people be blessed and the land from which this man came to participate in our struggle as an equal." A major study of the Warsaw ghetto mentions no such episode and points out that the Soviet Union, like the other allies, "did not come to the aid of the fighters in the ghettos." Ironically, spokesmen of the Polish Home Army believed that "the ghetto is no more than a base for Soviet Russia . . . the Russians were the ones who prepared the revolt in the Warsaw ghetto." Yisrael Gutman, *The Jews of Warsaw, 1939–1943* (Bloomington: Indiana University Press, 1982), 408, 409, 417. A Polish Communist historian also does not mention Red Army men in the two versions of his history of the Warsaw ghetto uprising. See B. Mark, *Powstanie w getcie Warszawskim* (Warsaw: Zydowski Instytut Historyczny, 1953; Idisz buch, 1963).
48. Israel Meyer, "*Dos Bulgarishe Folk hot geratevet di Yidn fun fashistisher oisrotung*," *SH* no. 6 (1967), 124.

49. See Esther Markish, *The Long Return* (New York: Ballantine, 1978), 152.

50. *SH* no. 2 (1963), 158.

51. Yudl Pertsovsky, "*Er hot farteidikt Moskve,*" *SH* no. 2 (1966).

52. Hoffman, "*Dos iz geshen in Taganrog.*" See also Dobin, "*Der koiech fun lebn.*"

53. "*Proyektn far a denkmol in Babi Yar,*" *SH* no. 3 (1966), 158. The Ukrainian writer Ivan Khomenko described how his mother hid a Jewish teenage girl for nine months. He published a poem, "*Di Yidishke,*" about the incident (*SH* no. 10 [1966]). Other items emphasized the friendship among nationalities in the ranks of the partisans (Letter from Avrom Hurman, *SH* no. 6 [1963], 122) and the sympathy of Gentiles for the massacred Jews (letter from Piotr Bulakh, *SH* no. 3 [1964]), 156–57.

54. Boris Polevoi, "*Doktor Vera,*" *SH* no. 3 (1967), 46.

55. *SH* no. 5 (1965), 3.

56. Mishe Lev, "*Der Riger Manuscript un zein autor,*" *SH* no. 5 (1962), 37.

57. See Iosif Yuzovsky, "*Faran in Varshe a denkmol,*" *SH* no. 4 (1967), 132.

58. M. Vesterman, "*Zeit vachzam!*" *SH* no. 2 (1963), 156–57.

59. "There's No Turning Back," *Pravda*, August 24, 1987, translation in *Current Digest of the Soviet Press* (CDSP), 39, no. 34 (September 23, 1987), 1.

60. Gennady Vasilev, "Journey to Russian America," *Pravda*, November 16, 1987, translation in *CDSP* 39, no. 46 (December 16, 1987), 21–22.

61. Yu. Kirilchenko, " 'Touchstone of Ill Will' " *Pravda*, August 23, 1987, in *CDSP* 39, no. 46 (December 16, 1987), 2.

62. One result of *glasnost'* was the possibility of opening up this issue. As one article put it, "Ignorance of history is kindling wood for the bonfire of fervent nationalism. But one has to admit that in the Baltic republics textbooks . . . suffer from a lack of objectivity and, with incomprehensible diffidence, pass over in silence, to put it bluntly, tragic periods in the life of Latvia, Lithuania and Estonia. . . . Anti-Soviet propaganda takes skillful advantage of this, filling the blank spots in the textbooks with malicious fabrications and fanning national enmity." O. Meshkov et al., "In a Foreign Voice," *Pravda*, September 1, 1987, translation in *CDSP* 39, no. 34 (September 23, 1987), 7.

63. V. Kazakov, "*Der goirl fun a held,*" *SH* no. 12 (1966), 12, translated from *Sovetskaia Rossiia*, September 24, 1966.

64. Reuben Ainsztein, *Jewish Resistance in Nazi-Occupied Europe* (London: Paul Elek, 1974), 373.

65. See, for example, G. A. Kumanev, ed., *Istochniki pobedy Sovetskogo naroda v velikoi otechestvennoi voine 1941–1945* (Moscow: Nauka, 1985), 187, 194, 197.

66. Among the biographies listed in one Western bibliography are four on Jewish heroes. At least one other biography, a second one of General David Dragunsky, has appeared since. See Michael Parrish, *The U.S.S.R in World War Two*, vol. 12 (New York and London: Garland Publishing, 1981). The later biography of Dragunsky is V. Z. Krivulin and Yu. I. Pivovar, *I eto vse v odnoi sud'be* (Moscow: Izdatel'stvo Politicheskoi Literatury, 1986).

67. Serafim Alekseev, "*Di operatsie in Adamov,*" *SH* no. 2 (1963), 145: "The Jewish fellows distinguished themselves by their discipline, courage, steadfastness."

68. For example, Guards Lt. Gen. Hirsh Plaskov, "*Frontovnikes,*" *SH* no. 5 (1966), 71–73. Plaskov writes about several heroic Jewish soldiers.

69. See, for example, Shire Gorshman, "*Zol feln a hor,*" in *SH* no. 5 (1966), 77–85.

70. These include: Aron Abramovich, *V reshaiushchei voine: uchastie i rol' evreev SSR v voine protiv natsizma*, vol. 1 (Tel Aviv: n.p., 1982) and vol. 2 (Tel Aviv: n.p., 1992); Gershon Shapiro, *Evrei—geroi Sovetskogo Soiuza* (Tel Aviv: n.p., 1982), (English translation is *Under Fire: The Story of Jewish Heroes of the Soviet Union* [Jerusalem: Yad Vashem, 1988]; Fedor Sverdlov, *Evrei: generaly vooruzhennykh sil SSSR* (Moscow and Jerusalem: Yad Vashem, 1993); Leonid Smilovitskii, "Minsk Ghetto: An Issue of Jewish Resistance," *Shvut* 1–2 (17–18), 1995, and the works cited therein.

71. A. I. Epshtain, ed., *Nash otvet klevetnikam* (Kharkov: Prapor, 1976).

72. See John Garrard and Carol Garrard, eds., *World War 2 and the Soviet People* (New York: St. Martin's, 1993).

73. John Garrard, "The Nazi Holocaust in the Soviet Union: Interpreting Newly Opened Russian Archives," *East European Jewish Affairs* 25, 2 (1995), 8–9.

74. R. M. Brodskii and O. Ia. Krasivskii, *Istinnoe litso sionizma* (Lvov: Kameniar, 1983), 34–39. On the *Judenraten*, see Shmuel Spector, "Getaot veyudenratim beshitkhay hakibush hanatsi bivrit hamoetsot (bigvulot September 1939)," *Shvut* 15 (1992).

75. L. E. Bernshtein, *Antikommunisticheskaia sushchnost' ideologicheskikh kontseptsii sionizma* (Kiev: Politicheskaia Literatury Ukrainy, 1984), 33.

76. L. Ia. Dadiani, S. I. Mokshin, and E. V. Tadevosyan, "*O nekotorykh voprosakh istoriografii proletarskogo internatsionalizma,*" *Voprosy istorii KPSS* (January 1987), 76.

77. Quoted in Yaacov Ro'i, *Soviet Decision Making in Practice* (New Brunswick: Transaction Books, 1980), 70.

78. S. Bugayev, "History Covered with Glory," *Krasnaia zvezda* August 15, 1987, translation in *CDSP* 39, no. 33 (September 16, 1987), 18. See also Yury Perechnev, "Ten Volumes on the War," *Moscow News*, September 20, 1987, in *CDSP* 39, no. 50 (January 13, 1988), 7.

79. V. Svirsky, "History Passes Over in Silence," *Izvestiia*, July 21, 1987, translation in CDSP 39, no. 29 (August 19, 1987), 6.

80. Yury Orlik, "Treat History with Respect," *Izvestiia*, August 8, 1987, translation in *CDSP* 39, no. 32 (September 9, 1987), 9–10.

81. See V. Dashichev, V. Kulish, and A. Mertsalov, "History of the War: Yet Another Revision?" *Izvestiia*, November 19, 1990, translation in *CDSP* 42, no. 46 (December 19, 1990), 27.

82. Interview with Major-General V. I. Filatov in *Voenno-istoricheskii zhurnal*, no. 4 (April 1991), translation in *CDSP* 43, no. 17 (May 29, 1991), 17.

83. Ibid.

84. "'*Chernaia Kniga' sushchesvuet,*" *Vechernii Kiev*, September 29, 1989. An over-

view of the materials now being unearthed in archives in the former Soviet Union may be found in Shmuel Krakowski, "Documents on the Holocaust in the Archives of the Former Soviet Union," in David Cesarani, ed., *The Final Solution.*

85. See the documents and testimonies in Sima Ycikas, "Lithuanian-Jewish Relations in the Shadows of the Holocaust," *Jews and Jewish Topics in the Soviet Union and Eastern Europe*, no. 1 (11) (Spring 1990), 33–66.

86. Some of the research on the Holocaust is reported in V. Shubinskii, "*Sobytiia kholokosta v materialakh gaisinskogo gorodskogo arkhiva*," and V. Shubinskii and V. Lukin, "*Katastrofa: po stranitsam 'ustnoi istorii*,' " both in V. Dymshitz, ed., *Istoriia evreev na Ukraine i v Belorussii* (St. Petersburg: Peterburgskii Evreiiskii Universitet, 1994). It is worth pointing out that the same author uses "*kholokost*" and "*katastrofa*" for the Holocaust. Some people are discussing how to teach the Holocaust in schools. See Anatoly Podol'skii, "Prepodavanie kholokosta v shkolakh Ukrainy: problemy i perspektivy," *Evreiskaia shkola* 4 (October-December 1994); and his "Vikladnnia golokostu: al'ternativi i perspektivi," in G. Aronov, ed., *Evreiska istoriia ta kultura v Ukraini* (Kiev: Asotsiatsia iudaiki Ukraini, 1995).

87. Henry Kamm, "Lithuania Halts the Reversal of War-Crimes Convictions," *New York Times* October 17, 1991. The Lithuanian government has refused to allow the Simon Wiesenthal Center, which tries to locate Nazi war criminals, to open an office in Lithuania. Wiesenthal Center representative Efraim Zuroff charges that "The Lithuanian government is afraid of the information which will be made public if we are allowed to do research and find witnesses. The nationalist opposition has incredible difficulty acknowledging the role played by Lithuanian collaborators in the mass murder of Lithuanian Jewry." John Crossland, "A Difficult Inquiry into Lithuania's Holocaust Bears Grisly Fruit," *International Herald Tribune*, April 22, 1994. Zuroff has been criticized in Lithuania as being irresponsible, anti-Lithuanian and sensation-seeking.

88. Dov Levin, "New Lithuania's Old Policy toward the Holocaust," *Jews in Eastern Europe* 2 (24), (summer 1994), 15.

89. Bandera and Stetsko, as quoted in Shmuel Spector, "The Attitude of the Ukrainian Diaspora to the Holocaust of Ukrainian Jewry," in Yisrael Gutman and Gideon Greif, eds., *The Historiography of the Holocaust Period* (Jerusalem: Yad Vashem, 1988), 277. On the attitudes of OUN factions toward Jews, see A. Vais, "Otnoshenie nekotorykh krugov Ukrainskogo natsional'nogo dvizheniia k Evreiam v period vtoroi mirovoi voiny," *Vestnik Evreiskogo Universiteta v Moskve* 2 (19), 1995.

90. Ibid., 278.

91. See Basyl Dmytryshyn, "The SS Division 'Galicia': Its Genesis, Training, Deployment," *Nationalities Papers*, XXI, 2 (Fall 1993). German accounts indicate that 80,000 Ukrainians volunteered for the division and 50,000 were provisionally accepted. Dmytryshyn generally downplays what he calls (always in quotation marks) "German-Ukrainian collaboration." See also Richard Breitman, "Himmler's Police Auxiliaries in the Occupied Soviet Territories," *Simon Wiesenthal Center Annual* 7 (New York: Philosophical Library, 1990).

92. Spector, 279.

93. Ibid. Further discussion of Ukrainian collaboration can be found in Aharon Weiss, "Jewish-Ukrainian Relations in Western Ukraine during the Holocaust," in Peter Potichnyj and Howard Aster, eds. *Ukrainian-Jewish Relations in Historical Perspective* (Edmonton: Canadian Institute of Ukrainian Studies, 1988). For documentation, see also B. F. Sabrin, ed., *Alliance for Murder* (New York: Sarpedon, 1991). A rationale for Latvian participation in the war on the side of the Germans is offered by a former high-ranking officer of the Latvia Legion: "Despite all the restraints by the German Civil Administration, the Latvians, totally isolated from the outer world, still regarded the German army as the only protection that could prevent a second occupation of their homeland by the Soviet Union and the spread of Communism in Europe. Consequently Latvians were willing to support Germany in its struggle against Communism." The author discusses Latvian SS units and "police" but never mentions Jews or the role of "police" and SS in the murder of civilians, Jews and non-Jews. Arthur Silgailis, *Latvian Legion* (San Jose, CA: R. James Bender, 1986).
94. John Garrard, "The Nazi Holocaust in the Soviet Union," 29.
95. David Marples, *Stalinism in Ukraine in the 1940s* (New York: St. Martin's Press, 1992), 80, 72. Marples says, "While those Ukrainians who carried out atrocities against Jews were for the most part individual policemen, not members of the UPA or SS Division, there was also a small minority of leaders known to hold anti-Jewish views," 77.

THREE

The Holocaust of Ukrainian Jews

Shmuel Spector

This chapter is a brief introduction to a complicated and contentious story, the massacre of Ukrainian Jewry. As other chapters in this book show, and as some of the documents illustrate most vividly, Ukrainian Jews, especially those who lived in areas ruled by Poland until 1939, had to try and survive in a particularly hostile environment. For reasons elucidated elsewhere in this volume, some Ukrainians perceived "the Jews" as collaborators with the Soviet Communists who had recently taken over West Ukraine and who had earlier presided over the collectivization of agriculture and a mass famine in the early 1930s, today regarded by some Ukrainians as their "Holocaust," in Soviet Ukraine. To the extent that Jews were identified with Communism and the Soviet regime, they were also perceived as enemies of the Ukrainian people and Ukrainian independence. Some part of the Ukrainian population looked to the Nazis to sponsor a Ukrainian state and rid the land of the detested Jews, Russians, and Communists. Others fought in the ranks of the Soviet Army against the Germans and their collaborators, and some aided and saved Jews. Today in independent Ukraine there is ambivalence about the role of Ukrainian forces during the war, symbolized by the fact that since 1992, on May 9, the "Day of Victory" over the Axis powers, in the largest Ukrainian cities there are two commemorations: one by Soviet Army veterans who mark the "liberation" of Ukraine from the Nazis, and the other by veterans of the Ukrainian Insurgent Army, which at various points fought both Soviet and German forces, marking the "occupation" of Ukraine by Soviet forces which had defeated the Nazis. On May 9, 1996, Ukrainian President Leonid Kuchma called for the two groups to commemorate together in the future, for, after all, both had "fought against Fascism." However the Ukrainians sort out who was doing what and why in the 1940s, there is no doubt that it was the Germans who were responsible for planning and attempting to implement the total annihilation of Ukrainian Jewry.

Organizing Mass Murder

The Nazi plan for "the final solution of the Jewish problem in Europe," the extermination of European Jewry during World War II, began in the Nazi-occupied territories of the Soviet Union. It started there because of the Nazi identification of the Jews with Bolshevism. This was one of the main foundations of the Nazis' ideology, and appeared frequently in Hitler's speeches and in Nazi propaganda. His speech in the Reichstag on January 30, 1939, can serve as an example: "Today I will once more be a prophet: If the international Jewish financiers in and out of Europe should succeed in plunging the nations once more into a world war, then the result will not be the Bolshevization of the earth, and thus the victory of Jewry, but the annihilation of the Jewish race in Europe."[1]

During the planning period of "Operation Barbarossa," the attack on the Soviet Union, on March 3, 1941, Hitler sent the Wehrmacht High Command (the *Oberkommandos der Wehrmacht*, or OKW) some corrected guidelines to the plan. He wrote, "This coming war is more than a fight with arms; it leads you to a conflict of two opposing *weltanschauungen*. To finish this war it is not enough to defeat the enemies' armies. The Jewish-Bolshevist intelligentsia, which until now has oppressed the nation, must be removed."[2]

Hitler's above-mentioned ideas were later included in "Directive 21 (Operation Barbarossa)" issued by the OKW. The *Reichsführer* SS was entrusted with the preparation of the political administration, "tasks which derive from the decisive struggle that will have to be carried out between the two opposing political systems."[3] The tools that Himmler created to carry out his tasks were "The *Einsatzgruppen* of the SD-SiPo." Since they were to operate in a military capacity, General Brauchitsch, Chief of the OKW, issued an order on March 28, 1941, which regulated relations between the Army and the *Einsatzgruppen*. The latter got full freedom in their activities and the full cooperation of the Army's Secret Field Police (GFP). The Army was to provide logistic aid in the form of rations, accommodations, communications, and so forth. Thus, the Wehrmacht was to help with the extermination of "Jewish-Bolshevist elements" in areas under its jurisdiction. In other words, contrary to what later became popular belief, the regular German army was directly involved in the wholesale massacre of Jews and other "undesirables."

Later, on June 6, 1941, the "Commissars' Order" repeated Hitler's ideas regarding the coming war:

> In the fight against Bolshevism it is not to be expected that the enemy will act in accordance with the principle of humanity or international

> law. . . . The army must be aware of the following:
> (1) In this battle it would be a mistake to show mercy or respect for international law towards such elements. They constitute a danger to our own security and to the rapid pacification of the occupied territories.
> (2) The barbaric, Asiatic fighting methods originate with the political commissars. Action must therefore be taken against them immediately, without further consideration, and with all severity.[4]

Thus, on June 22, 1941, four *Einsatzgruppen* marched into the Soviet Union together with the units of the German army. Two *Einsatzgruppen* operated in Ukraine: EG-C, commanded by SS Colonel Dr. Otto Rasch, was attached to the Headquarters of *Heeresgruppe Sued* (Army Group South) and numbered 700 to 800 men. It was divided into four *Kommandos*—4a, 4b, 5, and 6. EG-D was commanded by SS Colonel Professor Otto Ohlendorf. It numbered about 600 men and was attached to the 11th Army. It too was divided into four *Kommandos*—10a, 10b, 11, and 12. Each of the *Kommandos* operated almost independently. EG-C operated in the North and Central Ukraine, while EG-D operated in the South, Crimea, and Caucasus region.

The *Einsatzgruppen* acted according to oral instructions received during their formation on the eve of the war. On July 2, 1941, Heydrich sent his guidelines to the senior SS and police leaders in the occupied territories of the Soviet Union. In paragraph 4, "Executions," he wrote, "All the following are to be executed: . . . Jews in Party and State employment, and other radical elements."[5] Since in the centralized Soviet economy, everyone was employed by the state, this was in effect an order to kill all Jews.

The political struggle between opposing ideologies, and the need to destroy the bearers of the conquered ideology explained perfectly to the German troops in occupied Russia the need for the massacres. Hence, military voices were not raised in protest when all Jews—men, women, and children—were killed *en masse*.

Most historians agree that the mass murder of Soviet Jews was the first stage of the "Final Solution," although complete liquidation of Jewish communities apart from Kiev and a few other places was not achieved in the first months of the Nazi occupation. There were objective obstacles to the immediate extermination of all Soviet Jews in Ukraine. One was the small number of men available to do the actual killing; *Einsatzgruppen* C and D together numbered at most 1,400 men. They had to operate in a vast territory through which Jews were spread in many settlements. In the interests of efficiency, the *Einsatzgruppen* used many Ukrainian auxiliary police units or even rear-area units of the German army.

The main obstacle, however, lay in the needs of the German occupied forces. They relied on a broad range of local resources and services, including various skilled workers. Jews were prominent in many skilled fields, and the army therefore needed them. This is clearly expressed in a memo written by the Chief Inspector of the Armaments Department of the Army in Ukraine to General Thomas of the OKW. In paragraph C, "The Jewish Question," the Chief Inspector wrote,

> Settling the Jewish Question in Ukraine has been made more difficult because in the cities the Jews constituted a major part of the population. . . . The entire situation was complicated by the fact that these Jews carried out almost all the work in the skilled trades and even provided part of the labor for small- and medium-sized industries. . . . [Their] elimination was therefore bound to have profound economic consequences, including even direct effects on the military economy (supplies for troops). . . . It was only weeks, and in some cases months, later that the shooting of the Jews was carried out by the units of the Order Police specially set up for this purpose. . . . It was carried out entirely in public, with the assistance of Ukrainian militia; in many cases regrettably, also with voluntary participation of members of the Wehrmacht. These *Aktionen* included aged men, women and children of all ages, and the number of executions involved in this *Aktion* is far greater than any similar measures undertaken in the Soviet Union up to now. Altogether about 150,000 to 200,000 Jews may have been executed in the section of Ukraine belonging to the *Reichskommissariat*; up to now no consideration was given to the interests of the economy . . .

with the consequence being "elimination of urgently needed craftsmen, who were in many cases indispensable for the requirements of the Wehrmacht."[6]

The opinion of the *Einsatzgruppen* was quite similar. In their reports we find the following: "In Western and Central Ukraine, Jewry is identical with the urban stratum of workers, artisans and merchants. If we don't consider the Jewish labor force in its full capacity, the economic restoration of Ukrainian industry and the rebuilding of the city centers will be impossible."[7]

The territory of the Ukrainian SSR in its 1941 borders was divided by the Nazis as follows: Eastern Galicia (Lvov, Stanislavov, Tarnopol) was incorporated into the *Generalgouvernment* as "District Galizien"; most of Ukraine east of the Dniepr River remained under military rule; the southern edge, between the Dniestr and Bug rivers was handed over to Romanian administration as "Transnistria," and the west bank of Ukraine, including Volhynia, was handed over to German civilian administration as "*Reichskommissariat* Ukraine" with the capital in Rovno. In Eastern Galicia and Volhynia, both Polish provinces before September 1939, large-scale *Aktionen* were organized in some towns during the first days of occupation by the *Einsatzgruppen*, and many thousands of Jews were killed. In other settlements, small *Aktionen* were launched against "Soviet activists" and tens to hundreds were murdered in different towns. In many places, Ukrainians themselves organized anti-Jewish pogroms in which many thousands of Jews were brutally murdered and their property stolen. The largest of these occurred in Lvov, where thousands of Jews were massacred, among them Chief Rabbi Levin. The Germans welcomed the pogroms as "laudable activities against the Jews, that the Ukrainian population undertook within the first hours after the Bolshevik retreat."[8] The *Einsatzgruppen* ordered: "No obstacles are to be put before the self-cleaning of Communist circles and Jews. On the contrary, they are to be supported without hesitation."[9]

The Jews of western Ukraine were not viewed as heavily "Bolshevized" since they had spent only two years under Soviet rule. Therefore, only about 25 to 35 percent perished in the first wave of *Aktionen*. The bulk of the killings took place in the summer and autumn of 1942. In Galicia, many thousands of young Jews were left alive in labor camps, and worked on the construction of the Lvov-Kiev highway. Galician Jews were sent, for the most part, to die in the Belzec death camp.

In most of Ukraine, the Jews were murdered in the first weeks or months of the Nazi occupation, by the *kommandos* of the *Einsatzgruppen*. Thousands of artisans and skilled workers needed by the Wehrmacht, however, were spared temporarily. Several thousand were also left alive so that they could work on the construction of Hitler's headquarters in Vinnitza. By September 1941, the following mass murders had occurred: Berdichev—16,000 to 17,000 dead out of 20,000; Kamenets-Podolsk—13,000 out of 18,000; Vinnitza—7,300; Zhitomir—9,623. The "Final Solution" was fully implemented in Kiev, where *Einsatzkommando* 4a, headed by SS Colonel Paul Blobel and with the full cooperation of the city military commander General Eberhardt, executed 33,711 Jews on September 29 and 30, 1941, in the ravine called Babi Yar. These Jews presented themselves voluntarily, believing that they were to be evacuated. Thousands of Jews remained in hiding throughout the city, but due to roundups and denunciations by locals, most of them were caught and killed, also at Babi Yar. The commander of the Kiev SD-SiPo, Dr. Schumacher, testified after the war that the denunciations came in "by the basketful," in such quantities that his staff could hardly handle them.[10] Thus, Kiev quickly became a *Judenrein* city.

The skilled workers were usually allowed to live until the autumn of 1942, and very few were left alive by the spring and summer of 1943. During 1942, this group was decimated; only those with extremely valuable skills survived through 1943, only to be killed on the eve of liberation by the Soviet army.

Farther to the east, in the areas under military rule, the extermination of the Jews was carried out a short time after the occupation; for example, in Poltava after nine weeks, in Kirovograd after six weeks, in Kherson after six weeks, and in Kharkov after ten weeks.

In the Transnistria region, occupied by the Romanians, there were about 400,000 Jews, about two-thirds of whom were trapped by the German occupation. The *kommandos* of *Einsatzgruppe* D, which hurried through the region, murdered many of them. However, in October 1941, when the region was handed over to the Romanians, there were still many Jews living there. Soon Jews from Bessarabia and Bukovina were sent there, and settled with the local

Jews in the ghettos. Some of the locals died of hunger and disease, and many of the young were sent to work in the German-ruled areas, where they were killed when they were no longer needed. Nonetheless, an unknown number of Ukrainian Jews stayed alive until the liberation.

Ghettos and *Judenrats*

The first and most important orders regarding the Jews were issued by the commanders of the Rear-Area Army Groups or Armies (*Befelshaber des rueckwaertiges Heeresgebiets* or *Armeegebiet*). The orders dealt with the following subjects: forced labor service, special markings to be worn by Jews in public, and organization of *Judenrats*, councils of Jews which would cooperate with the German authorities. All this was done with the full cooperation and assistance of the *Einsatzgruppen.*[11] Jews were at first ordered to wear a white armband ten centimeters wide with a blue Star of David sewn onto it. In September 1941 this was changed to two yellow badges to be worn on the chest and back.[12]

The military orders also dealt with elections of *Judenrats*. Apart from a few settlements where there was some kind of election, in most cases they were nominated by the Germans with the advice of local Ukrainian authorities. In western Ukraine the *Judenrats*' members were usually former communal or party leaders or activists, because in these areas Jewish organizations had been disbanded only two years earlier, in September 1939, following the Soviet-German invasion of Poland. But even in Soviet Ukraine proper (that is, within the pre-1939 borders), despite the short period that the Jews were allowed to live under the Nazis, there were also *Judenrats*. The Jews called these "the Jewish Kehila," or in Russian "*Evreyskaya obshchina*," or sometimes the "Jewish Committee" (*Evreyskii komitet*). The head of the *Judenrat* was called "*Evreyskii starosta*" or "*Evreiskii starshina*" (elder).

In Transnistria, most members of the *Judenrats* were Romanian Jews, because they formed the majority in the Transnistrian ghettos, and because they could communicate more easily with the Romanian administration, which was important for survival. Nonetheless, the local Jews were also represented in the *Judenrats*.

No Jewish national organization had existed in Soviet Ukraine since October 1917. There were no Jewish activists there, since the only ones, the Communists, had fled before the occupation or were immediately killed by the Germans. In these areas, the *Judenrats* were composed primarily of the elderly and white-collar workers (doctors, engineers, and so forth) who were well known to the non-Jewish population that recommended them to the German authorities.

The *Judenrats* were responsible for the conduct of the Jews, and could be killed for failure to perform well. Their duties included registration of the Jews and supply of labor gangs.[13] They also had to fulfill all German orders regarding the collection of taxes, various goods, and so forth.

Outside western Ukraine, the ghettos were short-lived or even nonexistent. Usually the ghettos were set up in the poorest parts of the cities, for example in Berdichev, or in abandoned military barracks as in Vinnitza or Novograd-Volhynskii. In Kharkov the Jews were put in the barracks of the evacuated tractor factory. These barracks were without doors, windows (in the severe weather of December!), or sanitation facilities. In western Ukraine the ghettos were usually surrounded with wooden and barbed-wire fences. They usually lasted about one year before they and their inhabitants were destroyed.

How many Jews were killed in Ukraine? It is to be remembered that the Soviet Union was the only country in Europe with a huge "hinterland" to which refugees could flee in large numbers. In addition, in implementing the decision to leave "scorched earth" for the Nazis, the state organized a large-scale evacuation of human and material resources. Many Jews joined either the evacuation or the flow of refugees heading to the east. There were over 2,531,000 Jews in the Ukraine before the German occupation. From the newly annexed areas (western Ukraine, Bukovina, and Bessarabia) about 5 percent managed to flee or were evacuated. From the Zhitomir, Kamenetz-Podolsk, and Vinnitza districts, about a third fled or were evacuated, while from central and eastern Ukraine, some two-thirds were rescued either by flight or through evacuation. About 1,500,000 Ukrainian Jews were killed, and one million saved by evacuation or flight.

The experiences of the war years have left a bitter and contentious legacy to the peoples of now-independent Ukraine. Who sided with whom, for what reasons, and to what effects is a subject of heated debates among Ukrainians in Ukraine and in the large Ukrainian diaspora. Among Jews, there are those who see a direct line from the pogroms of 1648 initiated by Ukrainian national hero Bohdan Chmielnicki to the collaboration of thousands of Ukrainians in the murder of Jews almost 300 years later. Others argue that the Ukrainian people as a whole cannot be held responsible for atrocities committed by individual Ukrainians and even by explicitly antisemitic Ukrainian organizations or military groups. One thing can be agreed upon by all parties: the issue of Ukrainian-Jewish relations during World War II remains critical to the future relations between these two peoples.

Notes

1. *Documents on the Holocaust* (Jerusalem, 1981), pp. 134–35.
2. Hans-Adolf Jacobsen, ed., *Kriegstagebuch des Oberkommandos der Wehrmacht*, vol. 1 (Frankfurt am Main, 1961), p. 341.
3. *Documents on the Holocaust*, p. 375.

Shmuel Spector

50

4. International Military Tribunal, NOKW-484.
5. *Documents on the Holocaust*, p. 378.
6. Ibid., pp. 417–19.
7. *Ereignsimeldung* 86, September 17, 1942, p. 22 (Yad Vashem Archives 051/125/128).
8. *Ereignsimeldung* 24, July 16, 1941, p. 2 (Yad Vashem Archives).
9. International Military Tribunal, NO-2890.
10. Yad Vashem Archives, Tr-10/39, p. 67.
11. *Ereignismeldung* 25, July 17, 1941, p. 4, 43-4.8.1941, pp. 4–5 (Yad Vashem Archives 051/125/128).
12. *Volyn*, Rovno, no. 4, September 21, 1941, p. 4 (Ukrainian).
13. Yad Vashem Archives, DN 7/2.

FOUR

The Nazi Genocide of the Jews and the Ukrainian Population, 1941–1944

M. I. Koval

The extermination of the Jews was the most terrifying of all the numerous Nazi war crimes, considering its cruelty, scope, and consequences. Unfortunately, Ukrainian and Soviet historians for a long time have been held hostages of officially imposed false conceptions and ideological stereotypes and were unable to pay due attention to one of the most "delicate" topics in the historiography of World War II. Party ideologists, having driven out of use such notions as "the Jewish question," "Jewish culture," and "Jewish history" and substituting for the very name of the people—"Jewish"—an artificial neologism "Soviet people," thus took the theme of the Holocaust out of the purview of scholars.

Ukrainian historians, finally being able to leave the swamp of dogmatism and coming out to the "fresh air" of a scholarly approach, face the following fact: the question of the genocide of the Ukrainian Jews during 1941–44 has to be studied from "ground zero." At the same time it should be observed that the extermination of the Jews was just part of the Holocaust that all Ukrainian people went through, becoming the victims of Nazi maniacs and butchers. But, if the Slavs, and the Ukrainians especially, were being killed mostly because of their political preferences, the extermination of the Jews was based on an ethnic factor. The dubious status of the Jews in Ukraine is to be taken into account when we examine the essence of Jewish-Ukrainian relations during the German occupation. Also, centuries-old Jewish-Ukrainian relations, based on relatively firm economic premises, during the years of Stalin's terror acquired a certain political hue, conducive to the rise of antisemitism and the displacement of common tensions from the routine matters of everyday life to ethnic grounds. The Nazis made use of this circumstance.

By the time of the invasion of the USSR, fascist Germany had devised all necessary propaganda cliches, according to which Jewry was identified with Communism. Thus, "the Soviet Bolshevik state" was regarded as "the effort made by the Jews in the twentieth century aiming at establishing world control."[1] Hitler's ideas are fully reflected in the instructions by the Wehrmacht General Headquarters dated September 12, 1941: "The struggle against Bolshevism requires energetic and merciless actions first of all against the Jews, who are the main carriers of Bolshevism."[2] The conduct of an antisemitic propaganda campaign demanded big financial expenditures, broad use of media sources, archival data, and scientific research. On March 1, 1942, the special purpose staff headed by Rosenberg received the following order from Hitler: "Gather all material that can be used for the total moral annihilation of our enemy, primarily, the Jews, the Masons and Bolshevism."[3]

From the first days of the occupation of the republic the Nazi propaganda machine aimed at the Ukrainian population was working at full capacity. And its potential was considerable: almost 190 newspapers with a circulation of a million copies, sixteen radio stations, the movie industry, exhibitions of various kinds, a mobile propaganda center (special purpose battalion V3), and many other devices of the vast apparatus of occupation.[4] A lot of effort was devoted to the creation of hysteria around the notion of "Judaeo-Bolshevism." Shaped this way, the theme may be traced in 576 out of 700 issues of a Kiev newspaper, *New Ukrainian Word.* Propaganda movies such as *The Jews and NKVD* or *Stalin and the Jews* remained constantly in the repertoires of movie theaters.

Moral pressure on the Ukrainian population was supplemented by intimidation. The following orders would be posted out at military headquarters after the seizure by the Germans of a locality: "Should anyone give asylum to a Jew or let him stay overnight he, as well as the members of his household, will be shot by a firing squad immediately." On the same leaflet a considerable award would be offered for every Jew turned into authorities. Thus, the Germans, having outlawed the Jewish population, hemmed it in by "the pale of alienation." Intimidation was backed by instigation. In the instruction that dealt with the problem of how the native population should be treated, distributed by the Chief of Staff of the Rear Areas of the Army Group "South" on August 16, 1941, one reads: "It is necessary that our actions always appear to be correct. If an offender is not found, all subversive activity should be blamed not on the Ukrainians, but on the Jews and the Russians. In regard to them repressive measures ought to be used."[5]

Such an insidious policy was meant to involve the Ukrainians (or at least neutralize them) in "the final resolution of the Jewish question." It should be noted that in several cases Nazi casuistry attained its goal. The residents of Stanislav, Ternopol, and some other towns were incited to pogroms.[6]

Later on, the invaders tried to involve Ukrainians in extermination actions in western Ukraine. In late 1941 and at the beginning of 1942 a certain number of Jews still remained there even after the implementation of mass extermination campaigns. Thus, the invaders were in a hurry to finish their sinister job. Special attention was paid to the south of the republic. Here regular troops [Wehrmacht—ed.] took part in these actions side by side with special-purpose *Einzatsgruppen*. One of the reports of the Nikolayev military headquarters states that as of September 1941 not a single one of the 250 to 300 Jewish residents of the village of Snegurovka remained alive. In the same document there is a note on the "eviction" (Nazi euphemism for "execution") from this area on August 26 of three Jews who had "spread unfavorable rumors about Wehrmacht"; four Jews were "evicted" on September 1 for "subversive activity and Communist propaganda," one on September 10, and three on October 5.

On October 20 the headquarters of the 444th SS Division filed a report stating that "in Southern Ukraine the Jewish question is resolved once and for all."[7] They also emphasized that "the Ukrainian police did its best fulfilling police tasks. During the last five days they seized three Jews and turned them into SS headquarters in Nikolayev."[8] Almost the same was going on in other regions, so that on June 1, 1942, the Chief of Staff of the Rear Areas of the Army Group "South" stated: "The region that is subject to my control may be considered free of Jews."[9]

The newly created Ukrainian police units took part in these actions. But their involvement in pogroms and executions should not be identified with the attitude of the Ukrainian population as a whole. The police constituted no more than 1 percent of the local population, and it was despised and criticized by people.

Several times, reports emphasize the negative reaction of the overwhelming majority of the population toward anti-Jewish actions. On May 10, 1942, the Chief of Staff of the Rear Areas of the Army Group "South" sent to the 197 field headquarters an instruction: "It is essential that you use all means to prevent the population from witnessing possible acts of the elimination of the Jews by the SS."[10] And the department of propaganda of "Galichina district" in its report says, "The means and methods used for the eviction of the Jews are far from raising the population's respect for the German authorities."[11]

From the documents one can conclude that many Ukrainians regarded the horrible fate of the Jews as a foreshadowing of their own near future. A report filed by Kiev SS-SD in 1942 contains the text of a popular song: "The Germans have come—*gut;* for the Jews—*kaput;* for the Gypsies—*tozhe* [as well]; for the Ukrainians—*pozhe* [later]."[12] There is a similar idea expressed in a saying, which was popular among the population: "The Jews are used instead of water to make the dough, the Ukrainians will be used instead of yeast to knead the dough."

Mass executions of the Jews, conducted in every region in which they lived, had a horrible impact on Ukrainians' state of mind. After the Babi Yar executions in September 1941, the majority of Kiev residents suffered serious psychological stress. Their reaction can be judged from the words of V. M. Tverskoi, a professor at the Kiev State Teachers' Training Institute: "Had we been told by someone [about the killings] or [had information about them been] published somewhere, I would never believe this. But we saw it and had to trust our eyes. I think no villain of all time can be compared to these monsters [Nazis—M. K.]. Is it that on this blood [in Babi Yar—M. K.] they wanted to build the happiness of the Germans?"[13] The September executions were regarded by Kievans, no matter what ethnic group they belonged to, as an attempt to intimidate, demoralize, and force people into submission to the new regime. In any case, since that unforgettable September every honest person bore the burden of Babi Yar on his shoulders.

The new wave of terror rose in summer-fall 1942. It went from the eastern and southern regions to western Ukraine. By this time, 278,000 Jews remained in Galicia, i.e., one-third of the prewar population.[14] They were put into fifty urban ghettos. The rest of the Galician Jews either had been killed or had died because of the inhuman conditions of the ghettos. The food rations for Jews were smaller than for people of other nationalities. Moreover, some part of their earnings went to the German authorities.

In regard to these ghettos—or as Goebbels called them, "death trunks"—we have little information on the relations between their inhabitants and the local people. From a few known facts it can be concluded that in the places where local people, disregarding strict prohibitions, did dare to maintain economic contacts with ghetto inhabitants, the latter had better chances to survive, at least until the next elimination campaign. This was the case in Buchach (Buczacz), Borislav, Ozerpiany, and other ghettos. A former resident of the Chernivtsi ghetto recalls: "People helped us to survive, the people to whom I went, risking my life, to earn some potatoes. The people, the Ukrainians from the local villages, who were not afraid of coming to the ghetto, helped, did what they could, sympathized with us, even though sometimes they were punished for it."[15]

In general, the attitude of the Ukrainians toward the Holocaust seems to have been as follows: the insignificant minority supported the anti-Jewish actions, the overwhelming majority took a neutral stand. At the same time, many people managed to overcome prejudices and propaganda pressure, and opposed the pogrom makers and torturers, helping the victims.

To our great chagrin, it has to be said that in the USSR during half a century after the end of World War II everything possible was made to conceal the truth about the Jewish tragedy, about those who did their "dirty work" and those who opposed the genocide. That is why today it is difficult to reconstruct the developments or even the names of their participants. But something has been done lately.

There are hundreds of cases that we know about in which Ukrainians came to the aid of Jews. We also know that these people were in desperate need of the organization of their efforts. But what is curious is that in spite of the fact that there was a network of underground Communist Party organizations active in the Ukraine, there are hardly any notes in their reports on the assistance offered to the Jews, though the same reports contain profuse information on the aid to Soviet POWs and those deported to Germany. Looking for an explanation, we can assume that the Soviet underground simply was not directed by higher authorities to help the victims of the Holocaust.

The attempts at organizing assistance for the Jews came from quite a different side. And here we should note the role played by the Uniate Church and especially by its archbishop Andrii Sheptyts'kyi, and also by the Baptists in organizing such assistance. Sheptyts'kyi must have been the only Catholic priest in Europe to publicly raise his voice in favor of the Jews, as in his address "Thou shalt not kill" and the letter sent to Hitler, where he protested the involvement of Ukrainians in anti-Jewish actions. Moreover, Sheptyts'kyi in the above-mentioned address, distributed in Galicia, suggested that honest people should turn their backs on local murderers whose hands are covered with innocent blood. He himself gave asylum to 150 children and fifteen rabbis, thus saving their lives. About 500 believers helped their pastor.[16] In connection with this, Himmler was going to arrest Sheptyts'kyi, and Gestapo officers searched St. George's (Iura) cathedral during the service. Another time they even opened the tombs that were in this famous cathedral.

Sheptyts'kyi's example was followed by some other Uniate priests. In the Przemysl woods, with the assistance of foresters, they hid 1,700 people.[17] On several occasions, clergymen prevented pogroms against Jews. Two hundred Jews were killed during a pogrom in the town of Tovsto and its environs in 1941. But many were saved due to the interference of a priest, Izvolsky.[18] But there were also clergymen who regarded the Holocaust as "God's punishment" and refused any assistance to the Jews.

But the activity of Andrii Sheptyts'kyi, a man widely respected by much of the population, was emulated by hundreds of others. The inhabitants of Lvov (Lemberg, Lwow, L'viv) saved 2,000 people.[19] O. V. Masliak, the director of the Lvov library of the Academy of Sciences, gave asylum to eight Jews in his apartment. And in the library itself, 200 people were hidden. Twice Masliak himself almost perished. Once a Jew was found in the library during a search. Masliak was going to be shot, but he convinced the Germans that the room where the Jew was hiding did not belong to the library. Another time when Germans came, Jews were hiding under book stacks, and one even hid under the table on which a Gestapo officer sat. The director started trembling from fear. The Germans must have suspected something, but he treated them to some strong vodka and they left.[20]

Hiding potential victims of the Holocaust in cities was especially difficult. There was virtually no way to lead a clandestine existence in an apartment. The food situation was very difficult. Nevertheless, there are numerous facts about people who were saved in cities. This may be appreciated using Odessa as an example. A local newspaper, the *Legal Chronicle*, almost every day published the verdicts passed on those who, risking their lives, were selflessly saving Jewish compatriots. Among the convicted were Russians, Ukrainians, Poles, and even Germans. People were punished not only for giving asylum and arranging false papers for Jews, but also for the misrepresentation of people's identities.

Conditions for resisting the Holocaust were more favorable in the countryside, though the danger was still great. There were cases when Jewish families were saved by the entire commune of a village. Jewish families were given asylum in the villages of Torkiv, Stadnitsa, Grinenki, Kholodivka, Zarichno, Tarasivka, Mykhailivka, and Bratslav in the Tulchin region, Vinnitsa district. Hundreds of people knew where Jews were hiding, and there was not a single case of betrayal. These villages traditionally had strong economic relations with the Jews, and thus were inclined to treat them in a friendly manner.

In the countryside, natural hiding places could be used to assist large numbers of people. Thus, in the village of Kuialnik, Odessa district, the peasant V. I. Ivanov hid twenty-five people in catacombs.[21] During the entire occupation the peasants of the village of Rakovets, Lvov district, were hiding thirty-three families in attics.[22]

There is some information on people who, having escaped from ghettos or executions, were hiding deep in the woods in the bunkers and pill-boxes of the former front line. It is quite clear that they could not have lived there for years without the assistance of the local population. Such assistance was offered in the villages of Guta Peniatska and Ganachivka, Lvov district, Borodnitsa, Rovno district, and Bitle and Khusi, Stanislav district.

Our survey would not be complete if we did not mention the assistance offered by guerrilla units. Many of them, especially the mobile ones, in one way or another maintained contacts with Jews who were seeking help. As a rule, guerrillas would protect them, create camps for civilians, and accept them as fighters. Thus, 154 Jews fought in A. F. Fedorov's unit; 102 in V. A. Begma's; 97 in S. A. Kovpak's; 50 in A. M. Saburov's; 43 in A. Z. Odukha's, etc.[23] Where possible, national Jewish units were formed, such as D. Erlbaum's unit in the Lvov region, M. Vokalchuk's in the Rovno area, and the guerrilla group of the Kantorovich sisters in Odessa. But as a whole this subject needs a thorough investigation.

In this context it would be interesting to see what was the attitude of OUN-UPA (Organization of Ukrainian Nationalists—Ukrainian Insurgent Army) toward the Jewish question. Now, as all the artificial stereotypes of Soviet historiography are being torn down, we have a chance to explore this difficult question with due objectivity.

The first impression that one gets, having gone through relevant documents, is as follows: shortly before World War II and during its first years OUN shared in general the Nazi program on "the final solution of the Jewish question." In the records of the Second Krakow Congress of the OUN, one reads: "The OUN fights the Jews, regarding them as supporters of the Moscow-Bolshevik regime."[24] But under the influence of German atrocities, on the one hand, and the firm position on the Jewish question that was taken by Sheptytsky on the other hand, OUN changed its attitude, recognizing the right of minorities, including the Jews, to live in Ukraine. This change is reflected in the resolution adopted by the Third Extraordinary Congress of OUN (August 1943). Unfortunately, by that time there were no Jews left in western Ukraine.

For the Ukrainian resistance movement, which included different and often opposing forces, assistance to potential victims of the Holocaust became part of its everyday activity. By their self-sacrifice and devotion the participants in the resistance movement were striving to save the honor of the Ukrainian people, helping them to withstand this moral test. I would like to quote from the speech delivered by the Chairman of the Society for Jewish-Ukrainian Relations: "The selfless assistance offered by the Ukrainian people to the suffering and helpless Jews who went through an unprecedented genocide during World War Two is the brightest and most convincing expression of humanism, good will and faithfulness in the name of love for one's neighbor."[25]

Noting that only a small number of Ukrainians took part in the resistance movement, the former president of the State of Israel, Chaim Herzog, wrote in his address to the participants of a memorial ceremony in Babi Yar on October 5, 1991, "It is sad that very few non-Jewish neighbors gave them [the Jews—M. K.] a hand."[26] Those foreign authors who compare the number of the participants of pro-Jewish movements in Western Europe—6,000 people[27]—to the known analogous number from Ukraine, keep forgetting the especially harsh conditions imposed by the Nazi regime in the republic, conditions that were far more severe than in Western Europe.

Conceding that in fact this movement was not as widespread as we would like it to have been, it ought to be noted that the Ukrainians themselves were subject to Nazi terror. Of the overall number of the Nazi victims, two-thirds were Ukrainians, Russians, Poles, and others. The rest were Jews. Of course, for an ethnic group as small as the Jewish one the figure of a million victims [presumably in the Soviet Union—ed.] is very large. This loss can be felt in the Jewish population even today. Some people refrained from helping Jews out of fear of Nazi retribution, though they sympathized with "the persecuted and starving."

Decent Ukrainians, people from other ethnic groups, whatever their number might have been, did not turn their backs on the wretched victims of Nazism. In Galicia alone about a hundred Ukrainians were executed for this "crime." The data come from German court martial reports and media releases. But it is far from reflecting the overall picture. For instance, in 1942, the 4V SS unit executed the Ukrainian mayor of the town of Kremenchug, Sinitsa-Vershovski, for helping the Jews.

Now, fifty years later, we do not have complete information, and it is unlikely that we will get any information in the future. But each fact about the Jews saved by the Ukrainians must be perpetuated and brought to public attention.

We are pleased to note that the State of Israel, unlike the Ukrainian state, gives all the credit due to the participants of pro-Jewish movements. At the beginning of the list one can see the name of an average Ukrainian, a homeless and lonely old woman, Olena Grigorishina. This noble woman represents her other brave compatriots.[28]

A quite natural question arises: how many Ukrainian citizens of Jewish descent were saved? Unfortunately, there are no comprehensive data on this question, though it is known that in Galicia, for instance, only 2 percent of the prewar Jewish population was left after the Germans had been driven out.[29]

But there is another very depressing fact in this sad story, namely, that the horrible conditions in which the remnants of the Jewish population lived under the Nazi regime were far from being immediately improved after the return of Soviet power. The following document supports this assertion. On May 18, 1944, the chairman of the Jewish Anti-Fascist Committee, the renowned actor Shlomo Mikhoels sent a letter to the Deputy Chair of the Sovnarkom USSR Vyacheslav M. Molotov: "Every day we receive from the liberated regions alarming information regarding the extremely difficult moral and material situation of the Jews who survived extermination. In some regions (Berdichev, Mogilev-Podolski, Balta, Zhmerinka, Vinnitsa, Khmelnik, Rafalivka in the Rovno district) many survivors continue residing in former ghettos. They are not given back their housing, the belongings that were taken away and are now recognized by the owners are not being returned. After the catastrophe the Jews survived, local authorities are not only paying insufficient attention to their problems but sometimes violate Soviet laws. . . . The situation in regard to employment and material assistance is not better. . . . The assistance received by the Red Cross from various countries never reaches the needy Jews." Mikhoels asked Molotov to "take immediate actions that would remove all these negative developments concerning the Jewish survivors on the liberated territories."[30] There is a notation by Molotov on this letter: "Comrade Khrushchev, I am asking you to take care of these things. Comrade Beria, having read this letter, made some suggestions, concerning Ukraine, which I am enclosing here. June 4." Enclosed are extracts from Beria's letter:

> 1. The Ukrainian Central Committee and Sovnarkom must be sent instructions on the employment and living arrangements for the Jews who have gone through repression during the Nazi occupation (concentration camps, ghettos, etc.). Special attention [should be paid] to the arrangement of orphanages for the children whose parents have been either killed or are in great need.
> 2. The representative of the Central Committee and the Sovnarkom of the UkrSSR is to be sent to Chernovtsy and Mogilev-Podolski to investigate the causes of the overcrowding of these regions by Jews and to organize assistance in sending them to the places of their residence.[31]

As we see, nothing by way of practical steps was suggested. Thus, the people whom Mikhoels wrote about were already regarded as unfit, "the detritus of war," unimportant for the authorities.

Over the centuries, Jewish-Ukrainian relations had their ups and downs. But in any case the Jews and the Ukrainians lived on common soil, under a common sky; one sun shone on both peoples. And even during the war years they managed to survive and preserve the bridges of relations. There may be salvation for both in these relations as Dmitro Pavlychko justly put it.[32]

Notes

1. Adolf Hitler, *Mein Kampf* (Munich, 1941), p. 751.
2. The Ukrainian Central State Archives of the October Revolution. (UCSAOR), f. KMF-8, op. 2, case 149, ark. 136.
3. UCSAOR, f.4620, op. 3, case 378, ark. 11.
4. *Popular Resistance to the Fascist Invaders in Ukraine 1941–1944* (Kiev, 1985), v.1, p. 174.
5. Aaron Weiss, "Jewish-Ukrainian Relations in Western Ukraine during the Holocaust," in Howard Aster and Peter Potichnyj, eds., *Ukrainian-Jewish Relations in Historical Perspective* (Edmonton: Canadian Institute of Ukrainian Studies, 1988), p. 413.
6. UCSAOR, f. KMF-8, op. 2, case 157a, ark. 392.
7. Ibid., case 393, ark. 143.
8. Ibid., case 195, ark. 69.
9. Ibid., case 156, ark. 129.
10. Ibid.
11. Ibid., f. 3676, op. 4, case 475, ark. 639.
12. The Central State Archives of the Ukrainian Civil Organizations (CSAUCO), f.166, op. 2, case 179, ark. 2–3.
13. It must be noted that there are many vague and unclear "spots" in the history of this crime, especially in regard to the number of people shot in September 1941. German historians and the Nuremberg Trial documents give the figure of 37,771 (such precision looks strange especially since it is absent from many other reports of mass executions in Ukraine). On the other hand, there are some historians in our country who claim (without any sound evidence) that the number should be about 150,000. We consider as most valid the figures obtained by the State Extraordinary Committee for the Investigation of Nazi Crimes that worked in Kiev: 52,000 shot in Babi Yar from September 29 till October 3 (cited in *Ukr.SSR in the Great Patriotic War 1941–1945* [Kiev, 1975], v.1, p. 351). Demographic data support this figure. At the beginning of the war the population of Kiev was approximately 900,000. Two hundred thousand were drafted into the Red Army; 335,000 were evacuated from the city. According to the German census con-

ducted in January 1942, the population of Kiev was 330,000, of whom 30,000 were German personnel. Any emigration from or immigration to the city was prohibited. But at least 10,000 Kievans moved to the countryside prior to the conquest of Kiev or right after it. Thus, if we compare the prewar population with the above-mentioned losses, we get the difference that roughly corresponds to the figure announced by the State Extraordinary Committee.

14. State Archives of Lvov District, f. R-35, op. 9, case 47, ark. 5.
15. *Sovetskaya Bukovina,* January 6, 1989.
16. *Nasza Kultura*, (Warsaw), 1973, no. 2, pp. 11–12.
17. Ibid., p. 11.
18. *Pinkas Ha-kehillot*, Eastern Galicia (*Galitsiya ha-mizrahit*), (Jerusalem: Yad Vashem, 1980), pp. xxii, xxix.
19. CSAUCO, f. 166, op. 3, case 246, ark. 89.
20. Ibid., op. 2, case 219, ark. 13.
21. Ibid., f.1, op. 9, case 85, ark. 23.
22. *Lvov District in the Great Patriotic War (1941–1945): Selected Documents* (Lvov, 1968), p. 126.
23. UCSAOR, f. 4620, op. 3, case 102, ark. 16.
24. *Ukrainian Political Thought in the XX Century* (Munich, 1983), v. 3, p. 15.
25. *Vozrozhdenie* no. 6, 1991.
26. *Rossiia* (Moscow) no. 41, 1991.
27. Yad Vashem: National Institute of the Holocaust (Jerusalem, 1989), p. 37.
28. *Vozrozhdenie*, no. 6, 1991.
29. Weiss, p. 409.
30. CSAUCO, f.1, op. 23, case 3851, ark. 3–5.
31. Ibid., ark. 5.
32. *Vozrozhdenie*, no. 6, 1991.

Translated by Leonid Livak

FIVE

Metropolitan Andrii Sheptyts'kyi and the Complexities of Ukrainian-Jewish Relations

Shimon Redlich

Jews seem to remember primarily, and very often exclusively, their pain and tragedy. It seems that traumatization prevents them from admitting those relatively few instances of compassion and assistance "from the outside." Is this the correct way to view the past and remember it for the future? Shouldn't we rather seek a more realistic, though by no means artificially balanced, approach?

Jewish attitudes toward Metropolitan Andrii Sheptyts'kyi (1865–1944), archbishop of L'viv and head of the Ukrainian Uniate (Greek Catholic) Church in Galicia, could serve as an example of a "selective" memory and conflicting interpretations. This chapter examines Sheptyts'kyi's attitude toward Ukrainian nationalism and his theological stand vis-à-vis Jews. There is no question that Sheptyts'kyi remains a controversial figure. Some consider him a saint and a savior, while others accuse him of collaboration with the Nazis. What follows is an attempt to reconstruct a multidimensional Sheptyts'kyi, often motivated by conflicting interests and acting within changing and tragic realities.

The Setting

For centuries, Ukrainians and Jews lived side by side and were usually part of a "triangle," whose base was the ruling element, either Poles or Russians, and whose sides were formed by Ukrainians and Jews. Jews performed the role of economic middlemen between the Polish nobility and the Ukrainian peasantry. This, of course, caused hostile attitudes toward Jews. Ukrainians also tended to believe that the Jew had control over their churches, although historically this may be quite incorrect. The image of the Jew in Ukrainian folk tradition assumed the form of somebody who controls both property and spirit. Moreover, antisemitism became in time a significant component within evolving Ukrainian nationalism.

The Chmielnicki pogroms of the seventeenth century, a symbol and prototype of Jewish martyrdom, as well as the Haidamak atrocities of the eighteenth century had a traumatic effect on the collective memory of East European Jewry. Chmielnicki and the Cossacks, who represent to the Jews the very essence of cruelty, were and are perceived by the Ukrainians as symbols of national heroism. These diametrically opposed perceptions of historical personalities and events make mutual understanding and compassion very difficult. The pogroms of the 1880s and the early twentieth century, as well as anti-Jewish outbursts in the wake of the Bolshevik revolution, continued to reinforce the image of the Ukrainian as murderer and *pogromchik*. Attempts at Ukrainian-Jewish coexistence and cooperation within an independent Ukrainian state were short-lived.

Eastern Europe continued to form the major arena of Ukrainian-Jewish relations in the years between the two world wars, although considerable numbers of Jews and Ukrainians emigrated to the New World. Those who remained in Europe found themselves again close to each other in independent Poland and in Soviet Russia. There seemed to be a chance for improved relations on both sides of the border; but in spite of some efforts toward parliamentary cooperation in Poland during the 1920s, Ukrainians basically tended to view their Jewish neighbors as natural allies of the ruling Poles. The aggravation of the nationality problem in Poland in the 1930s and especially the growing oppression of the Ukrainian minority by the Poles presented new opportunities for fascist and Nazi influence in Ukrainian nationalist circles. Traditional antisemitism began to absorb the racist theories of Nazism.

As for the USSR, the new regime tried to eradicate antisemitism in the 1920s, and some parallel national interests of Jews and Ukrainians emerged in Soviet Ukraine. However, the onset of Stalinism in the 1930s caused a renewed inflammation of dormant antagonism. The growing role of the security apparatus, the Stalinist terror and, above all, the horrors of collectivization—became linked in the Ukrainian mind with the image of "Judeo-Bolshevism." This image grew even worse during the short but significant period of 1939–41, when eastern Poland was annexed by the Soviets. The Jew was again perceived by the local Ukrainian population as a collaborator with the hated Bolshevik regime. All this took place on the eve of the Nazi occupation of eastern Poland, densely populated by both Jews and Ukrainians. This was also the immediate background to the Holocaust.

What were Sheptyts'kyi's attitudes toward and relations with Jews before the war? Knowledge of Jews and Judaism was part and parcel of Sheptyts'kyi's intellectual and physical environment since his youth. At the age of twenty Sheptyts'kyi started his study of Hebrew, which he continued in his later life. Within a relatively short period of time he could both write and speak Hebrew. In August 1905, he traveled to the Holy Land with a group of Moravian pilgrims, and in September 1906 he returned there with a pilgrimage of about 500 Ukrainians, who visited various points of interest to Christians. Sheptyts'kyi apparently planned to found there a Greek-Catholic center for pilgrims.

Sheptyts'kyi devoted time and money to social and philanthropic activities, which became one of his major concerns. In the early 1920s, he traveled through Western Europe and North America to collect funds for the victims of World War I in Galicia, especially for orphans. His charitable projects provide a useful precedent and point of reference when considering his assistance to the Jews during World War II. Already during the early part of the century Sheptyts'kyi's philanthropic deeds extended at times to Jews. Sheptyts'kyi made regular contributions to the pre-Passover collection of funds for the poor of the Jewish communities in eastern Galicia.[1] Moreover, his major social project, the establishment in 1903 of the "*Narodnia Lichnytsia*" (The People's Clinic) in L'viv (Lemberg, Lwow, Lvov) (expanded to a full-scale hospital in 1938), was in fact a nonsectarian clinic which served Jews, as well as Ukrainians and Poles.[2]

A most indicative expression of Sheptyts'kyi's relations with Jews was his meetings with the elders of Jewish communities during his regular pastoral visits. A report on one such visit states that "he was greeted by church processions, the clergy . . . and also by rabbis with a Torah. He thanked the rabbis and the Jewish delegation in their Hebrew language."[3] The Metropolitan's contacts with Jewish religious and communal leaders in Galicia were apparently welcome and appreciated in Jewish circles. Thus, in July 1935, the Jewish daily *Chwila* published a greeting by the L'viv Jewish community on the occasion of Sheptyts'kyi's seventieth birthday. The greeting dwelled upon the Metropolitan's high moral and ethical standards, and also mentioned the friendly feelings toward Sheptyts'kyi among the Jewish population.[4] On that same occasion Sheptyts'kyi was personally greeted by the Chief Rabbi of L'viv, Dr. Ezekiel Lewin.

There is no doubt that genuine feelings of humanitarianism and compassion motivated Sheptyts'kyi in his relations with Jews. However, there were additional elements behind his Jewish-oriented activities. A pastoral letter entitled "My Hebrew Speeches," distributed by Sheptyts'kyi to Ukrainian Greek Catholic clergy in the early 1900s, may provide a clue to some of his religious and theological motivations.[5] Sheptyts'kyi apparently had been criticized for his "special" relationship with Jews. In his pastoral message, he reported that "antisemitic Viennese journals, having learned about such an event [Sheptyts'kyi's response in Hebrew to Jews greeting him with the Torah] accused me severely of Judaizing."[6]

It is also possible that criticism of his behavior was voiced among Ukrainian clergy. Sheptyts'kyi decided to respond to these accusations by discussing explicitly his "Jewish encounters." Since his letter seems to be quite significant for our understanding of Sheptyts'kyi's motivations, it will be quoted here at some length.

> . . . I believe that when a man who is granted by Christ the task of preaching the Holy Scripture faces nonbelievers, even for a single moment, he should not miss the opportunity to preach God's message to them. When I face assembled Jews, who are ready to listen to me, I cannot avoid considering them as fellow men exposed to eternal perdition. That is why I consider it my duty to take advantage of this opportunity to convey to them at least one word of the Lord's revelations. I accomplish this while talking to them. Indeed, I do it in their tongue and language, since this has been the custom of Christ's church for twenty centuries. The preachers of the Scriptures accommodate themselves to those to whom they preach. This is the only means to bring the represented truth closer to the listeners' souls. If such a speech while being greeted with the Torah were made in the Russian or German language[s], it could not have been the preaching of the Bible but would have made an impression of a secular talk. In such a situation, the preacher must arouse the interest of his audience and touch that part of its soul in which he can find a religious response. This could not be attained even by speaking in the German-Jewish jargon [Yiddish], since that would become a discussion of financial matters. A speech in Hebrew fits this need. Though not everyone of the listeners fully understands this speech, all are more or less familiar with some Messianic texts of the Old Testament. And if in the soul of any amongst them there is a spark of religious sentiment, it might be kindled under the influence of the uttered words of the Holy Scripture. That is why I usually start with a Messianic holy text. It has often happened that the listeners were so familiar with the text, that they recited it one word ahead of me. To these texts, I add some commentaries in the Christian spirit or another text which leads to a Christian interpretation of the former text. Thus, I offer them as far as possible, the thought of expectation, love, and the search for the Messiah. I do not expect great results. I am satisfied if even one lost soul finds in my words a distant reflection of God's truth and even for a second ponders upon those prayers which are being repeated daily perhaps without any attention. . . . [7]

Sheptyts'kyi then went on to explain his motivation for financial aid to the Karaites: "For that same reason I contributed a donation to the Galician Karaites, for the poor of their community, and I am ready to talk to them at the first opportunity. I believe that every thread of Christian love for one's fellow man which links the faithful with non-believers may become by the

Grace of God, an opportunity for bringing them nearer to Christ's teaching."[8] This explanation may apply as well to Sheptyts'kyi's donations to Jewish communities. Sheptyts'kyi had in mind, at some time, the establishment of Judeo-Christian communities modeled after similar groups in early Christianity. One such community is supposed to have existed in L'viv, but the overall results of this plan were negligible.[9]

The interwar period posed increasing problems and difficulties for Sheptyts'kyi. In the early 1920s, hopes for Ukrainian independence were thwarted by both Bolshevik Russia and nationalist Poland. The 1930s brought new oppression and suffering to the Soviet Ukraine and the "pacification" campaign in Poland resulted in growing frustration among the Ukrainians, which, in turn, bred violence and terror. Sheptyts'kyi, close to the moderates in Ukrainian political circles, consistently condemned acts of terror by Ukrainian extremists. His consistent prewar denunciation of violence and terror was a significant antecedent to his stand on this matter during World War II.

Sheptyts'kyi's attitude vis-à-vis Bolshevik Russia became increasingly critical. The Bolsheviks loomed in his mind as the personification of a double evil. They were committed in his view against both God and the Ukrainian people. Sheptyts'kyi's outspoken anti-Bolshevik and anti-Communist stand in the interwar years also had some effect on his attitude toward those Jews whom he identified with the hated regime and ideology. Thus, already in 1920, when an attempt was made to establish a Soviet republic in Galicia, Sheptyts'kyi criticized it severely and maintained that it was organized by a "Jew-dictator." A church publication close to Sheptyts'kyi wrote in 1936 about a "common front" of radicals, socialists, masons, and—Jews.[10] It should also be remembered that if throughout the 1930s Sheptyts'kyi expressed time and again his unequivocal criticism and opposition to Communism, to the Soviet Union, and to its supporters in the West, he did not show any similar critical sensitivity toward the expansion of Nazi totalitarianism.[11]

In the 1930s, Ukrainian public opinion became increasingly influenced by the right wing nationalist organizations and press, which presented an utterly negative image of the Jew. The major elements in the press were: "Judeo-Bolshevism"; the threat of international Jewry; the Jew as an alien parasite, and admiration for the fascist and Nazi models. Numerous anti-Jewish comments appeared in connection with the short-lived but ideologically and emotionally significant episode of Ukrainian Subcarpathian autonomy. Anti-Jewish sentiments were expressed not only directly but also via derogatory language and images, part and parcel of traditional Ukrainian antisemitic folklore. Though differentiation and diversification in respect to Jews and Jewish-related issues existed, explicit antisemitic views became increasingly visible. This must have contributed to the growing receptivity to antisemitic Nazi ideology and propaganda.[12]

We do not know the precise stand of the Uniate clergy on Jewish issues. We may assume that since many among them were nationalistically minded and since the radicalization of Ukrainian nationalism was accompanied by antisemitic overtones, anti-Jewish moods probably increased. However, there were also other voices. Bishop Ivan Buchko, a close associate of Sheptyts'kyi and an enthusiast of the Metropolitan's "Hebrew encounters" with Jews, spoke publicly against antisemitism and condemned Hitler's neopaganism. Buchko also openly supported the anti-Nazi criticism of Cardinals Faulhaber and Innitzer.[13]

The Soviet annexation of eastern Poland in September 1939 created additional tensions between the Jewish and Ukrainian populations. In spite of the disruption and suffering inflicted by the Soviets upon Jews and Ukrainians alike, the image of the Jew as a sympathizer with the new regime became prevalent among the non-Jewish population of the annexed territories. There was indeed some enthusiasm for the Soviets among Jews. In order to understand this, one should remember the rapidly deteriorating condition of the Jews in prewar Poland, their apprehensions of what might happen to them under Nazi rule, the atmosphere of lawlessness and violence during the disintegration of Polish authority after the German invasion, and Soviet propaganda concerning the solution of the Jewish problem in the Soviet Union.

Although Soviet condemnation of antisemitism in the annexed territories was far from comprehensive, some Ukrainians indeed were punished for antisemitic behavior, a fact which might have contributed to further emotional reactions on the part of the Ukrainians.[14] Another factor which undoubtedly affected Ukrainian attitudes toward Jews was the influx of thousands of Jewish refugees fleeing from the German-occupied territories of western and central Poland into western Ukraine. The "visibility" of the Jews thus became increasingly pronounced and contributed to the growth of an anti-Jewish mood. Such feelings were apparently expressed as well by some church officials in Galicia. One church report on the conditions in the Soviet-occupied section of Poland stated that the best-treated group there were Jews. A local bishop in Przemysl complained in his letter to Rome that the diocesan chancery office building had been given to Jews.[15] Sheptyts'kyi himself, in a letter to Cardinal Tisserant, spoke of the "immigration of an enormous number of Jews" who "make life more difficult." Discussing the disruption and changes resulting from the Soviet annexation, the Metropolitan went on to remark that, "The Jews invaded economic life in prodigious numbers . . . and gave the activities of the [Soviet] authorities a character of sordid avarice which one is accustomed to see only among Jewish petty merchants. . . . "[16] As the spiritual leader of the Christian Ukrainians, Sheptyts'kyi was particularly saddened and angered by Soviet atheistic education and indoctrination of local Ukrainian youth. In another letter to the Vatican he reported "our greatest fear is for school children and for youth in general. . . . Principals of these schools [under the Soviets] were often Jews or atheists. . . . "[17] Sheptyts'kyi's most vehement condemnation of Soviet rule was expressed in a letter written a number of weeks after those territories had been captured by the German army, in the summer of

1941.[18] An American authority on the subject commented that the nearly two years of Soviet rule in eastern Galicia "created a state of mind in which the Ukrainians of the area would at least initially welcome any force which opposed the Soviet Union."[19] It seems that in the eyes of many Ukrainians—and to some extent even in the mind of a man like Sheptyts'kyi—Jews were associated with the Ukrainian traumas resulting from their Soviet experience.

War: Occupation or Liberation?

The situation changed drastically on June 22, 1941, with Hitler's attack on the Soviet Union. German armies entered L'viv a week later. A basic question relevant to Sheptyts'kyi's attitude toward Jews during the Holocaust is that of Ukrainian attitudes toward the Germans in general and Sheptyts'kyi's reaction to German rule in particular. Without going into the details of the various Ukrainian political and national groupings and their respective stands vis-à-vis Hitler's Germany, one may argue that the overall reaction of the Ukrainian population was one of relief from the Bolshevik regime and hopes for Ukrainian sovereignty to be implemented by Germany. German concessions to the Ukrainian population included the reopening of churches, whose existence had been curtailed during the preceding two years of Soviet rule. This, together with Ukrainian national expectations must have increased pro-German sympathies among Ukrainian clergy.

The occupation of eastern Galicia by German forces resulted in acts of vengeance by Ukrainians against suspected collaborators with the Soviets. Moreover, the prevailing confusion as to German intentions in respect to Ukraine was used to proclaim Ukrainian statehood. Sheptyts'kyi's initial reaction to the rapidly unfolding events was positive and even enthusiastic. In a pastoral letter "to the Ukrainian people," the Metropolitan declared, "We greet the victorious German army as a deliverer from the enemy."[20] In a letter to the Vatican, written at the end of August 1941, Sheptyts'kyi stated in a similar vein, "We should support the German Army, which freed us from the Bolshevik regime." He also alluded to his hope that a German victory in the area would eliminate "atheistic militant Communism once and for all."[21] Sheptyts'kyi's national and religious interests and their impact on his initial attitude toward Germany, were clearly spelled out. In a letter sent to Hitler in February 1942, signed by Sheptyts'kyi and other Ukrainian personalities, a commitment to Ukrainian-German cooperation was repeated several times. The signatories expressed their hope and wish that Hitler's "New Order" in Europe would make possible the establishment of an independent Ukraine.[22]

Hitler's policies and intentions toward the Slavs were not yet fully apparent, and numerous Ukrainians, Sheptyts'kyi among them, assumed that the mutual Ukrainian-German hatred of Soviet Russia would suffice to cement an anti-Bolshevik alliance and ensure Germany's support for Ukrainian national objectives. At the very same time, the Nazi occupation of western Ukrainian lands portended the ever-growing suffering and ultimately the total annihilation of the Jews.

Immediately upon the arrival of the German army in L'viv, *Einsatzgruppe C* started to carry out violent acts, including killing local Jews. Ukrainians participated in these pogrom-like activities. Such anti-Jewish acts were motivated by traditional folk antisemitism and by the more recent Jewish-Bolshevik association in the minds of the local Ukrainian population. It should be remembered that Nazi antisemitic propaganda, prior to the war, used extensively the slogan of "Judeo-Bolshevism." An especially ominous Ukrainian allegation against the Jews was that they cooperated with Soviet security agencies in the arrest and murder of Ukrainians prior to the Soviet abandonment of the city.

Between June 30 and July 7, about 4,000 Jews were massacred in L'viv by German units with the assistance of the Ukrainian auxiliary police. On July 25–27, about 2,000 Jews were murdered in a pogrom-like fashion under the slogan of "Petliura days," signifying Ukrainian revenge for the assassination of Semen Petliura [head of the independent Ukrainian government after the 1917 revolution—ed.] by a Jew in France in 1926. All in all, some 30,000 Jews are estimated to have been murdered in this massive pogrom wave during the first few weeks of the Nazi occupation of eastern Poland. The Ukrainian militia assisted German police units during anti-Jewish "actions" which followed. Ukrainians were also used in German labor and extermination camps.[23] However, there were also Ukrainian organizations which did not engage in anti-Jewish activities.[24] There were also, of course, instances of Ukrainian individuals aiding and saving Jews. According to one estimate, hundreds of Ukrainians attempted to aid Jews and about 100 were executed as a result by Nazi authorities.[25] The Ukrainian nationalist underground was either indifferent or outright hostile to the Jews. Similar sentiments prevailed among Ukrainian clergy. This, then, was the general context within which Sheptyts'kyi's wartime attitudes and activities concerning Jews must be viewed.

The tragic and dramatic news of pogrom-like acts by Ukrainians and of the Nazi use of Ukrainian militia in the rounding up and killing of Jews must have reached Metropolitan Sheptyts'kyi. Dr. Lewin, Chief Rabbi of L'viv and a personal friend of Sheptyts'kyi, asked him to intervene with the rioting mobs. "Some time ago you told me that you consider yourself a friend of the Jews. I ask you now, in this hour of mortal danger, to give evidence of your friendship. I ask you to save thousands of human lives."[26] A young Ukrainian confessed to the Metropolitan, apparently at the same time, that he had himself "murdered seventy-five people in L'viv in one night."[27] However, it was only in early 1942 that Sheptyts'kyi expressed himself unequivocally on the matter of Ukrainian assistance to the Nazis in their crimes against the Jewish population.

It is possible that during the first few months after the German invasion the 76-year-old and ailing Sheptyts'kyi was overwhelmed by the unexpected events and still believed in the establishment of a Ukrainian national entity under German auspices. However, the situation must have become clearer in his mind as time passed. The regular and continuous use of violence by the

Germans, as well as the growing disappointment among the Ukrainians in German assistance for their national aspirations, must have had an effect. What disturbed him most was apparently the demoralizing and dehumanizing impact of Nazi behavior upon the local Ukrainian population, especially Ukrainian youth, many of whom adopted extreme stands already in the 1930s. Sheptyts'kyi expressed such concern on a number of occasions. In a letter to Heinrich Himmler, written in February 1942, the Metropolitan deplored German treatment of the local population, especially of the Jews, and protested against the use of the Ukrainian auxiliary militia in anti-Jewish activities.[28] Sheptyts'kyi considered this appeal of utmost importance. He spoke about it with Rabbi Kahana (one of the Jews assisted and saved by Sheptyts'kyi), and mentioned it in a letter to the Vatican.[29]

The summer of 1942 witnessed in L'viv, as well as in Warsaw and other localities, the intensification of the Final Solution in the form of mass deportations of Jews to the death camps. Whereas formerly German "actions" were carried out under various pretexts of "relocation" for labor purposes, the summer 1942 deportations were openly perceived as leading to annihilation. Massive deportations of Jews from the L'viv ghetto took place between August 20 and 23, the number of deportees reaching 50,000. The events of August 1942 were among the most shocking and cruel throughout the years of Nazi rule in L'viv. It is not surprising, therefore, that a highly dramatic condemnation of the Nazi regime by Sheptyts'kyi appeared in a letter to the Vatican, written in the wake of these events.

The letter summed up Sheptyts'kyi's disappointment with and accusations against the German rule. He wrote: "Liberated by the German army from the Bolshevik yoke, we felt a certain relief. . . . [However], gradually the [German] government instituted a regime of truly unbelievable terror and corruption . . . now everybody agrees that the German regime is perhaps even more evil and diabolic than the Bolshevik [regime]. For more than a year not a day has passed without the most horrible crimes being committed. . . . The Jews are the primary victims. The number of Jews killed in our region has certainly surpassed 200,000. . . ."[30] The murderous and inhuman nature of the German treatment of the Jews became increasingly exposed. "In time," according to Sheptyts'kyi, "they began to kill Jews openly in the streets, in full view of the public."[31]

Among the evils of the new way of life under German rule Sheptyts'kyi also mentioned "national chauvinism," alluding perhaps not only to its German aspect. The use of such expressions as "rabid wolves" and "monsters" in describing German rule revealed Sheptyts'kyi's moral judgment of the Hitlerite regime. What hurt Sheptyts'kyi most was the devastating influence of the Nazi-type frame of mind upon his fellow Ukrainians and Greek Catholics. In a letter to Cardinal Tisserant, written in September 1942, Sheptyts'kyi expressed once more his displeasure at the recruitment of Ukrainians into the auxiliary police and for using them by the Germans for "perverted purposes."[32]

Sheptyts'kyi's major attempt to influence the Ukrainian population and to counteract the immoral standards of Nazi rule was through pastoral letters. Some were printed, some were spread by word of mouth. It is nearly impossible to estimate the actual impact of these appeals upon the Ukrainian population and the clergy. However, the very fact that the Metropolitan felt the need to repeat them time and again points to the tremendous difficulties involved. To what extent were Sheptyts'kyi's pastoral messages meant to stop immoral deeds in respect to the Jewish population? The Jews were not mentioned explicitly in any of his public appeals known to us. One should keep in mind that terror was applied not only to Jews but also in Ukrainian-Polish relations and among the various Ukrainian factions. It is in this general context that the condemnation of crimes committed against Jews should be understood.

Sheptyts'kyi's most famous pastoral letter, issued in November 1942 under the symbolic title, "Thou Shalt Not Kill," deals with all forms of homicide.[33] Although political murder is mentioned as an example, it is sufficiently clear that the letter condemns all kinds of murder. Sheptyts'kyi seems to have been preoccupied with the fear of what he defined as "murder addiction," i.e., the acceptance of the killing of fellow men as a common norm of behavior. The fact that Sheptyts'kyi gave a copy of this letter to Rabbi Kahana in 1943, when the latter was hiding in the Metropolitan's quarters, indicates that Sheptyts'kyi himself considered it a Jewish-related appeal.[34] Yet another indication of Sheptyts'kyi's concern about the massive killings of Jews was his discussion with Dr. Frederic, a French expert on Eastern Europe who collaborated with the German Foreign Office and visited Sheptyts'kyi in September 1943. In their conversation, the Metropolitan expressed once more his opinion that "Germany is worse than Bolshevism," and accused the Germans of inhuman behavior toward Jews.[35]

The two major existing testimonies on Sheptyts'kyi's attempts to rescue Jews during the German occupation are those by Rabbi David Kahana, who served during the 1930s as the Rabbi of the Szatnochy Street Synagogue in L'viv, and by Kurt Lewin, the son of Rabbi Dr. Ezekiel Lewin, Chief Rabbi of the L'viv Reform Jewish community on the eve of the war. When Rabbi Lewin visited Sheptyts'kyi in his residence on St. George Hill on July 2, 1941, the Metropolitan urged him to remain there, but the latter decided to go back to his family and congregation. He was apprehended on the same day and murdered together with other Jews. It is perhaps symbolic of Ukrainian-Jewish relations at the time, that whereas the leading Ukrainian ecclesiastic personality offered his assistance to Rabbi Lewin, other Ukrainians took part in killing him.[36] After the Rabbi's death, contacts were maintained between Sheptyts'kyi and the Lewin family. On Sheptyts'kyi's recommendation, the Rabbi's two sons, Kurt (Isaac) and Nathan, stayed at various Greek Catholic monasteries and at St. George's cathedral complex until the arrival of the Red Army in L'viv in the summer of 1944.

Rabbi Kahana was sheltered on Sheptyts'kyi's recommendation starting in May 1943. Prior to that, during the major deportation "actions" in August

1942, Rabbi Kahana approached the Metropolitan with a request to help in saving Torah scrolls, to which Sheptyts'kyi readily consented. Most of the Jews rescued by Sheptyts'kyi and his assistants escaped from the L'viv ghetto and labor camp between August 1942 and May 1943. The ghetto was liquidated in June 1943, and the camp in the fall of the same year.

As for the organizational aspect of his assistance, it seems that the Metropolitan acted on behalf of the Jews through certain fully trusted personnel, such as his brother, Klementii, head of the Studite Order, and Mother Josefa. Another central figure was the Reverend Marko Stek, who seemed to act as a "contact man" between St. George and the various monasteries within and outside L'viv. Usually it was easier to shelter women than men, and children more so than adults. Rescued children were given false baptismal certificates, Ukrainian-sounding names, and were delivered to monasteries, convents, and orphanages. Some Jews were assisted by Studite monks to cross the borders into Romania and Hungary. It seems that a "network" of the most trusted, moral, and courageous among the ecclesiastic personnel were mobilized by Sheptyts'kyi to perform the complex and dangerous task of rescue. They were exposed not only to the external threat of the German authorities, but also to criticism and opposition from within.[37] The lower strata of the clergy were quite antisemitic and many among them must have been opposed to rescuing Jews. Rabbi Kahana, in an interview in the late 1980s, confirmed this assumption. Clergymen of the Ukrainian Autocephalous Church (one of the three principal churches in the Ukraine, the other two being the Orthodox and the Uniate) were apparently the most antisemitic. A survivor's testimony quotes a priest's sermon in which he implored his flock: "Dear merciful [*sic*] . . . people . . . do not give a piece of bread to a Jew . . . whoever knows about any hiding place of a Jew, look for him and inform the Germans."[38]

Metropolitan Sheptyts'kyi and the Churches

A discussion of Sheptyts'kyi's attitude toward Jews during World War II can never be complete without touching upon the issue of Christian theology and the stand of the Holy See. Traditional hostility of the Christian Church toward Jews and anti-Jewish theological myths led, at least partially, to an atmosphere of indifference and animosity among the non-Jewish populations of the Nazi-dominated countries. For a variety of reasons, such feelings ran particularly strong in East Central Europe. Some Christians perceived the Nazi-organized killings of the Jews as an unavoidable realization of the Christian call for the punishment and destruction of those who rejected Christ.[39] The debate concerning Pope Pius XII, including Rolf Hochhuth's *The Deputy* and John Morley's study of the Vatican's reactions to the Holocaust, seems to point to the moral failure of the Papacy during a period of extreme crisis and challenge.[40] Sheptyts'kyi's attitudes and behavior during these difficult and crucial years must be placed also within this context.

In a letter to Rome describing Nazi atrocities toward Jews, written in August 1942, Sheptyts'kyi remarked: "The only consolation one can have in these terrible times is that nothing comes to us without the will of our Heavenly Father. I think that among the massacred Jews there are many souls who converted to God, because never through the centuries have they been placed in a situation as they are in the present, facing for months on end the possibility of a violent death."[41] A discussion that occurred in September 1943 between the Metropolitan and Rabbi Kahana (as related by the latter in his memoirs) might shed additional light on Sheptyts'kyi's theological thought. According to Kahana, the Metropolitan told him: "Did you ever . . . ask yourself what the reason is for the hate and inhumane persecution against the Jewish people from the early times up to the present? . . . He asked me to locate chapter 27, phrase 25 in the Gospel according to Mathew, 'And all the people answered: His blood be on us and on our children.' "[42] Shortly after this discussion, Sheptyts'kyi apologized to Kahana: "In this grave situation, when the Jewish people is bleeding profusely and bearing the sacrifice of hundreds of thousands of innocent victims, I should not have mentioned this subject . . . please forgive me."[43]

As far as conversion and baptism of the rescued Jewish children are concerned, testimonies vary. Rabbi Kahana maintains that such tendencies were visible in Sheptyts'kyi's environment, especially on the part of his brother Klementii. However Kurt Lewin and Zvi Barnea (Chameides) testified that no such attempts were made. The latter stated that "In 1944, after our liberation, the Metropolitan returned the Jewish children to the remnants of the Jewish community in L'viv as soon as foster families for them could be found."[44]

In conclusion, an attempt will be made to answer two significant questions: why were Sheptyts'kyi's attitudes toward Jews complex and what determined this complexity, and how is he reflected in Jewish memory today?

Paul R. Magocsi, in his preface to a collection of essays on Sheptyts'kyi, stated that a constant dilemma in the Metropolitan's life was "how to make Christian morality the basis of everyday reality."[45] Another student of Sheptyts'kyi's early career argued that he was "an important ally of the Ukrainian national movement, but only in so far as this was consistent with Christian principles."[46] The tension between his Christian worldview and the realities pertaining to Ukrainian nationalism were to mark Sheptyts'kyi's attitudes and acts in the years to come. Already in the interwar period, but much more during the war and the Holocaust, Ukrainian nationalism became increasingly extreme, violent, and antisemitic. Sheptyts'kyi, as a leader of the Uniate Church and as a symbolic focus of Ukrainian national aspirations, was forced into an impossible situation. He tried to preach Christian morality while not dissociating himself from the nationalist elements. He was torn between his moral and humanist values and his compassion for frustrated Ukrainian nationalism.

John Conway, in an essay on Catholic attitudes toward Jews under Nazi rule, correctly remarked that one should not exaggerate the potential influence of the Church in times of inflamed nationalism and pointed out the Church's fear of exposing its ineffectiveness with the masses as a result of an unequivocal stand on the Jewish issue. Church leaders were striving to preserve their influence in circumstances of rapid erosion.[47] Sheptyts'kyi should be viewed in precisely this context.

His situation was even more difficult than that of his ecclesiastic contemporaries. His co-nationals, the Ukrainians, and particularly the young generation, were more extreme, violent, and antisemitic than most other populations in Nazi-occupied Eastern Europe. His deeds on behalf of the Jews should therefore be appreciated even more than those of other church leaders. As for the Jews, his stand stemmed from various sources: his humanist approach, his lifelong relations with Jews, but nonetheless from traditional Christian theology. Sheptyts'kyi's relations with Jews during the Holocaust fit the preliminary findings of a conference held in Jerusalem several years ago. They "yielded a complex picture of diverse and often contradictory reactions"[48] and indicated that "even in Eastern Europe the relation between the churches and the Jews during the period of Nazi occupation was more multifaceted than hitherto had been assumed."[49] In Sheptyts'kyi's attitude to the Jews one finds, likewise, complexities, tensions, and conflicts.

As far as the historical image and memory of Sheptyts'kyi are concerned, various—and at times conflicting—views prevail. The Jewish memory of the man and his deeds is seriously affected, not only by his stands vis-à-vis Ukrainian nationalists and Nazi Germany, but also by the traditionally negative Jewish view of Ukraine and the Ukrainians. The utterly hostile Soviet approach to Sheptyts'kyi may have also exerted its influence upon official Israeli decision makers. The fact remains that in spite of numerous appeals to the Yad Vashem Remembrance Authority, the granting of the "Righteous among the Nations" title to a man who initiated the survival of some 150 Jews and expressed his criticism of Nazi anti-Jewish policies—has been denied. As this essay shows, Sheptyts'kyi's attitudes toward Jews were marked by tensions, inconsistencies, and conflicts. Yet, compared with the churches and populations in Nazi-occupied Europe, Sheptyts'kyi's statements and deeds on behalf of Jews place him among that humane and courageous minority who during the time of trial believed that they were their brothers' keepers.

Notes

Reprinted, with revisions, from Yehuda Bauer, et al., eds., *Remembering for the Future* (Oxford: Pergamon Press, 1989), vol. I, with permission of the publisher.

1. David Kahana, *Yoman geto Lvuv* (Jerusalem: Yad Vashem, 1978), p. 157.
2. Ann Slusarchuk Sirka, "Sheptyts'kyi in Education and as a Philanthropist," to be published in Paul R. Magocsi, ed., *Morality and Reality: The Life and Times of Andrei Sheptyts'kyi.*

3. *Berezhan'ska zemlia: istorychno-memuarnyi zbirnyk* (New York, 1970), pp. 189–91.
4. *Chwila*, July 31, 1935. See also *Dilo*, August 1, 1935; and Yitshak Lewin, *Aliti mi-spetsyah* (Tel Aviv: Am Oved, 1946), p. 85.
5. *Poslanie pastyrske Andreiia Sheptitskoho Mitropolita Galitskoho, Arkhiepiskopa L'vovskoho, Episkopa Kaments'a Podol'skoho do Dukhoven'stva soedinenykh eparkhii. O kanonichnoi vizitatsii* (Zhovkva, 1902), pp. 16–19.
6. Ibid., p. 16.
7. Ibid., p. 18.
8. Ibid., pp. 18–19. In another pastoral letter, written two years earlier, Sheptyts'kyi expressed his religious toleration toward non-Christians, including Jews, as long as they fulfill "the divine will to the best of their power and ability." *Pravdyva Vira* (1900), reprinted in *Tvory Sluhy Bozhoho Mytr. Andreia Sheptyts'koho*, vol. 1: "*Pastyrs'ki Lysty*" (Toronto, 1965), p. 70.
9. Edward Prus, Wladyka Swietojurski, *Rzecz o arcybiskupie Andrzeju Szeptyckim (1865–1944)* (Warsaw: Instytut Wydawniczy Zwiazkow Zawodowych, 1985), pp. 157–58.
10. Ibid., p. 71.
11. For a discussion of German-Ukrainian relations during this period see Ryszard Torzecki, *Kwestia ukrainska w polityce III Rzeszy (1933–1945)* (Warsaw: Ksiazka I Wiedza, 1972).
12. Shimon Redlich, "Jewish-Ukrainian Relations in Interwar Poland as Reflected in the Ukrainian Press." Paper delivered at the International Conference on the History and Culture of Polish Jews, Jerusalem, January 31–February 5, 1988.
13. "Episkop I. Buchko proti antisemitizmu" (Bishop I. Buchko against Antisemitism), *Dilo*, September 18, 1936.
14. *The Jewish Chronicle* (London), December 29, 1939.
15. John F. Morley, *Vatican Diplomacy and the Jews During the Holocaust, 1939–1943* (New York: Ktav, 1980), p. 133.
16. Letter dated December 26, 1939, *Actes et Documents du Saint Siege relatifs a la Seconde Guerre Mondiale Vol. III: Le Saint Siege et la situation religieuse en Pologne et dans les Pays Baltes 1939–1945*, pt. I: 1939–1941 (The Vatican, 1967), Doc. 79, pp. 170–71.
17. Cyrille Korolevskij, *Metropolite Andre Szeptyckyj, 1865–1944* (Rome, 1964), p. 362.
18. Letter dated August 30, 1941, *Actes et Documents*, Doc. 297, pp. 437–42.
19. John A. Armstrong, *Ukrainian Nationalism, 1939–1945* (New York: Columbia University Press, 1955), p. 27.
20. Cited in Kost' Pan'kivs'kyi, *Vid derzhavy do komitetu* (New York and Toronto: n.p., 1957), p. 112.
21. Letter dated August 30, 1941, *Actes et Documents*, doc. 297, p. 440.
22. Roman Ilnytzkyj, *Deutschland und die Ukraine, 1939–1945*, vol. 2 (Munich, 1958), pp. 276–79.
23. Ukrainian attitudes toward Jews during the Holocaust are discussed in Philip Friedman, "Ukrainian-Jewish Relations during the Occupation," in his *Roads to*

Extinction: Essays on the Holocaust (New York and Philadelphia: Jewish Publication Society, 1980), pp. 176–208, and his *Their Brothers' Keepers* (New York: Crown, 1978), pp. 130–36. See also Shmuel Spector, *The Holocaust of Volhynian Jews, 1941–1944* (Jerusalem: Yad Vashem, 1986); Aharon Weiss, "Jewish-Ukrainian Relations in Western Ukraine during the Holocaust," in Peter Potichnyj and Howard Aster, eds., *Ukrainian-Jewish Relations in Historical Perspective* (Edmonton: Canadian Institute of Ukrainian Studies, University of Alberta, 1988); and *Ukrainians and Jews: A Symposium* (New York: Ukrainian Congress Committee of America, 1966), pp. 123–47.

24. See Philip Friedman, "Ukrainian Jewish Relations," p. 187.
25. Interview with Aharon Weiss, *Hotam, Al-Hamishmar*, September 4, 1987, p. 20.
26. Cited in Kurt A. Lewin, "Andreas Count Sheptytsky, Archbishop of Lviv, Metropolitan of Halych, and the Jewish Community in Galicia During the Second World War," *The Annals of the Ukrainian Academy of Sciences*, vol. 7, no. 1–2 (23–24), 1959, p. 1660. Sheptyts'kyi also urged Rabbi Kahana to tell him about the fate of the Jewish community in L'viv. See Kahana, *Yoman geto Lvuv*, pp. 154–55.
27. As stated in the "Frederic Report," quoted in Raul Hilberg, *The Destruction of the European Jews* (New York: Franklin Watts, 1973), p. 330.
28. At least three persons testified to have seen Sheptyts'kyi's letter to Himmler. However, neither the original nor a copy of the text of the letter is available. For details see Kost' Pan'kivs'kyi, *Roky nimetskoi okupatsii* (New York and Toronto: Kliuchi, 1965), pp. 29–39; Lewin, "Andreas Count Sheptytsky," p. 1661; and Kahana, *Yoman geto levuv*, p. 155.
29. Kahana, *Yoman geto levuv*, p. 155. The text of the letter to the Vatican dated August 29–31, 1942 is in *Actes et Documents*, vol. 3, pt. 2: 1942–1945 (The Vatican, 1967), doc. 406, p. 628.
30. See letter, dated August 29–31, 1942, Ibid., p. 625.
31. Ibid., p. 625.
32. Eugene Tisserant, *L'eglise militante* (Paris 1950), p. 14.
33. Andrei Sheptyts'kyi, *Pys'ma-poslannia Mytropolyta Andreia Sheptyts'koho ChSVV z chasiv nimets'koi okupatsii*, Biblioteka Lohosu, vol. XXX, part 2 (Yorkton, 1969), pp. 222–31. It should also be mentioned that as early as July 1, 1941, in a pastoral letter discussing the newly established Ukrainian Stets'ko government, Sheptyts'kyi urged its members to ensure the safety and well-being of all, regardless of religion, nationality, and social status. See Roman Ilnytzkyj, *Deutschland und die Ukraine*, p. 274.
34. Kahana, *Yoman geto levuv*, p. 155.
35. See note 27.
36. For additional details, see Yitshak Lewin, *Aliti mi-spetsyah* (Tel Aviv, 1947), pp. 27, 59, and a letter from Kurt Lewin to Roman Boytzun, December 6, 1984, with a copy to the author.
37. This summary of Sheptyts'kyi's rescue of Jews is based on Kahana, *Yoman geto levuv*; Y. Levin, *Aliti mi-spetsyah*; Kurt I. Lewin, "The Metropolitan Andrei Sheptyts'kyi in the years 1942–1944: Recollections of an Eyewitness," Paper de-

livered at the University of Toronto Conference, "Andrei Sheptyts'kyi: His Life and Work," November 23, 1984; Kurt I. Lewin, "Andreas Count Sheptytsky" and an interview with Kurt I. Lewin in New York City, December 24, 1984. For testimony on Sheptyts'kyi's rescue of the two sons of Rabbi Kalman Chameides, the former Rabbi of Katowice, see a letter by Zvi Barnea (Chameides) to the Editor, *The Jerusalem Post*, January 24, 1986, and a letter by Leon Chameides to the author, dated January 22, 1986. Both responded to my article "Sheptytsky and the Jews," *The Jerusalem Post*, December 13, 1985. See also Joachim Schoenfeld, *Holocaust Memoirs: Jews in the Lvov Ghetto, the Janowski Concentration Camp, and as Deportees in Siberia* (Hoboken, NJ: Ktav, 1985), p. 46 and interview with Rabbi David Kahana in Zahala, October 19, 1987.

38. See Shmuel Spector, *The Holocaust of Volhynian Jews*, p. 192.

39. Robert Michael, "Christian Theology and the Holocaust," *Midstream* (New York), vol. 30, no. 4, April 1984, pp. 6–9. Nazi Germany, the Churches, and the Holocaust are discussed in Otto D. Kulka, Paul R. Mendes-Flohr, eds., *Judaism and Christianity under the Impact of National Socialism* (Jerusalem: Historical Society of Israel, 1987).

40. See Carlo Falconi, *The Silence of Pius XII* (Boston and Toronto: Little, Brown, 1970); Saul Friedlander, *Pius XII and the Third Reich: A Documentation* (New York: Knopf, 1966); and John F. Morley, *Vatican Diplomacy and the Jews*, op. cit. For a "revisionist" view, see Owen Chadwick, *Britain and the Vatican During the Second World War* (Cambridge: Cambridge University Press, 1987).

41. Letter dated August 29–31, 1942, *Actes et Documents*, p. 628.

42. As related in Kahana, *Yoman geto levuv*, p. 157.

43. Ibid., p. 158, and interview with Rabbi Kahana, October 19, 1987.

44. Letter by Zvi Barnea (Chameides) to *The Jerusalem Post*, January 24, 1986. See also Yitshak Levin, *Aliti mi-spetsyah*, p. 175, Kurt I. Lewin, "Andreas Count Sheptytsky," p. 1665, and interview with Rabbi Kahana, October 19, 1987.

45. Paul R. Magocsi, ed., *Morality and Reality*, preface (forthcoming).

46. John-Paul Himka, "Andrei Sheptytskyi and the Ukrainian National Movement before 1914," to be published in *Morality and Reality*.

47. John S. Conway, "Catholicism and the Jews during the Nazi Period and After," in Otto Dov Kulka and Paul R. Mendes-Flohr, eds., *Judaism and Christianity under the Impact of National Socialism*, pp. 447–48.

48. "Introduction, *Judaism and Christianity*," p. 12.

49. Ibid., p. 16.

SIX

Antisemitism in Ukraine toward the End of World War II

Mordechai Altshuler

During the last quarter of 1943, the Red Army waged a major campaign to liberate Ukraine from its Nazi occupiers. Kharkov had been recaptured on August 23 of that year. On the eve of the war, that city had a population in excess of three-quarters of a million people, including more than 130,000 Jews. In October, the armies commanded by Generals Nikolai Vatutin (1901–1944), Ivan Konev (1893–1973), and Konstantin Rokossovskii (1896–1958) created three bridgeheads on the western bank of the Dnieper in preparation for the liberation of Kiev. The capital of Ukraine was retaken on November 16, 1943. Its 800,000 residents at the beginning of 1939 had included roughly a quarter of a million Jews. In early April 1944, the Red Army entered Odessa, whose Jewish population at the beginning of World War II had exceeded 200,000. Lvov, one of the most important cities in the western Ukraine, with a prewar Jewish population of at least 100,000, was liberated on July 27, 1944.[1]

Of the 2.5 million Jews who lived in Ukraine on the eve of the Nazi invasion of the Soviet Union (June 22, 1941), very few of those who were unable to flee eastward or join the Red Army survived.[2] Across the length and breadth of Ukraine, there were hundreds of places where Jews were murdered, but only the most prominent of these have ever received any public attention.

Following the liberation of each city and town, Jews began to return. These persons had escaped the Holocaust in one of three ways: (1) some were hidden or helped by the surrounding Gentile population;[3] (2) a few survived in Nazi concentration camps; (3) some spent all or part of the war in the forests or with partisan bands.

In addition to the hardships that the survivors suffered, they had witnessed the massacre of large numbers of Jews, generally including their closest relatives. They knew of and sometimes were eyewitnesses to the cooperation by part of the non-Jewish population in these murders and were aware that some of the locals had taken part in the looting of Jewish property. Alongside the survivors, officers and soldiers who had been demobilized for some reason or were on furlough came looking for their relatives in the cities and towns of Ukraine. A Jewish Red Army man recounts one such visit:

> I got away for two hours to Kiev. Kreshchatik [the most elegant street in the city] was devastated, all around were ruins, debris, and smashed bricks. . . . There is hardly a Jew in the half-empty city. . . . Across from me a lame old man was hobbling along, wearing a filthy hood. I stop him and ask what life was like in the city under the Nazis. "What can I tell you, my son? They had the power and we had our lives. We served them and licked their boots." I ask: "Where did the Jews disappear to?" The old man closed one eye and looked at me in amazement. "What? You don't know? All those who didn't manage to get away—they finished them off in Babii Yar. They desecrated the corpses, trampling them underfoot. . . . Our strong young people made an effort to entertain the Germans."[4]

Another soldier writes that after Sumy was retaken, a group of officers gathered at a mass grave near the town and asked an old teacher to tell about life under Nazi rule. The man said:

> It's hard for me to talk about it. . . . It's hard to talk about the atrocities I was an eyewitness to. It's shameful to say that in all the tracking down, torture, rape, and murder, local Ukrainians participated as well. I too am a Ukrainian. . . .

The teacher described the massacre of the Jews in detail and concluded:

> The Germans took the best [Jewish property] for themselves and the rest fell into the hands of local collaborators. . . . When I consider that former students of mine were among them, I am seized with horror. . . . In their heart of hearts, a number of people felt the Jews' pain and bowed their heads at their fate, but they were afraid of Hitler's beasts and their local minions.[5]

The few Jews who witnessed the atrocities with their own eyes or heard about them soon after the liberation of the communities from the Nazis felt that natural justice required the most severe punishment of active collaborators. The survivors viewed with hostility those who had looked on while their relatives were murdered near places where they had lived alongside their Gentile neighbors for generations.

While fierce battles were still raging in Ukraine, the residents of these districts who had fled on the eve of the Nazi invasion began to trickle back. In areas where there were large concentrations of refugees, representatives of the

Ukrainian authorities issued permits (*propuski*) for travel to the liberated districts. There is some evidence that these Ukrainian representatives tried to limit, to the extent possible, the number of permits granted to Jews. This aroused anger among the Jews, who saw it as discrimination. For example, the Soviet Yiddish author Itzik Kipnis writes that his daughter, who had been released from the army, came to him in Saratov and, in early 1944, applied to the local representatives of the Ukrainian SSR for a permit to return to Kiev. The Ukrainian officials received her cordially, but hinted that in practice there was an unwritten policy that "one should be somewhat restrictive with regard to Jews who wish to return to the liberated areas." Jews in other cities met with similar refusals.[6]

This policy is alluded to in a letter (September 1944) from the wife of a Jewish physician serving in the Red Army to the actor Shlomo Mikhoels, head of the Jewish Anti-Fascist Committee, requesting his help in obtaining permission for herself and her two children to return to her previous place of residence, the village of Kalinindorf. The woman, who had got as far as Simferopol on her own, wrote:

> It is impossible to get there without an official permit. I have received no answer to my repeated requests. In Kalinindorf I worked in the hospital. Now I would perform any kind of work. I am ready to work in a kolkhoz, if only I can live at home.[7]

A Jew who did manage to return to the Kalinindorf district wrote to Ilya Ehrenburg on September 4, 1944: "Many letters are arriving from evacuees asking for permits so they can return to their former places of residence. . . . But no one is making any effort to help the [Jewish] residents who used to live here return."[8] Thus it is not surprising that Shlomo Mikhoels and Shakhne Epshtein, in a letter on behalf of the Jewish Anti-Fascist Committee to the deputy prime minister of the Soviet Union, Vyacheslav Molotov, dated May 18, 1944, stated:

> The Committee is in possession of information that Jewish workers who were temporarily evacuated by the Soviet authorities to the remote rear are encountering obstacles in returning to their former places of residence. Despite the fact that among the evacuees there are skilled workers who could be of great benefit in the reconstruction of the devastated cities and villages, they are not being permitted to return.[9]

On this letter, which was sent on to Kiev, Molotov wrote (June 4, 1944):

> Comrade Khrushchev, please pay attention [to this matter] and take [appropriate] measures. Comrade Beria, to whom I sent this letter, made recommendations concerning Ukraine, which I am conveying to you.[10]

But this intervention from Moscow was not enough to change the difficult situation of the Jews in Ukraine or the plight of those who sought to return to the area where they had lived.

For many Jews this policy aroused deep feelings of pain and humiliation. They believed that in view of the Holocaust that had been wreaked on the Jewish people and of their loyalty to the Soviet Union during the war, not only should they not be discriminated against, they should even be accorded preferred treatment. Despite the limitations on the return of Jews to Ukraine from the East, the republic's Jewish population continued to grow, as Jews kept finding ways to return to the regions they had fled during the Nazi onslaught. Among those who returned in early 1944 was the Yiddish poet David Hofshtein (1889–1952), who wrote, shortly before his return to Kiev:

> For months I made preparations, I prepared myself for the shock, for the anguish. For months I have been stifling the first scream that will erupt the moment I see there everything I already know—our disaster, our catastrophe in its full dimensions.[11]

When Hofshtein returned to Kiev he tried to organize a memorial meeting at Babi Yar, the place that became the symbol of the mass slaughter of Soviet Jewry. Not only did the authorities forbid such a public meeting; they considered the idea of holding it to be an expression of Jewish chauvinism that ostensibly provoked antisemitism.[12] Denying the Jews the right to mourn publicly only increased the tensions between them and the surrounding population, whom many Jews saw as active or passive collaborators in the disaster that had befallen their families.

For several years the non-Jewish population of Ukraine had been subjected to an intensive German propaganda campaign that emphasized that the Jews were the source of all their suffering and troubles.[13] This propaganda, in which some Ukrainians also took part, directly or indirectly penetrated broad strata of the population. What is more, during those years hundreds of thousands of Ukrainians witnessed the degradation of the Jews, whose brutalization and murder became a daily event. During the years of occupation, the Ukrainians in the cities and towns, for whom Jews had always been part of their daily lives, got used to seeing their communities without Jews. Hence the reappearance of Jews there was perceived as surprising, unnatural, and perhaps even threatening. This feeling is reflected in the following testimony, taken in January 1962:

> We returned to Kiev in July, 1944. . . . First we entered the courtyard where we had lived for some 15 years. . . . The neighbors met us angrily. . . . When she saw us, the girl Lidia screamed: "I'm going to go tell the Germans that the Zhids have come!"[14]

The return of the Jews provoked resentment and even hatred in broad sectors of the population, especially when they became involved in the republic's cultural life. Such feelings are expressed in an anonymous letter sent to the Central Committee of the Communist Party of Ukraine in July 1944:

> The Kiev Conservatory has returned—99% of the Jews who had fled and two-and-a-half Ukrainians. The Jews immediately seized the executive positions: deans, assistant deans, and head of the pedagogical department. Next they arranged good jobs for their cronies and their wives. Because there weren't enough places for all, the Ukrainian teachers and some of the Russians trained in the same conservatory were thrown out. But a conservatory like this smells too strongly of garlic,[15] so they stuck a few Ukrainian "flowers" into the bouquet: Litvinenko-Vol'gemut,[16] Patorzhenskii, Ronskii. Now they can continue their policy, putting in their own people and shunting aside members of other nationalities.
>
> Does the list of Ukrainians capable of running the Ukrainian Conservatory of the capital city end with P. Panch,[17] P. Tychina,[18] and Korneichuk[19]—and this for the good of all the people and not just the dwarves and cantankerous boors?[20]

The rhetorical question at the end of the anonymous letter implies that the authorities preferred Jews over Ukrainians and were Judaizing the Ukrainian SSR. The authorities were sensitive to such opinions and raised obstacles not only to giving Jews prestigious positions, but even to accepting them in workplaces considered to be desirable because of the chances they gave for a "side" income—especially those connected with food.[21] Considerable segments of the Soviet apparatus, themselves tainted by such anti-Jewish attitudes, gave expression in both word and deed to the undeclared policy of limiting the Jews' opportunities in finding jobs in the Ukraine. This created a kind of symbiosis between public opinion and the policy adopted by large segments of the Soviet apparatus.

Many Jews refused to believe in the Ukrainian authorities' indifference or impotence in the face of antisemitic manifestations and were convinced that these were merely "deviations" by some apparatchiks. Accordingly, they sought assistance from the highest echelons in Moscow, but these appeals only intensified the local authorities' hostility. The Jews also approached the highest Party organs in Ukraine itself and requested that they institute an information and education campaign against antisemitism. Consider, for example, the following anonymous letter sent to the Central Committee of the Communist Party of Ukraine in September 1944:

> In Kiev, one finds antisemitism on a large scale. The Fascists left behind agents to fan hatred against the Jews. Every negative phenomenon, no matter how small, is blown up and ascribed to the Jews. What is more, we see that plants and institutions are not placing Jews in the highest positions, even when they are veteran Party members. Evidently, many of the senior officials have forgotten that our great Communist Party educates its members in the spirit of internationalism, and that the founder of Marxism, Karl Marx, was of Jewish origin. This theory was realized

> by Comrade Lenin and is also being realized by our leader, Comrade Stalin.
>
> I do not for a minute doubt that the Party is waging a campaign against the great evil of antisemitism. The Jews are the first victims of fascism. Tens of thousands of the Jewish proletariat and workers' families who were unable to be evacuated from Kiev were slaughtered down to the last one and thrown into Babi Yar.
>
> I think that the struggle against antisemitism, that great evil, must engage every Party member. For this reason, I propose holding closed meetings of Party members in Kiev to discuss the fight against antisemitism since it is increasing rather than diminishing.[22]

This and similar letters were carefully filed away but, to the best of our knowledge, no information and education campaign against antisemitism, which sometimes assumed violent forms, was ever instituted.

In Ukraine, as elsewhere, the economic situation after liberation was extremely difficult. One expression of this was severe food rationing based on coupons.[23] Alongside the almost total absence of goods and commodities in the stores, there was a black market where foodstuffs were sold at astronomical prices; people also sold off their household possessions there. The situation created severe social antagonisms, which were often directed at Jews, who were traditionally depicted as profiteers and middlemen. It is not surprising, then, that the market became a focus of coarse and sometimes violent expressions against Jews and against non-Jews believed to be Jews. Given the general antisemitic attitude, nurtured by the factors mentioned above, on occasion the tension spread beyond the market to the entire city, becoming a quasi-psychosis that threatened the entire Jewish population.

On the eve of World War II, especially in the large cities, the housing shortage was almost a permanent feature of life in the Soviet Union, including Ukraine. The housing shortage was exacerbated by the war; in some cities one-third to one-half of all buildings were destroyed, whether as the result of military activity or deliberate demolition by the retreating German army.[24] Apartments belonging to everyone who had fled to the east, including Jews, were occupied by those who had stayed behind during the Nazi occupation. Squatters also moved in to the apartments of the Jews slaughtered by the Germans. When Jews who had survived or fled eastward returned to Ukraine, the question of returning apartments to their previous tenants arose in its full complexity. The general policy was that such flats should be returned to their former tenants, and the authorities usually issued orders to this effect. This situation created grounds for conflict between those reclaiming their apartments and the current occupants, who were offered inferior accommodations and sometimes none.[25] The conflict between claimants and squatters did not concern only Jews. What was unique is that this conflict tended to go beyond mere friction between tenant and claimant and led to accusations that the Jews were taking over Ukraine, and sometimes even to attacks on Jews who were not directly connected with the specific dispute.

Another source of tension between Gentiles and Jews involved the return of property. In the Soviet Union, where most real estate had been expropriated many years previously, this referred chiefly to personal and household goods. Most of the Jews who fled east were unable to take all their household goods with them and left some of them behind in their apartments or with neighbors and acquaintances for safekeeping. The household goods and personal items of Jews murdered by the Nazis were plundered by the occupiers, who generally took the valuables, and by locals, especially by Nazi collaborators. When the Jews came back to Ukraine, there arose the sensitive problem of returning property to survivors or their heirs. There were two aspects to the Jews' vigorous demand for restoration of their property or that of their families: one of principle and one practical. As a matter of principle, the Jews believed that those who had collaborated with the invader or looted the property of murder victims should not be allowed to retain the fruits of their crimes after the liberation. As a practical matter, every garment or blanket was extremely valuable, given the drastic shortage of such items, and was often bartered for food. A significant proportion of the population refused to restore such property to its rightful owners or their heirs; in fact, a lively trade developed in goods stolen from Jews.[26] For their part, the authorities tried to ignore the claims of Jews who discovered their property and that of their relatives so as not to antagonize the local population. Many Jews found themselves standing helplessly by, despite their just claims, or were forced to take independent initiatives.

We see, then, that the gross manifestations of antisemitism in Ukraine at the end of World War II were fed by the traditional hostility toward Jews, which had been intensified by the Nazi propaganda and dehumanization, and by the desire of broad sectors of the population to see a Ukraine without Jews, an aspiration encouraged by the Soviet authorities. These manifestations were further exacerbated by the tensions created by the claims for the return of apartments and property.

Until now, information about antisemitism in Ukraine at the end of World War II has been based on the testimony of Jews who left the Soviet Union during that period or many years after the events; doubts as to its accuracy and credibility were unavoidable. The document published here has a more reliable provenance: it is a top-secret memorandum concerning this phenomenon throughout the republic, written by the head of the security services in Ukraine at the time.

Following a wave of antisemitic manifestations, Gersonskii, the deputy head of the Second Department of the Ukrainian NKGB (*Narodnyi komissariat gosudarstvennyi bezopasnosti*, the People's Commissariat for State Security), which was responsible for gathering information on current thinking among the intelligentsia, drafted a memorandum on antisemitic incidents in Ukraine, evidently in early August 1944.[27] The document was almost certainly reviewed by the head of the Second Department and the NKGB, People's Commissar for State Security of Ukraine, S. R. Savchenko.[28] On September 13, Savchenko submitted it as an official memorandum to the first secretary of the Communist Party of Ukraine and prime minister of Ukraine, Nikita Khrushchev. The memorandum, marked "Strictly Secret," has three parts. In the first part, the author assesses the factors that he believes have led to the rise of antisemitism, namely: (1) the influence of Nazi propaganda and of Ukrainian nationalist propaganda during and after the Nazi occupation; (2) "the very low percentage of Jews in the ranks of the Red Army"—here the writer is accepting as fact rumors spread by antisemitic elements;[29] (3) rumors spread by Jews that the Ukrainians are to be punished and the most important positions in the government of the republic filled by Jews; (4) the Jews' alleged evasion of conscription into the Red Army after liberation, especially in the Chernovtsy region, their refusal to enlist for work in the Donbas mines, and their involvement in profiteering. Of the four reasons cited by Gersonskii for the rise of antisemitism in Ukraine, the Jews themselves were ostensibly guilty of three of them. Hence it seems unlikely that the author of the memorandum was exaggerating in his description of the increase in antisemitic manifestations.

In the second part of the document, the author describes gross antisemitic expressions and events that almost certainly are no more than a representative sample, as the memorandum hints.

The third part of the document is devoted to examples of "Jewish nationalism," which, according to the author, is fanning the fire of antisemitism. According to Gersonskii, this "nationalism" is expressed in the following areas: (1) the attitude of Jews who seek to defend their brothers from antisemitic attacks; (2) the transmission of false information that the Jews in the United States live better than those in the Soviet Union, encouragement of emigration from the USSR, and manifestations of sympathy for Zionism; (3) the circulation of rumors that the Soviet authorities will give the Jews a territory where they can pursue their own national aspirations; (4) an appeal to the leaders of the Soviet Union to act against antisemitism in Ukraine; (5) the Jews' contention that the Central Committee of the Communist Party of Ukraine includes individuals with antisemitic attitudes, including the First Secretary of the Party, Nikita Khrushchev, who is for this reason about to be replaced by Andrei Zhdanov.

Against the background of available information as to the changes that took place among Soviet Jewry in the wake of the Holocaust, some of the claims about Jews made in this document seem logical. But the connection that the author draws between the trends prevalent among the Jews of Ukraine and the rising wave of antisemitism is artificial and unconvincing. This portion of the memorandum was intended to strike a balance of antisemitism and "Jewish nationalism"—the standard practice in the Soviet Union.

After Khrushchev studied the memorandum, he wrote on it on September 18, 1944: "Korotchenko [one of the secretaries of the Central Committee of the Communist Party of Ukraine]: Investigate and present recommendation to the Politburo of the Central Committee of the Communist Party of Ukraine." Korotchenko accordingly appointed a three-member commission, comprising Alidin, the deputy director of the Department for Organization and Instruction (*orginstruktorskii otdel*); Zhukovskii, the deputy director of the Personnel Department (*otdel kadrov*); and Zolotoverkhii, the deputy director of the Agitprop Department of the Central Committee of the Communist Party of Ukraine. The inquiry commission studied the matter for about two months and submitted its conclusions in November 1944. Its report was handwritten, evidently in a single copy, and marked "Extremely Confidential" (*strogo sekretno*). The commission summoned the individuals mentioned in the memorandum submitted by the head of the security services in Ukraine and took their testimony in writing. These depositions are included here in chapter 20. In its report, the commission proposed expanding information activities against antisemitism, Ukrainian nationalism, and Jewish nationalism; but the main thrust of its recommendations deals with intensifying the security services' actions to suppress Zionism and "Jewish nationalism," including the detention of those involved. The commission hinted that some of the blame for manifestations of antisemitism and "Jewish nationalism" redounded to the security services, which failed to act against them with sufficient vigor. It rejected the description of the situation presented in the memorandum and went so far as to recommend the dismissal of the deputy director of the Second Department of the NKGB in Ukraine, who had written the memorandum. It determined that the description of antisemitism presented in the memorandum was exaggerated and did not accurately reflect the situation.

It seems most likely that the report of the Party-appointed commission, with its overt criticism of the minister for security affairs for surrounding himself with inappropriate persons, was written in direct or indirect coordination with Nikita Khrushchev. Hence it may be that these documents open a small window on the various attitudes then prevailing in Ukraine, and perhaps elsewhere, with regard to antisemitic manifestations in the Soviet Union. The different assessments of antisemitism in Ukraine may also coincide with contrasting attitudes toward expressions of "Ukrainian nationalism." In any case, the Jewish question in general and antisemitism in particular became a "hot potato" tossed back and forth among the various organs of Party and government. This may explain the rumors concerning Khrushchev's replacement, since the Jewish question had implications far beyond the limits of the Jews' strained relations with the surrounding population and became part of the power struggles within the regime.

Notes

This essay was originally published, in slightly different form, in *Jews in Eastern Europe* 3, no. 22 (Winter 1993), pp. 40–51.

86

1. These statistics are based on the 1939 Soviet census, except for those on Lvov, which come from the 1931 Polish census.
2. The situation was described by the Russian Jewish writer Vassily Grossman in two articles entitled "Ukraine without Jews," which appeared in the Moscow Yiddish newspaper *Einikayt* (Nov. 25 and Dec. 2, 1943). The Russian journalist and author Tatiana Tess (1906–1983), who wrote for *Izvestiia* during the war and visited these communities immediately after their liberation, used the expression, "Odessa—a city without Jews" (S. Borovoi, *Vospominaniia* [Memoirs], [Moscow: Evreiskii universitet, 1993], p. 285). In late 1944, a survivor wrote to a relative in Palestine: "In Sarny, only 30 Jews have survived. In Rakitno—150, in Dabrowice—10, and in Rovno 500" (Joint Rescue Committee of the Jewish Agency for Palestine, *Bulletin*, February 1945, p. 10).
3. On the concealment of Jews by the Metropolitan Andrii Sheptitsky, see D. Kahana, *Yoman geto Lvov* (Lvov ghetto diary) (Jerusalem: Yad Vashem, 1978), pp. 135–56, and the chapter by Shimon Redlich in this volume. Testimony about non-Jews who helped Jews during the Nazi occupation can also be found in Walter Duchnyck, ed., *Ukrainians and Jews: A Symposium* (New York: Ukrainian Congress Committee of America, 1966), pp. 123–47. More Jews seem to have survived in western Ukraine than in the areas that had been under Soviet control prior to 1939. Rabbi David Kahana relates that a total of 2,705 persons were registered as members of the Jewish community of Lvov in November, 1944. D. Kahana, *Aharei ha-mabul* (After the Deluge), (Jerusalem: Mosad Harav Kook, 1981), p. 12.
4. Ia. Ben-Ami, *Vremia i pamiat'* (Time and Memory), (Tel Aviv, 1976), pp. 125–26.
5. M. Marshak, *Qol qore v-halakhti* (A Voice Called and I Went), (Tel Aviv, 1976), pp. 29–30.
6. I. Kipnis, *Tog un tog* (Day by Day), (Tel Aviv: Y. L. Peretz farlag, 1980), pp. 403–404. The discrimination against Jews who wanted to return to the areas recaptured from the Nazis was given artistic expression by the Russian Jewish author Vassily Grossman, who placed the following line in the mouth of one of his heroines: "In the city of Ufa they deleted from the roster of workers at the Ukrainian Academy of Sciences [who were to return to their previous places of residence] almost all the Jews, leaving only the doctors of science" (V. Grossman, *Zhizn' i sud'ba* [Life and Fate], [Moscow: Knizhnaya palata, 1988], p. 335). The historian Shaul Borovoi, who spent the war in Central Asia, relates that Jewish scientists and lecturers who did not hold the degree of doctor of sciences encountered many obstacles when they tried to return to their former places of residence (Borovoi, *Vospominaniia*, pp. 283–86). The correspondent of an Anglo-Jewish newspaper who spent time in Eastern Europe and met Jewish soldiers who had served in those areas reported that: "It is . . . recognized, equally by the Jews concerned and the Russian authorities, that because of the inflamed antisemitism among the people in areas formerly occupied by the Germans . . . it is undesirable for Jews to return there for the present at least" ("The Position of Russian Jewry Today," *The Jewish Chronicle* [Dec. 10, 1948], p. 11).
7. M. Altshuler, "The Jewish Antifascist Committee in the USSR in Light of New

Documentation," *Studies in Contemporary Jewry* 1 (Jerusalem: Institute of Contemporary Jewry, 1984), p. 270.

8. *Sovetskie evrei pishut Il'e Erenburgu* (Soviet Jews Write to Ilya Ehrenburg), ed. M. Altshuler, Y. Arad, and S. Krakowski (Jerusalem: Centre for Research and Documentation on East European Jewry, 1993), p. 151.
9. Tsentral'nii derzhavnii arkhiv gromads'kikh obednan' Ukrainy [Central State Archive of Public Associations of Ukraine], hereafter TDAGOU), f. (collection, hereafter f.) 1, opis' (inventory, hereafter *op.*) 23, spr. (file, hereafter spr.) 3851, pp. 3–4.
10. Here is an excerpt from Beria's letter relating to the proposal by Mikhoels and Epshtein:

    1. Order the Central Committee [CC] and the Council of People's Commissars [SNK] of Ukraine [and] Comrade Khrushchev to take the required measures to aid the Jews in the liberated areas who were subjected to particular repressions (concentration camps, ghetto, etc.) on the part of the German occupiers to establish themselves in terms of work and daily life. Specifically, in the first place to arrange placements in orphanages for orphans and for children who desperately require parental care.
    2. Send to Chernovtsy and Mogilev-Podolsk a representative of the CC and SNK of the Ukrainian SSR to ascertain the reasons for the accumulation [there] of a sizable Jewish population and to organize assistance for them to reach their [prewar] places of residence. And also to assign places of settlement for that portion of the Jews who are residents of not-yet-liberated territory and to help them when they are sent for resettlement. (ibid., p. 5)

11. D. Hofshtein, *Ich gloyb (milhome lider)* (I Believe: War Poems) (Moscow, 1944; New York: IKUF, 1945), p. 50.
12. Ibid., p. 66.
13. We cite here passages from two antisemitic posters distributed in Ukraine during the German occupation. One says: "A trustworthy word from Foma Smyslov—a veteran Russian soldier—on the cruelty of the German fascists. . . . We have all heard that they came to fight us and ostensibly to murder our wives and children. [The poster rejects these arguments and contends that] When the bad years came and there was chaos in Russia, the Kike deprived us of our freedom and settled down in the Kremlin. Wherever there's a purse, the Kike is there and the Russian loses his trousers. That's why the Germans got angry at the Kikes and began to liberate the nations. The Kike picked up his devil's tail and fled to the rear, while sending us to die for him. . . . When we finish off the Kikes we'll make peace" (TDAGOU, f. 1, *op.* 70, spr. 237, p. 41). The other, which concerns life in the rear, says: "So listen, brothers, to what I am telling you, there's no room in Russia for the Kike parasite! Give it to him in the neck, cock your rifle! When the Kike perishes, things will be good for us. Russia will be our country and we'll order the Kike with no nonsense to go to the devil, drop dead, don't dare prevent us from living free and happy!" (ibid., p. 40). On antisemitic German propaganda in Russia, see R. E. Herzstein, "Antisemitic Propaganda in the Orel Region

of Great Russia, 1942–1943: The German Army and Its Russian Collaborators," *Wiesenthal Center Annual* 1989, pp. 33–55.

14. B. Vest, ed., *Be-havlei kelayah* (In the Throes of Extermination), (Tel Aviv: Archion ha-avodah, 1963), p. 130.
15. "Garlic-breath" was a common anti-Jewish epithet.
16. Mariia Litvinenko-Vol'gemut (1895–1966), Ukrainian folksinger, graduated music school in Kiev in 1912 and performed in that city until World War I. Then she sang in Petrograd. After the Civil War she returned to Ukraine, where she performed in Kharkov and Kiev. In 1946 she became a professor at the Kiev Conservatory.
17. The Soviet-Ukrainian author Petro Panch (real name: Petr Panchenko [1891–1978]) published his first stories in 1921. During the 1920s, he was affiliated with the proletariarian trend in Ukrainian literature. Later he found his place in the Soviet Writers' Union and for many years was a member of its Ukrainian executive. He published short-story collections and novels on social themes.
18. Pavlo Tychina (1891–1967), poet and politician, whose poems and stories were first published in 1912, served as Ukrainian Minister of Education (1943–1948) and was later (from 1952) a member of the Central Committee of the Communist Party of Ukraine. He was a member of the Ukrainian Academy of Sciences from 1923. In his work he sharply attacked Ukrainian emigrants and praised the Communist Party.
19. Alexander Korneichuk (1905–1972), Soviet-Ukrainian playwright and politician. His first story, about Lenin, was published in 1925; his first play was staged in 1929. On the eve of World War II he published *Bogdan Chmielnicki*, a play that lauded the Russian annexation of Ukraine in the seventeenth century. During World War II he wrote plays about the war; later he turned to rural themes. At the end of the war he was one of the most prominent authors in Soviet Ukraine and enjoyed great prestige.
20. TDAGOU, f. 1, op. 70, spr. 175, p. 67.
21. See ch. 20, 1.
22. TDAGOU, f. 1, op. 23, spr. 1394, pp. 4–5.
23. On the nutritional situation at the time, see the description by a Western correspondent in the Soviet Union: Alexander Werth, *Russia: The Postwar Years* (London: Hale, 1971), pp. 11–12.
24. For example, in the city of Voroshilovgrad, 2,542 buildings were burned or destroyed; in Stalino, close to 4,000 buildings were destroyed (*Ukrainskaia SSR v Velikoi otechestvennoi voine Sovetskogo Soiuza* [The Ukrainian SSR in the Great Patriotic War of the Soviet Union]), (Kiev: Politizdat, 1975), vol. 2, p. 174.
25. For example, a Jew who returned to Odessa wrote to Ilya Ehrenburg (August 10, 1944): "I was evacuated for three years and recently returned to my city. The household items and furniture in my apartment were stolen and the apartment occupied. My two sons are officers defending the homeland, and I am elderly. . . . I sat in the entrance hall [of my apartment block] until a neighbor took pity on me and let me into his flat. The bureaucrats of the housing department [*zhilotdel*] have still not given me permission for an apartment" (*Sovetskie evrei pishut Il'e*

Erenburgu, p. 148). When Ehrenburg passed on an appeal in a similar case, he received the following reply from the chairman of the Snegirevka soviet of Kherson province: "Immediately upon the return [of the former tenants] the [people living in them] were evacuated and the houses returned to the rightful tenants" (ibid., p. 153). In response to another complaint forwarded by Ehrenburg, the party secretary of the Kalinindorf district wrote: "No appropriate steps have been taken by Comrades Polovko, chairman of the district soviet, and Druzhinin, the former secretary of the district Party Committee; they responded with a lack of sensitivity to the complaints of the evacuees concerning the return of their homes" (ibid., p. 156).

26. See Borovoi, *Vospominaniia*, pp. 291–92.

27. The last date mentioned in the memorandum is July 25, 1944. See chapter 20.

28. Sergei Savchenko served as head of the NKVD (NKGB) in Ukraine until 1946. A confidant of Lavrentii Beria, he was later transferred to Moscow, where he served as a department head in the Information Committee (*Komitet Informatsii*), which was directly subordinate to the Soviet government and engaged in overseas espionage. He tended to report to Beria rather than to the foreign minister, Vyshinsky, who had direct responsibility for the Information Committee (K. Andrew and O. Gordievskii, *KGB: Istoriia vneshnepoliticheskikh operatsii* [The KGB: History of foreign-policy operations]), (Moscow: Nota Bene, 1992), p. 391. After Stalin's death he was removed from his post. Given Savchenko's closeness to Beria, the memorandum printed here and the response of the Party apparatus to it may already reflect the bad blood between Khrushchev and Beria. It is also possible that Beria considered antisemitism to be a more serious problem than did Khrushchev. On Beria's attitude on the Jewish question, see the recent book by Amy Knight, *Beria: Stalin's First Lieutenant* (Princeton: Princeton University Press, 1993), pp. 146–50. I wish to thank Professor Shlomo Avineri for bringing this book to my attention.

29. To the best of our knowledge, there is no reliable estimate as to the number of Jews who served in the Red Army during World War II. The figure generally cited, half a million, is based on articles by Yakov Kantor: "Yiden oif dem gresten un vikhtikstn front" (Jews on the Largest and Most Important Front), *Folks-shtime* (Warsaw), April 18, 1963; "Zey zaynen der shtolts fun unzer folk" (They Are the Pride of Our People), ibid., May 5 and 6, 1965. Kantor never indicates how he arrived at this figure, and its accuracy is doubtful. What is more, during the four years of the Soviet-German war there were changes in the ethnic composition of the Red Army, including its proportion of Jews. The subject still awaits a comprehensive study based on archival material. Here we can offer only some figures that have a bearing on the question. On the eve of World War II (January 1939), Jews constituted 1.77 percent of the population of the Soviet Union, and 1.63 percent of those on active duty in the Red Army including career soldiers. See M. Altshuler, "A Note on Jews in the Red Army on the Eve of the Second World War," *Jews and Jewish Topics in the Soviet Union and Eastern Europe* 2(18) (1992), pp. 37–39. Most of those conscripted from the territories annexed to the Soviet Union in 1939–1940, including the Jews, served in national units. In 1943, the 43rd Estonian Division was 9 percent Jewish, and the 23rd Lithuanian Division, 23.2 percent Jewish. Jews constituted 0.73 percent of the soldiers

and officers of the 21st Army in April–May 1942, and 1 percent of the 40th Army in August 1942. For the most part these were new conscripts, mobilized after the main Jewish population centers had been overrun by the Nazis. Nevertheless, the percentage of Jews in combat units remained close to their percentage in the population before the war. Jews constituted 1.43 percent of the seven rifle divisions that fought on the Orlov-Kursk front. The elite units—the 52nd and 67th *gvardeiskie strelkovye divizii*—which bore the brunt of particularly fierce fighting, were 1.57 percent Jewish on July 1, 1943. The percentage of Jews in more than 200 rifle divisions, with more than a million soldiers, varied over time as follows: January 1, 1943—1.50 percent; April 1, 1943—1.56 percent; July 1, 1943—1.35 percent; January 1, 1944—1.28 percent. The declining percentage of Jews stemmed from the fact that as territories were liberated, many of the locals (Ukrainians and Belorussians) were called up, while the vast majority of the Jews who had remained in these territories had been massacred by the Nazis. This trend intensified as additional areas were liberated. By July 1, 1944, Jews constituted only 1.14 percent of the troops in 100 rifle divisions (A. Artem'ev, *Bratskii boevoi soiuz narodov SSSR v Velikoi otechestvennoi voine* [Moscow: Mysl', 1975], pp. 54, 56, 58–59, 142, 145). If we take into account that Jews constituted roughly 1.1 percent of the population of the Soviet Union after the war (according to the 1959 census), their proportion in the Red Army as a whole and in its combat units was proportional to their share in the general population.

SEVEN

Nazi Policy toward the Jews in the *Reichskommissariat Ostland*, June–December 1941: From White Terror to Holocaust in Lithuania

Michael MacQueen

Historian and political scientist Raul Hilberg, widely regarded as the dean of Holocaust studies, wrote in his history of the destruction of the European Jews:

> The annihilation phase consisted of two major operations. The first was launched on June 22, 1941, with the invasion of the USSR. Small units of the SS and Police were dispatched to Soviet territory, where they were to kill all Jewish inhabitants on the spot. . . . In essence, the killers in the occupied USSR moved to the victims, whereas outside this arena the victims were brought to the killers.[1]

This chapter is intended to be a contribution to the discussion of the periodization of the destruction of the Jews in the Soviet Union in the first six months of World War II, in the first of the major operations referred to by Raul Hilberg. My main argument is that in order to fully comprehend this aspect of the history of the war, we must be aware of Nazi policy toward the Jews of the occupied territories of the USSR at each stage of its evolution.

At the same time I must qualify the parameters of the study, for, as the title makes apparent, I am limiting it geographically to Lithuania, more specifically the *Generalkommissariat Litauen*, as the territorially embellished former Lithuanian state was known. I must also note that professional discretion places limits on the citation of original documents located in the Lithuanian State Archives at Vilnius which I have collected in the course of official investigations.[2] In this study, I have relied in the main on captured Nazi records from American and West German archives.

Lithuania did not become part of the USSR until June-August 1940, when the Baltic states were successively subverted and incorporated as union republics. Certainly, the experience of the Baltic states may not be wholly transferable to the rest of the occupied Soviet Union, but in terms of the development of the Holocaust in this region, Lithuania in particular is of crucial importance to the historian. It is in light of these historical facts that I assert my main thesis: the Holocaust in Lithuania was as much the product of pressures from below (i.e., low-level *Sicherheitspolizei* (SiPo) and SD commanders, commanders of collaborationist Lithuanian police and paramilitary units, local vigilante squads, persons of responsibility in the Nazi and indigenous civil administrations) as it was of the decrees issuing from the Nazi hierarchy; further, it was the development of these forces in conjunction with the specific ethnopolitical context of Lithuania that made possible the full development of the Holocaust.

In particular, I contend that in the first three months of the Nazi occupation the situation had more of the elements of a "White Terror," as, for example, in Hungary in 1919 after the repression of the Hungarian Soviet, than with the generally accepted view of the immediate and seamless introduction of a planned and systematic campaign of extermination. I will argue that the shift to systematic extermination was possible only when the Germans based their policy on harnessing the local forces, that is, when the Germans recognized fully the destructiveness of their Baltic collaborators.

There is not sufficient room in an essay of this length for a comprehensive discussion of the formation and preparation of the *Einsatzgruppen*, the situation in the Baltic states prior to their incorporation into the Soviet Union, the nature of Soviet rule in the region, or other vital background information which I must assume the reader possesses. In this chapter I will discuss three themes, each closely identified with a chronological period: 1) the situation in Lithuania just before June 22, 1941. The main topic will be the formation of the myth of Jewish responsibility for Lithuania's fall and injustices of the subsequent period of Soviet rule; 2) the period from June 22 to mid-August 1941, which, I will argue was a period of random pogroms (much as in Poland in the first weeks of Nazi occupation) and highly selective killings. This is the period I refer to as the "White Terror"; 3) the period from September 1941, which features the shift to organized and indiscriminate murder on a mass scale. It will be in the discussion of this period that I will focus, not on the killings themselves, but on the conjuncture which made them possible.

Lithuania before June 22, 1941

Lithuanian politics between the two world wars were a politics of practical, if not moral, failure. An authoritarian regime established by Antanas Smetona destroyed parliamentary democratic government in 1926. After Smetona's ascent to power, the main source of resistance to his rule came not from the smashed parties of the left but from the extreme right, from the conspiratorial groupings, such as the "Iron Wolf" (*Gelezinas Vilkas*) associated with the person of Augustinas Voldemaras. As in other Central European countries affected by a general shift to the right, this group found its primary constituency in the officer corps and among army veterans, national guard (*Siauliu Sajunga*) and the intellectual proletariat whose advancement had been blocked by the Great Depression. Somewhat paradoxically, organized antisemitism was not nearly as evident here as in other contemporary Central European countries; in Lithuania the minority Poles were the main foil for the negative energies which in other settings were directed at the Jews.

The Lithuanian government's legitimacy rested on the defense of the national interest against Poland (the Vilnius/Wilno question) and Germany, which pressed the demand for Memel/Klajpeda. In March 1938, the Lithuanians were humiliated by Poland's ultimatum, which forced an opening between the two countries while leaving Wilno Polish. In March 1939 the Germans extorted the retrocession of Memel. Defeated on these two vital fronts, the Smetona regime was demoralized, and its support swiftly eroded. Only Poland's fall and the subsequent attachment of Vilnius to Lithuania, granted under the Soviet-Lithuanian treaty of October 1939, served to make possible the temporary preservation of the existing political order. Soviet bases in Lithuania, freely agreed to under the October treaty, housed the agents who spearheaded the subversion of the Lithuanian state. Though there is clearly little likelihood that the Lithuanians could have resisted the imposition of Stalin's will, there is nevertheless a logical basis for the contention that Lithuania's fall may be attributed in part to the irredentist lust for Vilnius and the Smetona government's blind pursuit of this end which led to the acceptance of conditions so conducive to Sovietization. The Jews, blamed for ushering in Soviet rule, had nothing to do with it. And in the subsequent period (up to the Nazi invasion), the Jews as a group suffered as much or more than anyone else.

Once the Soviet Union established control over Lithuania the Bolshevik rulers appealed to several key groups as the basis for new, Soviet power. Among those specifically targeted were working and academic youth, the rural poor and the industrial proletariat, such as it was. These groups included some Jews, though large numbers of Lithuanian youth were also not shy about membership in the Komsomol.[3] As in other parts of Eastern Europe under Soviet occupation a skillful politics of "divide and conquer" was put into play, with Jews visible in positions associated with oppression, e.g. the police. The image produced by this practice overshadowed the reality of the essential powerlessness of the Jews as a group.

The segments of Lithuanian society which truly felt the wrath of the new authority included the capitalists and merchants, those associated with the old ruling structures, and all the institutions, e.g., religious communities, which were in contradiction to Soviet philosophy. These groups, in particular the urban bourgeoisie, included a substantial representation of Jews.

In the middle of June 1941, just prior to the Nazi invasion, the Soviet authorities organized mass deportations of "enemies" from the Baltic states. About 35,000 persons were rounded up in Lithuania by the NKVD; Jews constituted about 20 percent of the transports, well above their representation in the population (some 7.5 percent). Autochthonous and refugee Poles made up another 20 percent of the total. Yet when Nazi Germany invaded in June 1941, the Jews were singled out for the wrath of the conqueror and the collaborator.

Barbarossa and the Final Solution in Lithuania

No one can dispute that Hitler intended to extirpate the Jews of Europe root and branch in the course of the war and, indeed, to continue that policy for however long it might take. One can, however, allege that the achievement of this policy was not one of the immediate, clearly defined goals during the planning and launching of Barbarossa. The documentary record of Nazi intentions toward the Jews at this time is, at best, ambiguous.

The war diary of the German High Command for March 3, 1941, contains the draft "Guidelines for Special Matters" (*Richtlinien auf Sondergebieten*) for Operation Barbarossa, with the notation that these guidelines had been personally looked over and approved by Hitler. The only reference to the destruction of the Jews as a component of Nazi war aims is contained in a general outline for the political recasting of the Soviet state:

> The Jewish-Bolshevik intelligentsia, up to now the oppressors of the people, must be eliminated. The former aristocratic-bourgeois intelligentsia, especially its remnants of the emigration, also has no place. The Russian people reject it and anyway it is hostile to Germany. This applies particularly in the Baltic states.[4]

It is clear that at this stage of planning the intention was solely to destroy the leading elements, the *Führungsschicht*, of the Soviet state. The "Jewish-Bolshevik intelligentsia" referred to here is the appellation dictated by Nazi ideology, which stressed the purported role of an elite cadre of Jews as the bearer of the "Bolshevik bacillus."

There is no direct documentation of the instructions given to *Einsatzgruppe A* which would follow Army Group North through Lithuania and beyond. From the few relevant records which do exist it is clear that the subject of the Jews was raised only at the last minute, just before the *Einsatzkommandos* marched off.[5] We do know, however, what the orders issued to the *Einsatzgruppen* after the beginning of the invasion stated on the treatment of the Jews.

Reinhard Heydrich, as head of the RSHA (Reich Security Main Office) issued periodic orders to the *Einsatzgruppen*. The third such order, dated July 2, 1941, states clearly:

> 4) *Executions:* To be executed are all functionaries of the Comintern (and all other professional communist politicians); the higher, middle and radical lower functionaries of the Party, the Central Committee and the regional district committees; Jews in state and Party posts; other radical elements (saboteurs, propagandists, snipers, assassins, agitators, etc.). When in individual cases execution is necessary, it is of course to be carried out, but only after the case has been thoroughly investigated.[6]

This order can scarcely be interpreted as constituting a directive for the immediate and systematic annihilation of all Jews in the Barbarossa operations area. If we accept that the extirpation of the Jews was the central aim of Nazi racial policy in the East already at this stage of the war, regardless of its absence from the orders given the Wehrmacht and the SS/police apparatus, how then did the Nazis intend to proceed to this end?

The Pogroms in Lithuania and Their Origins

Heydrich's orders did contain a number of references to murderous pogroms. The most illuminating of these is a component of his first "Deployment Order" (*Einsatzbefehl*) issued on June 29, 1941. Referring to verbal orders which were issued in Berlin on June 17, presumably only to the SiPo and SD officers of the *Einsatzgruppen*, Heydrich emphasized:

> 1) the self-cleansing efforts [*Selbstreinigungsbestrebungen*] of anti-communist or anti-Jewish circles are not to be obstructed. On the contrary, they are to be unleashed, to be intensified when necessary and to be steered in the right direction. This must proceed without a trace, so that later the local "self defense circles" may not point to any decrees or political assurances.
>
> Since such actions are possible only in the first period of military occupation for obvious reasons, the *Einsatzgruppen* and *Einsatz kommandos* of the Security Police and SD, in cooperation with the military authorities, are to send advance squads into the newly occupied territories as quickly as possible to make the necessary arrangements. . . .
>
> The formation of *permanent* self-defense units under central leadership is to be avoided at first; in place of these it makes sense only to unleash popular pogroms, as outlined above.[7]

Lithuania was, at one time or another in the first weeks of the invasion, the operational area for several different *Einsatzkommandos* (*EK 9, EK 1b, EK 2,* and *EK 3*). As the first area of Nazi operations and home to the largest concentration of Jews in the Baltic it might be expected that the *Einsatzkommandos* would immediately commence killing actions. The process of its permanent assignment to the authority of *Einsatzkommando 3* under the command of *SS Standartenführer* Karl Jager commenced on July 2, 1941; his detachment did not consolidate control of all Lithuania until October. But before the SiPo and SD men of Jager's or any other of the *Einsatzkommandos* could commence organized operations, some 5,000 Jews had been killed, most of them in Kaunas. The Lithuanians who committed these spontaneous murders called themselves "partisans." Who were they?

For Latvia there exists a fairly substantial body of information on the establishment and activities of a paramilitary underground in the period of Soviet rule 1940–41. A large fraction of this underground was subsequently directly linked to the Latvian collaborationist units which engaged in the murder of Jews.[8] But for Lithuania there is only a fragmentary documentary basis on the history of similar phenomena.

When Lithuania fell to the Soviets in 1940 a number of more or less prominent Lithuanian figures, sharing a no doubt well-founded suspicion that their futures under the new system would be bleak and limited, fled to Germany. Some of them assembled in Berlin where the former Lithuanian Minister to Germany, Colonel Kazys Skirpa, attempted to form a sort of emigre representation. The group born of these efforts took the name "Lithuanian Activist Front" (LAF). Its membership was a mixed group, including both ardent Smetonists and Voldemarists.[9]

This relatively elite group was not alone in seeking refuge. In the aftermath of the Nazi-Soviet agreement on the "repatriation" of the ethnic Germans of the Baltic states, some 52,000 persons left Lithuania for the Reich. However, contemporary German sources estimated that there were only 35,000 Germans in Lithuania as of the beginning of 1940. It appears that the excess included many Lithuanians, in particular those who were aware that their past histories would be regarded as compromised. In this number were members of the once-extensive secret police (*Saugumas*) apparatus built by Smetona. They took advantage of a flexibly interpreted definition of *Deutschtum*, if not the deliberate connivance of Nazi intelligence, and left. Among these were former senior secret police officials such as Stasys Cenkus and Aleksandras Lileikis.

An individual of lesser importance but whose career is better documented is Pranas Lukys, a secret police official from the border town of Kretinga. Lukys was tried and convicted in the Federal Republic of Germany in 1957 for the murder of Jews and suspected Communists in and around Taurage.[10] The indictment charged that Lukys and some fifty other secret policemen crossed the border into Germany on June 17, 1940, and were interned in a labor camp near Tilsit. In December 1940 he and the other secret policemen were transferred, at the order of the Tilsit Gestapo, to Lublin. Lukys was assigned as a sergeant of criminal police to the *Sicherheitspolizei* post in Radzin near Lublin (many Lithuanians spoke Polish). Here he worked until some time in the spring of 1941, when he went to Memel (Klaipeda). On the night before the Nazi invasion he crossed into Lithuania with other Lithuanian secret policemen under the orders of a former captain in the Lithuanian Army. It was not made clear who briefed this captain. Their mission was to organize partisans against the Red Army. These infiltrators and the partisan units they created were the armed exponents of the LAF.

Nazi columns rapidly penetrated Lithuania. Soviet forces withdrew in confusion, the muddle heightened by the mutiny of a major portion of the Lithuanian component of the Red forces, the 297th Territorial Corps. In Kaunas, a group of LAF partisans, under the command of a one-time journalist named Algirdas Klimaitis, rose up and engaged the Soviets in battle for control of the city. By the evening of June 23 most of the city was in the hands of the insurgents. Klimaitis and his partisans then unleashed a bloodbath, which by June 28 had claimed 3,800 Jewish lives.[11] Dr. Walter Stahlecker, commander of *Einsatzgruppe A*, reported on these killings in his own fashion:

> When the German troops marched in, the Lithuanians' hatred of the Jews led to effective pogroms. . . . In these pogroms, conducted with the substantial assistance of the Sipo and the SD, the Lithuanians eliminated 3,800 Jews in Kaunas and 1,200 in the smaller towns.[12]

When the German military administration consolidated control of Lithuania, the partisans were ordered disarmed, and the pogroms, at least in this "spontaneous" and extraordinarily bloody form, came to an end. This period leaves us to speculate on two points. The first is that, regardless of the previously guaranteed cooperation between the Wehrmacht and the SiPo/SD, the pogroms carried out by the Lithuanians at the encouragement of the SiPo/SD were too gruesome for the German military commandant to tolerate; the fear may have also existed that the pogroms represented an unacceptable element of anarchy in an already confused and chaotic situation. The second point is, a complete lack of documentation aside, it appears that the SiPo/SD may have trained a cadre of Lithuanians to act as the spearhead in the organization of pogroms as may be true in the Lukys case, preparing them for this task at the same time as the rank and file of the *Einsatzgruppen* themselves were still being kept ignorant of the true nature of their own mission. Recent scholarship on the LAF has exposed the fact that radio broadcasts to Lithuania from Germany made by LAF propagandists explicitly urged the population to take harsh measures against the Jews; the evidence also suggests that the only path to expiation for Lithuanians who had compromised themselves via association with the NKVD, Komsomol, or other organs of the Communist government was through the spilling of Jewish blood.[13]

Organization for Death

I have noted above how Heydrich ordered that the formation of "permanent self-defense units" was something to be avoided. This was precisely the step taken in Kaunas, however, commencing on June 28. Colonel Bobelis, the Lithuanian provisional military commander of Kaunas, issued two orders on that day, no doubt at the direction of the Germans. The first announced the disbanding and disarming of the partisans; the second was a call for all former officers and men of the Lithuanian Army to register for duty.[14] Within days hundreds of former soldiers had flocked to join this unit, the Battalion for the Defense of National Labor. The military circles associated with General Rastikis were rejected both by the Germans, who were already suppressing the Lithuanian Provisional Government in which Rastikis was a leader, and by the Voldemarists of the officer corps, who quickly gained control of the Defense of National Labor units. By July 1 Erich Ehrlinger, commander of *Einsatzkommando lb*, who was in the process of turning Kaunas over to Jager, reported that

> auxiliary police troops in the strength of five companies have been created. Two companies are under the orders of the *Einsatzkommando*. One of these guards the Jewish concentration camp established at Fort VII and carries out the executions. . . .[15]

Similar formations were organized in Vilnius. Local police forces were also reorganized, with the erstwhile partisans playing a key role; indeed, a certificate confirming one's participation in the ranks of the partisans became a prized and necessary document for any official position. The secret police were re-formed as the *Litauische Abteilung* (Lithuanian Department) of the Nazi *Sicherheitspolizei*, under Stasys Cenkus, freshly arrived from Berlin. The reorganized *Saugumas* mirrored the pattern of division of responsibilities of the Nazi *Sicherheitspolizei und der SD,* with a separate section for Jewish affairs.

In Kaunas the Defense of National Labor units were large enough by mid-August to form two battalions, with a third, fourth, and fifth added in rapid order. Renamed Auxiliary Police Service Battalions, three of the Kaunas units (1st, 2nd, and 3rd Battalions) were directly subordinate to *Einsatzkommando 3* as part of the *Ordnungspolizei*. Of the units formed in Vilnius, a company-sized unit known as the Special Detachment (*Ypatingas Burys*) was established; it carried out the mass executions at the Panierai pits. These were the Lithuanian vanguard of the White Terror.

When I use the term "White Terror" I mean a regime of terror instituted as the temporary means of control of a population in a period of counterrevolution (useful, for example, in facilitating the ghettoization of the Jewish population without resistance). In applying this to Lithuania I must further specify that there was a second counterrevolution underway within the apparent counterrevolution against Soviet power, waged by the Voldemarists against the Smetonist legacy. In winning this more subtle of the two struggles, the Voldemarists assured a *Gleichschaltung* of the secret police, formerly the prop of Smetona's government, to the new order of things.

The Lithuanian (and other Baltic) police battalions were recognized and formalized by Himmler in an order published at the end of July 1941:

> The tasks of the police in the occupied territories cannot be fulfilled by those units of the police and SS already and yet to be committed. It is therefore necessary to organize additional protective units from the ethnic groups suitable to us in the conquered areas as soon as possible, as the *Einsatzgruppen* of the *Sicherheitspolizei* have already done.[16]

The auxiliary police battalions were accorded the title *Schutzmannschaft*, and the municipal and rural police forces in Lithuania were known by a modified form of this appellation (*Schutzmannschaft des Einzeldienstes*). The importance of the *Schutzmannschaft* units to *EK 3* in the completion of its tasks becomes critically apparent when we consider the size of the latter. As of February 1, 1942, *EK 3* had:

24 Gestapo officials
32 SS reservists
44 drivers
13 Criminal Police (Kripo) officers
9 SD officials
7 temporarily assigned personnel
3 radio operators
3 clerks (women)
2 administrators
2 communications staff

Total: 139 personnel[17]

It was this relatively puny force which carried out the White Terror. The terror started with a frenzy of executions in two days (July 4 and 6, 1941) at Fort VII, an old tsarist fortification outside Kaunas. There Lithuanian units shot 2,977 Jews, all men save forty-seven.[18]

Simultaneously Jager set up a flying squad (*Rollkommando*) under SS *Obersturmführer* Hamann. It contained "eight to ten proven (SS) men" and traveled with an unknown number of Lithuanians (it is here that the inclusion of such a large number of drivers in the strength of *EK 3* begins to make sense). From July 7 to 31, 1941, the flying squad scoured Lithuania, from Panevezys in the north to Marijampole in the south. They killed 4,400 people, all adults. The actions involved as few as one and as many as 288 victims. Of the total, some 184 victims were identified as Lithuanian or Russian Communists. In comparison with the total figure it is an insignificant number; what is significant is that almost every action involved a mix of Jews and Communists, e.g. the action in Marijampole on July 14, 1941, where the victims were "21 Jews, one Russian and nine Lithuanian communists," or in Kedainiai on July 23, with "83 Jews, 12 Jewish women, 14 Russian communists, 15 Lithuanian communists, one Russian *Politruk*."[19] These killing actions were meant to set an example, to terrorize, and to demoralize any potential opposition.[20]

In the first half of August 1941 the scale of the operations increased. From

August 1 to 14, Hamann's unit conducted ten *Aktionen* which claimed 4,788 victims. The number of alleged Communists shot declined, though the pattern of exemplary actions remained. This changed dramatically at the middle of the month.

Holocaust

In the course of two days, August 15 and 16, 1941, 3,200 Jews—men, women, and children—were murdered at the temporary concentration camp which had been established near the northern Lithuanian town of Rokiskis. It was the first time that children were included among the victims of organized slaughter. This marked the shift to the inauguration of the program to completely destroy the Jews of Lithuania. Including the Rokiskis *Aktion*, over 33,000 persons were killed in Lithuania in the latter half of August, of whom only about 1,000 were non-Jews (including 544 mental patients murdered at Aglona in accordance with the Nazi policy on the elimination of "useless eaters").[21]

By December 1941 *EK 3* listed 133,346 persons, the overwhelming majority of them Jews, as having fallen before the guns of its mixed killing squads. Some fell to the roaming *Kommandos*, great numbers to the stationary Schuma battalions at Kaunas and the "Special Detachment" at Vilnius, which was reinforced by local *Schutzmannschaft* units when deployed for major actions. Three thousand and fifty victims fell to *EK 3* across the border in Belorussia. Including the victims of the partisans (which he understated as a total of 4,000), Jager claimed 137,346 victims, murders committed with a force of 139 Germans, including secretaries and office workers.

Concluding Thoughts

The huge death toll registered by *Einsatzkommando 3* in 1941 cannot be attributed to fabled German efficiency or the skill and dedication of Jager's SiPo and SD men, including in their efforts the occasional assistance of various German reserve police battalions. Instead, Jager's "achievement" has to be considered largely as a triumph of managing the Lithuanian *Schutzmannschaft* forces (some 8,000 men by the end of 1941) and the Lithuanian police, without whom this deadly work would not have been remotely possible.

The role of the local police forces in facilitating the process is illuminated by documents from the Lithuanian State Archives. The head of the uniformed police, Vladas Reivytis, sent out identical orders to almost every police station in central Lithuania. These orders were issued in such quantity that, rather than being individually typed they were run off as mimeographed forms, with blanks spaces left for the names of the affected localities. In each, the local police chief was instructed to round up all the Jews in the town and to either hold them there or to move them to a nearby collection point. When the requisite number of Jews had been assembled, Reivytis would send a communication to Hamann informing him that so-and-so many Jews had been locked up at a given place, under conditions which presented the danger of the "outbreak of infectious disease." Hamann would then dispatch his flying squad to that place and conduct the *Aktion*.[22]

The utility of the Lithuanian units in mass killing was recognized and employed elsewhere. At the beginning of October 1941, the 2nd Lithuanian *Schutzmannschaft* Battalion, formed at Kaunas, accompanied the llth German Reserve Police Battalion to Minsk. At numerous locales in western Belorussia this unit helped kill some 17,000 Jews, Red Army prisoners, and others in the span of two months.[23] Other Lithuanian *Schutzmannschaft* units served in the *Bandenbekampfung* (antipartisan combat) units under operational command of the SS. Many such units acquired a reputation for their propensity to commit atrocities against civilian populations. One Lithuanian *Schutzmannschaft* battalion was sent to the concentration camp at Majdanek, where it formed a major part of the guard contingent; when its stint was completed there, it was replaced by another Lithuanian battalion.

One can only speculate as to the motivations of the collaborators. In some cases personal greed clearly played a role, the executioners robbing the corpses and property of the victims. In others, especially the adherents of the Iron Wolf, there was an ideological commitment as deep as that of the Nazis to the elimination of the Jews. Regardless, enough willing hands were found to make possible acts which the Nazis themselves, due to the paucity of their numbers, could never have accomplished. Jager's (and the other Baltic *Einsatzkommando* leaders') contribution lay in the observation, manipulation, stimulation, and management of these destructive powers.

One might further speculate that Jager engaged in a competition with the other *Einsatzkommando* leaders, in the expectation that demonstrated zeal in the pursuit of the racial goals of Nazi policy, above and beyond the guidelines established by Heydrich in his orders, would be rewarded. It is clear that he and the other *EK* leaders expressly violated the orders on the treatment of the Jews issued by the civilian administration of the *Reichskommissariat Ostland* and military-economic apparatus of the Wehrmacht.

The Wannsee conference did not take place until January 1942. How much did the experience of the *Einsatzgruppen* in the Baltic states, above all in Lithuania, contribute to the decisions taken at that suburban Berlin villa? At the very least, they demonstrated that that which emerged from Wannsee as policy was entirely possible.

Notes

1. Raul Hilberg, *The Destruction of the European Jews* (New York: Homes and Meier, 1985), vol. 1, p. 273.
2. I would note here that scholars interested in pursuing the study of the Holocaust

in Lithuania would be well served by consulting some of the Soviet-era publications on the topic, such as *Masines Zudynes Lietuvoje* (Mass Murders in Lithuania) (Vilnius: Mintis, 1965), two volumes. On the question of the Lithuanian *Schutzmannschaft* the highly flawed *SS Tarnyboje* (In the Service of the SS), (Vilnius: Lithuanian Academy of Sciences, 1961) contains useful references. The greatest value of these and other works (*Documents Accuse*, Vilnius: Mintis, 1970) lies in the fact that the archival references are accurate and, in most cases, contemporary.

3. At the time of the June 1941 invasion one of the primary tasks of the *Einsatzkommandos* was the seizure of Communist Party documentation. In Lithuania a relevant portion of this documentation—membership applications and lists—was turned over to the Lithuanian Security Police (*Saugumas*) for use in identifying and locating suspected Communists. In a large number of these lists, a substantial portion of which are to be found in Collection R 972 of the Lithuanian State Archives, the Lithuanian-Christian names easily outnumber the Jewish names.

4. Helmut Greiner and Percy Ernst Schramm, eds., *Kriegstagebuch des Oberkommandos der Wehrmacht—Wehrmachtführungsstab* (Munich: Bernard und Graefe, 1982), vol. I, pp. 340–41.

5. Most of the available knowledge on the instructions given to the men of the *Einsatzgruppen* comes from the interrogations and testimonies compiled by the West German judicial authorities in the course of postwar investigations of Nazi crimes; for Lithuania the key investigation was that of commander of *EK 3* Karl Jager. *Zentralstelle der Landesjustizverwaltungen* AR-Z 14/1958. Jager committed suicide while in pretrial custody.

6. July 2, 1941, Order of Heydrich, Chief of *Sicherheitspolizei* and the SD, to the Commanders of the *Einsatzgruppen*, *Bundesarchiv Koblenz*, document series R 70/SU, folder 32, pp. 4–10.

7. June 29, 1941, Order of Heydrich to the Commanders of the *Einsatzgruppen*, Bundesarchiv Koblenz, document series R 70/SU 32, pp. 1–2.

8. See the *Anklageschrift* (Indictment) against Viktor Arajs, Landgericht Hamburg, file reference 141 Js 534/60, dated May 10, 1976.

9. On the sovietization and the LAF see Seppo Myllyniemi, *Die Neuordnung der baltischen Lander 1941–1944. Zum nationalsozialistischen Inhalt der deutschen Besatzungspolitik, Dissertationes Historicae* (Helsinki, 1973), pp. 103–104; Leonas Sabaliunas, *Lithuania in Crisis: Nationalism to Communism, 1939–1940* (Bloomington: Indiana University Press, 1972).

10. Trial proceedings against Bernhard Fischer-Schweder et al., Oberste Landgericht Stuttgart, file reference Js 1/56.

11. Klimaitis, at one point thought to have emigrated to the United States after the war, was finally found in Hamburg, Germany in the late 1970s, living under his own name. The energetic investigation launched by the Hamburg State Prosecutor's Office was for nought; Klimaitis died before he could be brought to trial. It is interesting that his son, also Algirdas, was accused and imprisoned in 1992 by the authorities of independent Lithuania as a suspected agent of the KGB.

12. *Einsatzgruppe A, Gesamtbericht vom 16. Oktober 1941 bis 31. Januar 1942*,

National Archives and Records Adminstration, Nuremberg Exhibit L 180, p. 60. This is the document generally known as the "Stahlecker Report."

13. See the conversations on the LAF with American-Lithuanian historian Saulius Suziedelis published in *Akiriciai* (Horizons), Chicago, nos. 9 and 10, October and November 1991, and no. 1, January 1992.

14. Order of the Commandant of Kaunas, Colonel Bobelis, June 28, 1941; Circular of the War Commandant's Office, Kaunas, June 28, 1941, Lithuanian State Archives Collection R 1444, series 2, folder 2.

15. *Situations- und Lagebericht, Einsatzkommando 1b*, Kaunas, July 1, 1941. Bundesarchive Koblenz, document series R 70/SU 15, folder 15, p. 3.

16. Order of Reichsführer SS Heinrich Himmler: *Die Aufgaben der Polizei in den besetzten Ostgebieten*; National Archives and Records Administration, Record Group 242, Microfilm Collection T454 (Records of the *Reichskommissariat Ostland*), roll 100, frames 699–700.

17. Stahlecker Report, op. cit., Appendix 2, "*Stahrke der Kommandos.*"

18. *Gesamtaufstellung der im Bereich des EK. 3 bis zum 1. Dezember 1941 durchgeführten Exekutionen*, December 1, 1941, signed by head of *EK 3* Karl Jager, original held in Special State Archive of the Russian Federation, Moscow, collection R500, folder 1. Known as the Jager Report, it is the fundamental document on the chronological progression of the Holocaust in Lithuania for the first five months of the occupation.

19. Jager Report, op. cit.

20. One of the jobs of the Lithuanian *Saugumas* was to separate out the "honest Lithuanian youth duped by the Komsomol" from the doomed. Contemporary Lithuanian police records demonstrate that a more heavily implicated Lithuanian, for example a Komsomol activist, could expect about three months at forced labor as punishment. Of course, for any Lithuanian Jew formerly associated with the Komsomol, the only punishment was death.

21. Jager Report, op. cit.

22. See materials in Collection R 683 (Records of the Commander of Police), series 2, folder 2, Lithuanian State Archives, Vilnius. Mr. Reivytis died in West Germany under an assumed name in 1988.

23. *Lagebericht*, Kommandant im Weißruthenien beim Wehrmachtsbefehlshaber Ostland, November 10, 1941, Archive of the October Revolution, Minsk, collection 1275, series 3; also *Lagebericht Weißruthenien* of the *Hoherer SS und Polizeiführer beim Reichskommissariat Ostland*, October 17, 1941, Archive of the October Revolution, Minsk, collection 1275, series 3.

EIGHT

"Inventing" the Holocaust for Latvia: New Research

Hans-Heinrich Wilhelm

Recent publications on the Holocaust have prompted scholars to examine once again, and more closely, the events of the summer of 1941, a critical period in the unfolding Holocaust, a time when unsystematic killings became more systematic, deliberate, and "rational." This new research includes the work of two young Berlin-based scholars, Goetz Aly and Susanne Heim, who have published several articles on the "economy of the Final Solution" and are completing a major book on the topic. Basing their thesis largely on material from the Nazi-occupied territories of Austria and Poland, Aly and Heim have concluded that the so-called Aryanization of businesses and the annihilation of the Jews in these areas came about mainly as a result of Nazi efforts to eliminate at least visible poverty and of their plans for a more rational economic system.[1] In light of this thought-provoking and insightful work, the Baltic states under Nazi rule should also be examined to see if their thesis applies to that region during the first months of the Russian campaign in the summer and fall of 1941.

Professor Bernhard Press, a survivor of the Holocaust in Latvia, has published an impressive book on the killing of the Jews in that Baltic state.[2] In this account, based largely on his own recollections, Press emphasizes the role of Latvians in the annihilation of the Jews. He suggests that local forces began to arrest, concentrate, and murder their Jewish neighbors even before the German troops had occupied Riga and Dünaburg (Dvinsk, Daugavpils). Furthermore, Press suspects that there might well have been communications and agreements reached between the German authorities, operating clandestinely in Latvia, and various (Latvian) underground organizations, such as the Aiszargy, Perkonkrusts, former members of the police, security service, army, aviation clubs, student associations, and fraternities. Through these arrangements, the underground groups may have promised not only to support German military efforts to "liberate" Latvia, but also to "cleanse" Latvian cities of their Jewish population before or shortly after the advancing German troops arrived.

A former high-ranking Soviet intelligence (GRU) officer, writing under the name of Viktor Suvorov, published a book in which he argued that, at least on the Soviet side, the war did not commence on June 22, 1941, but had actually begun weeks or even months earlier. So-called dirty war operations had been launched long before the German panzer divisions invaded the "peaceful" Soviet Union. Furthermore, Suvorov argues that Stalin's Second Wave was already underway, formed mainly by NKVD troops from the interior of Russia, so-called wood cutter divisions in gulag uniforms needed for the general attack on Berlin or farther west. In addition, Suvorov maintains that Stalin had neglected defensive measures only because of his concentration of energy and resources on an aggressive war against the Third Reich.[3] Suvorov's book prompts historians to examine again the hypothesis that *both* sides, Nazi Germany and the Soviet Union, were using spies, agents, and fifth-column representatives. Scholars need to ask if such preparations were in fact taking place and what impact they had on the Holocaust.

In an important study of forced sterilization in the Third Reich,[4] historian Gisela Bock points out a continuity between a policy of sterilization and the later policy of genocide, not noticed before and dating back for years which almost everyone believed had not begun before 1939 or 1941. Sterilization as an alternative to mass killings was not first discovered in 1939 or 1941. The *Ostjuden* or the Jews in general were not the only targets of German racism and "social hygiene"; attention was given as well to work shirkers (*Arbeitsscheue*), prostitutes, pimps, homosexuals, Gypsies, the mentally retarded, and individuals with hereditary diseases. In regard to forced sterilization and other matters, Hitler and his followers would look to authorities writing long before 1933, and not only in Germany. This literature must have penetrated Scandinavia, Russia, and the Baltic states, and this may have gained some importance in 1941–42. What were, for example, the tasks of the German Hygienic Institute in Riga, in addition to its involvement in medical experiments and in the development of the "gas-wagon?" How was it possible that a physician from Bausk (southern Latvia), assisted by an army surgeon, proposed to the local German authorities that all young Jews of the town be castrated? The physician indeed received the permission to carry out this macabre plan, and the bulk of the population of Bausk, especially the women, allegedly enjoyed this horrific joke.[5] Additional research on these topics is urgently needed.

In the last several years a number of significant regional historical studies have come out of Latvia. For example, Peter Krupnikov's book on Latvia and Latvians in German and Baltic-German writings from 1895 to 1950[6] sparked considerable interest and discussions at home and abroad. An article by Margers Vestermanis[7] challenges many assumptions concerning the Holocaust in Latvia. Vestermanis emphasizes especially the differences in policy and action between the German and non-German authorities in different places during the first weeks of the occupation of Latvia, and these enormous differences lead to the conclusion that at this date, there could not have been a single general directive, and that the later policy of mass and total annihilation needed at least weeks to develop by trial and error.

Older historical publications have offered little insight into the complicated antecedents of the Holocaust in east-central Europe. The deficiencies in such works become apparent when one reads a book like Klaus Schloegel's marvelous case study, *Jenseits des Grossen Oktober. Das Laboratorium der Moderne, Petersburg 1900–1921* (Berlin, 1988). Similar social-historical treatments of the Baltic states for the interwar years are desperately needed.

A Latvian-born American scholar, Andrew Ezergailis, has written extensively in recent years on the Holocaust in Latvia. His work has focused on the so-called Arajs Kommando, an auxiliary police unit operating out of Riga, responsible for the killing of tens of thousands of Jews. More research on this unit and other aspects touched by Professor Ezergailis in conference papers and articles is needed, but his work has undoubtedly already filled an important gap in Holocaust historiography.[8] Knowing very well not only the contemporary German documents and the decision of the Hamburg court against Viktor Arajs, the former head of this *Selbstreinigungskommando*, but also the other *Ermittlungsakten* (files of investigations) with dozens of eyewitness accounts, Ezergailis emphasizes that those Latvians involved in the Final Solution, especially those who served with Arajs, were volunteers, highly motivated, and well paid. The Arajs Kommando was responsible not only for most "actions" in Latvia, but also for war crimes and crimes against humanity in other regions as well, which in its eagerness to help the Germans, is comparable only to certain Lithuanian and Ukrainian *Schutzmannschaft* battalions.[9]

For many years the perpetrators, those involved in the killings, did not publish books. But that might be changing now, judging from the recently published memoirs of Baltic-German Jürgen Ernst Kroeger, which confirm in many aspects Bernhard Press's view of the events.[10] A former member of *Einsatzkommando* 2, Kroeger was born and raised in Latvia; he was not a *Reichsdeutscher,* as were most members of Dr. Rudolf Lange's Kommando, and he seems to be a sensitive historical witness, trying his best. There are a few other such memoirs, from Otto Braeutigam, Peter Kleist, Hugo Wittrock, and Ernst Turmann.[11] The passage of time has made it easier to avoid apologetic tendencies, as can be seen in Kroeger's book. For those interested in the long-term development of xenophobia, chauvinism, antisemitism, and "typical" Baltic-German *Herrenmenschen* (supermen) mentality in Latvia and in Germany, there is Dorte von Westernhagen's book, in which she comes to terms with her father's and her grandfather's generation. A member of the RSHA VI (SD-foreign nations) until March 1941, von Westernhagen's father later served in

Hitler's personal guard. Her grandfather, a Riga dentist, had left the Baltic after the revolution in 1919.[12]

Finally, there is a rich body of judicial records available to scholars at the Central Office for the Administration of Justice in Ludwigsburg and a number of other state attorney or court offices in Germany. Copies of much of this material have been used by the U.S. Department of Justice's Office of Special Investigations in its work, and some copies are at the Yad Vashem Institute in Jerusalem. It is a pity that more scholars have not taken notice of these important collections, for this is truly a wealth of new material.

Until the early 1980s, most scholars and the public believed that the annihilation of Europe's Jews in Soviet territory during the second half of 1941 was the result of a Führer Order, a direct order from Hitler instructing his soldiers to carry out genocide. It was supposed that at least the leaders of the *Einsatzkommandos* who moved into the Soviet Union just behind the combat troops had received such instructions before they crossed the border. The instructions, it had been assumed, were direct and specific: kill as soon as possible as many Jews as possible in the occupied areas, in part for alleged security reasons and in part as acts of revenge against the remnants of Stalin's "Jewish-Bolshevik" terror regime. Although the pretexts for actions against Jews varied, they were in reality not necessary; Hitler's order would have been sufficient justification.

Explanations that the Führer had ordered it were often heard from defendants at the Nüremberg Trials, as they sought to legitimize, explain, and defend their murderous actions. In some of the recent trials, similar comments were heard as the same line of defense was attempted. Even though some contemporary documents support this logic, doubts have arisen in the past several years.[13]

Still, the question remains and has become more important: are these explanations really sufficient? Or must scholars look more deeply at the events of the summer of 1941 with mass killings all along the eastern front?

Progress in the historical profession will depend to large degree on a very close analysis of all circumstances in 1941 and on the precise reconstruction of the decision-making process as it developed. Latvian scholar Margers Vestermanis has recently done such research for some parts of Latvia, but a great deal still needs to be done. Although scholars may never precisely determine the motivations of the participants at all levels of the Holocaust, reconstructing the day-to-day chronology will be of considerable assistance in deepening our understanding. And, of course, scholars must be keenly aware of the real historical situation and context when attempting to judge half a century later the culprits, perpetrators, victims, and bystanders of 1941–42.

How can a historian understand the actions and thought process of an individual in urban (or rural) Latvia during mid-July 1941 unless he or she has read the newspapers of the day and has listened to the broadcasts received from, say, the BBC, Radio Moscow, the Wehrmacht Special Reports, or other broadcast sites in Scandinavia or the Baltic states? Scholars need to know what the major topics of the day were, and they also need to be aware of what friends, neighbors, and relatives in these communities were talking about. What did they, for example, hear from a group of refugees from Vilnius the week before, or from a single Red Army soldier who passed through the village earlier that day? How did this information spread? What impact did it have on the unfolding events?

Total identification with the actors of that time, even for a moment, will not be possible and is not necessary. But some compensations for that should be found to get at least a feeling for the specific atmosphere of certain situations. Scholars need a lot of information if they are not to interpret the events ahistorically, i.e., falsely or with prejudice. Correct insight may be gained only from a very solid knowledge of what actually happened, of what really went on, of what people were concerned about. Correct evaluations cannot be expected if we do not care about historical reality. The question of historiography today is neither "*Sinngebung des Sinnlosen*" (making sense of the senseless) à la Theodor Lessing, nor "*Alles verstehen heisst alles verzeihen*" (to understand all is to forgive all), and nobody is interested in a historiography "*aus staatsanwaltlichen Perspecktive*" (from the government attorney's perspective) (Nipperdey). What we need is a "*Geschichtsschreibung des Moglichen*" (historiography of the possible), and it should not be impossible to describe things exactly. The often impatient readers will have to learn again that even very complex descriptions are sometimes unavoidable, and that no one is able to make good judgments and gain sound understanding before hearing both sides. *Audiatur et altera pars.* Even those long gone must be heard. "Democracy for the dead?" Well, why not?

To be sure, assembling the mosaic of Latvian social history and describing in great detail the events of 1941 will not be without gaps. But scholars should not give up prematurely. Many sources have not been used to this point. For example, no scholar has provided insight into what the neutral and the enemy intelligence services knew about the Final Solution before and after June 22, 1941: in Moscow, Stockholm, London, Bern, and Tokyo. Even the intelligence agencies of the Reich's allies must have known considerably more than has been revealed—from Vichy and Rome to Budapest and Bucharest. Furthermore, the extent of knowledge of the German military intelligence and its local representatives has not been reconstructed in a systematic fashion, though this agency may well have been the best informed, next to Heydrich's Security Service.

Walter Laqueur's book, *The Terrible Secret*,[14] was a very disillusioning first step, showing that some channels of information did exist and that some details of the actions against Jews reached London and Washington via Switzerland. The files of the OSS in the National Archives, Washington, D.C., show that there had been more channels, and as a newcomer, OSS was certainly not the best informed of the intelligence services. Another interesting source may be former members of the civil and military intelligence services of the Baltic states. After the Soviet occupation of their countries, numerous agents fled to Berlin, only to return in 1941. After the war many went to Canada, Australia, Great Britain, or the United States, where they found employment as experts on East European affairs, radio commentators, journalists, political advisors, historians, and even formal members of the intelligence services of their new homelands. Some had been involved in the Holocaust, though perhaps not to the same extent as a Klaus Barbie or Panzinger, the former chief of *Einsatzgruppe* A and prominent functionary in the RSHA who worked for a number of years in General Reinhard Gehlen's Federal Intelligence Service (in Germany).

Another important source of information may be the various national newspapers and their articles on aspects of the Final Solution. For example, what did the *Deutsche Zeitung im Ostland*, the semi-official organ of the German occupation governments in the Baltic states, write about such topics as the establishment of the ghetto in Riga (or other cities), police actions in Minsk, Jewish forced labor in Vilnius, or the activities of partisans in the Nevel district? What was published in Kovno newspapers on the great massacres in Lvov? Might it be that Latvian volunteers in the auxiliary police forces were influenced by alarming news from Ukraine? Had the Latvian pogromists in Riga already heard of such actions in the capital of Lithuania? How did German correspondents, sent by Goebbels along with the *Einsatzgruppen*, report on the events they witnessed? What did the Scandinavian newspapers, whose correspondents had long been in the Baltic region, report on German occupation?[15] What was known in Warsaw, or for that matter in Athens or Madrid? Who was better informed—the average citizen of the Baltic states, or the German troops at the front as it advanced rapidly eastward?

There are additional unanswered questions. Did all members of the indigenous governments fulfill their "duties" only reluctantly? Were there any indications of surreptitious solidarity between Latvian clerks, policemen, or ghetto guards and the Latvian and German/Austrian Jews? While the ultimate authority rested with the German occupation government, all routine tasks of governance were in the hands of the far-better-informed local Latvian authorities. Only conflicts which could not be resolved by the Jewish *Ordnungsdienst* (police) and the advisory committee (*Aeltestenrat*), on one hand, and the Latvian militia and the Latvian civil administration, on the other, were to be decided by *Einsatzkommando* 2, *Einsatzgruppe* A, or by the Higher SS and Police Leader of the *Reichskommissariat Ostland* and of the Military Administrated Region Russia-North. As a means of increasing their influence and authority as well as their responsibilities, local officials tended to solve problems without asking too many questions. And that may have meant that higher officials such as Reichskommissar Lohse, who were often absent from the area, heard of events in, say the Riga ghetto or the Salaspils concentration camp, only in piecemeal fashion, and only well after the fact.

Unfortunately, we have little information on Lohse's recruitment of his *Reichskommissariat* personnel and those who served in Drechsler's *Generalkommissariat*. But even less is known about those who served in the indigenous civil administration. What was the percentage of ardent antisemites among these administrators? Who came from the old political parties? Who sympathized with the Nazis (and since when)? Who wanted a rapid "Germanization" of Latvia? Who enlisted in the Latvian Legion of the Waffen SS? What role did they play in the Holocaust in Latvia? How did these individuals react to the killing of the Jews?

It does appear that virtually all inhabitants of Riga were very well informed about what was going on in their streets, in their central prison, in the nearby forests of Bikernieki and Rumbula, in the internment and concentration camps at Kaiservald, Jungfernhof, and Salaspils. But in Riga there were only scattered indications of any solidarity by the citizens with the persecuted Jews, in contrast to cities with far larger Jewish communities, such as Amsterdam and Berlin.

What could soldiers on both sides of the front in 1941–42 have known? Most modern armies have units responsible for censoring mail sent home from the front. Up to now, no scholar has determined whether soldiers writing home commented on the unfolding Holocaust. What were the contents of the letters from, say, Hungarian cavalry officers, Russian pilots, Romanian gunners, members of Franco's Blue Legion, Italian parachutists, volunteers from Denmark and Norway, German panzer generals, and other members of the various belligerent armed forces? Are all the letters lost?

Recently, I received information about a former Luftwaffe physician who "rescued" thousands of letters, his entire wartime correspondence with his wife which continued through his internment as a prisoner of war. Has not anyone rescued the summary reports of the German field post and its equivalent in the other armies? Or have the historians simply not asked the military archives for this type of material, as most of them have avoided the press departments of archives and libraries?

Ad fontes! Even in private collections! The historical profession needs more publications like *Schoene Zeiten: Judenmord aus der Sicht der Taeter und Gaffer* and *"Gott mit uns": Der deutsche Vernichtungskrieg im Osten. 1939–1945*, outstanding documentary collections edited by Ernst Klee, Willi Dressen, and Volker Riess.[16] We also need well-trained scholars with sharp eyes and keen insight. For example, a large collection of requests for weapon permits from Riga at the *Bundesarchiv* Koblenz would have continued to go unnoticed had it not been for an American colleague, Steven Rogers, who discovered and immediately recognized their significance: many came from members of the infamous Arajs Kommando. In some instances, these requests contained the first hint or the only solid documentation that these individuals served in the unit which had been established to "cleanse" Latvia of all Jews and Communists as quickly as possible. Other applicants themselves mentioned their participation in "actions against Jews," or in one case "in the destruction of the Jews."[17]

Historians ought not to cruise through crucial elements of the Holocaust as Arno Mayer has done in *Why Did the Heavens Not Darken? The "Final Solution" in History*[18] when he attempted to date Hitler's decision to annihilate all the Jews of Europe to a time when all chances of victory for the Third Reich had already vanished. Mayer did this without any evidence. His thesis is that Hitler was well aware of the invariable defeat of the German armed forces, and he *therefore* decided to kill all the Jews. The thesis is not completely wrong, but it needs to be modified. Perhaps Mayer is overemphasizing the importance of the Wannsee Conference.

The initial preparations for a Final Solution began in the summer of 1941 when no one in Berlin believed that the war in the East could be lost. In the winter months, all killing operations had to be stopped because of the weather. The strategic situation was stabilized not before February-March, but even in the crisis of late December and early January Hitler remained confident, in contrast to some of his military advisers. A different problem arose from German shortages in railway transportation capacities, the demands on which were increasing drastically when offensives were prepared and had to be "nourished." In that respect, the ideal month for Eichmann's plans in 1942 might well have been late February and early March. With the end of the muddy season Hitler had wanted to launch the decisive summer offensive, and the transport authorities needed at least two to three weeks for the necessary preparations.

In later years, Hitler and some of his followers did indeed fear Jewish revenge, and they did all they could to decimate Jewry in order to prevent it even after a totally lost war. But in July and August 1941 no one took seriously the occasionally mentioned threat of Jewish revenge. In fact, the point of no return might well have been Friedrich Jeckeln's unexpected "success" at Babi Yar at the end of September, which seemed to show that even in cities like Kiev massacring almost the entire Jewish population was possible and much easier than all the "experts" had believed.[19] A short time later, Jeckeln was transferred to Riga and received the order to proceed there as far as possible in the same way, while in Berlin, the *Heerestransportchef* (chief of military transport) tried to coordinate Eichmann's demands with Hitler's plans for Operation *Taifun* and his last blow in the south before the winter would stop all German offensives for this year. The result was Jeckeln's Bloody Sunday in Riga and the deportation of thousands of *Reichsjuden* (Jews from the Reich itself) to Kovno, Riga, and Minsk, where most of them were killed immediately upon their arrival. The planned mass murder of the remaining Jews was delayed by a variety of factors: climate, local protests, recognition of a manpower shortage in war industries in the Reich and in the conquered territories, the total collapse of the Wehrmacht organization for Soviet prisoners of war, Quartermaster General

Wagner's logistical debacle, Leeb's and Bock's inability to conquer Leningrad and Moscow, and, perhaps, other reasons that gave authorities in Riga the opportunity for further postponement. After that, deportation did not automatically mean physical destruction; otherwise some of those Jews deported from the Reich would never have survived the war.

Historical processes seldom are one-way streets, and most are very complicated networks of changing interrelationships. The decision-making process for the Holocaust also cannot be isolated from its historical context and must be evaluated and examined in this context.

Some suggestions for gaining better knowledge of the context and better parameters for evaluations have already been provided. What might be said, on the basis of our current knowledge, about the decision-making process itself?

Whether written or not, the Führer Order quoted by Himmler and others must have in fact existed, but hardly before early July 1941. The German military had already occupied Riga when Heydrich, possibly at the request of Stahlecker, instructed the four Higher SS and Police Leaders (HSSPF) operating in the East on July 2nd, that "only" Jews in official state or party positions should be killed. During the first two weeks of the campaign, the massacres carried out near the German-Lithuanian border, in Kovno and elsewhere, had been masked as either so called self-cleansing actions (*Selbstreinigungsbestrebungen*), as German countermeasures undertaken to break Soviet resistance, or as resprisals for Soviet war crimes or "cruelties" committed by the NKVD. In small villages the actions of German police units, killing all male Jews as reprisals for, say, acts of sabotage or shootings in which German civilians or soldiers were wounded, might remain undiscovered and not widely known. In communities with hundreds or even thousands of Jewish citizens, the German occupation forces had to operate more cautiously. But Stahlecker's men found ample reasons for strong actions and most often focused their acts of revenge on the local Jews (copying the German practice in Serbia). Of course, this was genocide, but not without a legal-looking facade. There are statements in the OSI files in Washington, D.C., from certain commandos of the Security Police and Security Service in which they assert that they never killed Jews only because of their faith or their race, that they always had their plausible legal reasons. But such statements might well be doubted, especially for the forces operating in Latvia. Partisan warfare was always a convenient excuse, a more than sufficient reason for carrying out acts of retribution, and Stahlecker knew that. However, in Latvia, partisan activities had all but disappeared in 1941.

Occasionally, Security Police and Security Service "overreacted"; in other cases they had to invent Soviet cruelties as justifications for harsh retribution; rumors were believed and exaggerated. The German troops carried with them their experiences in Poland, France, and Greece, and they made use of them in characteristic fashion. The reasons for the first massacres in Riga and in Daugavpils are still being discussed, and they may well have been based on rumors. But in other places evidence was quite overwhelming and therefore documented in all details by well-trained criminologists, journalists, doctors, clergymen, etc. Hitler and his general staff knew very well that terror and terror propaganda gave them additional advantages in their *Blitzkrieg*, and they did not hesitate to use them. Their teachers had been J. F. C. Fuller and Chengis Khan.

The total war was not only a regular war in the style of the nineteenth century. Especially in the East, German warfare had all the characteristics of an irregular war as well: civil war, "dirty" war, partisans, ideological warfare. Hitler's "unconventional" soldiers first of all wanted to be revolutionaries, and they had learned and should have learned a great deal not only from Fuller and Chengis Khan but also from Stalin, his army, and his commissars, their only respected enemies. (Jeschonnek, chief of staff of Goering's Luftwaffe, wrote after learning of the plans for the invasion of the Soviet Union, "at last a proper war.")[20]

When local forces went "too far" in their eagerness to "cleanse" the countryside, the German authorities tried not to take notice. Superiors were criticized by their subordinates, but often hesitated to intervene. Many were glad they had been told that they had nothing to do with the "inner conflicts" of Lithuania and Latvia. Leeb's *Befehlshaber des rückwahrtigen Heeresgebietes* (commander of the rear area) waited until August 3 to intervene, prohibiting unsystematic and arbitrary executions by local forces without German supervision and authorization, fully aware of the problem that the means were missing to compel his Latvian, Lithuanian, and Estonian auxiliaries to follow his advice.[21]

Everything seemed to be a question of dimensions. No one objected to "severe retribution against the Jewish-Bolshevik sub-humans" as long as the proportions seemed "appropriate." After all, Stalin's oppressive system had a very bad reputation throughout Europe, and colonial warfare in Asia might indeed require methods and means not appropriate to Belgium, France, Greece, or Norway. The conduct of the war might change with war theaters, as had been the case under Napoleon when his troops had fought in Italy, Egypt, Spain, and Russia.The old colonial powers were used to it, but the Germans too had learned very quickly to act in different ways in World War I in Africa, Turkey, France, and Russia. No diabolic Hitler was needed to create such Machiavellian war theories. Himmler and Rosenberg had studied the British colonial experience in India; Auschwitz commandant Hoess had fought in Palestine; relatives of Goering and Bach-Zelewski had returned from Africa. . . . But latecomer Hitler hoped to outrule all of his predecessors, as the greatest military leader of all times, greater than Hannibal and Alexander the Great, Julius Caesar and Scipio Africanus, Sherman and Grant, Foch and Napoleon.[22] (Heydrich was "only" ambitious enough to be Hitler's Fouche', as portrayed by Hans von Hentig, the famous criminologist, and Stefan Zweig.)[23]

Manstein's and Reichenau's often-cited orders demanding understanding among the troops for the strong punishment exercised by the SS and Police did not date from late June or the middle of July 1941, but from the middle of October and November 20. Their background was Babi Yar and the new policy of total extermination, even in huge cities with populations of tens of thousands of Jews. The great massacres in eastern Ukraine and the Crimean peninsula, the Romanian treatment of the Jews in Odessa and in "Transnistria," were not as well understood as the Wehrmacht "cleansing operations" in Belorussia which were carried out only in locations with less than a thousand inhabitants, such as Fegelein's punitive expeditions in the Pripet regions or Nebe's attempts to slaughter the Jewish intelligentsia in Vilnius and Minsk. "Actions" of this size represented a new dimension. The escalation in the months prior, however, had passed by almost unnoticed, as a rather dissonant background music to a new type of war, the hoped-for last confrontation of the two antagonistic ideologies.

Most observers had expected that the NKVD terror in Eastern Europe would be followed by a wave of White Terror, much the same as had taken place after World War I. Former Baltic Germans coming from the Warthegau or all those who had been for some weeks in Hans Frank's General Government had at least an inclination what *harter Volkstumskampf* (difficult struggle of the nation) might mean to Himmler's SS. Many participants of World War II had already fought in World War I and knew that conditions on the eastern front had been hardly comparable with those on the western front; the normal price of human life had been quite different. Even on the allied side, there had never been equal rights for a French poilu or his Russian comrade, the "poor" muzhik, and their treatment as POWs had been incomparable. Verdun had been hell, but what about Przemysl? "Galizien" remained synonymous with corruption, treason, smuggling, espionage, racketeering, moral insanity, an anarchy of the worst possible type and a standard invective of so-called unprejudiced antisemites of the positivistic school who believed only their own experiences.

"Domestic conflicts" between Poles and Russians, Ukrainians and Belorussians, Jews and non-Jews, separatists in Finland, Estonia, Latvia, Lithuania, or in the Caucasus had been used and nourished before the revolutions of 1917 quite in the same way as they were in World War II. The latest volume of the *Militargeschichtliche Forschungsamt* series on World War II, far more than had been the case for a long time in German historiography, quite correctly emphasizes the continuities between World War I and World War II.[24] The results are very interesting indeed. In 1930, Soviet intellectuals had engaged in a highly emotional discussion of the so-called Remarquian problem: that German school pupils, having read the famous pacifistic novel, *All Quiet on the Western Front*, were deeply impressed by pacifism, but, in their majority, not converted to it. On the contrary, the pupils frankly admitted that they would not want to miss the next conflagration.[25] If foreign journalists would have asked the same pupils if they would have found it attractive to return to Galicia, as described even by authors such as Joseph Roth and Karl Kraus, they surely would have gotten different answers.[26]

As a number of scholars, including Hermann Glaser, have already pointed out,[27] Hitler was not an original thinker. He was a synthesizer, and a very mediocre one, taking his ideas where he could find them, often misunderstood and popularized without mercy: a very successful "terrible simplifier," destroying everything he touched. As Glaser observes, Hitler represents the "genius of the mediocre, though his mediocrity was above average; so his mediocrity became the fate of a people which enabled him to rob them step by step of their humanity, in both theory and practice,"[28] step by step, by many people, not by a *Sündenfall* (sudden fall from Grace), dating somewhere in May or June 1941.

Seldom had Hitler's military campaigns been planned as carefully as Operation Barbarossa, but even Barbarossa was no grand design, carried out exactly as it had been planned. It emerged as an improvisation after the first four or five days, and Hitler's general staff experts were not surprised. They regarded strategy as a "*System von Aushilfen*" (system of ad hoc decisions—Clausewitz) and had argued that precise, long-term plans would never work in their profession. There had been scenarios and war games, of course, to test different options, and there had also been a general political outline, but modifications started very early on in the campaign, and after some weeks perhaps more flexibility was needed on all levels of the general staff hierarchy than in the hectic weeks after the success in France. Halder's diary documents this for the military sector. Heydrich's Situation Reports, USSR, (*Ereignismeldungen UdSSR*) demonstrate that SS and Police had the same problems. The day-to-day orientation offered by this important *Führungsinstrument* (instrument of command) would not have been given had not the Reich Main Security Office been convinced that its local representatives (and all concerned ministries in Berlin) needed for their decision-making process a daily *tour d'horizon,* including not only security aspects but also the military situation and the most relevant political events. The RSHA always encouraged self-initiative. Himmler and Hitler wanted activists, revolutionaries, "*mitreissende Persönlichkeiten*" (charismatic personalities who attract followers), "*mit- und vorausdenkende, verantwortungsfreudige Untergebene,*" (people who are happy to take responsibility, make decisions and plan ahead), but they often got "*Bremser*" (people who put on the brakes), "*typische Beamtenseelen*" (typical clerk-types), "*widerliche Konjunkturritter*" (disgusting opportunists), "*katzbuckelnde Speichellecker*" (sycophantic bootlickers), "*Miesmacher und Defaitisten ohne jede Ausstrahlung*" (killjoys and defeatists without any sparkle). They hated apparatchiks, bureaucrats, technocrats, commissars, and GPU methods but could not avoid them in the former Baltic states. The inhabitants compared their new nomenclature with their old one and came to the conclusion that there were no remarkable differences (except in the question of corruption).

The general SS was no elite corps, and SSPF Schroeder's SS and police in Latvia was not a very impressive group. It consisted of thousands of individuals in different uniforms, and in very heterogeneous units: a minority of German

Sipo-, Kripo-, SD-, and Orpo-"experts," a squad of Waffen SS, some dozens of Baltic German interpreters and secretaries, the already mentioned Arajs Kommando, incorporated in the Latvian Auxiliary Security Police, the "normal" Latvian police, now called Latvian Auxiliary Police, the German Police Battalions and Reserve Police Battalions passing through Latvia, and "Hiwi" formations from other regions, if needed for special purposes, etc. The monolithic *Fuhrerstaat* often performed in everyday life like a multicolored, ramshackle polycracy on the move, and each SD *Einsatzgruppe* acted like a little RSHA on wheels. The terrible efficiency of instruments such as these was not so easy to explain. (Some very surprising explanations for often neglected partial aspects are to be found in the files of the Office of Special Investigations and articles by Professor Ezergailis!)

For our attorneys, engaged in prosecuting war criminals, the question "Who did it?" has remained the most interesting. If there had been a Führer Order from the beginning all was clear: the criminal Hitler had operated on base motives. No law on earth allowed anyone to kill innocent people for racial reasons. Hitler's followers might have been "only" his accomplices and accessories, but were also clearly responsible and guilty. (If some of them had murdered people without order or permission, they could be regarded as were the so-called excess perpetrators who had exceeded their orders, for example, by acting with "unnecessary" brutality.)

If there had been *no* Führer Order, the offender had to be found. If he could not be identified, doubts might remain that base motives had been of decisive importance. No judge would risk convicting an accessory if these doubts remained. If the offender could be found, he was most likely to deny his racist motivations, especially if he had done it already in contemporary documents. In any case, things got much more complicated for the attorneys. One and the same action might be interpreted very differently. Murder (*mord*) was not the same as manslaughter (*Totschlag*).

Most war crime convictions in the Federal Republic of Germany were soon covered by an amnesty, and only the so-called *NS-Verbrechen* (Nazi crimes) remained indictable (insofar as they did not fall under the statute of limitations). In cases of accessory, the statute of limitation was not the same as in cases of direct responsibility. Premeditation could be substantiated only if the offender admitted his real intentions—and that would not be likely to occur so often. The chances of winning a case grew smaller with each passing year. Today in Germany only very few of these offenses are still indictable. And that might explain why so many cases are dismissed, even though they had looked very promising to nonlawyers.

Assuming that a Führer Order had existed from the beginning has been favorable not only for historians, who like clear deductions, but also for judges notoriously short of time and, last but not least, for many defendants who might have received different sentences if the partial exoneration by the fiction of a distinct Führer Order had not taken place. (As it seems now, Ohlendorf invented it in his Nuremberg prison cell.)

One of the first skeptics was Alfred Streim, director of the Regional Center for the Administration of Justice in Ludwigsburg, and one can imagine that the reaction was not only friendly applause when he dared say publicly what he had found. Now not only attorneys but also historians will have to search for the real perpetrators and their perhaps less sensational motives in the first phase, and they will have to search for the real date of the Führer Order if they won't admit that *Reichsführer* SS Heinrich Himmler and others did not tell the truth when they referred to it later in the war.

The OSI documentation on Latvia gives not the slightest indication that the motives identified by Aly and Heim for Austria and Poland may have been of any relevance to the Soviet Union in 1941. The *Saubermanner* (seemingly innocent) of Latvia were not interested in the poor Jews or in the elimination of visible poverty, but were in their majority pogromists of a well-known type. They hated the local Jewish intelligentsia, all left-wing politicians, Jewish bankers, shopkeepers, journalists, etc. They despised the newly rich, the assimilated Jews as a whole, from the so-called Saloon Bolsheviks on the left of the old political party spectrum, through moderates and liberals, to the conservatives who had converted to Protestantism or who still went to their Orthodox synagogue every Friday evening. Their main target was not the poor Jew, but the rich Jew.

The dominant role of some Jews in Latvia during Stalin's short rule from 1940 to 1941 gave them an excuse for their pogroms. They cried revenge, but meant the property of the Jews, their warehouses and their villas in Riga's elegant Kaiserwald area. As Vestermanis has put it, an "Eldorado-Psychose" had been unleashed. Everyone hoped to find hidden golden treasures, and when these riches did not materialize they became very angry. Others were hunting attractive Jewish women, the younger the better. Sexual envy, as in most revolutions, was a powerful motive. *Rassenschande* ("defiling" the Aryan race by sexual relations with non-Aryans) presented Arajs and his "Burschen" with no dilemma—until German racists stopped the nightly orgies at Arajs downtown headquarters much later. Especially the Arajs Kommando lived in "*Saus und Braus*" (corrupt luxury) gorging, drinking, plundering at least until August and September 1941. Its "high life" was interrupted only when "duty" called them by bus to the next massacre on the outskirts of Riga or elsewhere in Kurland.

As Bernard Press has written, "a bloody, drunken orgy seized the land and whoever did not raise his hand to kill, at least tried to browbeat us. No one comforted us, no one stood up for us. Suddenly we became strangers in our own homeland; our supposed friends of yesterday turned us in to the police. Cleaning women who ate Jewish bread for years threw the property of their employers down into the street to demonstrate their national feelings. We were surrounded by a sea of hatred. For what sins, one asks oneself. . . ."[29] Press and his fellow victims received no theological explanation in 1941. The Latvian churches preferred to remain silent, or "neutral," with some exceptions documented in the SD Report of Events, in contrast to Bishop Brizgys in

Lithuania who wholeheartedly cooperated with the German SS and Police authorities and urged his clergymen to follow his example.[30]

There were no rational explanations, of course, acceptable to "enlightened" individuals brought up with the values of 1789. But the mass movement described by Press and Vestermanis was for historians not a totally new phenomenon. In fact, such mass hysteria has occurred in history, and it still does, as we can see from the daily newspapers.[31]

Shortly after World War I, Ludwig Thoma, the famous humorist and satirist in upper Bavaria, had expressed his hope that the whole nightmare of Bolshevik rule in Russia might end, as usual in that country, in a giant pogrom. This forgotten quip created a considerable stir when Thoma first uttered it, and in the 1990s as well when it was reprinted in Munich. The article is surely worth reading in its entirety and in its original context: an anonymous commentary in the *Miesbacher Anzeiger*, in those days a journal read only by intellectuals outside of Miesbach who admired Thoma and his frank way of speaking. Did Thoma represent the so-called *gesundes Volksempfinden* in this case? Or was he only misunderstood?

Thoma had begun his career as a lawyer in Dachau, had written for *Simplizissimus*, and always criticized the hubris of Wilhelminian Germany and "Prussianness." But Thoma collaborated with Admiral Tirpitz in founding the Fatherland Party during World War I in an effort to stir up all the patriots, in Bavaria as well as in Prussia. And he remained a xenophobic chauvinist even after the defeat, fighting "*Zuogroaste*" (tourists, travelers, and settlers from outside of Bavaria) and "*Nordlichter*" (non-Bavarian intellectuals), *Schwabinger Caféhausliteraten* (Swabian coffeehouse intellectuals) and *Räterepublikaner* (red republicans of 1918), Ultramontane (ardent Roman Catholics) and Jews, *Franken* and *Schwaben* as so-called *Beutebayern* (captured Bavarians), the Ullstein journalists and the Berliner *Borsenjobber* (stock exchange employees), sometimes with self-irony and humor. In 1941 Thoma had been dead fifteen years, but the expectation that Stalin's empire might crash in a great *Kladderadatsch*[32] (mess, tohu-bohu) had survived. Hitler himself called the Soviet Union a "colossus with clay feet" in discussions with his military advisers. And Goebbels wrote in his diary on May 29 that, in reference to the latest reports from Estonia, Bolshevik mismanagement might lead to the Germans being received as demigods. The concept of self-purgation seems to have been the favorite concept in the "solution of the Jewish question in the Soviet Union" for many Nazi leaders, and as late as October *Einsatzgruppenchef* Stahlecker deplored the fact that it had been impossible to solve this question in that fashion.

That *Juda* had to perish seemed quite clear, not only to Julius Streicher and his "strong believers." Goebbels had published his proscription list already in his 1936 Parteitag speech.[33] Emigration and forced departures were only half measures for strong believers, who were convinced that sterilization and euthanasia were the only adequate means of healing a badly infected "people's body." Emigration would not work and would be endangered if so-called parasites and deadly foes of the German people were allowed to survive, and reproduce, just outside the borders of the Reich. Even Field Marshal Ritter von Leeb, a cautious Catholic, one of the most conservative generals in the Wehrmacht and its only specialist in defensive strategy with an international reputation, believed in mass sterilizations as an alternative to mass killings. Leeb did not protest the Kovno massacres and, perhaps, he never heard of the mass castrations in Bausk. He may, however, have used his channels to suggest that more discreet and "humane" methods be adopted—long before Nazi propaganda picked up Theodore Kaufman's proposal to sterilize "some 48,000,000" Germans in order to immunize the world forever "against the virus of Germanism," a call which had been published in February, commented upon ironically in *Time* at the end of March, and "counter-attacked" in the *Volkischer Beobachter* and in a Diewerge booklet two months later.[34]

Security Police and SD officials wrote in retrospect that orders existed from the beginning of the conflict to kill all Jews. But still in August 1941 they had participated in discussions which demonstrate that the "Jewish question" was still open for the survivors of the first wave of massacres. The so-called Jewish danger had to be removed, they agreed, but the SiPo and SD proposed to maintain Jewish forced laborers in ghettos and in restricted areas. Male and female Jewish workers ought to be separated, they concluded, in order to stop the breeding of more "subhumans" and to protect the Latvians against contaminations. The Jews were to organize their own housing and form an almost autarchic economic entity with agriculture, forestry, highway construction, etc. At a later date they might get their own workshops and industrial plants, and eventually they might be transferred to a Jewish reservation outside of Europe. The "total cleansing of European territory of all Jews" referred to in the same document, was not synonymous with physical destruction.[35] This rather "moderate" program was not only written down to mislead Lohse's civil administration, but was implemented, at least until Jeckeln came from Kiev to stop such "dangerous" experiments, and Heydrich modified Stahlecker's ideas at the Wannsee conference.

It was not always the Security Police and the Security Service that had the lead role or the most active part in dealing with Jews. In Latvia, the "Jewish question" had already been "solved" in several places before these troops arrived. The initial measures—carrying of IDs, registration, conscription to a work detail, concentration in a ghetto—had been initiated mostly by local military authorities. In Riga, everyone knew of Arajs and his "boys," but most inhabitants had never heard of a German *Einsatzkommando* 2 and only very few knew the name of Dr. Lange, later the KdS of Latvia, a position he held until 1944. And it was not Lange who received the nickname Schustin, the name of the Jewish KGB boss of Latvia in 1940–41, but Viktor Arajs who took it with humor and was proud of it. If Arajs and his gang could have acted without German supervision, their record of murdered Latvian citizens might have been far larger. As had been the case in Lithuania, German authorities complained even in their official reports to Berlin how difficult it had been to teach the local auxiliary troops "German principles." Of course, there were always exceptions. Relatively moderate people could be found on all levels of the SS and police hierarchy. But niches for upright policemen certainly had existed not only on the basic level, where "poor innocent" Latvian auxiliaries were suppressed by German "monsters," as is often believed. A different question is how frequently these slots were filled, and by whom. Perhaps a realistic answer at this moment might be very disappointing.

Already in 1965 two Latvian historians published a book that maintained that Nazi agents had been present in Latvia months or even years before the German forces invaded and that this fifth column was deeply involved in Hitler's mass extermination plans.[36] The authors provided names and current addresses for those allegedly involved. To check on this information, virtually every sentence of the book would have to be studied and verified, a tedious task but one which might prove fruitful. To be sure, there existed *vorgeschobene Agenten* (planted agents whose function was to mislead) and *V Leute* (fifth columnists). One of the most important was Edgar Klaus, born in 1879 in Riga and a typical product of the so-called *deutsch-judische Kultursymbiose*, but hardly the right person to organize antisemitic demonstrations or organize pogroms.

Others are represented or mentioned in the documentation assembled by the Office of Special Investigations: the Libau *Seekommandant*, Dr. Kawelmacher, a former member of the *Abwehr* who changed his name "on advice of an official" in the Federal Interior Ministry in Bonn after the war to avoid prosecutions by Soviet or East German authorities; and Hans Dressler, born in Moscow in 1913, brought up in Denmark and Latvia, former member of the so-called Wannsee-Institut in Berlin and of RSHA VI (5D-Ausland), who contacted the RSHA agents already in Riga immediately after his arrival there in early July. It is too early for hypotheses in this area, but it will hardly be avoidable at least to try to determine who these people were. For they may not only have played a key role as propagandists of antisemitism but also in the genesis of the Final Solution.[37]

Notes

1. Goetz Aly and Susanne Heim, "Die Oekonomie der 'Endlosung': Menschenvernichtung und wirtschaftliche Neuordnung," in *Beiträge zur nationalsozialistischen Gesundheits und Sozialpolitik*, vol. 5 (Berlin, 1987), pp. 11–90. Aly and Heim, "Sozialplanung und Volkermord. Thesen zur Herrschaftsrationalitat der nationalsozialistischen Vernichtungspolitik," *Konkret* 10/89, pp. 82–87. See the replies by Ulrich Herbert, "Rassismus und Rationalitat," *Konkret* 11/89, pp. 56–60, and Christopher Browning, "Vernichtung und Arbeit," *Konkret* 12/89, pp. 64–69. Also, see the discussion of the Aly-Heim thesis, "Gab es eine Oekonomie der

Endlosung?" at the Institut für Geschichtswissenschaft, Technical University of Berlin, 6 February 1990.

2. Bernhard Press, *Judenmord in Lettland, 1941–1945* (Berlin, 1988).
3. Viktor Suvorov, *Der Eisbrecher: Hitler in Stalins Kalkül* (Stuttgart, 1989).
4. Gisela Bock, *Zwangssterilisation im Nationalsozialismus: Studien zur Rassenpolitik und Frauenpolitik* (Opladen: Westdeutscher verlag, 1986).
5. On the events in Bausk, see the article by Margers Vestermanis (footnote number 7).
6. Peter Krupnikov, *Lettland und die Letten im Spiegel deutscher und deutschbaltischer Publizistik. 1895–1950* (Hannover, 1989).
7. The article by Margers Vestermanis appears in an anthology entitled *Im Schatten der vergangenheit: Impulse zur Historisierung des Nationalsozialismus*, ed. Uwe Backes, Eckhard Jesse, and Rainer Zitelmann (Berlin, 1990), pp. 426–49.
8. Professor Ezergailis is well along in his writing of a book on the Holocaust in Latvia and has done extensive research in the Latvian archives. See his unpublished papers "Who Killed the Jews of Latvia?" (April 1986) and "Sonderkommando Arajs" (June 1987), and his article "The Arajs Kommando," *Bulletin of the Academy of Science of the Latvian SSR*, no. 10/495 (1988), pp. 2–49.
9. Ibid.
10. Jürgen Ernst Kroeger, *So war es: Ein Bericht* (Michelstadt, 1989).
11. Ernst Turmann, *Pickwa: Ein baltisches Leben—erlebte Zeitgeschichte* (Tübingen, 1975).
12. Dorte von Westernhagen, *Die Kinder der Tater: Das Dritte Reich und die Generation danach* (Munich, 1987).
13. See, for example, Helmut Krausnick and Hans-Heinrich Wilhelm, *Die Truppen des Weltanschauungskrieges. Die Einsatzaruppen der Sicherheitspolizei und des SD 1938–1942* (Stuttgart, 1981), pp. 348 and 533–39.
14. Walter Laqueur, *The Terrible Secret: Suppression of the Truth about Hitler's "Final Solution"* (London, 1980).
15. Just how widespread antisemitic prejudice was, even in conservative circles, is demonstrated by a reprint of the memoirs of the former Chicago *Herald Tribune* correspondent in Riga and Stockholm, David Day's *Onward Christian Soldiers: 1920–1942* (Torrance, California, 1985. Reprint of the 1942/43 edition).
16. Ernst Klee, Willi Dressen, Volker Riess, eds., *"Schoene Zeiten": Judenmord aus der Sicht der Taeter und Gaffer* (Frankfurt am Main, 1988), and *"Gott mit Uns": Der deutsche Vernichtungskrieg im Osten. 1939–1945* (Frankfurt am Main, 1989).
17. Dr. Steven Rogers is Senior Historian with the Office of Special Investigations, U.S. Department of Justice.
18. Arno L. Mayer, *Why Did the Heavens Not Darken? The "Final Solution" in History* (New York, 1989). For a critical review, see Istvan Deak, "The Incomprehensible Holocaust," *The New York Review of Books* (September 28, 1989), pp. 63ff.
19. Krausnick and Wilhelm, *Truppe des Weltanschauungskrieges*, pp. 189ff.
20. *Das Deutsche Reich und der Zweite Weltkrieg*, vol. 4, *Der Angriff auf die Sowjetunion* (Stuttgart, 1983), pp. 285ff.
21. Wilhelm Ritter von Leeb, *Tagebuchaufzeichnungen und Lagebeurteilungen aus zwei*

Weltkriegen (Stuttgart, 1976), pp. 62ff., especially n. 146 (diary of Fhr. v. Gneissenbach, entry August 11, 1941).

22. Most of these military leaders had been portrayed before in separate biographical sketches by Basil H. Liddell Hart, the military correspondent for *The Times* of London and favorite foreign author of the "modernists" in the German General Staff.

23. Hans von Hentig, *Fouche': Ein Beitrag zur Technik der politischen Polizei in nachrevolutionahren Perioden* (Tübingen, 1919) and Stefan Zweig, *Joseph Fouche'* (Berlin, 1929). Hentig emigrated to the United States and became one of the "founding fathers" of the FBI. Zweig collaborated with Richard Strauss as librettist ("*Die schweigsame Frau*") and committed suicide three years after his emigration to Brazil in 1942.

24. *Kriegsverwaltung, Wirtschaft und personelle Resourcen. 1939–1941*, vol. 5, part 1 (Stuttgart, 1988).

25. N. S. Pawlowa, P. M. Toper, O. W. Jegorow, eds., *Blick nach Westen: Fortschrittliche deutsche Literatur im Spiegel sowjetischer Kritiken. 1919–1942. Eine Dokumentation* (Berlin, 1989), pp. 20, 184–200, and 668.

26. For the "traditional" interdependence between racial prejudices and "hygiene," see Gisela Bock, *Zwangssterilisation im Nationalsozialismus,* op. cit.

27. Hermann Glaser, *Spiesser-Ideologie: Von der Zerstahrung des deutschen Geistes im 19. und 20. Jahrhundert und dem Aufstieg des Nationalsozialismus* (Frankfurt, 1985).

28. Ibid., p. 27.

29. Press, *Judenmord in Lettland*, pp. 43ff.

30. See Hans-Heinrich Wilhelm, "Der SD und die Kirchen in den besetzten Ostgebieten 1941/42," *Militargeschichtliche Mitteilungen* 29(1981), pp. 55–99.

31. For parallels in Lithuania, see Leonid Olschwang, " 'Die Morder werden noch gebraucht', Judenmassaker in Lituaen 1941—was aus den Tater wurde," *Der Spiegel*, no. 12 (1984), pp. 123ff.

32. From 1848 to 1944 this was also the name of a famous satirical journal.

33. "Der Bolschewismus in Theorie und Praxis" (Munich, 1936).

34. "Das Kriegsziel der Weltplutokratie: Dokumentarische Veroffentlichung zu dem Buch des Preasidenten der amerikanischen Friedensgesellschaft," in Theodore Nathan Kaufman 'Deutschland muss sterben' " (Germany Must Perish), (Berlin, 1941). Theodore Nathan Kaufman, *The Book that Hitler Fears. Germany Must Perish!* (Newark, New Jersey, n.d.). W. Benz, "Juden Vernichtung aus Notwehr? Die Legenden von Theodore N. Kaufman," *VfZG* 29 (1981), pp. 615–30.

35. See Hans Mommsen and S. Willems, eds., *Herrschaftsalltag im Dritten Reich, Studien und Texte* (Düsseldorf, 1988), pp 467–71. A different interpretation of this document can be found by Helmut Krausnick in E. Jackel and J. Rohwer, eds., *Der Mord an den Juden im Zweiten Weltkrieg* (Stuttgart, 1985), pp. 100ff.

36. J. Silabriedis and B. Arklans, *Political Refugees Unmasked* (Riga, 1965).

37. Ingeborg Fleischhauer, *Die Chance des Sonderfriedens: Deutsch-sowjetische Geheimgesprache. 1941–1945* (Berlin, 1986), passim.

NINE

Jewish Refugees from Poland in the USSR, 1939–1946

Yosef Litvak

The Flight from Western to Eastern Poland

The Jewish-Polish refugee population on Soviet territory was created by two waves. The first wave, that of refugees who fled the German-occupied zone to the Soviet-occupied zone, was on the move mostly during September-December 1939 and somewhat less so in 1940. These refugees were, from a legal and civic point of view, residents of the Soviet-occupied zone, who were then imprisoned and exiled for various reasons to places of detention and exile inside the USSR. In the second wave were refugees who fled the Soviet-occupied zone to areas far from the war front at the onset of Hitler's attack on the USSR in the last week of June 1941. To this wave one must add the Jews who were residents of the Soviet-occupied zone and refugees from the German-occupied zone who were drafted into the Red Army during 1940 and in the first half of 1941 and who, because of their military service, found themselves in the interior districts of the USSR.

The refugees began moving eastward immediately upon the war's outbreak on September 1, 1939. The Germans conducted a vicious war, not only against the Polish army, but also against the civilian population, primarily the urban sector. They heavily bombed the cities, communication lines, train tracks, and roads. The purpose of the bombing was, *inter alia*, to curb Polish army movements and the flow of reserve soldiers to their bases. The Germans tended to use incendiary bombs which burned entire streets and complete neighborhoods. In this way they heightened the atmosphere of terror and panic and greatly damaged the morale and stamina of the population, both at the front and in the rear. The movement of the refugees was a headlong flight. The number of Jews among the escapees toward the east was especially large because of their great proportion among the urban population and because of the terrifying image they had of the occupying Nazis. The panicky flight lessened substantially with the end of resistance by the defeated Polish army, and their capture by the Red Army upon its invasion of Poland on September 17. It ceased completely with the surrender of Warsaw on September 28.

The end of the fighting did not bring peace to the Jews in the occupied country. The opposite was true: now began a period of harsh persecution and edicts, including acts of plunder, rape, and murder. The Soviet takeover of eastern Poland raised hopes among many Jews in the German-occupied zone that, as people persecuted by the Nazis, the Soviets would offer them shelter in their occupied zone. Until the invasion of eastern Poland by the Red Army on September 17, many Jewish and non-Jewish refugees flowed into the area without difficulty, excepting, of course, the usual "technical" difficulties and obstacles: shortages in means of transportation, shortages of gasoline for the limited number of motorized vehicles available to the refugees, and German bombings of transportation routes. These difficulties limited the traffic of refugees and made the trip possible primarily for young, healthy people who could stand the hardships of the trip, on foot, primarily at night, on side, dirt roads and in all weather conditions. Before September 17 there were instances when refugees tried to request shelter with the Soviets on the territory which had been Poland before the invasion, but they encountered flat refusals from the Soviet border guards who threatened to open fire on anyone who dared defy them and tried to cross the border without permission.[1]

The borderline between the two occupied zones, the Soviet and the German, was finally delineated along the Pisa-Narew, Bug, and San rivers on October 8, 1939. This was after Foreign Ministers Molotov and Ribbentrop signed a new pact on September 28, 1939, which included amendments to the earlier agreement signed on August 23, 1939. In the three weeks between September 17 and October 8, the Soviet and German armies moved back and forth, conquering cities and retreating from them. This continued until the final agreement on the border, which lasted until June 22, 1941, when Hitler began his military campaign for the conquest of the USSR. The Germans temporarily conquered broad areas which were designated for the Soviets in the agreement mentioned above. This was because the Polish army ceased to exist before the Red Army succeeded in gaining control of these districts. When the Red Army entered, it also continued to move toward the agreed upon line. The specifics of the line between the two occupied zones were finally summed up in a Soviet-German protocol signed in Moscow by Molotov and the German ambassador, Friedrich Schulenburg, on October 4, 1939.[2] On October 8, the Soviet-Lithuanian agreement was signed, according to which the Vilna area was to be turned over to the Soviets.[3]

During those 3 to 4 weeks when the Soviet and German armies were moving back and forth, the Jewish population in the area was greatly confused. It seems that the Soviet commanders in the territory did not have instructions as to how to proceed with regard to the Jews in Soviet-held territory. Should they, for example, allow, or even encourage the Jews to leave with the Soviets, or should they be prohibited from joining them? Without clear instructions, each area commander acted according to his own understanding and inclinations. There were those who looked favorably upon the Jews' joining the Soviets and even allotted train cars or trucks for those who asked to be evacuated. There were instances in which notices of evacuation were hidden from the population until the last minute and even instances of depriving Jews of any chance to leave. Jewish soldiers and officers generally assisted those who asked to be evacuated, and there were even those who tried to convince them to evacuate by warning the hesitant about the dangers expected at the hands of the Nazis.

Soviet Policies toward the Refugees

On October 22, 1939, the Soviets arranged elections in their occupied zone for two "National Assemblies." One of these was expected to convene in Lvov (Lwow), the main city of western Ukraine, and the other in Bialystok, the main city of what was now western Belorussia. In these "assemblies" the "elected" representatives of the inhabitants of these two areas were to make public their request to be annexed to Ukraine and Belorussia. Until October 22—election day—the Soviets did not close the new border between their occupied zone and that of the Germans. Their goal was to allow the millions of refugees who arrived from the western half of Poland during the battle period to return to their homes. The Germans also left their border open at that time for refugees returning to their homes, except for the Jews. On September 20 the German headquarters ordered the troops that were stationed in the new border area not to permit Jews to cross the border into the German-occupied zone.[4] On September 25 Hitler himself ordered his army's commanders to limit the crossing of the border just to *volksdeutsche* and Ukrainians who were "active," that is to say, those Ukranians who were willing to serve the Nazis.[5]

On November 16 (according to Soviet sources) or on November 3 (according to German sources) the two occupying powers signed an additional agreement which was aimed at settling, in a basic and final way, the issue of exchanging populations between the two occupied zones according to their national-ethnic characteristics. According to this agreement, the Germans allowed "ethnics" (*volksdeutsche*), residents of the Soviet-occupied zone, to cross over to the German zone while Russians, Ukrainians, Belorussians, and Ruthenians (Rusyns, or a group of Ukrainians, residents of the Carpathian region of Czechoslovakia during the interwar period, annexed by the USSR in 1944), who were residents of the German-occupied zone were permitted to cross over to the Soviet-occupied zone.[6] Jews were not included because neither occupying power wanted them. In spite of this, Jews did move from one occupied zone to the other, causing only small disruptions as long as the borders between them were open. After the borderline between the two occupied zones was agreed upon and marked, it remained open in both directions for legal commercial passage. Passage was allowed to workers who held official positions and to citizens whose passage was approved by the two occupying powers. As previously noted, Jews were not included. At the same time, the number of Jews in the German zone seeking shelter on the Soviet side under the pressure of increasingly harsh decrees and persecution by the occupying Germans grew daily.

From the time the Soviets closed the border they acted harshly, with no concessions and in more than a few instances even with great viciousness toward the Jewish refugees who were running to them for shelter from the Nazis. Refugees who were caught at the border were forced to return to the German side. Those caught near the border after they had succeeded in crossing were imprisoned for a number of years. The excuse for the harsh punishment was that in addition to their having escaped over the border they also came to spy for Germany or other Western countries. Many of these prisoners were gathered into the prisons and camps in the gulag. One of the most vicious acts committed by Soviet soldiers during the incarceration of the Jews was the forced separation of family members. In young families they separated the couple from one another, and both were separated from their small children, including nursing babies. This was presented as a humane step, as there were no adequate facilities for keeping and raising children in the prisons. The NKVD, the authority for the care and handling of the refugees, did not find it necessary to inform separated couples of their mates' or children's whereabouts. Except for a few lucky ones, these particulars never became known to the refugees.[7] Refugees who were able to get some distance from the border were not imprisoned if they succeeded in claiming that they arrived on the Soviet side previously, when the border was still open.

The Soviets also did not allow permanent Jewish residents of their territory to return to their homes and families on the Soviet side. These were Jews who, for various reasons, found themselves temporarily in areas that later became German territory. For example, there were several hundred Jews from Lomza (northeastern Poland), located in the Soviet occupied zone, but, like scores of other towns, it had been occupied by the Germans for a number of days before the Soviets arrived. In the few days of their rule the Germans expelled hundreds of local Jews to work and hard labor, and murdered some of them. After several weeks the Jews finished their work, and those who survived were permitted to return to Lomza. Despite the fact that they had papers proving their residence in Lomza, they were not allowed by the Soviet guards to return home. Those who evaded the guards were imprisoned and sentenced to five to eight years in prison for "illegal crossing of the border."[8]

In November and December 1939 there was not yet a clear Soviet stance with regard to the Jewish refugees from the German-occupied zone. It is possible that this was one of the factors behind the failure to publicize the Soviet citizenship law of November 29, 1939, which was also intended to include the refugees. The decision regarding the fate of the Jewish refugees was not postponed for long. The hundreds of homeless, unemployed refugees with no source of income, concentrated primarily in cities, very quickly became an unbearable burden for the populations among whom they attempted to find support, and for the Soviet authorities. When tens of thousands of Party members were brought from the USSR to take key positions in the large Soviet bureaucracy, a serious housing problem was created. Others needing housing were the clerks who were brought in, and the hundreds of thousands of soldiers and officers of the occupying Soviet army. There was, of course, no space for hundreds of thousands of foreign Jewish refugees who were "superfluous" anyway. Only a small proportion of "useful" professionals such as doctors, engineers, highly qualified technicians, distinguished artists, scientists, researchers, and lecturers in higher education, were relatively easily absorbed if no fault was found in their personal political dossier or in their class status.

It soon became clear that the Jewish refugees were not returning to their homes on the German side and, furthermore, even if they wanted to return they were not able to do so due to German opposition. Despite efforts to prevent the Jews from crossing the border, and despite the dual challenge posed to Jews by Soviet and German border guards, the infiltration of Jews, albeit in smaller groups and on a limited scale, continued in the beginning of 1940, though on a smaller scale than in the last months of 1939. The authorities therefore decided to evacuate the Jewish refugees from western Ukraine and to send them to various areas in the interior of the USSR where there was a need for labor. The Soviet economy, which was not based on profit, did not have any limitations on absorbing new laborers, as in a capitalist economy. The tremendous development of enterprises in the ambitious five-year plans enabled the Soviets to absorb large additions of manpower as long as those in charge were ready to provide it.

During approximately four months—November 1939 to February 1940—tens of thousands of refugees were sent, if they agreed, to work in enterprises in the interior of the USSR and especially in Donbas, a coal-mining area in the Donetsk basin in Ukraine which was at the time at the height of its development. There were places where refugees were absorbed without many problems. The authorities did their best to absorb the new workers in the best conditions possible. However, unfortunately for the refugees, the quarters, food, and clothing were worse even than their low standards in Poland from whence they had come. The most critical problems were the many work accidents, primarily in Donbas. These were caused by the lack of safety measures in the mines and the refugees' lack of experience in this kind of work. News about deadly accidents, serious injuries, and other difficult conditions caused panic among the refugees and led some to a fatal decision to return illegally to the places from which they had come in Ukraine and western Belorussia. Spontaneous traffic-stopping demonstrations broke out in the train stations in Kiev, Minsk, and other places after refugees were refused train tickets. This kind of behavior was hardly tolerable in Stalin's USSR, but luckily for the refugees the authorities restrained themselves and allowed the refugees to return to the cities in which they were drafted to work.[9] In these cities there was no housing or work for the refugees. Their problem forced the governments to find a solution.

Passportization

In February to April 1940, there was a decree on passports in which identification papers were issued ("passports," in Soviet terminology) to all residents, including recently arrived refugees from the German-occupied zone. No other state bestowed citizenship upon refugees, especially Jewish refugees fleeing the Nazis' grasp. However, in light of the disappointing experiences with the Jewish volunteers in Donbas and similar places, the Soviet authorities decided to arrange a "loyalty test" for each of these refugees. This would bestow Soviet citizenship upon all those who were eligible. The exam was given only to Jewish refugees. That is not to say that the authorities were totally certain of the loyalty of the non-Jewish residents of Ukraine and western Belorussia, or of the non-Jewish refugees. To test their loyalty, however, the government was satisfied with the standard system which had been available since the beginnings of the Soviet regime, one run by the NKVD with great fervor from the first days of "Ukraine's and Belorussia's liberation from the yoke of the Polish Pans [masters]," as the official line put it.

In arranging the loyalty test for Jewish refugees the Soviets used cruel trickery. Announcements, publicized throughout Ukraine and western Belorussia, called on refugees from the German-occupied zone to appear at the NKVD offices where they would receive new citizenship papers. Those who went were told that they could choose between receiving Soviet citizenship or returning to their places of origin on the German-occupied side. They were told that this option was being offered them due to the agreement by the Soviets and Germans on population exchanges between the two parts of what was once Poland, according to which the Germans agreed to accept anyone who came from their territory, had been displaced by the war, and asked to return. The fraud was obvious. The agreement about the population exchange from November 16, 1939, did not, as previously mentioned, apply to Jews and Poles. Not only did the Germans not want Jews to return to their occupied zone, but they actually pushed Jews forcibly and by trickery into Soviet territory. Even had the Germans agreed to accept Jews they would certainly not have trusted the Soviets' judgment regarding who was allowed to pass to the German side. Indeed, when the agreement regarding the switching of the populations was decreed, on November 16, 1939, an SS German delegation was active in Ukraine and western Belorussia. The SS group was 307 strong, and personally checked each German who registered to cross over to the German side. Before arriving at the

German delegation each of these Germans was checked by Soviet NKVD personnel. A Soviet delegation operated similarly within the German territory and checked every Russian, Ukrainian, Belorussian, and Ruthenian who asked to pass over to the Soviet side.

Among the Jewish refugees who were registered to return to the German side were many intellectuals. It is odd that they didn't understand that it was illogical that the Soviets alone could have been authorized by the Germans to register and approve Jews who asked to return to their homes on the German side. The Germans assisted the NKVD with carrying out this fraud upon hundreds of thousands of Jewish refugees by admitting on May 13, 1940, one train with close to a thousand Jewish refugees who wanted to return to the German-occupied zone in Brest-Litovsk. Additionally, it was illogical to assume that in February-May 1940, when Soviet-German friendship was flourishing and while the SS was still active during February on the Soviet side, the Soviets would publicize the fact that Jewish refugees were registered to return to the German side with the permission of the Germans, had the Germans had not agreed to this publicity.[10]

More than half the refugees from the German-occupied zone were registered to return to their homes on the German side. Most of those registered to return were lone individuals, hoping that in this way they might be reunited with their family members. They saw this as a moral obligation after they had lost hope of bringing their families to them on the Soviet side. The NKVD usually allowed Jewish refugees the freedom of choice between Soviet citizenship and registration for return to the German side. However, there were places in which efforts were made to persuade the registrees to opt for returning over citizenship. On the other hand, there were several places in which refugees were persuaded to choose Soviet citizenship over returning.[11] The feeling of despair and fear of what would happen to them on the Soviet side was particularly heightened in February 1942, when the NKVD expelled hundreds of thousands of permanent residents from the Soviet-occupied zone. Most of these people were ethnic Poles, but Ukrainians, Belorussians, and Jews who were defined as "anti-Soviet" elements were also included. In addition to the expulsion of large groups of the population, many permanent residents and refugees were also arrested and sentenced to many years in prison or exiled. They were accused of "transgressions" such as "speculation," the buying and selling of produce, or of criticism of the hardships and difficulties of daily life, which were collectively defined by the authorities as "anti-revolutionary and anti-Soviet propaganda."

Imprisonment and Expulsion

In June 1940 an operation was launched in western Ukraine and western Belorussia to imprison and expel Jewish refugees who were registered to return to their homes in the German-occupied zone. The climax of the operation came on the night of June 29 when hundreds of thousands of people were arrested, most of whom were Jewish and the rest Poles. As mentioned above, not only refugees were arrested, but also Jews who were permanent residents of the occupied Soviet zone: leading members of Zionist organizations as well as other political parties, especially the "Bund," former representatives in the Polish Sejm and senate and local authorities, some wealthy people and rabbis, as well as people who were suspected informants and collaborators with the Polish police against Communists. The Jewish refugees, with all other prisoners and "exilees" of the NKVD in Ukraine and western Belorussia at the time, were divided into two groups, depending upon their ages and family structure. Each group was then dealt with differently. One group was made up of single and young people and the other of families of all ages, including children and the elderly.

The jailers treated the prisoners harshly, with no regard for their health or the fact that they were without the rest of their family members. People who were seriously ill, including mothers about to give birth, or newly born infants, were gathered with their healthy family members and brought to the train stations from which they were sent to their destinations in northern European Russia, Siberia, and eastern Kazakhstan. Many died on the trains. Children were arrested and sent alone if they had been detached from their home or from one or both of the parents. The NKVD never allowed the unification of families, nor did it make it possible for them to get information about the whereabouts of family members who had been arrested individually, in spite of the fact that this information was readily available to the NKVD.

Travel conditions were barely tolerable. Prisoners were sent in freight cars in which three layers of bare wooden "couches" were normally arranged. Adults could not sit or stretch, the quarters were extremely cramped, and the air was stifling. There were cars in which there was a hole in one of the corners through which the travelers were forced to relieve themselves in front of everyone. But there were also cars in which the NKVD had, by chance or on purpose, forgotten to make such a hole. Despite this the train often did not stop for many hours. In fact, most often the train did not even stop within a 24-hour period to allow the passengers to relieve themselves in the open fields. In the winter a small "oven" was placed in each car. The Jewish fugitives who were arrested in June and who were still traveling to their destination in July and August suffered especially from the oppressive heat, intensified by the overcrowding in the sealed cars. Passengers had only a small amount of water, despite the fact that the trains were traveling through areas with plenty of fresh water. Once every couple of days "low quality" bread was rationed to the cars. Each loaf weighed two kilograms, which allowed for half a kilo per person. In addition to the bread, passengers were sometimes given modest amounts of salt herring which did not alleviate their hunger and served only to increase their suffering from thirst. In these circumstances many diseases of the intestines (especially dysentery) and of the skin (mostly scabies) were spread. Among the fugitives there were also doctors, although not in every car, but they did not have medical supplies or medication with them.

There were caravans of fugitives on their way for weeks at a time in the trains and later in cargo ships where conditions were similar to those on the trains. Naturally, the death toll increased as the trip became longer. Approximately 10 percent of the refugees died on those trips before arriving at their "final" destination. There were caravans of fugitives who were brought to urban settlements to work in industrial and construction enterprises. Some were brought to kolkhozes (agricultural collectives) and sovkhozes (state-owned agricultural settlements). Most of the families were scattered in farms across Kazakhstan, but there were those who were brought to especially harsh places such as north Yakutia (Siberia). Some caravans were taken to completely empty places, after marching for days across tens of kilometers on paths that had never previously been traveled by foot. The fugitives were told, upon arrival, that if they wanted shelter they were to build themselves lean-tos and huts, although appropriate tools were not always made available to them. Many fugitives were brought to immense forests in which they chopped trees and prepared them for shipment by river to railway stations. There were places in which new evacuees found established refugees and installations, and there were places in which they were the first settlers. In this chapter we shall dispense with a description of the living conditions in the compulsory work camps and in the deportation camps. These camps were under the supervision of the NKVD and were part of the gulag (the acronym of the branch of the NKVD which managed the thousands of places—*Glavnoye upravleniye lagerei*—the chief administration of the camps).

The Refugees of June 1941

After the Nazi invasion of the USSR on June 22, 1941, an additional wave of tens of thousands of Jewish refugees flowed to the interior of the country. These refugees were from the Soviet-occupied zone in eastern Poland. Only a small part of the Jewish population in this zone, which totaled approximately 1.2 million people, could be evacuated with the Soviets who retreated in a panic in the face of the rapid German advance. As had been the case in western Poland in September 1939, the Jews escaped almost entirely on foot. The lack of vehicular transport restricted the number of Jews who could evacuate. Trains served the Soviet army and administration which came at that time from the "east" (the Soviet heartland). The Soviet authorities did not have time to prepare for an organized evacuation. They did not especially concern themselves with the evacuation and rescue of Jews.

Many Jews did not even attempt to escape. The German army attacked the USSR after it had gained control, by blitzkriegs, of Eastern and Central Europe, and it seemed to be an immense, unstoppable force. The Nazis were victorious in battle after battle, and liberation was not visible on the horizon.

Some therefore perceived the Nazi advance as a natural disaster from which there was no escape. Young Jews, the only group at the time that had the option of escaping, did not do so: they regarded the fact that the Soviets (in contrast with the Germans) were drafting Jews into their army as an important and viable argument against escaping. The war was just beginning, and the chance that draftees would survive it seemed low indeed. Although many Jews certainly wanted to participate actively as Jews in the war against the Nazis, it seemed in those days that it would be engaging in a lost cause from the start.

Soviet military and civilian authorities did not succeed, except in a few extraordinary circumstances, in setting up organized evacuations of the civilian population during the week in which they were still in power in a dwindling number of locations in Ukraine and western Belorussia. On June 28 the Germans conquered Minsk (east of the old border) and on June 30, Lvov. By July 2 they already controlled all the territories which until September 1939 were part of Poland. Nonetheless, not only did the Soviets not encourage the Jews to flee (non-Jews, excepting a few who were identified as collaborators with the Soviets during their occupation, did not ask to be evacuated and many waited for the Germans as saviors) but they hindered their evacuation in Vilna (Vilnius) and western Belorussia. They did not allow them to cross the pre-September 1939 border between Poland and the USSR. Those young Jews who asked to be drafted into the Red Army were rejected. In contrast, in western Ukraine, eastern Galicia, and Volhynia, from which the Soviet retreat was slower, young Jews, especially doctors, whose service was urgently needed, were taken into the army.

Thousands of Jews, residents of western Ukraine, Belorussia, and the Vilna area, as well as refugees from the German-occupied zone who received Soviet citizenship, were drafted into the Red Army through 1940 and until June 1941. In August 1941 almost all of these draftees were transferred from active military duty to "work battalions" (*Stroitelnye bataliony*—also generally called *Trud-armiya*). This transfer occurred after it became clear that most of the draftees, especially the Ukrainians, had deserted to the Germans. Jews, whether they were pro- or anti-Soviet, obviously did not desert to the German side. Nevertheless, the order regarding removing *Zapadnik*s (Westerners) from the combat troops didn't differentiate between Jews and non-Jews. There were more than a few instances where, in spite of the order, "Western" Jews were not released from the active fighting army, perhaps because the order did not reach all of the army troops, some of whom were in the midst of battles or of a hasty retreat. Another possibility is that there were local officers who ignored the order because of the chaos. During the few weeks in which "Western" Jews were still fighting, hundreds, perhaps thousands, fell in combat. An unknown, but certainly not insignificant, number of "Western" Jewish soldiers were in the troops captured by the Germans and were executed as Jews by their captors. The percentage of victims among those who went to the *stroitelnye* *bataliony* was, of course, much lower than among the fighters, although conditions were very difficult and many died of work-related accidents and illness.

The Soviet-Polish Agreement and the Jewish Refugees

On July 30, 1941, a pact was signed in London between the Soviet government and the Polish government-in-exile, headed by General Wladyslaw Sikorski. The agreement renewed diplomatic relations between the two governments. The Soviets promised to grant clemency and to release all of their prisoners, refugees, and Polish army captives, that is, everyone who had been a Polish citizen before the outbreak of the war. In addition, the two sides agreed to establish a Polish army and embassy on Soviet soil which would take under its umbrella those people who had been Polish citizens. In order to establish such a protective umbrella it was decided that twenty Polish delegations would be set up in twenty cities around which the majority of the Polish population would be found after liberation, according to the clemency agreement. This Polish population would need material aid, health care, education, cultural and religious services.[12] The clemency order for Polish citizens was announced on August 12, 1941. In that same month the Polish ambassador, Stanislaw Kot, arrived in Moscow with a group of Polish diplomats who opened the embassy. They began to organize a Polish army under General Wladyslaw Anders.

Due to Soviet opposition, the pact did not specify Poland's postwar borders. On this issue, the Poles and Soviets differed from the start. The Soviets saw Ukraine, western Belorussia, and the Vilna area, which were annexed at the time by the USSR, as Soviet territory. The Poles insisted that Poland return to its prewar borders. Although all of Poland was occupied by the Germans, these differences of opinion were not of only theoretical importance, but also of practical significance to a large part of those who had left Poland and come to the USSR, among them Jews. The Soviet stance went through several changes in connection with political changes occurring in both countries, and, indeed, worldwide because of developments in the war front. In contrast, the Polish stance did not vary as long as the Western allies, the USA and Britain, supported it.

In line with their position on the question of the border between the USSR and Poland, the Soviets continued to view the refugees as Soviet citizens. These refugees included those from the Polish territories absorbed by the USSR in 1939–40, and those who left the German-occupied zone and received Soviet citizenship during the imposition of passports in 1940. Despite this, in order to fulfill the Soviet-Polish agreement of July 1941, they acknowledged the Polish citizenship not only of people who left the German-occupied zone, and who were exiled in the summer of 1940 because of their refusal to receive

Soviet citizenship, but also of those who left the Soviet-occupied zone, that is, those who were granted clemency on August 12, 1941. The clemency included all prisoners and refugees who were Polish citizens until September 1939 without regard to their reasons for imprisonment. On their release papers it was noted that they had been released as Polish citizens.

The agreement with the Polish government-in-exile was thrust upon the Soviets against their will at a particularly difficult time. It contradicted their long-range plans for Eastern Europe in general and for Poland in particular. As soon as it was signed, the Soviets displayed an obvious reluctance to carry it out. They created obstacles to the agreement, ignoring various items, sometimes completely and sometimes partially, and introduced changes in its interpretation. This characterized Soviet tactics in carrying out the agreement until its abolition and the breaking of relations with the Polish government-in-exile on April 26, 1943. It must be noted that not all of the difficulties, delays, and distortions in the implementation of the agreement stemmed from the Soviets' not wanting to implement it. Many difficulties arose due to the war conditions which affected all aspects of life in the country and impeded the effectiveness of all government offices and state services.

Clemency was implemented gradually. The officers in the gulag camps were not eager to comply with the orders to liberate the prisoners. Some camps were made up largely of Poles, but there were those in which the Poles were a small percentage of the prisoners. Thus, releasing those to whom clemency was to be granted was likely to hinder the construction plans of these camps, which were in some cases vital to the war effort. Release also raised a question as to the need for the NKVD staffs; their work in the camps was what kept them exempt from service at the front. There were also many camps and places of exile to which the clemency orders did not arrive at all, either because of malice, error, or hardships caused by the times. In many places the climate allowed for tens of thousands of people to travel from the camps to a more comfortable climate only during a few months of the year. When weather conditions allowed for a mass movement south there were insufficient means of transportation. It was not only the different camp managements across the empire of the gulag who delayed the release of many prisoners as much as possible under various pretexts. The central authorities were also committed to hindering the release and the massive flow of hundreds of thousands of prisoners from north to the south during those difficult days of the second half of 1941 and all of 1942. That was when the Germans neared Stalingrad and threatened the center of the petroleum industry in the Baku area.

Because of the poor timing of the release of hundreds of thousands of Polish prisoners and fugitives during the most critical months of the defensive war against the German army, the Poles who were released suffered horribly. Their situation was in many ways worse than it had been before liberation. The released refugees, many of whom were disease stricken and exhausted, all of them starving, clad in rags and lacking in everything, streamed primarily to the Central Asian republics in the hope that they might escape from the danger of another winter in the cold north. The governments did not succeed in controlling the traffic of civilian refugees from the front to the rear in the east and south or the flow of released Poles who were trying to get to the south.

Jews were a large majority of the Polish refugees who traveled southward. The ethnic Poles were mostly exiles who were sent away by the mass exile decrees with all of their family members. As they were burdened with elderly people and children they could not endanger themselves by wandering about in the horrible conditions of the second half of 1941 and 1942. In contrast, the Jews were mostly young and male, who had dared to flee the German occupied zone in Poland. In 1942 they were already experienced nomads. There was an additional motivation for many young Jews to reach the south. They aspired to reach the borders of Iran and Afghanistan in the hope that the "storm" of the war would afford them the opportunity to cross these borders and reach Palestine (Israel). This hope was not realized, as the Soviet authorities found ways of preventing attempts at border crossings even during the war.

Many people were gathered at rail junctions, and they stormed any sort of train possible, including open, unprotected shipping cars. They grabbed any and all space, even on the roofs and in the passageways between cars. The congestion was unbearable and the filth caused a lice epidemic and pestilence. Many of the refugees who arrived after many difficult wanderings to the long-awaited south were bitterly disappointed. They learned that it was very difficult to find housing and appropriate work, that food was not easily available, and that in the hot, dry summer climate epidemics were much worse than they were in the northern areas from which they had come. Needed professionals found work and thus also received "privileges" of housing and "*propiski*" (residence permits). However, whoever did not find work also did not receive housing rights and were required by the local authorities to leave and look for work on collective farms. There was plenty of work but no income there, because according to prewar arrangements the collectives in Uzbekistan grew only cotton and no produce, which they were supposed to receive from other areas. From the outbreak of the war all supply plans broke down, and produce was not received. Small private plots were the only source of food for the farm workers and their families. Members of the collective farms were left without bread: they certainly did not want to share the little they had with newly arrived foreign refugees. Many refugees who arrived at the collective farms died of starvation and many others were forced to leave under the pressure of (imminent) starvation.[13]

Refugees in the cities were also exposed to hunger and epidemics. Hospitals were full, and there was nobody to care for thousands of sick people and those on the brink of death. In the city of Guzar the sanitation workers would gather dozens of refugees' corpses every morning and bury them in mass graves without coffins or religious services, and without recording their identity. In the same city there was also a Polish army camp in which dozens of soldiers died daily. These soldiers were buried in the camp after their identities were recorded. On the day on which it was the turn of the writer A. Zak to work in the burying detail, forty people, nine of whom were Jews, were buried.[14] In Bukhara, the deaths of approximately 3,000 Polish Jews, who were buried in a Jewish cemetery, were recorded. Many deaths were not recorded.[15] A. Zak writes about the atmosphere of despair and helplessness among the refugees in Tashkent due to the epidemic, where news "arrived daily of more and more deaths. As typhus spreads like wild fire in the city it creates an atmosphere of fear. Refugees are the main victims. No one pays attention to them. They die alone. People are dying in the streets and in the '*Chaikhanes*' [Uzbek tea houses]. Nobody mourns them and accompanies them to their eternal rest. Their bodies are removed as if they were corpses of dogs in a no-man's land."[16]

As the Poles increasingly pressed for accelerating the releases, the Soviets needed to contrive new interpretations for the clemency article in the Soviet-Polish pact of July 30, 1941. In letters to the Polish embassy dated November 19, 1941, the Soviet Ministry of Foreign Affairs established that criminals and Nazi agents had not been and would not be released.[17] According to unofficial information received at the Polish embassy, the refugees—almost all Jewish—were categorized as criminals if they had been caught crossing the border from the German-occupied territory to Soviet territory! This categorization had secondary benefits for the Soviets: it heightened the conflicts and tensions between Jews and Poles. Afterward they took additional steps which further heightened this tension. There were many instances in which Jews who complained that they were not being released were told to complain to the embassy and the Polish government, which were the bodies preventing their release. The imprisoned Jews, of course, had no opportunity to check the truth of these claims. These claims were definitely false, because the Poles, due to their own political calculations and not necessarily because of philosemitism, supported the release of all of their citizens as stipulated by the original contract.[18]

On December 2, 1941, the Soviets instituted a new decree which once again primarily affected Jews and was not timed coincidentally. On that day General Sikorski, head of the Polish government-in-exile, met with the Kremlin leaders. Just then the Soviet Ministry of Foreign Affairs notified the Polish embassy that the USSR recognized only the Polish citizenship of ethnic Poles but not that of the national minorities: Ukrainians, Belorussians, and Jews. Therefore, official authorization was given to end the release of the minorities under the clemency act and to stop discriminating against the minorities with respect to assisting them and drafting them into the Anders army. In addition, by denying their Polish citizenship and turning them into Soviet citizens they were prohibited, in theory, from having any contact with Polish offices which were considered foreign agencies. In actuality, the Soviets did not rigorously enforce this decree, except in instances which they chose to show their principled stance. Thus, a large group of Jews, Ukrainians, and Belorussians were drafted into labor battalions in the fall of 1941 in Alma-Ata, Kazakhstan, whereas only a few weeks earlier they had been liberated under the clemency agreement and they had release papers identifying them as Polish citizens.[19] On February 21, 1942, eleven Jews who were also initially granted clemency were arrested and accused of initiating contact with the Polish delegation which was active in the city.[20]

In both cases the Polish embassy protested to the Soviet Ministry of Foreign Affairs. The Poles argued that the Soviets were contravening the Soviet-Polish agreement of July 30, 1941, as well as international law and the Hague Convention. The Soviet Ministry of Foreign Affairs rejected Polish protests, claiming that the matter concerned people who had become Soviet citizens as a result of a Supreme Soviet decree of November 29, 1939. Therefore, the Polish embassy had no grounds for dealing with them. The Soviets and the Poles continued to differ, tensions increased, and each side ignored the claims of the other. This resulted in a complete break in relations in April 1943. Naturally, matters were resolved in favor of the more powerful Soviets.

However, there were instances in which the Poles seemed to overtly sabotage Soviet instructions and demands. They continued to issue Polish identification papers and other permits to Jews until the Soviets specifically prohibited them from continuing. They also continued assisting Jewish refugees who were registered in their offices. As noted, this was possible because the Soviets were uninterested, at this juncture, in consistently checking on the implementation of their instructions regarding the expropriation of Polish citizenship from minorities, especially Jews. Their concern was to stick to their official position in official letters, documents, and activities which were publicized, especially those which were known to the Western powers. Their steps were designed to show their intransigence regarding the future boundaries of Poland. For the same reason, the Poles fought as hard as they could to uphold their position that the pre-1939 borders should not be changed at all. At the same time, the Poles, who were aware of their inferior position, were careful not to push their position too hard. They were careful not to assist or have any contact with refugees from eastern Poland who had Soviet citizenship from 1940, those being the refugees of June 1941, draftees into Soviet army, and the labor battalions.

During the years being discussed, the debate over the future border was purely theoretical, because all of Poland, Ukraine, and Belorussia were under German occupation. Ethnic Polish refugees naturally sided with the position of their government-in-exile, especially after the Soviets themselves recognized it and also recognized their Polish citizenship on the grounds of their ethnicity. The Poles could not rely on the Ukrainian and Belorussian refugees because of their immense fear of the Soviets and because of the tremendous care they took not to be accused of a lack of loyalty, or worse, of being traitors to their country. The Poles claimed to the British and the Americans that the Jews from Lvov, Vilna, and Bialystok were deeply attached to their Polish citizenship and were asking to return to their places of origin on condition that they remain Polish citizens. The Poles used this as decisive proof that these areas were and remained an integral part of the Polish state.

Jews from eastern Poland who had been arrested and exiled by the Soviets, were released, under the clemency agreement, as Polish citizens. Their release papers served them as identification papers testifying to their Polish citizenship. They saw their life preserver and their hope in these papers, because they allowed them to return to Poland and, most importantly, to leave the USSR after the war. In the interim, they placed many hopes on Polish protection and on Polish material assistance, extremely vital in those years of hunger and distress. For example, the Zionist leader from Lvov, Dr. Emil Sommershtein, a deputy in the Polish Sejm, turned for assistance to the Polish embassy immediately upon his release from Soviet prison. Indeed, the Polish embassy had looked for him and tried to locate him and secure his release.

As stated, the Soviets were concerned chiefly with the political repercussions of their principled stand on the Soviet citizenship of the national minority refugees. In practice, they did not act to revoke the Polish citizenship of the Jewish refugees and thus cut them off from the offices which were branches of the Polish government-in-exile in the USSR. Soviet policy was inconsistent. In their desire to "grab the stick at both ends"—to get the political benefit from their principled stance and, with that, not to detach Jews from Polish authorities and institutions—they could not overlook the Jews because they had assigned them important roles in both their short- and long-range plans. For the long term, the Jews were assigned a very important job in plans for controlling Poland and making it into a Soviet colony after winning the war against Germany. Jews were assigned important tasks in organizing the administrative apparatus of Poland while they were still on Soviet soil. A short-term role, less important but not insignificant, was assigned to the Jews as early as the second half of 1942, when relations with Sikorski's government were faltering. The Soviets saw to the removal of the Anders army from the USSR to Iran and to the closing of the Polish delegations. Due to the fact that educated Poles would be leaving with the Anders army, an important role in administration was thrust upon the Jews, namely running and maintaining services for the refugee population. The ethnic Polish refugees were mostly simple peasants, lacking the skills and talents needed for this work. The Soviets also gained other benefits from the continuation of contact between the Jews and the Polish authorities. Polish animosity toward the Jews, expressed especially in the Polish army, raised the tension between the two peoples. The Soviets were actually helped by the antisemitism of some of the Poles because it lowered the latter's standing in Western public opinion.

The welfare service was run directly by the embassy beginning in February 1942 and was based on a broad network of branches spread across the entire USSR. It was made up of twenty-one delegations, each responsible for twenty people. In all there were 381 local branches headed by "trustees." Each branch had several refugee camps from the nearby area assigned to it, which made for a total of approximately 2,600 such camps in thirty-five districts. In urban settlements and farms beyond the reach of this network there were approximately 200 more camps in some ten districts. The Polish embassy received supply shipments for refugees and for maintaining the Polish army from the American Lend-Lease Administration, from the London government-in-exile, and from various philanthropic organizations, mostly from the United States, among them Jewish organizations, chiefly the American Jewish Joint Distribution Committee. In addition, the Soviet government granted the Polish embassy a loan of 100 million rubles and one of 300 million rubles to the Polish army. The most important aid was in the form of food, clothes, shoes, blankets, and medicine. A vital financial allowance was also given to those in need. It could be used for the rationed portions of food, rent, train travel, postage, etc., for which one had to pay in cash. However, in light of the prices of produce in the black market, this financial aid had a very limited value. Approximately 52 percent of the aid was designated for the maintenance of 807 special institutions for the handicapped, sick, elderly, and orphans. There were clinics and shelters, mostly for children. There was not a single Jew among the delegates, but when the Polish embassy closed, after the Soviet government broke off relations with the Polish government, there were eighty-two Jews among the 387 trustees. The whole aid administration totaled 3,847 workers, 1,828 of whom (47.5 percent) were Jews.

The attitude toward the Jews in the delegations and local branches depended upon the personal attitude toward Jews of those who had these jobs. Anti-semites among them prevented Jews from obtaining any support. Ambassador Stanislaw Kot wrote in his memoirs that he instructed all of his subordinates to treat all refugees equally, regardless of race, nationality, and religion. However, the documents he includes in his own books and in the appendices attached to them and in the two volumes of documents (*Documents on Soviet Political Relations*) published by the Sikorski Historical Institute, do not include any such document. Moreover, there is no indication of its existence in the hundreds of files in the Szwarcbard Archive, nor in the report on welfare written by Ludwik Zeidenman, published by the Polish embassy in the summer of 1943 right after the rupture in Soviet-Polish relations, a report designed to gain the sympathy of Jewish public opinion for Poland.[21] Even had there existed such an order there was no inspection, and there was no technical possibility to have such an inspection on the part of the embassy, not only of the execution of such an order but also of the general activity of hundreds of trustees, given the conditions in the thousands of settlements of the Polish diaspora across the USSR.

Moreover, the aid service was active in the hardest days experienced by the USSR; starvation, epidemics, and very severe poverty were the lot of the entire population. The relief shipments included materials which were in very short supply. They were intended to reach thousands of distribution points and so had to pass through thousands of hands and eyes, not only of the Polish welfare workers, but also of postal employees, train drivers, clerks, police, and Soviet and Polish guards. Naturally, parts of these shipments were stolen and robbed. In order that the remainder reach the offices distributing the aid it was necessary to bribe those with power and authority with the relief supplies and not with money, which had little value. However, the last stations, which were the warehouses of the distribution offices governed by the trustees, were often broken into. In the absence of any kind of inspection, there was no one to prevent the trustees themselves from transferring a large part of the merchandise to the black market. In order to ensure their proper and legal activity the trustees had to bribe local Soviet administrators, commanders of the NKVD, and the police. It is only natural that thanks to bribery and good relations with these men in power, the trustees were able to ensure their own black market businesses.

In July 1942, only five months after the aid service began operations, the Soviets closed all the delegations and arrested 118 of their employees, including all of the delegates. The pretext for the arrests was spying by one of the delegates who collected information about the difficulties and failures of the Soviet draft bureau in his area (Akmolinsk, Kazakhstan). The local bureaus continued operation with the permission of the trustees. The Soviets were not interested in stopping the aid work, since this sort of a break was certainly likely to rouse the anger of the Americans, who were supplying aid both to the Soviets and to the Polish refugees. Moreover, the Soviets had internal reasons for not stopping this activity. It would have further worsened the living conditions of the Polish refugees, who were at the bottom of the ladder anyway. Increased sickness and epidemics in the refugee community also hurt the Soviet population among whom the refugees lived after their release. Besides, it was likely that a heightening of the distress would cause the Polish refugees to be even more hostile toward the Soviet government, and this was at a time when this government was preparing to appease them in line with its long-term plan.

Ironically, the Jews gained from the aggravated relations between the Soviets and the Polish government-in-exile. In March and August 1942, the Polish army, under the direction of General Anders, left the USSR for Iran in two phases. Approximately 37,000 civilians left with the army, many of them educated or members of the intelligentsia who worked with the welfare services. There was an urgent need to fill the open positions in the aid agency and its administration. Many Jewish refugees were suitable for those posts. The Soviets did not continue to oppose contacts between Jews and Polish officials, nor did they oppose Jews dealing with the aid agency or their right to benefit from aid coming from the agency. The Polish ambassador and his staff were also ready to be helped by the Jews, and they hoped that eliminating anti-Jewish discrimination or at least curbing it would raise their standing in the eyes of American Jews and of the American government. (Wendell Willkie, President Roosevelt's emissary, visited the USSR during those months and warned Ambassador Kot that he personally, and the public he represented, would not support the Poles if it became clear that they were "guided by antisemitism.")[22]

After their great victory in the battle of Stalingrad, the Soviets decided that conditions were ripe for a complete break of relations with the exiled Polish government. From then on they were free to work openly and without hesitation for their plans for Poland. On January 16, 1943, they announced that all refugees who were Polish citizens in the past, including ethnic Poles, were considered from that point on Soviet citizens. In February they seized the aid agency, its entire administration and all warehouses of relief supplies from the Polish embassy. On April 26 they broke diplomatic relations with the Polish government-in-exile. The Polish embassy left the USSR, and the aid agency was placed under the auspices of the Union of Patriotic Poles (*Zwiazek Patriotow Polskich*, ZPP), which from then on served as a Polish partner for the continuation of contacts and discussions about the future of the refugees from Poland in the USSR. Summarizing the activities of the Polish aid agency in the USSR, it would be fair to say that although this agency was not free of anti-Jewish discrimination, it seems that there was no antisemitic direction from above. Ambassador Kot also tried to eliminate antisemitic tendencies among his subordinates in this agency. The service was also not free of corruption, a phenomenon which lasted throughout the period. Some of the corruption was hidden, but it was obvious when it had to do with the relief supplies that didn't get to the refugee population and the needy. Nonetheless, the service contributed significantly to easing the poverty and suffering of the refugees, including Jews, at a very tough time for the entire Soviet population, and above all for the refugee population.

After the Soviet government cut off diplomatic relations with the Polish government-in-exile and established the ZPP, responsibility for refugee welfare was transferred to that organization. Aid to the refugees was diminished significantly because the American government did not allow government agencies, such as Lend-Lease, or philanthropic organizations to send aid as long as the Soviet government did not arrive at a reasonable arrangement with the Polish government-in-exile, the only government which the Americans would recognize at the time as representative of the Polish nation.

Fortunately for the Jewish refugees from Poland, the American Jewish Joint Distribution Committee came to their aid. As long as the Soviet Union had contact with Nazi Germany, the Joint and other Jewish organizations were not able to get permission from the Soviet authorities to give aid to the refugees, including those from Poland. After Germany's attack on the Soviet Union and the renewal of relations between Moscow and the Polish government-in-exile, the Soviets and the Poles were interested, each side independently, in receiving the supplies that the Joint and other Jewish organizations were ready to supply to help the Jewish refugees. The Soviets demanded that the aid be presented to the Soviet Red Cross, which aided all war refugees regardless of nationality or religion, and they promised that Jews would not be discriminated against in the division of the supplies. In conjunction with this they adamantly refused to allow a representative of the Joint to enter the USSR to check what were the immediate and vital needs and the fastest methods of meeting them. The Polish government also refused to include a representative of the Joint in the Polish Red Cross delegation, which was allowed to operate in the Soviet Union, or with any other delegation of Polish representatives in the USSR (embassy, army, etc.). Without options, the Joint made do with a modest flow of supplies by means of the Soviets and by means of the Poles, just as long as they could be sure that the Jews would at least enjoy a significant part of the supplies donated for their benefit.

In the summer of 1942, with the arrival of the Anders army deportees in Iran, the Jewish world found out about antisemitism and discrimination against Jews in the Polish government delegation in the Soviet Union and about the very seriously distressed situation of the Jewish refugees. Joint leaders then decided to review its policies and mode of operation in the Soviet Union. As a first step, Harry Witeles, a Jewish American who lived in Jerusalem at the time, was assigned to Iran in order to investigate the situation and present his suggestions regarding ways of sending aid to the Jewish refugees. Witeles visited Teheran in November 1942 for three weeks. He met with the American, British, Soviet, and Polish ambassadors and with high officials in their respective embassies. He also met with the heads of the Red Cross from the four countries, representatives of the government of Iran, delegates from Palestine, representatives of the refugees from across the ideological spectrum—Zionists, Bundists, orthodox, and assimilationists—and with the heads of the local Jewish community. The complaints and the harshest blame, not only from all of the Jewish representatives, but also from the Americans and from Iran's delegation, were directed toward the Poles. They were not only blamed for acts of discrimination against Jews, but in general for grave criminal acts, thievery and embezzlement. Incidentally, during Witeles's visit in Teheran, the directors of all five Polish refugee camps in the city, and also the director-general of the Polish office for refugee matters, were arrested and charged with stealing relief supplies and passing them on to the black market.

Upon his return, Witeles suggested to the Joint leadership that aid packages be sent to the refugees' private addresses and not by means of any Soviet or Polish organizations or institutions. The Soviets did not look favorably upon this arrangement. They did not prohibit the shipment of these packages because they did not want to become involved in a dispute with the Americans. However, they levied heavy taxes on the private packages. An average package cost the Joint $28.32, seven-and-one-half times the price of the goods in it. Of this, $9.56 went to Soviet fees and taxes, and the rest was the cost of packaging, shipping, and insurance.[23] In early 1943 the Joint made do with supporting the Jewish Agency's project of sending the packages. Until July 1943, the Joint's money sufficed to send 3,132 packages.[24]

In June 1943, a new representative of the Joint, Charles Passman, arrived in Teheran. He volunteered to direct the Joint relief project for Jewish refugees in the Soviet Union for two years. He was a keen businessman with many connections. Within a few months he was able to discover new sources for supplies with goods available inexpensively and some even free. He took advantage of the problems of the Polish government-in-exile which had lost contact with the Poles in exile in the USSR after the break of relations with the Soviets. He made a deal with the Polish Red Cross according to which the organization would give the Joint the relief supplies which they received in abundance from American Lend-Lease and the Joint would increase the number of packages to be sent directly to the USSR by a few times the planned number. Half of these would go to addresses supplied by the Red Cross and the other half to Jewish Polish citizens according to addresses that the Joint had. Thus, the number of packages grew, and beginning in April 1944 some 10,000 packages arrived per month.[25] Passman also succeeded in acquiring goods directly from the Lend-Lease which were not being transferred through the Polish Red Cross.[26]

Paralleling this were aid packages that were sent by individuals in Palestine to their refugee relatives in the USSR and those sent by Zionist organizations. Passman pointed out that the small Jewish population in Palestine sent the refugees in the USSR a great amount of aid in comparison with what the American Jews put forth.[27] According to an agreement with the Joint, HIAS (Hebrew Immigrant Aid Society) began in 1944 shipping packages to the refugees in the USSR. These came from their relatives in North and South America, and accounted for most of the shipments.[28]

At the end of 1944, there were already 40,000 Jewish refugee families from Poland who were receiving an aid package from the Joint every three months. The value of the goods in each package varied between 1,500 and 4,000 rubles, at a time when the monthly wage for a worker came to 300 rubles.[29] The project of sending packages to the USSR continued throughout 1945 in quantities similar to those from 1944 because the mass return of refugees to Poland began only in February 1946. From then on the Joint replicated its activities in Poland, benefiting the few surviving Jews of Poland. The Joint's relief project for Jewish refugees from Poland in the USSR saved tens of thousands from death by starvation.[30]

Religious Life and Cultural Activity

The refugees were initially unorganized in their settlements. Uprooted and foreign, they found themselves in "night shelters" in hostile environments. Horrible news came of the loss of their relatives and of their homes to which they had hoped to return after the war. On January 6 and April 22, 1942, Soviet Foreign Minister V. M. Molotov made public announcements detailing "the acts of robbery, destruction, massacre of citizens and ruthless monstrosities at the hands of the Germans in the Soviet territories which they had occupied." Among other things announced was the massacre at Babi Yar in Kiev, where 52,000 Russians, Ukrainians, and Jews were murdered.[31]

But the desire to live had its effect. An atmosphere of a viable Jewish population slowly began to emerge in the refugee camps. Due to both external and internal policy the government stopped the persecution of adherents of all religions, although this policy was not declared officially. Nonetheless, the public sensed this and acted accordingly. On the High Holidays the refugees gathered in synagogues and in private homes. Even nonreligious Jews who previously had not attended synagogue services felt an emotional need to identify with their brethren and to shed a tear together for those dear to them, as well as for the destruction of their people. Slowly and hesitantly Jews expanded their religious activities. They were helped in this by the Jews of Uzbekistan ("Bukharans") who were at the time still primarily traditional, as well as by Orthodox Jews amongst the veteran Soviet Jews and war refugees. In Dzhambul, in southern Kazakhstan, thousands of Jews from Poland were concentrated, among them approximately ten rabbis. They established a *yeshiva* for twenty youths, and a *Talmud-Torah* for seventy children. A *mikvah* (ritual bath) was built with 34,000 donated rubles, and a rabbinic court was active. An underground *yeshiva* was also active in Samarkand, used both by refugees from Poland and strictly observant Khabad Hasidim.[32] Orthodox Jews were also assisted by the Bukharan Jews in activating a burial society, since each Jewish community of Uzbekistan still had separate cemeteries and burial societies.

There were also attempts at organizing secular cultural activities. A traveling Yiddish theater troupe made up of Polish refugees performed across Central Asia. Among them were the two famous comedians, Shimon Dzigan and Yisroel Shumakher, as well as David Lederman, Mark Moravski, Mitek Rotshtein, Yoel Bergman, and others. Included in the group's writers were Moshe Nudelman, one-time editor of the weekly humorous supplement *Der Krumer Shpiegel* in the Warsaw daily, *Moment*, and Yosef Goldstein, former editor of the weekly humorous supplement *Kol-Boinik* in the Warsaw daily, *Haynt*. Dzigan and Shumakher, who were imprisoned when they were in the Anders army, had the luck to arrive at the camp ITEL in the city of Aktyubinsk, a large industrial city in Kazakhstan. There were thousands of Jewish refugees in that camp. In the vicinity of the ITEL camp there was also a camp which housed many Polish Jews. The camp government allowed theatrical performances in the context of "cultural activities." Dzigan and Shumakher presented skits to mock the Nazi enemy. The performances were purely in Russian, although sometimes they managed to include a Yiddish song. They aroused great emotion in the audience, especially when they sang the popular song, "*Mayn shtetele Belz*," which was very famous among Polish Jews before the war, in Russian translation with the singer Khayim Lebin, also a refugee from Poland.[33] The Jewish content of the cultural activities and of the secular entertainment was very thin. In spite of that, they strengthened ties among the refugees and helped create a feeling of togetherness.

Physical and emotional distress led, among other things, to the development of mutual assistance among the refugees. One of the most significant and well-known such events was managing the release of Dzigan and Shumakher for the large sum of 1.5 million rubles paid as a bribe to the NKVD commander in Lublin. The money was donated by three religious Jews who maintained that in the circumstances of those days, the "ransom of captives," traditionally an important religious duty, was top priority.[34]

Relations with Soviet Jews

The majority of the Jews of Poland had lived under the tsarist Russian government until World War I, and were in their religious culture very close to the Jews of European Russia. There was only a twenty-four-year break (1915–1939) in Russian rule, and so the renewed contact was usually warm. The initial contacts began on the first day of the Soviet invasion, Sunday, September 17, 1939. The invading army had many reserve troops who were drafted in Soviet Ukraine and Belorussia, especially for the purpose of "liberating" Ukraine and western Belorussia, and there was a relatively high proportion of Jews in this group. Local "Polish" Jews were happy to host their "Russian" brothers. In many instances the guests found relatives, even parents and siblings, among their hosts.

Jewish reserve soldiers—people in their thirties and forties—had received their education before the revolution. Many had studied in "*kheyder*," grew up in traditional homes, spoke Yiddish, and remembered the Jewish holidays. The process of assimilation of those inclined to assimilate was still incomplete. Therefore, it is not surprising that the encounter with the Jews of the "liberated" areas awakened powerful sentiments and longings for the Jewish milieu. Of course, there were those who identified with the Soviet regime's negative view of religion, the Jewish past and culture. However, there were many among the Jewish soldiers who were pleased by the opportunity to visit a synagogue on Yom Kippur, which fell just a few days after the Soviet invasion, and to be guests in a Jewish home on the Sukkot holiday.

There were instances in which the Jewish soldiers in the Red Army, guarding the border between the German- and Soviet-occupied zones, allowed refugees to cross into their zone. Sometimes an argument would ensue because of this between Jewish and non-Jewish soldiers. An excellent example of help for Polish Jews from the Jewish soldiers in the Red Army is the incident when such soldiers passed a group of Zionist pioneers over the border. These pioneers had been caught by Soviet guards while trying to cross over to Lithuania before it was absorbed by the USSR. The soldiers served as translators for their commander, who questioned the escaping pioneers. After they heard their story the Jewish soldiers took responsibility, despite the high risk, for guiding them over the Lithuanian border.[35]

Among the "Easterners" there were also dozens of people active in Yiddish culture who were hoping to find a base for their activities, which at the time stood at the brink of extinction in the Soviet motherland. Jewish cultural activists faced a void, their livelihood collapsing in front of their own eyes. They hoped that the state's interest in gaining the sympathy of the local population including Jews, would compel the authorities to extend the life of Yiddish culture in the "liberated" zones. Most of the guests from the East came only for visits, in order to lay foundations for activities which they hoped to guide from their permanent places of residence in Kiev and Minsk.

The theater troupe established in Bialystok in the summer of 1940 by refugee actors from the German-occupied zone—including three famous actors of the time, Ida Kaminska, Shimon Dzigan, and Yisroel Shumakher—was permitted to perform in several central cities in the Soviet Union, including Moscow, Minsk, Kharkov, and Dnepropetrovsk. Many Jews, among them people with high positions in these cities, received the actors with great excitement. In Dnepropetrovsk the troupe was invited to perform before a high-ranking Jewish officer in the local NKVD. Dzigan described in his colorful Yiddish the general atmosphere that was created around the troupe wherever they performed: "*Alle hobn zikh getuvlt in der benkshaft tsu Yiddishkeyt*" (Everyone drowned in longings for Yiddishkeit).[36]

National and religious sentiments were awakened in Soviet Jews under the influence of Jews from Poland. A number of examples follow: in one of the ITEL camps in the far north, the Jewish wife of an officer of the NKVD made a traditional Passover seder, in her husband's absence, for a group of Polish and Soviet Jewish prisoners. She prepared a lot of food and one of the prisoners, who had been a ritual slaughterer, read the Haggada.[37]

In 1943, Moshe Grossman worked in Samarkand in a cooperative with a Jewish director. Two Jews once came to ask for a donation for a *Khevre Kadisha* (burial society). The director threw them out but called Grossman immediately afterward, gave him 300 rubles for them, and asked him to pass the money on to them and to tell them to return every month for his donation.[38]

Jerzy Gliksman, a Bundist activist, tells of his meeting with a Jewish engineer from Moscow in an ITEL camp. The engineer asked him for as many details as possible about Palestine, kibbutzim, Tel Aviv, and the like: "When I told him, I saw one thousand sparkling lights in his eyes . . . the man was exploding with feelings—the ancient walls of Jerusalem, Mount Carmel, blooming orchards. . . . "[39] In the ITEL camp in Aktyubinsk, which held thousands of Soviet and Polish Jewish prisoners, Polish Jews organized small groups for studying Hebrew. Soviet Jews who were learning the Hebrew alphabet for the first time participated in the groups.[40]

Polish Jews came into contact with Soviet Jews in all sectors of Soviet society in the most turbulent period in the history of both groups, and of the Jewish people generally. The shocking news of the murder of Jews in all areas occupied by the Germans brought home to Russian and Polish Jews, including the assimilated ones, that they shared a common destiny. The rise of antisemitism in all strata of Soviet society strengthened the feeling of solidarity. Even assimilated Soviet Jews and devout Communists were moved to extend assistance to coethnics who were in deep trouble, sometimes even if it involved personal risk.

But there were also instances of misunderstanding, indifference, and even cruelty in the relations between Soviet and Polish Jews. Some Soviet Jewish women in Stalinabad (now Dushanbe, Tajikistan) resented the fact that Polish Jews were "not fighting" while their own husbands were at the front. Some Soviet Jews were harsh toward the Polish refugees in the belief that this would ingratiate them with their superiors. But the instances of solidarity and mutual aid far outnumbered those where negative feelings were expressed. It can be asserted that this encounter contributed to strengthening the Jewish consciousness of the Soviet Jews and planted seeds which were to bear fruit in the appearance of a national Jewish movement one generation later, after the Six Day War in the Middle East (1967).

Conclusion

Half a million Polish Jews sought refuge in the USSR between September 17, 1939, and June 22, 1941. Their fates were determined by the "objective" circumstances of a war which was more cruel and of greater magnitude than any other. But to a large extent, and sometimes in a decisive way, their fate was decided also by Soviet policies and attitudes toward an uninvited and unexpected population. There was no planning or even elementary preparation for receiving the refugees and dealing with them. Inconsistencies in attitude, and contradictory, improvised policies caused the refugees much suffering, but also caused Soviet authorities on various levels a good deal of work and presented them with perplexing situations. Improvised and hasty solutions often led to new problems and further suffering.

At the same time, it would be a mistake to see Soviet dealings with the Polish Jewish refugees in a completely negative light. The Soviets did not want them, but their policies were not atypical. Even the "enlightened" democracies of the West, including prosperous America, closed their doors to Jews persecuted by the Nazis. Great Britain went further and closed the gates of Palestine which, the British had announced in 1917, was supposed to be the national home of the Jews. Moreover, the Soviet Union was a poor country plagued by shortages because of its unsuccessful social and economic socialist experiment. Nevertheless, after they had "succeeded" in early 1940 in stopping the further influx of Jewish refugees from the Nazis, the Soviets reconciled themselves to the existence of hundreds of thousands of Jewish refugees who had arrived legally before the doors were shut and even to the presence of those who came illegally. In this instance they displayed greater generosity than any other country. They offered the refugees full citizenship, including the right to work and study. They provided refugees housing and food, within their limited means, to those who agreed to work in large enterprises. Of course, they could not give the refugees better conditions than those enjoyed by their veteran citizens.

This is not to excuse the acts of cruelty the Soviets visited upon the refugees. They closed their borders to refugees when it was technically feasible to admit them; they tortured those who were caught when trying to sneak over the border and sent them back to the Germans; they sent to the gulag those whom they could not hand over to the Germans. One cannot excuse at all the viciousness of the NKVD's large-scale activity, in cooperation with the Gestapo, of registering thousands of despairing refugees for supposed repatriation to their homes and then sending them to their deaths in the gulag and the notorious camps. Still, a quarter of a million Polish Jews were saved in the Soviet Union and, in the end, were permitted to return to Poland.

The Poles, as well as the Soviets, were decisive in determining the fate of Jewish refugees in the USSR. From August 1941 until April 1943 those refugees who had not accepted Soviet citizenship in 1940 enjoyed the limited protection of two Polish government agencies, the Polish embassy and the army organized in the USSR headed by General Wladyslaw Anders. There were antisemitic tendencies in both institutions, though they differed in their intensity. Ambassador Stanislaw Kot, a professor and professional diplomat, placed the interest of his nation and government above all else. He was a moderate antisemite but thought it would be wise to present to the allies an image of a democratic regime free of antisemitism. He protected "his" Jews from the Soviet authorities and tried to free them according to the law on clemency. He saw to it that freed Jews would receive Polish identity papers, and these generally protected them against being drafted into labor battalions, though in many instances this did not work. On the one hand, he protested to Anders about discrimination against Jews who wished to serve in the army, or in the evacuation to Iran, but, on the other, he presented Jews in a negative light and accused them of disloyalty to Poland and of harboring anti-Polish sentiments. Among other things, he justified discrimination against Jews by Anders and his officers, criticizing them only for doing this publicly and crudely, so that foreign newspapers got wind of this and Poland's good name was damaged thereby.

Anders, by contrast, was an extreme antisemite who took no pains to hide his opinions of Jews except when he thought this might harm him. He rejected the majority of Jews from his army and kept only 3 percent of them in its ranks to serve him as an alibi. He tried to exclude them from the evacuation to Iran and almost succeeded. Only under Soviet pressure did he allow 3,500 Jewish soldiers and 2,500 civilians, among them about 1,000 children, to leave for Iran.

The best period for Polish Jewish refugees was from May 1943 until the end of July 1946 because Stalin had assigned them a role in the process of transforming Poland into a "peoples' republic" and a Soviet satellite. All told, about a quarter of a million Jews returned to Poland, where they encountered murderous hostility. Over a thousand were killed before security organs could protect them. The murders reached a climax in the pogrom in Kielce on July 4, 1946, in which forty-two survivors were killed and eighty wounded by a mob. This led to a massive Jewish exodus from Poland to the displaced persons camps in American-occupied Germany and Austria.

Blind luck and certain character traits, such as courage and wisdom, determined the fates of individual Jews, within the parameters established by Soviet and Polish policies. Soviet goodwill, mitigated by cruelty, and some actions by both nationalist and pro-Communist Poles allowed some Jews to be saved. But neither the Soviets nor the Poles saw the Jews as a group which deserved to make its own decisions about its needs and aspirations. For them, Jews were an object and an instrument which they could use for their own purposes, including the conflict between them.

Notes

1. *Contemporary Jewish Record*, vol. 2, no. 6 (November-December 1939), p. 71; *Sho'at Yehudey Polin* (Jerusalem, 1940), vol. 1, p. 44. Report of Shimon Zeidenman.
2. *Documents on German Foreign Policy, 1918–1945* (London: HMSO, 1949–1964), Ser. D., vol. viii, no. 193, p. 62.
3. *Documents on Soviet-Polish Relations, 1939–1945* (London, 1961), no. 62, p. 62.
4. Gerald Reitlinger, *The Final Solution* (London: Valentine Mitchell, 1953), p. 51.
5. *Documents on German Foreign Policy, 1918–1945*, op.cit., Series D, vol. 8, no. 135, p. 95.
6. *Yad Vashem* Archive (Hereafter Y.V.A.). Jerusalem. Report from the German Ministry for Foreign Affairs, no. JU3335.
7. Y. Yekhiels. *Fun Bug biz Pechora* (Tel Aviv, n.p., 1966); YIVO Archive, New York, *Eydes [testimony of] Marie Ansman*. R.G. 104. Second series.
8. *Pinkas Lomza* (New York, 1957). p. 186.
9. For a complete description of the acts of cheating and collaboration of the NKVD and the Gestapo, see Y. Litvak, *Plitim Yehudim mepolin bebrit-Hamo'atzot 1939–1946* (Jerusalem: Institute for Contemporary Jewry, Hebrew University, 1988), pp. 123–88 and references therein.
10. Yuli Margolin, "Biymay hakibush ha-Sovieti," *Sefer Pinsk*, vol. B (Tel Aviv: Irgun yotsai Pinsk, 1977), p. 313; Y.V.A. Testimony no. P *(Peh)* 483.143, T.A.P. no. 2(20).
11. *Documents on Soviet-Polish Relations*, vol. 1, pp. 140–42.
12. Y.V.A. Testimony no. 1438/843-2; YIVO Archive, Testimony no. 1000.
13. Avraham Zak, *Oyf shliyakhn fun hefker* (Buenos Aires: Yidbuch, 1958), vol. 1, p. 168.

14. G. Lustgarten, *In vander un gerangel 1939–1968* (Tel Aviv, 1968) p. 200.
15. Zak, op. cit.
16. *Documents on Soviet-Polish Relations,* vol. 1, p. 220.
17. Ibid., pp. 228–30.
18. Ibid., p. 200.
19. A.S. ("*Aleph Shin*"). Folder 11–2/329. Report of the Polish Embassy about the condition of the Jewish citizens of Poland in light of official documents and activities of the Soviet authorities, October 11, 1942.
20. Report on the Relief Accorded to Polish citizens by the Polish Embassy in the USSR with special reference to Polish citizens of Jewish nationality, September 1941–April 1943. Final report of the Polish Embassy compiled in Teheran in August 1943 for the use of the charitable institutions concerned.
21. A.S. ("*Aleph Shin*"). Folder no. 11–2/325.
22. AJDC Archives, New York. Folder "Relief Supplies," Polish Refugees in Russia, May-December, 1943. Temporary Report, September 20, 1943.
23. Ibid. Report of Charles Passman on his visit to Teheran, July 14–23, 1943.
24. AJDC Archives, New York.
25. Ibid. S.T.A. Announcement, June 2, 1942.
26. AJDC, ibid. Passman to AJDC, NY, July 31, 1944.
27. Ibid. The Joint-HIAS Announcement to the Press, February 28 and March 21, 1944.
28. AJDC Archives, New York. Folder October 1944–1945. (Passman, Jerusalem to Levit, New York, November 2, 1945).
29. Zak, 1958, vol. 2, p. 253.
30. Stanislaw Kot, *Listy z Rosji do Generala Sikorskiego* (London: St. Martin's Printers, 1956), pp. 465–66.
31. Ya'akov Cohen, *Unter di sovyetishe himlen* (Tel Aviv: *Y.L. Peretz farlag,* 1961), pp. 326–28.
32. Lustgarten, *In vander*, p. 186.
33. Shimon Dzigan, *Der koyekh fun yidishn humor* (Tel Aviv: *Gezelshaflikhn komitet tsu fayern 40 yor tetikayt fun Shimen Dzigan oif der Yidisher bine*, 1974), pp. 269–86.
34. *Al masu'ot Polin,* Merkhavya, Palestine, 1940, p. 98.
35. Dzigan, op. cit., pp. 163–70.
36. Eliezer Pomerants, *Berdifah akhar ha'emet—derekh khayav shel komunist l'she'avar* (Haifa: *Pinat sefer*, 1966), p. 133.
37 Moshe Grossman (P. Grim), *In farkisheftn land fun legendarn Dzhugashvili* (Paris: *Emes un freiheit,* 1949), p. 112.
38. Jerzy Gliksman, *Tell the West* (New York: Gresham Press, 1948), pp. 322–23.
39. Ezra Rivlis, *Barzel me'ever lamasakh* (Tel Aviv: Moreshet, Sifriat Poalim, 1981), p. 214.
40. Kalman Goldvasser, *Fun der veysel bizn taykh kizil-Sy* (Paris, 1972), pp. 147–55.

TEN

Jewish Warfare and the Participation of Jews in Combat in the Soviet Union as Reflected in Soviet and Western Historiography

Mordechai Altshuler

The dualist language of the title obliges us first of all to define the distinction between "Jewish warfare" and "the participation of Jews in combat." The fighting of Jews in the ghettos, in Jewish partisan units, in the Jewish Brigade, and the like is certainly to be understood as "Jewish warfare," since all the combatants in these units were Jews, their conduct stemmed from their identification as such, and it drew its impetus from the distinctive Jewish fate and the singular situation in which the Jewish communities found themselves during the Nazi occupation. The difficulty arises in attempting to categorize the actions of the hundreds of thousands of Jewish soldiers who engaged in combat alongside the masses of soldiers of other nationalities. Although the combatants in this case were likewise Jews, we must ask ourselves whether we can regard their fighting as a peculiarly Jewish endeavor. Can it be considered specifically *Jewish* warfare, or was it essentially the participation of Jews in combat?

In order to draw the thin line between these two categories, we must examine the motivation behind the fighting, for, in this context, motive was the decisive criterion. This same distinction must be applied not only to the Jews fighting in the ranks of the Red Army and partisan units in the Soviet Union, but also in examining Soviet and Western historiography on these topics. To illustrate the essence of the distinction, let me cite one example of an act of valor credited to a Jew serving in the Red Army.

On April 25, 1945, in the bitter battle fought by the Red Army near Breslau (Wroclaw, Poland) Josef Bumagin, a native of the Jewish town of Horodok and a resident of the city of Birobidzhan, blocked an embrasure of a German fort with his own body and, by his death, ensured a Russian victory in an important military action.[1] Bumagin took the motivation for his action with him to his grave, but for the historian there is significance to the question of whether his bold move derived from his Soviet education, his loyalty to the Communist Party (of which he had been a member since 1932), or from his Jewish education and a desire to avenge the deaths of his relatives who had been brutally murdered in the cities and towns of Belorussia. Then again, perhaps it was the attitude of contempt toward the Jews in his unit—as in so many other units—or the allegation that a Jew is incapable of self-sacrifice that drove Josef Bumagin and others like him to act as they did.

One's Jewish identity sometimes took pride of place in the constellation of factors to be weighed by junior officers and even individual enlisted men in making fateful decisions. Thus, we know of many cases, for example, in which a small unit found itself surrounded by the enemy and most of its soldiers saw no choice but to surrender and be taken prisoner. Often, it was the Jewish soldier who vigorously objected to this decision because he knew that as a Jew his fate would differ from that of the rest, especially since his comrades-in-arms might well inform their captors of his identity. To the degree that this and similar motives dictated the behavior of the Jewish fighter, his actions should be regarded as *Jewish warfare*. It goes without saying that many motives coexist in any given situation, but this does not release the historian from the duty to trace the motives peculiar to the Jewish fighter.

In turning to a review of Soviet and Western historiography we must adopt different criteria. For in Western countries, historiography can be viewed as the sum total of the studies and works written on the subject. Most of these studies are the product of the creative efforts of scholars. And while scholars obviously are not wholly detached from the worldview, mood, and outlook of the society in which they live, their first duty is to intellectual and scientific honesty. That, in turn, obliges them to contend with the material at hand in an honest attempt to breathe life into the information by viewing the historical event from a variety of standpoints and drawing conclusions based upon the facts.

These aims were not similarly incumbent upon Soviet historians, however. Soviet historiography was by definition Marxist historiography, that is, guided *a priori* by an immutable outlook that explains the events under examination, essentially the diametric opposite of what is acceptable in the West. Naturally, one can claim that there is nothing particularly remarkable about historians adopting a specific approach to their subject, but that is on condition that they strive to examine it as objectively as possible and that the writing of history serves as a vehicle for grappling with competing worldviews, ideologies, and political outlooks. This was not the case in the Soviet Union.

Even more detrimental to Soviet historiography were the pragmatic demands made upon the historian. In describing the science of Soviet historiography, the *Soviet Historical Encyclopaedia* of the 1960s explicitly stated that "the science of history in the Soviet Union has assumed a respected place among the social sciences, which are called upon to serve as an instrument for communist education of the workers."[2] This statement unequivocally declares that all the social sciences, including the writing of history, must fulfill a socio-educational purpose.

If that is the aim of writing history, then it is not historical truth which must be the scholar's prime concern. Rather the scholar is enlisted in the service of educational objectives by means of writing history. And because educational objectives for the masses were determined by the Communist Party—or, to put it differently, by the regime—in serving educational demands, the historian was essentially serving the political aims of the regime at any given moment. Considering these circumstances, it is justified to regard Soviet historiography in general, and the historiography of World War II in particular, as political writing. And from this standpoint it seems equally appropriate to regard the attention to or avoidance of Jewish subjects in Soviet historiography as an expression of the regime's stance on the Jewish question. Because all historical writing in the Soviet Union was governed by the solitary aim noted above, there are substantive grounds—at least insofar as the present subject is concerned—for including in the category of historical writing not only classic research based upon archival material, attended by scientific apparatus, and written in the cautious and meticulous language demanded of the scholar, but also such "borderline" literature as semipopular works, memoirs, and articles of various kinds.

Soviet historians, publicists, and memoirists had been raised on the precept that their writings must serve political-educational ends. In the course of writing, therefore, the material was sifted through a filter of self-censorship, a winnowing of the facts and events that were best ignored—in keeping with the general line pursued by the regime at any one time. Major works of scholarship—primarily collective ones—were deliberated once or more by the scholarly institutions that sponsored and produced them. During this process scholars and writers were told to avoid certain subjects and stress others. The final stage at which each publication was examined was that of official censorship, which followed the regime's explicit and secret directives. Hence, every work that reached us from the Soviet Union had undergone a series of inspections, from the writer's initial selection of subject (often no less important than the others) through official censorship. All these filters sharpened the political character of the historical works and "borderline cases" that we have included in our discussion. The earliest Soviet historiography on the fighting in World War II, in its broadest sense, dates to the war itself, when pamphlets and articles were published to extol the heroic acts of the Red Army and partisan fighters. Publications of this kind continued to appear during the latter half of the 1940s, and the subsequent period of the "thaw" saw a new wave of writing about World War II that touched on subjects and issues that had been taboo at the end of the Stalinist era.

The historical treatment of combat during World War II continued to expand in the subsequent decades to such an extent that it is difficult to survey it. Suffice it to say that by the middle of the 1970s, more than 9,000 books and pamphlets and some 6,000 articles in scholarly journals had been published about World War II in the Soviet Union—and that does not include belles lettres on the subject.[3] Obviously it is all but impossible to address the full range of material, but it appears that we can classify it into six main categories.

1. Collections of documents (published in the form of special books or in historical journals) that generally comprised the directives of the Communist Party or other arms of the regime.[4] This type of material, covering either the country as a whole or specific geographical areas, did not, and essentially could not, make direct or indirect reference to the Jews.

2. Collections of documents that included reports of combat units, whether of the Red Army or of the partisan movement. An example of this type of publication is the three volumes of documents of the partisan movement in Belorussia published in Minsk (in 10,000 copies) from 1967 to 1982.[5] These collections make reference to at least 150 partisans whose names clearly indicate that they were Jewish. Although the nationality of the partisans is not explicity stated, publications of this sort can certainly be regarded as primary evidence and a source for determining the exact dates of events. However, due to the biased attitude of many scholars who are convinced that Soviet publications contained no material relating to the Jews, this type of literature has not been sufficiently exploited—even though it is sometimes the only evidence available about specific events. Take, for example, the case of the following report by the commander of the Kirov Company of partisans dated June 16, 1943:

> At three in the morning on June 9, 1943, Germans surrounded the village Vulka (7 kilometers from Luninetz), removed 156 families, and transferred them to the Luninetz ghetto. . . . On the evening of June 11, 1943, a group of partisans under the command of the political commissar A. Svitzov was sent to the city of Luninetz to make contact with the members of the police . . . who were in touch with the [partisan] company and would liberate 150 families from the ghetto. The mission was carried out on the night of June 11/12, 1943; 127 families escaped and 28 remained in the ghetto.[6]

Although there is no question whatsoever that these families were Jewish, the officer who wrote the report did not identify them as such, for reasons best known to him. In the same way, the editors of the collection did not see fit to cite this fact, so as not to highlight that the purpose of the partisan action was to rescue Jews. Hence we see how the Jewish element has been muted in publications of this sort, though it is not absent altogether.

3. Specific studies that focus on military, economic, and social analyses of the warfare of the Red Army and partisan units during the various stages of the Soviet-German war. These works all but ignored the Jews completely, though from time to time the names of outstanding Jewish officers received mention.

4. General works on the history of the Soviet Union or of certain geographic or administrative districts during World War II. The best-known of these works is a five-volume study entitled *The History of the Great Patriotic War*. Similar books exist for various republics; it is sufficient to cite the three-volume history, *The Ukrainian Soviet Republic in the Great Patriotic War of the Soviet Union*. Publications of this type, which were of what the Soviets called a "popular-scientific" character, tried to recreate and explain the broader canvas of events in the country, or in a specific area, during a difficult or decisive period of the war.

The works that fall into the third and fourth categories are marked by a clear tendency to play down, though not entirely disregard, the role of Jews in the war against the Nazis. Thus, for example, the general history of the Ukraine during World War II notes that the Jew Yefim Fomin took part in the heroic defense of the fortress of Brest.[7] In most cases, however, the names of the fighters are given without citing their nationality. Moreover, in order to obscure the role of Jews in the fighting, their first names and patronymics are given as initials—a system used by the tsarist authorities during World War I whenever Jews were mentioned in dispatches.

5. The prolific memoir literature, which includes reminiscences about World War II published by senior officers—commanders of fronts, armies, and the like—junior officers, and even enlisted men in both the army and partisan movement. Many Jewish fighters are cited in these works, although usually only in passing and without any emphasis on their distinctly Jewish character. In an Uzbek, Ukrainian, or Tartar account, for instance, the author usually hints at the nationality of his character (when he does not note it explicitly) by describing his house, his family, the foods he likes, and similar traits that point to a specific ethnic background. But in most of the memoirs, the Jew is devoid of any ethnic characteristics, and if his name does not specifically indicate his origin, it is difficult to draw that conclusion on the basis of any other evidence.

Of course, it can be argued that Soviet Jews, particularly the young men who fought in the ranks of the Red Army or in the German rear, no longer exhibited any uniquely Jewish traits, conduct, or responses, and therefore these did not find expression in the memoirs. But it is highly doubtful that a young Jew from Moscow or Leningrad was wanting in these differentiating ethnic traits, while any Jew who had recently left his *shtetl*—and there was no lack of such Jews in the ranks of the Red Army, to say nothing of the partisan movement—

was certainly distinguished by them. It would therefore appear that avoiding identifying Jews as such stemmed primarily from writers' understanding that it was best to play down the Jews as much as possible, and, as a result, they tried to steer clear of introducing "too many" Jewish characters into their works.

Within the context of this general approach, there were, of course, different interpretations of how far one could, and should, go in making reference to Jews. And where writers left off, censors often added their personal interpretations of what was permissible in these terms. Consequently, some memoirs feature more Jewish characters and others less, but the general trend is to mute this subject, though not shun it entirely.[8]

6. Collections about Heroes of the Soviet Union . . . that were published by almost all Soviet republics, many districts, and sometimes even by subdistricts. For the most part, these works are made up of short biographies and descriptions of the subjects' feats of heroism, usually composed by journalists or writers and occasionally by professional historians. They are based mostly on archival material and documents originally published in the press, but also on conversations and interviews with the fighters themselves or members of their families. These publications include entries on outstanding Jewish soldiers who were born or lived in the area covered by the work. Explicit reference to the subject's Jewish nationality is generally made—though this principle is not necessarily observed. The aim of these pieces is threefold: to honor the fighters, pay tribute to the residents of the area for their role in the war against the Nazis, and set an example for the younger generation. They provide a relatively large amount of information on outstanding Jewish soldiers.

Yet, here, too, little attention is paid to the specific motivations of the Jewish fighter, and the portrayal of his deeds is served up in classic Soviet cliches—a mixture of grandiloquent phrases and bombastic slogans. Other than the citation of his name and nationality, the Jewish fighter is usually devoid of any real national relationship or attachment—in contrast to the fighters of other peoples whose national origins often receive special emphasis.

Thus, an analysis of the basic categories of Soviet publications on the fighting in World War II indicates a clear tendency to play down the role of the Jews in the battles against the Nazis and to deliberately ignore the phenomenon of "Jewish warfare." The natural question is to what degree this trend was part of the general approach of the Soviet historiography of World War II, which tried to deemphasize nationalist aspects, and to what degree it was a qualification applied specifically to Jews.

The approach of Soviet historiography to the national background of fighters in the Red Army and the partisan movement during World War II is marked by a striking dichotomy. Out of a desire to stress the unity of all the peoples of the Soviet Union and the burden shared equally by the country's entire population, historians and other writers fell back on such phrases as the "warfare of the Soviet people," the "fighting of the Soviet people," the "fighters of the Soviet Union," and the like. Indeed, the reply of the Defense Ministry's Institute for Research on Military History to the approach of a group of Jews in September 1976 was entirely in keeping with this spirit. In the course of preparing for a symposium on Jewish culture, Soviet-Jewish activists turned to this official institution and asked whether it engaged in research on the role of the Jewish people in the war against fascist Germany. In response to this query, Nikolai Shekhovtsov, the deputy director of the institute, told the organizing group:

> The Institute's publications bring the public information on the participation of the entire Soviet people in the Second World War without according a special role to any one people among the nationalities that populate the Soviet Union.[9]

This answer was not, in fact, incorrect, but it comprised only one facet of Soviet historiography. The other facet of that historiography, in the broadest sense of the term, was the desire to stoke the pride of the various Soviet peoples in their contribution to the war effort. In the service of this aim publications celebrating the role of the peoples of each republic, national district, and the like were produced. This division was not on a territorial, but rather on a national (ethnic) basis. One chapter of the three-volume history of Ukraine during World War II, for example, bears the title "The Contribution of the Ukrainian People to the Strengthening and Reinforcement of the Armed Forces of the Soviet Union."[10] More than a few scholarly articles were devoted to the contribution of various peoples to the war effort;[11] the roles of the Kirghiz,[12] the Belorussians,[13] the Armenians,[14] and other peoples even merited special books. The Georgian historians outdid themselves in publishing a work on the part played by the Georgian people in the liberation of Ukraine, in which a special chapter was devoted to the Georgians in the Ukrainian partisan movement and their participation in the liberation of the Crimea.[15] All these publications related to the subjects on a national, not territorial, basis. All highlighted the second facet of the Soviet historiography of World War II, which stressed the contribution of the various peoples along essentially national lines.

Publications of this kind emphasized the fighters' loyalty not only to the Soviet Union but to their national groups. Thus, for example, Ukrainian fighters are portrayed as excelling in battle in order to avenge the damage done by the Nazis to Ukrainian cultural treasures. Yet, particularist explanations of this sort are completely lacking when it came to Jewish fighters. The deemphasis of the Jewish role in the war against the Nazis is all the more conspicuous against the background of this dichotomy in the Soviet historiography. For the most part, Jewish warfare per se was disregarded altogether.

Soviet historiography was designed to serve public and educational objectives. The idea of publishing documents and articles on the service of the Jews in the Red Army during World War II was first mooted publicly by Ilya Ehrenburg at the second session of the plenum of the Jewish Anti-Fascist Committee in February 1943. Publications of this sort were conceived as a propaganda instrument against antisemitic contentions that the Jews were evading service in combat units and found themselves more comfortable positions in the rear.[16] But as early as mid-1944, the plan proved unfeasible, as we can see from Ehrenburg's remarks in his memoirs:

> In the summer [of 1944] I was asked by the Sovinformburo[17] to appeal to the Jews of America about the brutality of the Hitlerites and the need to defeat the Third Reich as quickly as possible. One of A. S. Scherbakov's aides—Kondakov—rejected my wording on the grounds that the heroic deeds of Jews, soldiers of the Red Army, must not be mentioned [because] "That is arrogance."[18]

Considering this policy, there was obviously no point in discussing the publication of a special book, in Russian, on the part played by Jews in the Red Army.

Yet despite the difficulties, Jewish public figures did their best to bring some information about the valor of the Jewish fighters at least to the attention of Jewish readers. In 1943, three pamphlets dedicated to the Jewish Heroes of the Soviet Union were published in Yiddish: one by the Russian military correspondent and later poet Semyon Gudzenko on Leyzer Papernik, who fought to the last bullet and, after running out of ammunition, blew himself up with his Nazi prisoners;[19] one by the Yiddish writer A. Khashtshevatski on Chaim Diskin, who, with a single cannon, stopped an assault of German tanks;[20] and one by R. Kovnator on Yoysef Makovski, an outstanding tankist in the war against Finland.[21] Nineteen forty-four saw the publication of a pamphlet by the Russian writer of Jewish origin V. Kaverin about the submarine captain Yisrael Fisanovich, who was awarded the Hero of the Soviet Union medal in 1944 for his deeds of valor.[22] In 1946, the Yiddish writer Shmuel Persov published a pamphlet about Moshe Khokhlov, who was awarded the Hero of the Soviet Union for his outstanding performance in the crossing of the Dnieper, and in 1947 a Yiddish translation was published of the pamphlet about David Dragunski by A. Bezymenski.[23] Just before the liquidation of all Jewish culture in the Soviet Union in 1948, a pamphlet was published by R. Kovnator about the celebrated Jewish woman pilot, Polina Gelman.[24]

These seven pamphlets were constructed along much the same lines and included a brief biography of the subject, his or her outstanding performance in combat, and the heroism for which he or she was awarded the medal of "Hero of the Soviet Union." Most of the pamphlets were written by non-Jews, and in those cases where the motives for such heroism were addressed at all, they were usually generalized in the accepted Soviet phrasing, such as in response to the Hitlerite barbarism or loyalty to the Communist Party and the Soviet Union. Some of the pamphlets are likewise peppered with popular Soviet catch phrases of the time, such as "a loyal son of the Soviet people and the Jewish people."

The pamphlets published in Yiddish and meant exclusively for Jews tried to convey the message that the Jews, too, had their war heroes, just like any other people—though these pamphlets are similarly weak in their analysis of the motives for the hero's conduct. Even so, years later, when some of these articles were published in Russian for the benefit of the non-Jewish reader, the few passages that might possibly have hinted at the special motives of the Jewish fighter were carefully expurgated.

Shmuel Persov's pamphlet on Moshe Khokhlov contains the following description of his subject's chance meeting in one of the liberated settlements:

> In one of the villages, as the mortarmen were sitting in a peasant's hut hungrily lapping up borscht, a Jew walked in. Looking around him he slowly whispered: "Are there any Jews among you?"
>
> "Members of all peoples," said Geynutdinov, and Khokhlov added, "I am a Jew."
>
> The guest was as delighted as if he had met his own son. "I am from here," he began in Yiddish. "The Jews have been living here since time immemorial, but now I am the only one left of the Jewish town. I literally escaped from the grave."
>
> "Speak so everyone can understand," one of the fighters spat.
>
> Khokhlov briefly reported what the Jew had said, and Yefim Ivanov added: "So why are you standing? Sit down and use my spoon." Geynutdinov pushed a piece of bread toward the Jew and then the bowl of borscht. As the Jew ate the borscht, tears fell from his eyes and dripped onto his beard. Wiping them away with his hand, like a child, he addressed Khokhlov again:
>
> "Where are you from and what is your name?"
>
> "My name is Khokhlov."
>
> "A Jew, and your name is Khokhlov?"
>
> "Yes, yes," Khokhlov said defensively. "I am from Dubrovna."
>
> "Yes, Dubrovna," the Jew turned and lapsed back into Yiddish. "They used to make wonderful *taleisim* there."
>
> Before leaving, the Jew shook hands with each of the fighters.
>
> "Don't forget, my son, make them pay for the innocent blood that has been shed. . . . "[25]

This passage, which may have intimated the special feeling of the Jewish fighter, was omitted from the Russian translation published in 1959. Yet this tendency to edit the Jewish aspect out of the Russian translation, was not a phemonenon of the late 1950s and thereafter, but was already widespread in the 1940s.

Three books that hold a special place in Soviet-Jewish historiography belong by definition to the realm of Jewish warfare: Avraham Sutzkever's book on the Vilna ghetto, which devotes an entire chapter to the fighting in the ghetto and the forests; M. Yellin and D. Galpern's book on the partisans from the Kovno ghetto; and H. Smolar's book on the Minsk ghetto, in which many sections describe the resistance in the ghetto and within the ranks of the partisan movement.[26]

In 1947, Smolar's book was published in Russian translation under the title *Avengers of the Ghetto*.[27] A cursory comparison of the two editions is sufficient to show that passages were deleted and cuts were made in the Russian edition—some stemmed from the translation itself, but others were deliberate. Thus, for example, the Yiddish text notes that, with the approval of the partisans, the Underground in the ghetto decided to establish independent units—Jewish units—but in the Russian edition the words referring explicitly to the Jewish units have been omitted, and all that remains is a vague reference to independent units.[28] In another place the author speaks of the attempt to establish a joint partisan unit of forty armed fighters from the ghetto and thirty railroad workers. But there was a hitch in the course of founding the unit, and the Belorussians returned to the city. "But what would the Jews do?" the author asks, stressing the fact that they did not have the option of returning to the ghetto.[29] That is how the author implied the special circumstances in which the Jewish fighter, as distinguished from his Belorussian comrades, lived and operated. But this implication was deleted from the Russian edition, so that the accent on the uniqueness of Jewish warfare was blunted. In another place Smolar quotes a commander of the Soviet partisan unit as saying, "The Jews of the ghetto are now the ones in my unit who excel in their bravery in battle,"[30] but these words were deleted from the Russian translation for fear that they would be taken by the non-Jewish reader as "Jewish arrogance."

Examples of such differences between the Yiddish and Russian versions of Smolar's book signify that, as early as the 1940s, there was a tendency to soft-pedal certain aspects of Jewish warfare, particularly in publications that were also destined for a non-Jewish readership. This policy was followed scrupulously in the last book on the subject of Jewish fighting against the Nazis (published in Russian just prior to the liquidation of the Jewish Anti-Fascist Committee): *The Partisan Brotherhood: Reminiscences of the Combat Activities of the Jewish Partisans of the Great Patriotic War*.[31] Most of the pieces in the collection were penned by non-Jews, and in no case are special motives ascribed to the Jewish partisans. On the contrary, emphasis is placed upon the sense of brotherhood that was achieved between the Jewish and non-Jewish fighters in the partisan units. Yet, despite the limitations and constraints reflected in this work, it was an expression of the desire to prove that Jews, too, fought in the war—at least to the same degree as the members of the other Soviet peoples—and may have served as a rebuttal to the many antisemitic contentions to the contrary. But even this Soviet-Jewish historiography—poor in content, limited in quantity, and pale in its Jewish character though it was—ceased to appear after the liquidation of Jewish culture in the Soviet Union at the end of 1948.

Nevertheless, the discounting of Jewish warfare continued to trouble many Jews in the Soviet Union, particularly in light of the relentless claims that the Jews had evaded service during the war. Some sought an answer to their sense of distress, and among the outlets we can cite the article by Yaakov Kantor published in the Warsaw Yiddish paper *Folks-Shtime* and the piece by A. Pribluda and Y. Bergman published in *Sovietish heymland*, which is virtually brimming with Jewish Heroes of the Soviet Union.[32]

The emotional need to prove to non-Jews—and perhaps first and foremost to the Jews of the Soviet Union themselves—that the Jews played just as great, and perhaps an even greater, role in the war against the Nazis as all other Soviet peoples was also evident among Jewish-nationalist circles in the Soviet Union. It is therefore not surprising that the quasi-legal Jewish publications (the *samizdat*) devote considerable space to the role played by the Jews in the Red Army during World War II.[33] The overwhelming majority of material on this subject in Jewish *samizdat* comes from Soviet publications and therefore bears the stamp of their classic spirit and style. Comprising articles from official Jewish sources such as *Sovietish heymland*, these works were designed to commemorate and highlight the role of the Jews in combat as a response to the downgrading of this subject in the official Soviet historiography. They cannot, however, be counted as analytical works of scholarship.

It is therefore possible to say that the Soviet-Jewish historiography on the subject of Jewish warfare never advanced beyond the incipient stage, even within the framework of general Soviet historiography. The first manifestations of writing on the subject were immediately nipped in the bud with the liquidation of Jewish culture. What remained intact was an enormous need in the Jewish community to know more about the subject, especially in light of the many Soviet publications extolling heroism during the war that deliberately play down the Jewish factor.

The earliest historiography on Jewish warfare in the Soviet Union published in the West—and this is particularly true of the writing on the partisan units in the annexed territories—is credited to combatants who had recently laid down their arms. Their writing was based on personal experience and random testimonies and is certainly not free of political coloration. The most outstanding effort in this genre is Moshe Kaganovich's book *The Participation of the Jews in the Partisan Movement of the Soviet Union*, published in Rome in 1948 by the Historical Committee of the Union of Jewish Partisans. For purely political reasons, the author included a quote from an order supposedly issued by the president of the Soviet Union stating, *inter alia*, that:

> Because the enemy is behaving savagely and brutally and is totally liquidating the Soviet citizens of Jewish nationality, I hereby order that they are to receive priority in evacuation to the distant regions of the Soviet Union.[34]

This order, which—his quote notwithstanding—the author never actually saw (as he himself testified in later editions of the book),[35] was almost certainly a figment of the mood of the period and underscores the caution that historians must observe in relying on material of this kind.

A generation was to pass before a scholarly historiography on this subject began to crystallize in the West, yet here, too, it dealt mostly with the territories that had been annexed to the Soviet Union during the war. The Jewish communities in these territories more closely resembled their counterparts in Poland and Romania than traditional Soviet Jewry. To a large extent, Jewish political movements and organizations survived there despite the fact that they had been formally disbanded during the brief period of Soviet rule. Moreover, the independent scholar had access to a relatively large body of material on the Jewish fighters in these territories, in contrast to the areas which had been part of the Soviet Union longer.

It is therefore not surprising that the earliest research on Jewish warfare and the participation of Jews in combat in the Soviet Union focused on these annexed territories. Worthy of mention in this context is Dov Levin's work on the Jews of the Baltic countries,[36] Yitzhak Arad's work on the Jews of Vilna,[37] Shalom Cholawski's work on the Jews of western Belorussia,[38] and Shmuel Spector's on the Jewish community in Volhynia.[39] In all of these studies, the authors address the focal subject of Jewish warfare and combat by examining the features unique to each area. Their research is based on a large and varied corpus of material, which they have tried to corroborate and analyze by using the finest tools of critical research. It can therefore be said that at least insofar as many sectors of the territories annexed to the Soviet Union are concerned, there is a body of historical writing on the role played by the Jews in the war against the Nazis. The same cannot be said regarding the Jews of the Soviet Union in its prewar borders.

Considering the paucity of material at the writer's disposal, many scholars were loath to approach this subject. The first to rise to the challenge was Yosef Guri, who made a serious and systematic attempt to summarize the information about the Jews who were awarded the medal of Hero of the Soviet Union and Jews in high positions of command. He was followed by Dov Levin, who engaged in an even deeper analysis of the data collected by Guri.[40]

The wave of immigration to Israel from the Soviet Union in the 1970s prompted a revival of interest in the participation of Soviet Jews in the fighting against the Nazis. It is thanks to this interest that we have been rewarded with two very detailed, thick tomes about Jews in the Red Army. One is Gershon Shapiro's book *Under Fire: Stories of Jewish Heroes of the Soviet Union*;[41] the other is Aharon Abramovich's work *The Decisive Battle: The Participation and Role of the Jews of the Soviet Union in the War against Nazism.*[42]

Both works serve the dual aim of commemoration and education. But other than their common objectives, they are distinctly different in structure and content. Shapiro's book is a collection of pieces culled from Soviet sources on Jews who were awarded the medal of Hero of the Soviet Union (some of these had previously appeared in quasi-legal publications in the Soviet Union). From many standpoints these articles hardly differ from the style of writing common in the Soviet Union. The book discusses the Jews who distinguished themselves in battle, but the author is not always successful in capturing the element of Jewish warfare, even when intimations to that effect could be perceived in the Soviet publications on which he based himself. These failings notwithstanding, the collection is a noteworthy contribution to the subject by virtue of its concentration of the material.

Abramovich's book, which is the initial volume of a larger publication, is the first attempt to draw a comprehensive picture of the role played by Jews in the Red Army. The author has invested tireless effort in poring over dozens of memoirs and hundreds of articles that appeared in the Soviet Union, as well as in collecting every piece of information on the distinguished conduct of Jews in battle. He has brought together information about the Jews in the broader framework of the fighting on the various fronts during different stages of the war. Abramovich has made every effort to identify names of Jews and to be meticulous about military details and factual circumstances. His book cites hundreds of acts of valor by Jewish fighters and the names of hundreds of Jews who were scattered throughout the length and breadth of the rapidly shifting front. That his sources were primarily Soviet has left its mark on the book's style and limitations. But despite its shortcomings, this work certainly serves as an impetus to further research.

From a review of the Soviet, Soviet-Jewish, and extra-Soviet historiography, it emerges that the matter of Jewish warfare in the Soviet Union during the war against the Nazis has still not been the object of thorough—to say nothing of exhaustive—research. Most of the works published to date tackle the subject of Jews in combat in one way or another, meaning a description of Jewish participation in the fighting in some sector of the struggle against the Nazis. But the cardinal question of whether and to what degree this fighting stemmed from specifically Jewish conditions, factors, and motives—or, phrased differently, whether and to what degree this was "Jewish warfare"—remains open, awaiting the kind of scholarly inquiry that will exploit not only the Soviet publications but also the thousands of witnesses who may well shed new light on the full array of issues.

Notes

An earlier version of this essay was published in Yisrael Gutman and Gideon Greif, eds., *The Historiography of the Holocaust Period: Proceedings of the Fifth Yad Vashem International Historical Conference* (Jerusalem: Yad Vashem, 1988).

1. *Eynikayt*, May 1, 1946. I. Davidovitsh, "Baym keyver fun undzer folks held" ("At the Grave of our National Hero"), *Folks-Shtime*, December 13, 1959. M Bruzh, "25 Yor nokh der bafrayung fun Vaysrusland" (Twenty-Five Years after the Liberation of Belorussia), ibid., September 13, 1969.

2. *Sovetskaia istoricheskaia entsiklopediia*, vol. 6, Moscow, 1965, p. 476.
3. *Sovetskii tyl v velikoi otechestvennoi voine* (The Soviet Rear in the Great Patriotic War), vol. 1, Moscow, 1974, p 190.
4. See, for example, *Kommunisticheskaia partiia v velikoi otechestvennoi voine* (The Communist Party in the Great Patriotic War), Moscow, 1970.
5. *Vsenarodnoe partizanskoe dvizhenie v Belorussii v gody velikoi otechestvennoi voiny* (The Popular Partisan Movement in Belorussia during the Great Patriotic War), Minsk, 1967–1982.
6. Ibid., vol. 2, book one, p. 456.
7. *Ukrainska Rsr u velikii vinchiznianii viini Radians'kogo Soiuzu 1941–1945rr* (Ukraine in the Great Patriotic War), vol. 1, Kiev, 1967, p. 64.
8. We are able to apprehend the personal influence of the writer on the degree to which Jews are mentioned in memoirs from a comparison of I. Satsunkevich's book with V. Agadzhanian's book.The former concentrates on the area of Minsk; the latter on the vicinity of Mogilev. While Satsunkevich's book almost totally ignores the role played by the Jews, Agadzhanian's work does make reference to it. I. Satsunkevich, *Surovaia byl'* (A Difficult Story), Minsk, 1969; V. Agadzhanian, *Dorogi partizanski* (The Ways of the Partisans), Minsk, 1979. Worthy of note is A. Okorokov's memoir, in which he pays affectionate tribute to many Jewish fighters: A. Okorokov, *Slovo vedushchee v boi* (A Word that Leads to Battle), Moscow, 1980.
9. *Evreiskii samizdat,* vol. 15, Jerusalem, 1978, p. 36.
10. See note 7 above, pp. 95–105.
11. See, for example, Ia. Pavlav, "Pomoshch Belorusskogo naroda frontu, letom, 1941" (The Support Given by the Belorussian Nation to the Front, Summer 1941), *Vestnik An BSSR*, no. 5, 1970, pp. 114–23.
12. A. Kazanskii, *Kirgizskii narod v velikoi otechestvennoi voine Sovetskogo Soiuza, 1941–1945* (The Khirgizian People in the Great Patriotic War), Frunze, 1954.
13. I. Kravchenko, A. Zalesskii, *Belorusskii narod v gody velikoi otechestvennoi voiny* (The Belorussian People during the Great Patriotic War), Minsk, 1959.
14. A. Mnatskanian, *Armianskii narod v velikoi otechestvennoi voine 1941–1945* (The Armenian People during the Great Patriotic War), Erevan, 1954.
15. I. Babalishvili, *Voiny-gruziny v boiakh za Ukrainu v gody velikoi otechestvennoi voiny* (Georgian Fighters in the Battles for Ukraine during the Great Patriotic War), Tbilisi, 1969.
16. "Tsveyter plenum fun Yidishn antifashistishn komitet in FSSR" (The Second Plenum of the Jewish Anti-Fascist Committee of the USSR), *Eynikayt*, March 15, 1943.
17. The Soviet Information Office, established at the start of the war handled the distribution of official information on the war activities and the organization of all propaganda within and beyond the borders of the Soviet Union. The office was evidently disbanded in 1948.
18. I. Ehrenburg, "Liudi, gody, zhizn" (People, Years, Life), *Sobranie sochinenii*, vol. 9, Moscow, pp. 376–77.

19. S. Gudzenko, *Held fun Sovetnfarband—Leyzer Papernik* (Leyzer Papernik, Hero of the Soviet Union), Moscow, 1943.
20. M. Khashtshevatski, *Khaim Diskin—der held fun Sovetnfarband* (Khaim Diskin, Hero of the Soviet Union), Moscow, 1941.
21. R. Kovnator, *Der held fun Sovetnfarband—Yosef Makovski* (Yosef Makovski, Hero of the Soviet Union), Moscow, 1943.
22. V. Kaverin, *Der held fun Sovetnfarband—Israel Fisanovitsh* (Israel Fisanovitsh, Hero of the Soviet Union), Moscow, 1944.
23. Sh. Persov, *Moshe Khakhlov—Der held fun Sovetnfarband* (Moshe Khakhlov, Hero of the Soviet Union), Moscow, 1946. A. Bezimenski, *David Dragunsky*, Moscow, 1947.
24. R. Kovnator, *Held fun Sovetnfarband—Polina Gelman* (Polina Gelman, Hero of the Soviet Union), Moscow, 1948.
25. See Persov, op. cit., pp. 21–23, and cf. S. Persov, *Ocherki o geroiakh* (Vignettes of Heroes), Moscow, 1959.
26. A. Sutskever, *Fun Vilner geto* (From the Vilna Ghetto), Moscow, 1946. M. Ielin, D. Gelpern, *Partizaner fun Kaunaser geto* (Partisans from the Kovno Ghetto), Moscow, 1948. H. Smoliar, *Fun Minsker geto* (From the Minsk Ghetto), Moscow, 1946.
27. H. Smolar, *Mstiteli Getta* (Avengers of the Ghetto), Moscow, 1947.
28. Cf. p. 73 of the Yiddish version, p. 56 of the Russian translation.
29. Yiddish original, p. 73.
30. Ibid., p. 119
31. *Partizanskaia druzhba; vospominaniia o boevykh delakh partizan evreev uchastnikov velikoi otechestvennoi voiny* (The Partisan Brotherhood: Reminiscences of the Combat Activities of the Jewish Partisans of the Great Patriotic War), Moscow, 1948. A Hebrew translation with slight cuts is found in B. West, ed., *Hem hayu rabim* (They Were Many), Tel Aviv, 1968.
32. Y. Kantor, "Yidn oyf dem grestn un vikhtikstn front" (Jews on the Greatest and Most Important Front), *Folks-Shtime*, April 18, 1963; see also idem., "Zay zaynen der shtoltz fun undzer folk" (They Are the Pride of Our People), ibid., May 5–6, 1965; "Undzer haymland hot zay g'kroynt mit rum" (Our Fatherland Crowned Them with Glory), *Sovietish heymland*, vol. 5, 1970, pp. 43–47. See also ibid., vol. 8, p.40.
33. The publications of the Jewish *samizdat* in the Soviet Union were copied and published in Israel and included the following items: "Evrei v voine protiv Hitlerovskoi Germanii" (Jews in the War against Hitler's Germany), *Evreiskii samizdat*, vol. 9, Jerusalem, 1975; G. Shapiro, "Ocherki o Evreiakh-geroiakh Sovetskogo Soiuza" (Vignettes of Jewish Heroes of the Soviet Union), ibid., vol. 14, 1989; V. Vagner, "Evrei v voine, 1941–1945 GG" (Jews in the War, 1941–1945), ibid., vol. 18; "Evrei na Maloi Zemle," ibid., vol. 19, 1979.
34. M. Kaganovich, *Der Yidisher ontayl in der partizaner bevegung fun Sovet-Rusland* (The Participation of Jews in the Partisan Movement in the Soviet Union), 1948, p. 188.
35. Solomon Schwarz called the existence of such an order into question as far back

as 1951 (Solomon M. Schwarz, *The Jews in the Soviet Union*, Syracuse, 1951, p. 221). In an expanded edition of his book, published in Tel Aviv, in 1954, Kaganovich writes: "According to the testimony of Jews who were in Russia at the outbreak of the war, toward the end of 1941 the presidency of the Supreme Soviet issued an order regarding the preferential evacuation of the Jewish population from areas where it was endangered by the German invasion. According to these witnesses, the local authorities were ordered to provide special means of transport toward this end. However, no document has ever been found corroborating this evidence" (Moshe Kaganovich, *The War of the Jewish Partisans in Eastern Europe,* Tel Aviv, 1954, p. 202). The author repeats this exact wording in his Yiddish book, published in Buenos Aires in 1956 (vol. 1, p. 370).

36. Zvi A. Baron and Dov Levin, *The History of an Underground: The Fighting Organization of the Jews of Kovno in the Second World War*, Jerusalem, 1962; Dov Levin, *Fighting and Defending Themselves! The War of Lithuanian Jewry against the Nazis, 1941–1945*, Jerusalem, 1975; idem., *With Their Backs to the Wall: The Fight of the Jews of Latvia against the Nazis, 1941–1945*, Jerusalem, 1978.

37. Yitzhak Arad, *Ghetto in Flames, The Struggle and Destruction of the Jews of Vilna in the Holocaust*, Jerusalem, 1980.

38. Shalom Cholawski, *On the Neman and Dnieper Rivers: The Jews of Western Belorussia in the Second World War*, Jerusalem, 1982.

39. Shmuel Spector, *The Holocaust of the Jews of Volhynia, 1941–1944*, Jerusalem, 1982 (doctoral dissertation), pp. 229–317.

40. Y. Guri, "The Jews in the Red Army in the Second World War"; Y. Slutzki and M. Kaplan, eds., *Jewish Soldiers in the Armies of Europe*, Tel Aviv, 1967, pp. 135–48; Guri, "The Jews of the Soviet Union in the War against Nazi Germany" in M. Mushkat, ed., *Jewish Fighters in the War against the Nazis*, Tel Aviv, 1971, pp. 20–75; Dov Levin, "Facts and Evaluations about the Jews in the Red Army during the Second World War," *Masuah*, vol. 10, 1982, pp. 79–105.

41. G. Shapiro. *Under Fire: Stories of Jewish Heroes of the Soviet Union,* Jerusalem, 1988.

42. A. Abramovich, *V reshaiushchei voine*, (In the Decisive War), Tel Aviv, 1982.

ELEVEN

Jewish-Lithuanian Relations during World War II: History and Rhetoric

Sara Shner-Neshamit

On the night of June 22/23, 1941, German planes bombed the cities of Lithuania. At 11:30 AM on the first day of the war, Radio Kaunas announced the Lithuanian revolt and the formation of a temporary government headed by J. Ambrazevicius, a member of the Christian-Democratic party. The Soviet government and its institutions were replaced, and along the joint Lithuanian-German border crowds of Lithuanians welcomed the invading Wehrmacht with bouquets of flowers.

While the Red Army soldiers were still retreating eastward along the roads of Lithuania, men with white armbands could already be spotted on the streets. These Lithuanians were the "partisans" who had revolted against Soviet rule. In the first days of the occupation, before the German Wehrmacht completed its takeover of Lithuania, the country was in the hands of "The Activists' Front of Lithuania"[1] and its murderous gangs. Jewish lives and property were at their mercy.

The Germans entered Kaunas on June 24; that very night a mass slaughter of Jews took place in the suburb of Slobodka (Viliampole). According to the report of Nazi General Franz Stahlecker, commander of *Einsatzgruppe* A, in Kaunas alone, 1,500 Jews were murdered that first night, and in the course of the following nights an additional 2,300 people were killed.[2] The Lithuanians grabbed Jews off the streets, broke into their homes, and slaughtered them with knives and axes.

The "partisans" arrested masses of Jews and incarcerated them in Fort VII, one of the fortresses on the outskirts of Kaunas dating from the tsarist period.

Seven thousand people, among them women and children, were imprisoned in the fortress, and much has been written about the tortures and brutalities that they suffered.

The news from the villages was also hair-raising: stories of the physical and mental torture of community leaders and brutalization of rabbis and the Jewish intelligentsia were common. In *The Destruction of Lithuania*, Rabbi Ephraim Oshry, the rabbi of the remnant of Lithuanian Jewry after the war, describes the events based on the oral testimony of eyewitnesses who survived these murders:

> In the town of Butrimonys, which is close to Kaunas, the commander of the Lithuanian police brought the Jewish doctor and his wife to the village and there ordered that they be sealed in with bricks while they were still alive. The wife went crazy; the doctor managed to escape.[3]
>
> In the town of Gargzdai, the men were murdered, and afterwards the women and children were led to the graves of their loved ones and were commanded to dance on them.[4] In Ukmerge, immediately upon the arrival of the Germans, they arrested the rabbi of the city, Zusmanovitz, the doctor, Karlinski, and the Jewish lawyers. They severely tortured the teachers from the gymnasium and other community leaders. They stuck rubber pipes down their throats and turned on the water until their bodies burst.
>
> They took the rabbi, Dr. Karlinski, and other community notables to the village of Pivonya, locked them up in a furnace and burned them alive.[5]
>
> In Kaunas, the Lithuanians murdered dozens of Jews with metal rods, while the Germans looked on.[6]
>
> On June 28, in the courtyard of an agricultural-machine cooperative in Kaunas, the Lithuanians taunted their Jewish victims. They stuck air pumps into the throats of sixty Jews and pumped water into them until their innards burst. Those who remained alive were then killed with billy clubs and iron bars.[7] In Panevezys in September 1941, the "partisans" caught sixty Jews and ordered them to drag barrels of oil, each weighing 200 kilograms. Whoever collapsed under his burden was murdered. Afterwards the Lithuanian superintendent, V. Andziulis, turned to them and said: "For your good work you will now have a hot shower, and afterwards you can cool yourselves off." The Jews who survived the first brutality were taken to a cement factory with large pits of unslaked lime. The murderers ordered them to fill the pits with water, and when it began to boil they threw the unfortunate Jews in. The Jews had to keep afloat in the pits so as not to be sucked into the lime. The few who survived were returned to the ghetto.[8]

It is impossible to record all that the Lithuanians did to the Jews on their own initiative, without any orders from the Germans. Why did this people, with whom the Jews had lived on relatively good terms for hundreds of years, exhibit such cruelty?

There was a definite political motive. The Lithuanians believed that the Germans would help them overthrow Soviet rule and reestablish Lithuania's independence. By murdering the Jews, the Lithuanians wanted to prove their loyalty and dedication to their new masters and thereby help gain their own political independence. There were also Lithuanians who explained their cruel attitude to the Jews as a desire to avenge the "Jews' sell-out of Lithuania to the Bolsheviks," or because "they had helped exile the Lithuanians to Siberia."

Concerning their relationship to the Jews after the overthrow of the Soviet regime, a leaflet was published by the "activists" on March 19, 1941—well before the German conquest. It stated:

> . . . The hour of Lithuania's liberation is near. . . . You will be notified of this immediately by radio or some other means. . . . You must take over the government. . . . You must arrest all local Communists and all other traitors in Lithuania. We will pardon the traitors only if they actually prove that they have killed at least one Jew. You must already notify the Jews that their fate is sealed.[9]

During the first days of the slaughter of the Jews in Kaunas representatives of the Jewish community turned to Lithuanian leaders and the heads of the Catholic Church and requested that they appeal to their people to stop the wanton murder. Bishop Vincentas Brizgys, acting head of the Catholic Church, replied that he could do nothing but pray.

The chairman of the Organization of Jewish Fighters in the Lithuanian War of Independence, attorney Yaakov Goldenberg, and other representatives turned for help to J. Vileisis, who had been mayor of Kaunas for several years and was considered an enlightened man. But Vileisis answered, "What's the outcry? Our young men will run wild a little and [then] will stop!"[10] Only three people tried to protest and say something in defense of the Jews, and only a few were actually active in saving Jewish acquaintances.[11]

Lithuanians in the Service of the German Military and Police

The Lithuanians hoped that they would be allowed to establish a Lithuanian army and that the "partisans" would form the nucleus of this national army. But the Germans were interested only in exploiting the Lithuanian forces for their own needs. On June 26, the Germans disarmed the "partisans" and began organizing new police and army units, which were called "Battalions for the National Preservation of Work."

Additional units were established with different names, for example, "The Lithuanian Regiment." At first, these armed Lithuanians were assigned guard duty at military installations, on the city streets, and in prisoner-of-war camps.

In Vilna, three battalions of "Service for the Rehabilitation of Vilna" were organized. "Police Punishment Units" were established for "special duties," i.e., murder. Later military-police formations (called *Lietuviu savisaugos batalionai*) also operated.[12]

In the different military units, there were soldiers and officers from the 29th Corps of the former Lithuanian army, as well as from the army marksmen troops (*Sauliu pulkai*). Many members of the old military, nationalistic organization that dated to the days of Lithuania's War of Independence—*Sauliu Sajunga*—also volunteered.[13] The officers were former Lithuanian military and police officers, but the high command remained in German hands. Changes in these units continued over a long period of time, and the various names by which these police/army units were called have caused quite a few headaches for historians. It is difficult to establish how many Lithuanians participated in the murder of Jews, as the perpetrators were not only members of these police/army organizations, but also included many nonorganized civilians.

At first, the partisans numbered 100,000 men.[14] By the end of June 1941, when the Germans spread them out and set up dozens of different armed units under the general name of *Litauische Schutzmannscharteinheiten* (Lithuanian Guard Units), their numbers dropped to 16,000. But this fluctuated throughout this period.

A German document from August 1942 notes that in the police battalions that operated outside the Lithuanian borders there were 341 officers, 1,872 junior officers, and 6,275 privates; a total of 8,388 men.[15] An SD report of May 13, 1942 (*Lagebericht*), stated that the Lithuanians had established seventeen battalions (*Bataillone Schutzmannschaften*) that remained in Lithuania and six or seven battalions outside the borders: the Second Battalion that operated in the Minsk area; one in the south of Lake Ilmensee and one to the east of Velikiye Luki, which was partially destroyed. In March a battalion was sent to Dno, and two or three battalions operated in Belorussia and in the General Government (Poland).[16] In August 1942, there were twenty police battalions, of which seven were sent abroad from Lithuania. Their murderous rampages covered Warsaw and the Belorussian, Russian, and Ukrainian cities of Baranovich, Minsk, Stalino, Pskov, Dedovitchi, Korosten, Kirovograd, Slutsk, and many other places.[17]

The military units were assigned guard duty in the ghettos as well as during *Aktionen* against the Jews. They participated in the large deportation from the Warsaw ghetto to Treblinka in July-September 1942, and escorted the transports to the extermination camp. They were coopted in the fighting against Soviet partisans and were employed in the extermination camp Majdanek near Lublin, Poland. At times they were even more cruel in their behavior than the Germans.[18]

Carl, the German commander of the city of Slutsk, requested of his superior that he redeploy the soldiers of the Lithuanian battalion, who, in an *Aktion* against the Jews of Slutsk on October 27, 1941, behaved with uncontrolled cruelty in front of the Belorussian residents of the city. They had fired indiscriminately and had killed Christians who happened to be present. Carl claimed that the Lithuanians' actions stained the name of Germany(!) and that he was forced to imprison two Lithuanians who, in the midst of the *Aktion*, had engaged in pillage.[19]

Those serving in the Lithuanian battalions were volunteers. They enjoyed special privileges and higher salaries. Land that had been nationalized by the Soviet government was returned to the sons of affluent farmers. There were also draftees who tried in this way to escape from the refugee camps, where conditions were difficult. The fighters in these units published newspapers that called on the Lithuanians to "liberate Europe from the Jews, from world democracy and from the worst enemy of all—Bolshevism." These volunteers took bribes, stole outright, and beat and tortured the Jews of the ghetto when they went to and from forced labor. In the Ninth Fort in Kaunas, they murdered not only Lithuanian Jews but also thousands of Jews who were brought there from France, Czechoslovakia, and other countries.[20]

Disappointment in the Germans and the Change in Attitude to the Jews

The Germans had never considered granting Lithuania her independence. They had never even given an explicit promise. The Germans dispersed the temporary Lithuanian government, drafted Lithuanians to work in the Reich and, for the most part, did not return the land appropriated by the Soviet government, but handed it over to the German inhabitants.[21] Nevertheless, the Lithuanian battalions served the Germans as hangmen and executioners in the conquered East European countries.

In 1942, the first signs of disillusionment began to appear among the Lithuanians, as they realized they had been tricked. In 1943, particularly after the German defeat in Stalingrad, the Lithuanians came to the conclusion that the time had come to settle accounts with the Germans. In the same year, the Lithuanian insurgence began to develop. Youths refused to be drafted into the Lithuanian army unit that was established to fight for Germany. Community leaders, including the heads of the Catholic Church, who, in 1941–42, had willingly cooperated with the Nazi conqueror and even went so far as to pardon the sins of the Lithuanian battalions as they left on their murderous operations, now began to seek alibis for themselves.[22]

There was also a certain newfound willingness to help the Jews. Indeed, more and more Jews could find shelter on estates whose owners had previously rejoiced at the Jews' misfortune. In the villages, more aid was extended to Jewish acquaintances, albeit usually in exchange for payment. There were also Righteous Gentiles who saved people without remuneration, even to the point of endangering their own lives. Several hundred Jewish children were hidden with the help of priests, although frequently with the intention to convert them.[23]

The Emigres

With the retreat of the German army beyond Lithuania's borders, many Lithuanians who had murdered Jews escaped. Other Lithuanians simply feared Soviet rule, for example, members of the former ruling class, high government officials, officers in the independent Lithuanian army, as well as clergymen. For a certain time they lived in the refugee camps in Germany and from there emigrated to the United States and Canada.[24]

Those who had cooperated with the Germans covered up their pro-Nazi past and became citizens of their new countries of residence. They established social and cultural organizations and founded a flourishing Lithuanian press. The Lithuanian emigrants did not reconcile themselves to Lithuania's Sovietization and, together with Latvians and Estonians, lobbied at the UN for their political independence.[25]

Historiography in Soviet Lithuania

We will not analyze the publications on the partisan movement in Lithuania and the role the Lithuanians played in the ranks of the army, but we will survey the important publications that dealt with the fate of the Jews in occupied Lithuania. From 1960 to 1963, the State Scientific Publishing House published a series of pamphlets under the inclusive name "The Facts Accuse" (*Faktai Kaltina*), containing the testimonies and documents on the annihilation of the Jews and Communists.[26]

Footsteps of Death Near Ponevezh[27] is a collection of testimonies on the murder and torture of Communists and Jews in the city and district of Ponevezh during the occupation and the first year after the expulsion of the German army. Many of those who cooperated with the Germans or served as soldiers in the murdering military units escaped after the war to forests or hid in villages. There they were involved in terrorism and the murder of activists in the reconstructed Soviet government. They murdered Jews who had returned to their villages in order to retrieve some of their property or to look for relatives. They also murdered Lithuanians who had saved Jews. Some of their compatriots who had escaped with the conquering army to Germany now infiltrated back to Lithuania and joined them.

We Will Not Forget[28] is a collection of the crimes of the Lithuanian nationalists in the district of Mazeikiai. *Nazi Murderers in Kretinga*[29] deals with the murder of Jews and Lithuanians, opponents of the government, in the city of Kretinga. *The Bloody Soil of Dzukya*[30] is a pamphlet on the murders in the district of Alitous in 1961. *In the Service of the SS*[31] is a collection of testimonies and documents of the crimes perpetrated by the Lithuanian military units compiled from the archives of the Lithuanian Academy of Sciences.

The most important of these publications—which includes German and Lithuanian documents on the murder and torture of Jews and the names of the murdered and murderers, as well as of the high-ranking Lithuanian officials and Lithuanian officers who cooperated with the German invaders—is *Mass Murders in Lithuania*, which appeared in two volumes.[32] A similar volume also appeared in English.[33] In 1966, a collection of articles, *The Nazi Occupation of Lithuania*,[34] was published in Russian, and in it is a long article on the annihilation of the Jews in Lithuania, including photographs.

In 1966, Meir Yellin's book, *The Fortresses of Death*[35] was published on the fortresses of death surrounding Kaunas, in which the Jews of the city, as well as Jews brought from Western Europe and Soviet prisoners of war, were murdered. Additional pamphlets were published on the Ninth Fort by O. Kaplan (Vilna, 1962) and Z. Kondratas (Vilna, 1961). These books were also published in Russian, English, and German.[36] The author of the pamphlet *Facing Death*[37] tells about his experiences in the Ninth Fort and his escape to the partisans. The Russian author, a Lithuanian citizen, was forced as a prisoner to chop wood for the pyres on which the victims' bodies were burned; after his escape, he was a partisan in a Lithuanian-Russian unit.

In 1970, *The Nationalists' Aid to the Nazis* was published. Its subject is the Lithuanian volunteers who collaborated with the Germans. This collection of documents was published by the National Academy of Sciences.[38]

One of the most shocking pieces was published in Vilna in 1977—*What Are the Pines Whispering in Ponar?*[39] It is a diary of a Polish journalist, Witold Sokovsky, in which he describes the murder of the Jews of Vilna. Sokovsky lived in the village of Ponar and witnessed the murders, as he was stationed at the roadblock that led to the murder site. Sokovsky recorded what he saw and heard and kept his diary buried in the ground. The last entry is dated November 4, 1943: "I am afraid to follow what is being done, lest they suspect me. Lately, they have already begun to send glances in my direction." Possibly this was the last day of the diarist's life, because he, too, was murdered. The diary was discovered years later when a tractor plowed up the area; more years passed until the diary's author was identified.

In a historical yearbook of 1975, an article was published on the Lithuanian Jews in the concentration camps.[40] The author tells of two transports to Auschwitz: on September 23, 1943, from the Vilna ghetto, and a Jewish children's transport from the Kaunas ghetto on March 27, 1944. An extraordinary episode is the escape of the Jew Yudl Vinovsky from Auschwitz on September 20, 1943.

Jews were transferred to Stutthoff in March and April 1944 from the Kaunas, Vilnius, and Shavli (Siauliai, Shavel) ghettos. On June 19, 1944, 4,000 additional Jews arrived (it does not say from where); in the summer of 1944, Jews were again brought from Lithuania and Latvia. The author does not tell about the fate of the Stutthof Jews, about the ship that sank in the Baltic sea, nor about the unique fate of the Vilna, Kaunas, and Shavli women.

Regarding Dachau, on March 26, Jewish children and old people unfit to work were brought there from the Kaunas ghetto. On the transport of July 6, 1944, in which 4,000 Jews were brought from concentration camps in Poland, there were also Jews from Lithuania. On July 6, 1944, when the evacuation of the Kaunas ghetto began, 600 to 700 people were brought there. On the transport of August 13, 1944, out of 1,000 people transported from Kaunas, 500 were children aged five to twelve.

Jews were sent from Lithuania to the ghetto in Riga and to concentration camps in Latvia and Estonia. In June 1944, while retreating, the Germans took approximately 4,000 Lithuanian Jews from concentration camps in Estonia to camps in Germany.

Although the statistics on the dispatch of Lithuanian Jews to the various camps are not completely accurate, they are valuable in the sense that they give a general picture of the annihilation of the Lithuanian Jews—in contrast to the few Lithuanians who were sent to the German concentration camps—a picture that stands in total contradiction to the Lithuanians' many claims about the Lithuanian people's suffering during the German occupation.

We value the contribution of these Soviet publications, as similar documents are not usually available in other countries in which the population and authorities played a significant role in the extradition of the Jews to the Germans. But we must also point to several errors.

Soviet historiography concentrated on the members of the nationalist bourgeoisie as though only they cooperated with the German conquerors. In fact, the nationalist bourgeoisie were not the only guilty ones: political leaders, former officers of the Lithuanian army who, with Sovietization lost their economic and political positions, their well-paying employment, and even their property, were the ones who organized the destruction and led its implementation.

The actual murderers—those who grabbed Jews on the street, tortured, and murdered them, who dragged Communists and members of the former Soviet government from their houses, imprisoned, tortured, and shot them—came from all strata of society, and a substantial percentage were the sons of peasants and workers.

German documents speak of the general feeling in the various strata of Lithuanian society and the attitude toward the Nazi conquerors.[41] There is also a report on the general feeling within the Catholic Church. To illustrate, I quote from a secret report of the SD of August 16, 1941:

> Thus, it may be said that the Catholic clergy in Lithuania, led by Bishop Brizgys, was entirely in favor of the German measures. In general, the clergy's position with regard to the Jewish question was un-

equivocal. Bishop Brizgys had, moreover, forbidden the clergy as a whole to intercede on behalf of the Jews in any way whatsoever.[42]

A report of July 25, 1941, by a member of the Abwehr, Bluemchen, states that the peasants and workers were on the whole gratified by the expulsion of the Bolshevists: "Many workers were active in partisan warfare. Farmers expressed enthusiasm and delight at the expulsion of the Bolshevists."[43]

Soviet historiography was very careful not to blame the Lithuanian people and emphasized that the "people" (*liaudis*) fought the German occupation.[44] It should be noted that not all Soviet authors who wrote about the Nazi occupation in Soviet Lithuania drew an accurate picture of the period. Books were published on resistance, partisan fighting, and loyalty to the USSR in which there is not a single word on cooperation with the Nazi conqueror and the annihilation of the Jews.

One example is the book by Mecislavas Gedvilas, who served as minister for Internal Affairs and later prime minister of Soviet Lithuania. His book, *The Fateful Change*,[45] which relates to the years 1940–45, contains his essays and speeches—his appeals from Moscow to the people during the war years. There is no mention of the murder of Jews by the Lithuanians. The author does talk about Lithuanian traitors who served the enemy, sowed destruction, and spilled innocent blood in the homeland, but not about the extermination of the Jews. About the Lithuanians' cooperation with the enemy, he says: "We Lithuanians can claim with pride that there are few traitors among us" (p. 224).

Emigre Historiography

There is little historiography to be found in Lithuanian emigrant concentrations. Aside from individual memoirs, "historical" Lithuanian writing appears in newspaper articles and periodicals and is primarily of a polemic nature.

Three of the few books that deal with the Nazi occupation of Lithuania are the two-volume work by Stefanija Rukiene, *The Return to Freedom*,[46] the memoirs of the priest Dr. Aleksandras Pakalniskis, and the essay by Bishop V. Brizgys, *The Catholic Church in Lithuania 1940–1944*. Rukiene complains about the Jews' hatred of Lithuanians: "The Jews express their hatred of the Lithuanians and their desire for revenge. They frequently state that they will yet pave the streets with Lithuanian heads" (vol. 2, p. 391).

In the second book, the author, who is from Plunge, tells about the Jews and their customs and includes a chapter on the extermination of the Jews in his town.[47] He also quotes several comments made by Lithuanians during the Soviet period, which describe how they planned the murder of the Jews and how they implemented the extermination. One typical remark was: "Just as soon as the Germans cross the border, we in Plunge will already wallow in Jewish blood." This priest relates that during the murder of the Jews of Plunge, there were only two Germans present in the town: they stood on the sidelines and did not involve themselves in the *Aktion*. The imprisonment of the Jews, rounding them up in the synagogue, starving them, torture, and finally murder was done only by Lithuanians. In response to his accurate description, the author "merited" a highly critical article in which he was accused of disseminating false accusations against innocent Lithuanians.[48]

The essay by Bishop Brizgys is simple apologetics; he attempts to clear the Lithuanian clergy of the accusations of collaboration with the Germans in the extermination of Lithuanian Jewry, but is unable to hide his own antisemitic inclinations.

The Controversy Erupts

On April 25, 1947, there was a meeting in Munich of Jewish survivors at which the Lithuanians were denounced as murderers of the Jews.[49] This public denunciation stained the name of the Lithuanians in world public opinion, threatened the position of the many Lithuanian immigrants in the United States and Canada with Nazi pasts, and elicited a wave of denials in the Lithuanian immigrant newspapers. Almost everyone denied their part in the annihilation of the Jews and emphasized the help they had extended to the persecuted.

The Lithuanians' responses to the Jews' accusations included the following [assertions]: 1) The Lithuanian people are not guilty of the crimes committed by individuals, degenerate criminal types, whose number was very small. 2) The Jews themselves, in their Communist activities, nourished the Lithuanians' hatred of them. 3) The Jews exhibited shocking ingratitude for the Lithuanians' favorable treatment during the hundreds of years that they had lived in their country and had been granted complete civil rights. As soon as the Soviet army arrived, the Jews turned their backs on the Lithuanians and began enthusiastically serving the Bolshevik invader. In truth, the Lithuanians did not murder Jews, but the Jews helped the Bolsheviks exile Lithuanians to Siberia and thus destroy the Lithuanian people. 4) The Lithuanians saved masses of Jews while endangering their own lives and the lives of their families, and now the Jews were ungratefully sullying the name of the Lithuanian people.

Among the first who responded to the Munich conference declaration was Juozas Salna, who published a series of articles entitled "Lithuanians in the Struggle for the Jews' Freedom" in *Naujienos*, the organ of Lithuanian emigrants in the United States.[50] The writer claims that the Lithuanians did not kill Jews—except for a few—and that most Lithuanians began rescue operations as soon as the Germans arrived.

In answer to the question of why acts of revenge against Jews were committed even by a few, Salna claims that the Jews made themselves hated by the Lithuanians because many of them participated actively in the arrest of Lithuanians and their exile and the Lithuanians were angry "that the Jews were behaving in their country as though they were the rightful owners."

Contrary to Soviet historiography, Salna claims that "in the revolt against the Bolshevists the masses—workers, clerks, and ordinary citizens—were the most active." Nevertheless, people from all classes of society began to save Jews, and only "a very small group of riffraff acted against the Jews," and the "intelligentsia acted with restraint." Salna lists names of numerous Lithuanians who supposedly saved Jewish adults and children. "Primarily, the Lithuanians hid Jews in the days of the first German attacks. Notables and priests turned to the German government on the issue of saving Jews."

The truth was that precisely in the first period, in the days of the temporary Lithuanian government, the Lithuanians were unrestrained in their abominable murders, until the Germans disbanded the government, took the "final solution" into their own hands, and installed "order" in the killing.

How the Lithuanian people behaved, how the intelligentsia behaved during those first days of occupation can be gleaned from the diary of the Righteous Gentile, Elena Kutorgiene. Excerpts from this diary were published by Ona Simaite, former librarian of the University of Vilna:

> All the Lithuanians—aside from isolated exceptions—and primarily the intelligentsia, which lost its standing in the days of the Soviet rule, hate the Jews. The crude Lithuanian mass, in contrast to the intelligentsia's total indifference, behaved with animalistic cruelty, until by comparison, the Russian pogroms look almost humane. I cannot believe my eyes and ears. I am totally shocked by the power of the blind hatred which they fan in order to satisfy the most primitive instincts.[51]

It is noteworthy that this paragraph and additional paragraphs were omitted from the diary in the Russian translation, which was published in a Russian periodical.[52]

A cynical attitude toward the murder of the Jews was expressed by J. Deltuvis in an article in the Canadian-Lithuanian newspaper *Teviskes Ziburiai.* In response to the extermination of the Jews in his city, Telsiai (Telz), he wrote, "It was also a big deal when youngsters pulled a bit at their rabbi's beard."[53] In the author's opinion, the Jews deserved punishment because they were so impudent as to dare to accept positions in the Ministries of Interior and Commerce during the Soviet period. The shocking torture of the Jews of Telz is related in Rabbi Oshry's book (p. 241) and in the open letter of Jacob Oleisky to the priest Prunskis.[54]

The Flood of Responses

In 1976, articles by Jacob Oleisky and Dr. Dov Levin were published in the newspaper *Teviskes Ziburiai.*[55] These essays, in which the authors spoke of the Lithuanians' guilt of participation in the annihilation of the Lithuanian Jews, were obviously not well received by the Lithuanians in the United States and Canada.

On January 10, 1977, the priest Prunskis, a member of the Association of Lithuanians, suggested to the Association of Lithuanians in Israel that they publish in English newspapers a manifesto on Lithuanians who saved Jews: "Now the American newspapers have published accusations against the Lithuanian people, as if only they murdered the Jews. You well know this is not true. If the Nazis found individual criminal types, there were many Lithuanians who saved Jews, and therefore it is not justified to accuse the entire Lithuanian people."[56]

Oleisky answered Dr. Prunskis in a long article published in the same newspaper. These were his main points: 1) It was not a small group of Lithuanians that helped the Germans murder the Jews, but several thousands. 2) It was not a group of riffraff that took part in the crimes, but public leaders who were in charge of municipal authorities, members of the intelligentsia, officers, and government officials. 3) Jews are accused of exiling Lithuanians, yet the fact that Jews and heads of national Jewish parties—up to 8,000 people—were exiled is overlooked.

Dr. Levin's article, which was also published in the journal *Forum*,[57] and in which the author accused the Lithuanians of murdering Jews, aroused angry reactions among the Lithuanians. One of the polemicists, A. Kalnius, suggested to strike a bargain: the Jews would publish a retraction of the decision taken at the Munich conference, at which Lithuanians were blamed for murdering Jews, and purge the libraries of books that sullied the name of the Lithuanian people. In return, the Lithuanians would stop accusing the Jews of Communism and of exiling Lithuanians to Siberia, and then "the Jews will be the friends of the Lithuanians."[58]

In the same newspaper there was also an open letter from A. Zemaitis. In his opinion, one should not blame the Lithuanians, because the Lithuanian intelligentsia is not guilty.[59] Again, the truth is exactly the opposite: at the head of the "partisans" stood engineers, lawyers, teachers, principals, officers, and priests. One of the most wanted criminals was the priest Lionginas Jankauskas, who organized the killing in the town of Skuodas, during which many Lithuanians were also murdered. Lithuanian public figures asked the city of New York to bring this priest, now called Jankus, to trial. He was living a peaceful life in Brooklyn, passing himself off as a Red Cross representative who had aided war victims.[60]

A lengthy list may be compiled of members of the Lithuanian intelligentsia who organized the murder of Jews and, at times, were personally involved in their torture and murder. Only a few names can be cited here: Engineer Vacys Deveikis participated in the murder of the Jews of Ukmerge; Kostas Milcis, headmaster of the high school in Vieksniai, brutally maltreated the township's Jewish residents; Vytautas Sakalauskas, headmaster in the village of Galiniai, captained a band of murderers in the township of Kraziai; agronomist Grigaliunas plundered and tortured Jews in Jonava; the priest Biliackas in Linkuva acted as advisor to police chief Sintaris in his torture of Jews; vice district attorney Grigaitis and Alisiunas, headmaster of the local high school, maltreated local Jews in Panevezys. Clerical leaders refused to help: when the Jews of Telz (Telsiai) appealed for aid to Cardinal Staugaitis, chairman of the Lithuanian parliament in independent Lithuania, he replied: "This is your punishment for bringing the Bolshevists to Lithuania."[61]

The heights of absurdity, however, were attained by the polemicist V. Domeika, who accused all the Jews of Communism, especially those who were fighting the Nazis. He averred that even the Jewish Fighting Organization in the Warsaw ghetto was Communist, and Mordechai Anielewicz "had already been involved in Communist activities in the Vilna ghetto."[62]

Other Voices

A few responsible voices stand out in the chorus of responses by Lithuanians who, by and large, deny or minimize the extent of their crimes. Dr. St. Sereika has said:

> All the essays on this question which were published in the newspaper *Teviskes Ziburiai* claim that we, the Lithuanians, are not guilty of the murder of the Jewish people in Lithuania in 1941. I am not satisfied with this answer, and I was glad to read Dov Levin's essay. He said that dialogue between the Jews and the Lithuanians has been impossible until now. We Lithuanians lack a pure heart, the innocence of a child and the sincerity to hear and tell the truth. Dov Levin has told the truth. Why don't we acknowledge this truth? The truth can only be a great help to the Lithuanian people and a comfort to the Jewish people who suffered so much in Lithuania.[63]

M. Goberis, whose comments were published in another newspaper, responded similarly to Dr. Sereika.[64] Sereika and Goberis were accused of slandering the Lithuanian people. A. Kalnius responded: "The Lithuanians will not beg for pardon. The Lithuanians cannot do so and will never do so. Because the Lithuanian people really did not kill a single Jew."[65]

Dr. Sereika was also criticized by Birute Kemezaite, who asserts: "The Jews, and not the Lithuanians, tortured the Lithuanians and poured boiling water on their hands and faces." She quotes from a work by Antanas Venclova who, she claims, traveled throughout Lithuania in an attempt to clarify the question of whether Jews were murdered by the Lithuanians and concluded that "the Germans most definitely never succeeded in tempting the Lithuanians to participate in Nazi crimes."[66]

Two others wrote while still living in the Soviet Union. Thomas Venclova, a poet and lawyer who in 1977 emigrated to the United States, published a lengthy essay in *samizdat* called "The Jews in the USSR" which contains a chapter on the fate of Lithuanian Jews.[67] He, too, merited a scathing attack from a Lithuanian who assumed the name Zuvintas. This essay was republished in the Lithuanian journal in America, *Akiraciai*.[68]

A. Terleckas defended his colleague, Professor Venclova. His essay was also first published in *samizdat* on October 8, 1978, and then published in a German magazine.[69] Terleckas was sentenced in 1957 to four years' imprisonment in a Soviet forced-labor camp. In 1973, he was imprisoned for the second time, and in 1979, for the third time. In his article, "Reflections on the Relations between the Lithuanians and the Jews," Terleckas admits to the Lithuanians' guilt for the mass murder of Jews, but also points to the guilt of other nations. His guilt, he wrote, robs him of his peace of mind to this day. He quotes Thomas Venclova:

> Evil remains evil and guilt remains guilt. Nothing can erase the fact that at the end of June 1941, the Lithuanians killed defenseless people in front of Lithuanian masses; nor the fact that in the twentieth century, many nations—almost all of them—perpetrated similar acts. I, as a Lithuanian, feel a personal responsibility to speak about the Lithuanians' guilt. (p. 168)

Terleckas calls for understanding between the Lithuanians and the Jews. To this end, one must employ the proper criteria in order to assess the guilt of the adult generation of the 1940s: "When I am concerned about the future of my people, I dream that in the future not one Lithuanian will ever again shoot an innocent man" (p. 177). The author predicts additional upheavals in human history in the future; the Lithuanians can guard against pogroms only if they unequivocally defend innocent people.

Notes

An earlier version of this essay was published in Yisrael Gutman and Gideon Greif, eds., *The Historiography of the Holocaust Period* (Jerusalem: Yad Vashem, 1988), 291–314.

1. Known as the LAF, *Lietuviu Aktivystu Frontas*. See also A. Rozauskas, ed., *Nacionalistu talka hitlerininkams*, Vilnius, 1970.
2. Military International Tribunal (MIT), L-180.
3. Ephraim Oshry, *Khurbn Lite*, New York-Montreal, 1951 (hereafter, Oshry), p. 204.
4. Ibid., pp. 208–209.
5. Ibid., pp. 222–23.
6. A German driver from the Wehrmacht unit's bakery chanced to be driving past and photographed the massacre. His pictures were printed in the German periodical *Politik*. Two of the photographs were printed with their German captions

in the Lithuanian album *Lietuvos partizanai*, Vilna, 1967 (hereafter, Lithuanian Album), p. 49.

7. Dr. Samuel Grinhaus, "Khurbn Lite," in *Fun letztn khurbn* no. 7, Munich, May 1948, p. 11; L. Garfunkel, *Kovna ha-Yehudit be-Hurbanah*, Jerusalem, 1959, pp. 31–32; *Masines zudynes Lietuvoje*, vol. I, Vilnius, 1965, p. 11; J. Vicas, *SS Tarnyboje*, Vilnius, 1962, p. 42.

8. Oshry, p. 281.

9. The directive was sent to the LAF Underground, which was already active in Soviet Lithuania, by the Lithuanian Ministry of Information in Berlin. *Masines zudynes Lietuvoje*, pp. 10, 49. See also Vicas, p. 33; Sara Neshamit, "Bein Shituf Peulah le-Meri," in *Dapim le-Heker ha-Shoah ve-ha-Mered*, second series, vol. I, Beit Lohamei HaGetaot, pp. 153–54.

10. Yaakov Goldenberg, "Bletlekh fun Kovner eltestenrat," in *Fun letzten khurbn* no. 7, p. 31.

11. According to the Lithuanian article by Juozas Salna, "Lietuviai kovoje del zydu laisves," *Naujienos*, September 21, 1948 (hereafter, Salna), they were the elderly Dr. K. Grinius, former president of Lithuania, clergyman M. Krupavicius, and Professor Y. Alekna. The three sent the German governor, von Rentlen, a memorandum condemning the murder of the Jews in Lithuania. The incident is not mentioned in Jewish historiography.

12. *Masines zudynes Lietuvoje*, pp. 332–35; Vicas, pp. 12–16, 30–31, 42–50.

13. Ibid., p. 16; *Masines zudynes*, pp. 19–21.

14. Prapuolenis's memorandum in the name of the LAF dated September 23, 1941, to von Rentlen, from the Lohse documents, YIVO Archive, New York. Microfilm in the archive of Beit Lohamei HaGetaot (hereafter, BLH).

15. *Masines zudynes*, p. 322; Vicas, pp. 16–17.

16. *Lagebericht der Sipo und SD*, March 28, 1942.

17. See list in *Masines zudynes*, p. 323; Vicas, pp. 68–69. The author lists eighty-seven towns and townships in which the Lithuanian battalions murdered Jews.

18. Ibid., pp. 69–70, lists thirteen villages that were burned by the 13th Battalion in reprisal for Soviet partisan activity; see also Noemi Szac-Wajnkranc, *Przemineto z ogniem*, Lodz, 1967; *Gitlerovskaia okkupatsiia v Litve, sbornik statei*, Vilnius, 1966 (hereafter, *Gitlerovskaia okkupatsiia*), pp. 33–34.

19. MIT, PS-1104.

20. *Documents Accuse*, Vilna, 1966; Karys, no. 2, 1941. On the massacres in the Ninth Fort, see nn. 36, 37, 35.

21. A warning issued by the Lithuanian organization Lietuvos Laisves Kovotoju Sajunga. The headline in the German translation ran: *Litauer, Litauen wird schon kolonisiert*, from the Lohse documents, YIVO archive OccE 3b, copy in the BLH archive. See also Prapuolenis's memorandum in *Gitlerovskaia okkupatsiia*, pp. 33–34; *Masines zudynes*, p. 8, *Lietuvos TSR Istorija*, Vilnius, 1958, pp. 416–17.

22. *Hitleriniai zudikei Kretingoje* (n. 29), p. 19; *Masines zudynes*, pp. 51–53, 319–20; Yaakov Goldenberg, p. 32. On Bishop Brizgys's change of tactics in 1943–44, see letter from Leib Garfunkel to Sara Neshamit, May 15, 1974, BLH archives;

testimony of Rachel Levin concerning the priest, Prunskis, BLH archive, file AYZ/1494 (temporary no.).

23. Testimonies of Jewish survivors concerning the Lithuanians who saved them in the BLH archive, file AYZ/1499 (temporary no.). Sara Neshamit "Hatzalah be-Lita bi-Shnot ka-Kivush ha-Nazi," in *Nisyonot u-Feulot Hatzalah bi-Tkufat ha-Shoah*, Jerusalem, 1976, pp. 238–75.

24. In view of the impossibility of enumerating all the murderers and collaborators who escaped from Lithuania upon the arrival of the Red Army, we shall mention only a few examples: Impulevicius, the commander of the 2nd Battalion (12), lived in the United States until his death and was neither handed over for trial nor punished in any way, despite demands to that effect; Marijus Blynas of the SD's Lithuanian staff in Vilna, is living in the United States; P. Jakys, a murderer from Kretinga who fled to Germany, was arrested and brought to trial in Ulm, Germany, in 1958, at the Tilsit Gestapo war criminals trial. The following infiltrated into Lithuania after the war but were captured: Captain Juozas Noreika, who is accused of the massacre of the Jews of Plunge; M. Maciukas; P. Masiulis, who is still living in Brooklyn, New York; clergyman Lionginas Jankauskas, who organized the murder of the Jews of Skuodas and of many Lithuanians; Rauka, one of the organizers of the massacre in the Kaunas ghetto, lived in the United States; Klimavicius, commander of one of the killer bands (now standing trial); and many others who have not yet been caught and placed on trial. Bishop Brizgys also lives in the United States.

    Of the Righteous Gentiles who left Lithuania, we would cite Bronius Gotautas, nicknamed "Broliukas," who died in (West) Germany; Ona Simaite, who died in Paris. See Sofija Binkiene (Sudartoja), Ch. Lifsicaite (Redaktore) *Ir be ginklo kariai*. Mr. and Mrs. Efertas, who saved Tamar Lazarson, live in Canada (see *Yomanah shel Tamarah*, BLH and Hakibbutz Hameuchad, 1976).

25. On the organization and activities of emigre Lithuanians, see among other newspapers, *Naujienos*, a weekly published in Chicago; *Teviskes Ziburiai*, a weekly published in Canada; *Darbininkas*, a periodical issued by clerical circles (see no. 5, February 1982, for lobbying to end the current investigation of Lithuanians supected of war crimes); *Akiraciai*, a monthly published in Chicago, and others. Also, *Musu desimtmetis*, Sao Paulo, 1982, a publication of the organization of Lithuanians in Brazil. The editor is Halina Mosinskiene, who was honored in Jerusalem with the title "Righteous Gentile." The pamphlet includes memories of front-line duty by Petras Babickas, a member of the Lithuanian Legion, an auxiliary of the German army. Needless to say, Babickas does not mention the massacre of the Jews.

26. See notes 27–30.

27. A. Vabalas (Spaudai paruose), *Mirties pedsakai prie Nevezio (Faktai kaltina)*, Vilnius, 1960.

28. G. Erslavaite (Spaudai paruose), *Neuzmirsime (Apie burzuaziniu, nacionalistu nusikaltimus hitlerines okupacijos metais Mezeikiu apskrityje) (Faktai kaltina)*, Vilnius, 1960.

29. B. Baranauskas (Spaudai paruose ir redagavo), *Hitleriniai zudikai Kretingoje*, ar-

chyviniai dokumentai, I rinkinys, Vilna, 1960. Among other things, the witnesses describe the murder of the local Jews.

30. A. Vabalas (Spaudai paruose), *Krauja sugere Dzukijos smelis (Faktai kaltina)*, Vilnius, 1960.

31. J. Vicas, *SS Tanyboje, Dokumentinis leidinys apie Lietuviu apsaugos daliu jvykdytus nusikaltimus*, Vilnius, 1961.

32. *Masines zudynes Lietuvoje, 1941–1944, dokumentu rinkinys, I dalias*, Vilnius, 1965, II dalis, 1973.

33. B. Baranauskas and K. Ruksenas (redagavo), *Documents Accuse*, Vilnius, 1966.

34. O. Kaplanas, *Gitlerovskaia okkupatsiia v Litve: sbornik statei*, Vilnius, 1966.

35. M. Eglinis-Elinas, *Mirties Fortuose*, Vilnius, 1966.

36. L. Kondralas, *IX Fortas*, Vilna, 1961; O. Kaplanas, *Devintasis fortas kaltina*, Vilnius, 1970; identical, *Das 9 Fort klagt an*, Vilnius, 1963.

37. M. Kurganovas, *Mirties akivaizdoje*, Vilnius, 1960.

38. B. Baranauskas, R. Ruksenas (rinkini paruose), and E. Rozauskas (redagavo), *Nacionalistu talka hitlerininkams*, Vilnius, 1970.

39. S. Bistrickas, *Ka osia Paneriu pusys*, Vilnius, 1977. Translated into Hebrew by Sara (Shner) Neshamit and published in *Zmanim* no. 12, summer 1983.

40. Kazys Ruksenas, "Lietuvos gyventoju naikinimas hitlerines Vokietijos koncentracijos stovyklose," *Lietuvos istorijos metrastis*, 1975.

41. In Lageberichte; also Ereignismeldungen sent by the SiPo and SD commanders in Lithuania to their superiors; also reports by Abwehr (counterespionage) agent in Lithuania, Bluemchen.

42. No-2849 Ereignismeldung UdSSR No. 54, pp. 17–18.

43. From the Lohse documents in the YIVO archive, New York, OccE 36. Microfilm in BLH archive.

44. For example, on p. 5 of the introduction to the Lithuanian Album (*Lietuvos Partizanai*) it says: "the general abhorrence of the occupiers and their allies—the bourgeois nationalists created favorable conditions for the burgeoning of the partisan movement." Similarly in the introduction to *Masines zudynes*, pp. 3, 5.

45. Mecislavas Gedvilas, *Lemiamas posukis*, Vilnius, 1975.

46. Stefanija Rukiene, *Grizimas i laisve*, vols. 1, 2. The quote is according to Zemaitis's article of March 5,1981, in the newspaper *Teviskes Ziburiai*.

47. Aleksandras Pakalniskis, *Plunge*, Chicago, 1980. He wrote seven memoirs on the period. In the seventh he described the massacre of the Jews of Prienai and was subsequently accused or falsifying facts.

48. A. Kalnius, "Kas sunaikino Plunges zydus?" *Teviskes Ziburiai* no. 23, June 3, 1982.

49. According to the article by Dov Levin, "Faktai kaltina," *Teviskes Ziburiai* no. 28, 1976; V. Domeika, "Perdideli kaltinimai lietuviams," ibid. no. 26, June 24, 1982.

50. Juozas Salna, "Lietuviai kovoje del zydu laisves," *Naujienos*, April 21, 1948–March 31, 1949.

51. M. Sudarski, ed., *Lite*, vol. I, New York, 1951, 1966.
52. E. A. Buivydaite-Kutorgiene, "*Keunaski Dnyvnik*," *Druzhba narodov* no. 8, Moscow, 1968.
53. "Nedidelis dalykas, jei ten paaugliai papesiojo rabino barzda," in Dov Levin's article, "Opuji klausima gvildenant."
54. In *Teviskes Ziburiai* no. 6 (1669), February 4, 1982.
55. J. Oleiskis, "Kadaise zydai gyveno Leituvoje," ibid., issue of June 24, 1976; Dov Levin, "Faktai kaltina," ibid. no. 28 (1370), July 8, 1976; J. Oleiskis, "Kadaise zydai gyveno Leituvoje," *Teviskes Ziburiai* June 21, 1976.
56. Kun. Juozas Prunskis, "Lietuvos zydai Kaltina Lietuvius," *Teviskes Ziburiai* January 10, 1977.
57. *Idem.*, D. Levin, "1939–1941, The Intermediate Period and Its Implication for the Holocaust. The Jews of Eastern Europe Under the Soviet Regime," in *Forum* 37 (Spring 1980).
58. A. Kalnius, "Valia dziaugtis valia ir liudeti," *Teviskes Ziburiai* no. 38 (1701).
59. Aleksas Zemaitis, "Atviras laiskas kaltintojams," *Teviskes Ziburiai* no. 9 (1620), February 26, 1981; no. 10 (1621), March 5, 1981.
60. *Who is Hiding in Grand Street*, Vilnius, 1964.
61. *Yahadut Lita*, vol. 4, p. 290.
62. V. Domeika, "Per dideli Kaltinimai lietuviams, netikslus ir nepagristi, Dov Levino priekaistai," *Teviskes Ziburiai* no. 26 (1689); no. 27 (1690); no. 28 (1691), June-July 1982.
63. Dr. St. Sereika, "Opiuoju klausimu," *Teviskes Ziburiai* no. 28 (1691), April 8, 1982.
64. *Akiraciai* no. 5, 1982.
65. See note 58.
66. Birute Kemezaite "Kalte atsakombe ir zydai," *Teviskes Ziburiai* no. 43 (1768).
67. Thomas Venclova, *Die Juden in der UdSSR*. Quoted in the article by Terleckas (n. 69, below).
68. Ibid.
69. Antanas Terleckas, "Uberlegungen zum Verhaltnis zwischen Litauern und Juden," *Kontinent* no. 12, pp. 167–68.

TWELVE

Lithuanian-Jewish Relations in the Shadow of the Holocaust

INTRODUCED AND ANNOTATED BY

Sima Ycikas

Lithuania, the first republic to exercise the right to secede from the USSR, faces complex political and economic problems. Particular importance accrues to the domestic consolidation of the population and the related issue of interethnic relations.

According to the Soviet census of 1989, the population of Lithuania amounted to 3,690,000, with Lithuanians accounting for 80 percent of the population, Russians 9 percent, Poles 7 percent, Belorussians 2 percent, and other nationalities 2 percent.[1] Among the "other nationalities," along with the Tatars, Karaites, etc., are the Jews, who number 12,000 (in mid-1996, the Jewish population was estimated at between 6,000 and 8,000).[2]

The Lithuanian government requires the support of the entire population, and it has adopted a policy of satisfying the national requirements of the peoples who reside in Lithuania. In consideration of the fact that its relation to the Jewish question is one of the factors that influence world opinion, the Lithuanian government removed barriers to cultural and educational activity of Jews much earlier than the leaderships of other Soviet republics. The revival of Jewish life was facilitated by the support of Sajudis, the Lithuanian movement for reform, in which representatives of the Jewish community also participated.

Lithuanian-Jewish cooperation has not removed or resolved one of the most fundamental problems—that of Lithuanian-Jewish relations during World War II. Discussion of this problem began in the late 1940s in the West. Participating in it were some surviving Lithuanian Jews and Lithuanian emigrants, among whom there were a number of war criminals. The Jews accused repre-

This essay was written as Lithuania was emerging as an independent state in 1989–1991. It has been edited to reflect developments since that time. —ed.

sentatives of all strata of the Lithuanian population of collaborating with the Germans. At a congress of Lithuanian Jews who were former concentration camp inmates, which took place in Munich on April 14–15, 1947, a declaration was adopted which said:

> We, the small remnant of Lithuanian Jewry, which had numbered 160,000,[3] are living witnesses to the cruelty of Lithuanians toward their Jewish neighbors. Each of us can testify to cases of crying villainy committed during the years of occupation by Lithuanians against the Jewish population, which was innocent and defenseless. Unfortunately, we must add that all Jewish communities of the Lithuanian provinces, without exception, were destroyed by Lithuanians, while in the large towns, this was done with their active participation.[4]

The Lithuanians who took part in the discussion considered the first mass murders of Jews as an expression of national wrath evoked by the participation of Jews in the deportation of the Lithuanian population and in other actions of the Soviet authorities in Lithuania. Such discussions have been renewed from time to time, particularly in the 1970s and 1980s.[5] In Lithuania itself they were not reflected, at least in the official press, although the latter did have much to say about the collaboration with the Germans of "Lithuanian bourgeois nationalists" and about bringing war criminals to justice.[6]

The subject of Lithuanian-Jewish relations has recently become particularly topical, as indicated by the wealth of materials appearing in official and independent Lithuanian publications. The documents below include materials published in 1989 and give an idea of what readers in Lithuania then could learn about our topic. It is worth paying attention, however, also to certain aspects and materials not included in our selection which have direct relevance to this topic.

In Lithuania today there is a tendency to idealize the period of independent Lithuania, 1918 to 1940. Some authors, while paying tribute to the cultural autonomy of those peoples living in Lithuania, at the same time prefer to pass over the fascist orientation of President Smetona and his nationalistic slogan "Lithuania for the Lithuanians." The past of the Jews of Lithuania tends to be idealized: it is forgotten that the privileges granted by the royal authorities were intended to protect the Jews from anti-Jewish attacks of the local population, that the Jews suffered from blood libels, heavy tributes, and taxes. It is forgotten that hatred toward the Jewish "Christ-killers" over many years was incited by the Catholic clergy. Negative images of Jews are found also in the works of Lithuanian writers and publicists and in Lithuanian folklore, which hardly encouraged the establishment of ideal relations with the Jewish population. Thus, the weekly *Gimtasis Krastas*, following this tradition, as late as 1988 published an illustrated article with detailed descriptions of masks of Jews used in folk ritual to evoke mockery of their behavior.[7]

In 1989, the day of the beginning of mass deportations—June 14, 1941—

was first officially declared a Day of Mourning and Hope. In articles prepared for this date authors did not indicate the national origin of those subject to deportation. In materials by Lithuanian authors there is no indication of those deported activists of the Zionist movement, of the Bund, of participants in other Jewish organizations, of Jewish religious leaders, industrialists, and merchants. It is possible to attribute this to the fact that until just recently the documents and statistics were not available to researchers in Lithuania. Only in 1990 (in no. 1 of the journal *Pergale*) did there appear a translation of the article by the Israeli scholar Dov Levin,[8] which indicates that 7,000, or 20 percent of those deported, were Jews, and that they amounted to 3 percent of the Jewish population of Lithuania, as compared to 1 percent of the Lithuanian population which was deported. Thus, the Jews suffered proportionately from the deportations more than the Lithuanians.

The deportation was carried out by the KGB republic staff (established in May 1941), which depended on local operational groups whose members included Soviet activists and sympathizers with the new regime. Among these were Jews, some of whom worked in the investigative bodies. One of these was Danielius Todesas, who has written:

> The orders of Stalin were carried out, they were not discussed. If someone had dared to doubt the utility of the deportations (not to mention whether they should be allowed), and to speak out—that would have changed nothing. But I am certain that no one had any doubts.[9]

Todesas admitted that the deportations did not attain theirs goal, but rather turned against their organizers and provided moral justification for the accomplices of the Germans—the opponents of the Soviet regime.

During the first days of the war, despite the disorderly retreat of the Red Army, the lack of preparation for evacuation, and anarchy, the dispatch of trains of deportees and reprisals against those arrested by Soviet authorities continued. The Lithuanian press in the early 1990s paid considerable attention to the events in the Rainiai forest where, with the retreat of the Red Army, NKVD troops on June 26, 1941, shot seventy-three Lithuanians who were being held in prison in the town of Telsiai. Local inhabitants discovered the bodies after several days when the Germans were already in the city and the "white-belts" (local Lithuanian policemen) forced the Jews to dig up the corpses and bury them in a common grave. The majority of the white-belts belonged to the Lithuanian Activist Front, which was established in 1940 in Berlin. It functioned in Lithuania as a fifth column, committing reprisals against activists of the Soviet regime and Jews as "a Bolshevik nation."

At present, as previously, the actions of the white-belts are condemned by some authors. Thus, in his article "Rainiai," Stasys Kasauskas writes with indignation about those who participated in the killing of hundreds of Jews in Rainiai, Geruliai, and Vesvenai: "It is not Germans who will shoot, tirelessly guzzle vodka, grab up Jewish gold and burn. . . ."[10]

During the first days of the war, on June 25, a massacre of Jews took place in the Lietukis garage in Kaunas. All writers on the Holocaust in Lithuania discuss these bestial murders. Some recent publications reflect the view of former Nazi accomplices who served sentences in Soviet camps. Typical of these is the publication presented below from the weekly, *Gimtasis Krastas*. Violence against the Jews is presented as a fight against Stalinism. The attitude of the editors to the discussion evoked by this publication can be gauged by the letter of the editor-in-chief of the weekly, A. Cekuolis, to a Jewish reader, Z. Sh.:[11]

> We received your letter. Thank you. We are obliged to curtail discussion about the murders in the Lietukis garage. Letters streamed in from all sides, including from emigres who are trying by various means to slander the Jewish people for the events of 1939–1941, recalling facts which now everyone would be better off not to recall. . . .
>
> You can imagine the tension here, particularly in regard to the nationality issue. The Jews living in Lithuania are fine politicians and good allies, and it will be of no use to anyone if to some charges others are added, etc.
>
> Our newspaper was the first to take up the topic of the tragedy of Lithuanian Jewry. We wrote much about it, we continue to do so, but we shall endeavor to be constructive.

Ninety percent of the Jewish population of Lithuania perished during World War II. Only a small proportion of Jews was saved by the local population. The book, *Fighters without Weapons*,[12] contains testimonies of Jews who were saved and of the Lithuanian saviors. There were few of the latter righteous people. The Lithuanian press writes much about the nobility and heroism of these people.The former editor-in-chief of the newspaper *Tiesa* and the journal *Kommunist*, Genrikas Zimanas, noted: "It is painful that precisely this page which so much helps one comprehend the real humanism of these people is omitted from their official biographies."[13] In citing examples and names of saviors, he includes the physician Olga Landsbergiene, the mother of the first post-Soviet president of Lithuania, Vytautas Landsbergis.

Many of the saviors have remained unknown, either due to their modesty or to the long-standing policy in Lithuania of maintaining silence about the Holocaust. However, there is another aspect which has also been omitted from the Lithuanian press. That is fear—the memory that after the war some people paid with their lives for having saved the lives of Jews. They were victims of reprisals of the Forest Brethren, who continued their activities right up to the early 1950s. The latter included many who did not manage to escape along with the German war criminals, but there were also those who resisted the Soviet regime. Now there is a tendency to completely rehabilitate the Forest Brethren as freedom fighters. At the same time there are other voices urging people not to confuse the executioners with the victims. Moreover, no one recalls that at the hands of the Forest Brethren there perished some Jews who survived the war, mainly Jewish mothers who were seeking their children in the provinces and Lithuanian peasants who hid these children.

The cruelty of the Lithuanian police units, which exceeded even that of the Germans in the annihilation of the Jews of Lithuania and Belorussia, and the bloody terror of the Forest Brethren were used as arguments in ideological battles by extremist Soviet military circles, which tried to highlight negative aspects of the Lithuanian people. For this purpose they adduced evidence presented by Jews. For example, *Voenno-istoricheskii zhurnal* (no. 2 [1990], pp. 84–86) published a German document and commentary on it from the book published in Israel by Y. Damba, *V krovavom vikhre*, about the bestiality and sadism of the Twelfth Lithuanian police battalion in the city of Slutsk during an action against Jews.[14]

Today much is openly said about Lithuanian-Jewish relations. From the Lithuanian side there are now attempts to improve relations with Jews in Lithuania, in the West, and in Israel. One sign of this was the telegram sent to Israeli President Herzog on Israel's forty-second Independence Day. Another manifestation was the following declaration, published in *Tiesa* on May 11, 1990:

> Declaration of the Supreme Soviet of the Lithuanian Republic about the Genocide of the Jewish People in Lithuania during the Years of the Hitlerite Occupation.
>
> The Supreme Soviet of the Lithuanian Republic in the name of the Lithuanian People declares that it unequivocally condemns the genocide of the Jewish people which took place in Lithuania during the years of the Hitlerite occupation and with sorrow notes that among the executioners who aided the occupiers were also citizens of Lithuania. There is not and cannot be any justification for the crimes committed against the Jewish people in Lithuania and beyond its borders, or for a statute of limitations for their criminal persecution.
>
> The Supreme Soviet of the Lithuanian Republic calls on all organs of state authority and administration, public organizations and citizens to create for the Jews of Lithuania, as for other national communities, the most favorable conditions for the restoration and development of their culture, education, scholarship, religious and other institutions.
>
> The government of Lithuania will concern itself with the preservation of the memory of the victims of the genocide of the Jewish people. The Lithuanian republic will not tolerate any manifestations of anti-Semitism.
>
> Chairman of the Supreme Soviet
> of the Lithuanian Republic
> Landsbergis
> Vilnius
> May 8, 1990

The future will tell how such efforts will affect the fate of the Jews remaining in Lithuania and relations between Lithuanians and Jews elsewhere.

1. Jews and Lithuanians[15]

Tomas Venclova[16]

[This article by a distinguished Lithuanian writer and scholar was first published in a Jewish *samizdat* journal in 1976 and aroused considerable debate. Deletions indicated by [. . .] in the documents in this article were made by Sima Ycikas when she originally published them and are preserved here.]

I have a daughter; she is two years old. According to the laws of the state of Israel, she is a Jew. I am a Lithuanian by any laws and primarily by that internal law which I have assumed for myself. Some day my daughter will ask about what happened between our peoples during the years of World War II. I shall try to answer her now.

Before the War there were approximately 240,000 Jews in Lithuania, amounting to 8 percent of the country's population. That was rare in Europe. Some 80,000 Jews lived in Vilnius, which was called the Jerusalem of Lithuania: it had a huge Jewish quarter, ancient synagogues, publishing houses, and libraries, a Jewish scientific institute, a museum. In Kaunas, which was considered the second Lithuanian capital, there were 40,000 Jews. Since the eighteenth century the Jews had their own traditional section—Vilijampole (Slobodka) (although many of them lived outside its precincts)—their synagogues, schools, a press, and writers. In the villages the Jews comprised one-third of the population. According to the 1970 census, there remained 23,600 Jews, 16,500 in Vilnius and just over 4,000 in Kaunas. Now there are undoubtedly fewer; many are leaving the Soviet Union. Lithuanians are also leaving.

During the war hundreds of thousands of people were murdered in the woods of Paneriai (Ponary)[17] near Vilnius, in the fortress of the Ninth Fort[18] near Kaunas, in the Vilnius and Vilijampole ghettos, and in Lithuanian shtetls. They were annihilated not only by Germans, but also by Lithuanians. Many perished in the first days of the war, when the Germans entered Lithuania, but did not yet control it. Then there occurred the Kaunas pogroms about which much evidence has been preserved. It is estimated that on June 25–26, 1941, 3,800 Jews were slaughtered in Kaunas. Several hundreds of them met their death in the garage on Vytautas Prospect. I know how they died, but I will scarcely tell my daughter about that.

The first months of the war I myself spent in Kaunas. I was then four and I lived, as the expression goes, "with good people": my father,[19] a Soviet people's commissar of education, had left for Moscow, and my mother had been arrested. She was accused of being a Jew. The investigator stated that it made no sense to try to prove otherwise since it was well known that all people's commissars were married to Jews. My mother still proved that she was a Lithuanian and had been baptized (both of these things were true). After some time, she was released.

I did not see the murders. In my childhood and also in my youth hundreds of times I passed the garage on Vytautas Prospect without knowing its history. Nevertheless, I am implicated in it. The Jews were murdered by Lithuanians, and I am a Lithuanian. The Jews were murdered in Kaunas, and Kaunas is my city. I know its every house, every tree on Laisves Avenue, I know its dusty gardens, its cramped movie theaters. I cannot exist without the Lithuanian language—it is my natural space; I write poetry only in Lithuanian. There are cultures which are much greater than the Lithuanian one, but for me it is still incommensurable with any other. I know that one can say many good things about it. My people for centuries has had a sense of its own worth, honor, steadfastness, and goodness. It has a sense of history which is not characteristic of all people: it remembers its past and usually knows how to make its present comparable with it. I am proud also of the fact that in the vast majority of cases the Lithuanians behaved well in the camps; the most famous contemporary Russian writer[20] has told of this, and he knows whereof he speaks.

I love the Jewish people. Its cultural role and its fate are so significant that for me they are the main proof of the idea which has defined our historical being. What happened during the first days of the war was a catastrophe for the Jews, but was a far worse catastrophe for the Lithuanians.

How is one to understand what happened? When the issue is one of death and irredeemable guilt one can always produce a number of rational and deterministic explanations, but in the final analysis they are not worth anything. That was known long ago by Oedipus. Christianity knew it even better. Nevertheless, I have many times attempted to clarify all this, have read documents, spoken with friends, with Jews who survived, and with Lithuanians.

I was struck most of all by the fact that the Kaunas pogroms contradicted the whole Lithuanian historical tradition. Whoever is familiar with the disgusting common antisemitism which now infects very many Lithuanians (I would be lying if I said that I had never in my life given way to it) considers it to be a permanent phenomenon. Yet undoubtedly that is not so. And in any case, in its best periods Lithuania was a country where the Jews experienced justice and protection. Our peoples lived together for 800 years. Grand Prince Vytautas, to whom Lithuanians relate as the Russians do to Peter the Great or the French to Napoleon, in 1388 granted privileges to the Jews in the first known document relating to the position of Jews in Lithuania. It is worth recalling some of the thirty-seven articles of this charter of privileges. Vytautas forbade accusing Jews of ritual murder; if a Jew was accused of murdering a Christian child (in an ordinary, not a ritual murder), the charge would have to be corroborated by six witnesses—three Jews and three Christians. Any accuser who did not prove his charge was subject to the same punishment which the accused murderer would have faced if found guilty. If a Christian damaged something in a Jewish cemetery, he was liable to confiscation of his property. Strict punishment was to be meted out to a Christian who did not respond to the cry for help of his Jewish neighbor. The Jews in the garage on Vytautas Prospect cried for help. A crowd of onlookers witnessed their deaths. The majority of this crowd considered themselves to be Christians. It did not occur to them that they were insulting not only Christ, but also Prince Vytautas, for whom the Prospect was named, although later it was renamed Lenin Prospect. [. . .]

Nevertheless, despite the long experience of contact, Lithuanians and Jews basically lived in separate worlds. We Lithuanians knew little about Polish culture, something about German and Russian culture, but about Jewish culture which was being created under our very eyes, in our country, we had not the slightest idea. The religion, language, alphabet, and customs were too great a barrier. The Jewish community was considered an exotic inclusion unconnected to us spiritually. Of course, this was a serious mistake. The Jews also knew little about Lithuanian traditions and culture. Those who assimilated usually adopted the Russian language or occasionally German. Two national revivals—a Lithuanian one and a Jewish one—took place simultaneously and alongside each other, but in different spaces. [. . .]

It seems to me that the spiritual lack of communality was the cause of much woe. But whether due to it or, more likely, parallel to it, there arose something worse: the division of people into types, the supercilious and distant relation to the Jews by which one does not speak of a "good person," but says "a Jew, but a good person anyway." The word *zydas* in Lithuanian is not derogatory (unlike the Russian word *zhid*, i.e., "kike"), but has the same meaning as the Russian *evrei* (a neutral word for "Jew"); when used by antisemites it requires the additions of suffixes or epithets; and still on the lips of many Lithuanians this innocent word sounds in a way that makes me ashamed. [. . .]

From a particular pronunciation of the word *zydas* to a pogrom—this distance seems to be considerable. But in the spiritual world it, apparently, is quite small and collapsible. Whoever separates some group of people, on the basis of nationality, religion, class, etc.—and considers himself internally unconnected with it, in essence is paving the way for pogroms, concentration camps, for a totalitarian regime. This is an elementary truth but, like all such elementary truths, it is quite often forgotten. [. . .]

In 1940 Soviet tanks entered Kaunas and soon thereafter Lithuania was incorporated into the USSR. The directives were issued by the infamous Dekanozov,[21] who many years later was executed along with Beria. For almost a year things were relatively quiet. However, in mid-June 1941, Lithuania finally entered the twentieth century—with the wave of repressions which engulfed her. In terms of horrors and numbers of victims, it approached the pogroms which followed two weeks later. The postwar Soviet press mentioned these events without fanfare and sometimes even with criticism. For example, in his memoirs my father said a bit about them. In five or six days tens of thousands of people disappeared—members of the intelligentsia, white-collar workers, priests, officers, peasants; by the usual Stalinist methods the cultured stratum of the Lithuanian people was liquidated. It is claimed that exile was the fate even of Esperantists and philatelists, for their ties with people abroad. I suspect that this is true simply because one does not make up such things.

In the official bodies which carried this out there were Jews. Of course, there were also Lithuanians. Their names are well known [. . .] and I will not mention them here. One must say that Jews were also arrested and exiled. It is said that in terms of percentage more of them were exiled than Lithuanians since many Jews belonged to the bourgeoisie.

During the first days of the war power fell into the hands of the Lithuanian partisans; this was made possible partly by the underground front of activists (LAF), and partly, one assumes, it occurred spontaneously. A government was formed which declared the restoration of an independent Lithuania. We do not know much about this. [. . .] It is clear that the Lithuanian government was playing with the Germans a game that was complicated and doomed to fail. By June 25 the Germans had practically stymied the activity of the government. In the speech of Prime Minister Ambrazavicius, published in a Soviet collection of archival documents, it was said that the government therefore was powerless to halt the pogroms. It was also stated that the pogroms were directed by German SS officers, although they made efforts to conceal their involvement (this was mentioned at the war crimes trials in West Germany). On August 5 the government, after issuing a protest to the Germans, ceased to function. Its members were later persecuted by the Germans.

Those who were implicated in Stalin's repressions, of course, managed to get out of Lithuania. In their haste they even abandoned their papers. Hatred and vengeance were vented on the Jews; there were many of them, they did not manage to escape, and everyone remembers that the residents of Vilijampole had welcomed the arrival of the Soviet tanks.

What can I say after hearing this evidence? Yes, totalitarianism distorts the human countenance and human motives; yes, violence begets violence, but evil always remains evil, murder—murder, and guilt—guilt. Nothing in the world will alter the fact that in late June 1941, in front of a Lithuanian crowd, Lithuanians destroyed defenseless people, not even the fact that in the twentieth century practically every nation committed something similar. And I, a Lithuanian, am obliged to speak about the guilt of Lithuanians. Sadism and robbery, scorn and shameful indifference to people cannot be justified. Worse than that, they cannot be explained, they exist in such dark corners of individual and national consciousness that to seek rational reasons for them is a fruitless exercise. Some will say "after all, the Jews were murdered not by Lithuanians, but by fools [or even better, by 'bourgeois nationalists'], they have no relation to the Lithuanian people." I myself have said something similar. But that is not true. If one considers the people a huge personality, then everyone in the nation—saint and sinner alike—participates in this personality. Every sin committed burdens the conscience of the whole people and the conscience of each member of it. One cannot cast the blame onto other peoples. They themselves will sort out their own affairs. It is for our people to sort out our affairs and to repent for them. That, indeed, is the meaning of belonging to one people or another.

I do not know how many Lithuanians will read these words, but I have to write them. Repentance is a complicated matter. It is not at all a squaring of accounts with murderers, no matter who they might be. It is not a tearing of garments—people repent internally. But we must speak about all that has happened, without holding ourselves back, without internal censorship, without propagandistic distortions, without national complexes, without fear. We must always understand that the destruction of the Jews is the destruction of ourselves, the humiliation of the Jews is the humiliation of ourselves, the destruction of Jewish culture is an attack on our own. At present the Lithuanians and Jews of the USSR basically share one fate; but still there are specific Jewish (and Lithuanian) problems, and one should take this into account. We have lived together for 800 years; perhaps this period is coming to an end. At such an hour we cannot be either enemies or be indifferent. We do not have the right to claim that Jewish affairs do not affect us. We are affected by every antisemitic outbreak. We are directly affected by the fact that silence is beginning to cover the destruction of Jews in the Ninth Fort, and other less significant pages of history are being blown out of proportion. Every inhabitant of Vilnius often passes the area of the former ghetto. During my school days this was an area of wild ravines; in their center there stuck out the shell of the ancient synagogue—it could have been restored, but it was removed (at the same time the Jewish museum was liquidated). Now there one finds a pseudomedieval quarter of cheap restaurants and displays of Lithuanian art. There is not a single word to recall what had been on this spot. This quarter pleases many (it also used to please me), but, in fact, it is our national shame.

Of course, there is not only shame, and this should be known too. We did not have a king like the one the Danes had; but there were Lithuanians who saved Jews and perished for this. In 1967 (the year is important here) in Vilnius the book *Fighters without Weapons* appeared. It notes the many dozens of Lithuanians who were not indifferent. [. . .]

Yes, we did not have a king like the one of the Danes. But a middle-aged Jewess who survived the ghetto recently told me a story that is also worth recalling. A young Lithuanian who had married a Jewess did not want to divorce her even though this would have saved his life. He lived in the ghetto and once started to have an altercation with a Lithuanian guard; the latter called him a Jew-face and shot him. It is said that before he died, he said: "It is good that I am dying as a Jew." Perhaps he didn't say it; myths are quick to arise. His grave was in the ghetto cemetery in Vilijampole among the new postwar housing. Perhaps it no longer exists. I hope that there will always be found Lithuanians who have the spirit to act the same way.

2. No Justification for the Murder of Lithuanian Jews[22]

[This article was written in 1978 but published only in 1989 in a Lithuanian emigré journal.]

During the German occupation of Lithuania a horrible tragedy took place—the murder of approximately 200,000 Jews. To this day the question burns and disturbs our peace—who is guilty? Why did Lithuanians, who for centuries had been distinguished for religious and national tolerance, in the mid-twentieth century raise their hands against innocent people?

I also have long been trying to find the answer. No one in my native Krivasalis shot at Jews, no one close to me was besmirched with the blood of innocents. And, still, for many years I have experienced an irrepressible feeling of guilt.

I once spoke with Tomas Venclova about the responsibility of the Lithuanian people for the destruction of its Jews. As I recall, our views coincided. His reaction to this human drama was published in the journal *Evrei v SSSR*. It reflected talent, cleverness, and conscience. It was hard to imagine that it could insult any Lithuanian (with the exception, of course, of those who had fired the fatal shots).

To our shame, the underground publication *Ausa* published a "rebuttal" to Venclova under the pseudonym Zuvintas. *Ausa* did not find it necessary to present before the court of its readers the criticized article itself. This antisemitic article of Zuvintas was reprinted by the emigre *Akiraciai*. I fear that this polemic, which has already begun, may turn into a justification of the murderers. [. . .]

And what does Zuvintas have to say about the guilt for the destruction of the Jews in Lithuania? His answer is very simple—the Jews themselves are responsible! It is easy to say what his "arguments" are worth.

1. The Jews in June 1940 welcomed the Red Army with flowers. Thus, they demonstrated to the Lithuanian people blatant ingratitude, for which they were punished a year later. Of course, it was not right to annihilate the Jews, but one must try to also understand the *pogromshchiki* who just got a little out of hand. [. . .]

Tsarist Russia was a prisonhouse of nations in which the Jews were particularly oppressed. And the Jews welcomed the creation of an independent Lithuanian republic, hoping that its establishment would facilitate the national and religious development of the Jewish people. [. . .] The Jews paid for this broad cultural autonomy one hundred times over—with their blood in the fight for an independent Lithuania. [. . .]

However, to be fair, one should recall that the Jews were not equal in rights to the Lithuanians. For example, they could not own land, nor could they serve as officers in the army. [. . .] After the overthrow of the government which brought Smetona[23] to power, the Jews were removed from government. This was used by Stalin's propaganda, which promised the Jews to abolish all legal restrictions. And since the Jews knew Stalin only from the newspaper *Izvestiia* circulating in Lithuania, they believed him.

There was another—in my view, the main—reason for the loyalty of the Jews to the Soviet regime in 1939. Only the naive rulers did not grasp the covert meaning of the agreement between Stalin and Hitler. Throughout the world people were saying that Lithuania would soon be occupied by German troops. For Lithuanian Jews this meant the ghetto, concentration camp, death. With the arrival of the Russians rather than the Germans, of course the Jews rejoiced since for them this meant—life!

Why did they not think about our people? When in late 1941 we ecstatically welcomed the German army, were many of us thinking of the Jews? We complain that the world cannot understand why we greeted the occupiers with flowers. Then why do we not understand the Jews, who had analogous, if not more weighty, reasons for rejoicing at the arrival of the Red Army?

2. Among the NKVD personnel there were many Jews, including real sadists. Zuvintas recalls the monster Rozovskii.[24] One can extend the lists of Jews who worked in the NKVD. But were the Jews really more prominent than the Lithuanians? The occupier's press depicted in black colors the Jewish sadist type in order to stir up antisemitic sentiments. However, today also it is being used to frighten the people. [. . .]

One often hears that when in July 1940, on the eve of elections to the so-called Seimas (parliament), arrests took place, only Jews (and a sole Lithuanian) took part in them. This was a tried and true tactic: when the Gestapo arrested Poles, at least one Lithuanian had to take part in the action, and when they arrested Lithuanians, the participation of a Pole was obligatory. . . . The Judeophobes Beria and Stalin used the same tactic.

3. The Jews constituted a majority of the ranks of the Communist Party of Lithuania. Zuvintas points to the fact that as yet there has not been published a breakdown of the ethnic composition of the Communist Party of Lithuania during the interwar period. This, most likely, can be explained by the fact that the underground organizations consciously inflated the number of their personnel. We shall attempt to utilize indirect data.

On October 19, 1933, Sneckus and twenty-four other Lithuanian Communists were exchanged for Lithuanian priests arrested in Russia (among them was the archbishop Matulenis). Among the twenty-four were fourteen Lithuanians, i.e., more than half. According to the Lithuanian security service, on the eve of World War II, the Communist Party of Lithuania had only 600 to 650 members. Let us assume that there were approximately 300 Jews among them and, even, as some do, that all of them committed crimes against Lithuania—what was the guilt of those 200,000 Jews who were killed? It somehow does not even seem serious to explain that in 1940 the Soviet regime was supported not only by Jews. In the so-called popular government there was only one Jew—the Minister of Health, L. Koganas.[25]

Hitler's propaganda made great efforts to convince part of the Lithuanian population that every Jew was a Communist and every Communist a Jew. In fact the majority of Jews were either deeply religious or indifferent both to religion and politics.

Such is the value of Zuvintas's "arguments."[. . .]

It is difficult to imagine the extent of the suffering of the Jews in the ghetto daily facing new and varied "actions." Even only in one's imagination the picture is terribly unbearable of people brought to the place of execution, of older children grasping their mothers' skirts while the mothers were pressing the infants to their breasts. And the two-legged beasts tore them away—their little ones—and bashed their heads in with spades.

Can one really forget this, forgive it, justify it? Only a person for whom nothing is holy can find objective arguments for murder!

The antisemite is a pitiful scoundrel, a vile and cowardly nonentity who dares to raise his hand only against the weak. But he is at the same time a marionette which the strong of this world employ for their most foul deeds. Those who raised their hands against the Jews with equal facility also destroyed their own countrymen.

Every people has its own Cains and its wandering sheep. But there is not and cannot be a court in the world which would dare condemn a whole people and the Jews do not need a speech from me in their defense. It was not the Jews who shot the Lithuanians, but the reverse. The murder of Lithuanian Jewry is also a tragedy for the Lithuanian people. [. . .]

The Lithuanians are no worse and no better than other peoples. Only a handful of Lithuanians are Judeophobes. This is attested to by the memoirs of Jews themselves: "In the fall of 1941 all the Jews from the nearby villages were forced into the big ghetto in Pasvalis. It was planned to destroy the ghetto, but by the appointed day people willing to do the shooting were not found" (*Fighters without Weapons*, comp. S. Binkiene, Vilnius, p. 271). [. . .]

We are called upon to resolve the problem of restoring the unity and confidence between Jews and Lithuanians. As the Jews themselves say, their position in Lithuania is much better than in other Soviet republics. However, much more should be done. And first of all—to appreciate the scale of the tragedy and degree of guilt of the generation of the 1940s. Then, after getting rid of preconceptions, to better understand the Jewish people, its culture and traditions. Only thus can we arrive at coexistence, mutual understanding, and cooperation. [. . .]

It has been the lot of the Lithuanian people to suffer much—such was the will of Providence. Concerned only about the future of my own people, I dream that never in the future will Lithuanians shoot innocents and the defenseless. The world has no guarantee that there will not be even more horrible catastrophes. One can save the Lithuanians from participating in pogroms (this time of non-Jews) only by unambiguously condemning the murder of their civilian population.

Let us respect the memory of the Jews who perished. Their fraternal graves have become overgrown with moss. The Church may assume the initiative of seeing to it that memorials are placed at the sites where Jews were shot. On Memorial Day I too shall bring a wreath to the Svencioneliai cemetery for the fraternal grave where Lithuanian Jews lie. I hope that on this day I will not be alone. [. . .]

3. Not All Lithuanians Are Guilty

[This statement by Sajudis, the movement which started out supporting Mikhail Gorbachev's reforms but organized the move toward Lithuanian independence, was made in 1989.]

Greetings of the council of the Parliament (Seimas) of Sajudis, the Lithuanian Movement for Reform[26] to the founding meeting of the Society for Jewish Culture in Lithuania.[27]

Dear Brothers!

In sincerely hailing your honorable gathering, one wants to say something important. Lithuanian-Jewish relations were not hostile in Lithuania of old. Beginning in the fifteenth century, the Jews were protected by the privileges granted by Vytautas and, subsequently, by the traditional tolerance typical of Lithuanian culture. Therefore, Lithuania, when it was incorporated into the Russian Empire, became a country, one of the few in Eastern Europe, where there were no pogroms against Jews. Tensions which arose on the basis of competition were usually resolved in a civil manner. The Jews accepted the restoration of Lithuania with loyalty, defended its independence on the battlefield, participated in the establishment of the administration of the Lithuanian Republic, in its sciences and its health-care system. For its part, the Republic of Lithuania guaranteed the cultural autonomy of its constituent peoples: Jewish houses of prayer, schools, and public organizations operated unhindered here.

The situation changed when Lithuania once again lost its independence. Between 1940 and 1944, a terrible fate overcame many inhabitants of Lithuania, both Jews and Lithuanians. Attacks on culture mercilessly destroyed Jewish institutions. Later, during the occupation of Lithuania by the Nazi army, the majority of the Jewish inhabitants of Lithuania were annihilated. [. . .]

Among Lithuanian Jews then there were also those who, out of conviction or careerist considerations, approved Stalin's arbitrariness—people of this nationality also were among those who were sent from the USSR as functionaries of the organs of repression. This fact was quickly seized upon and used in the psychological arsenal of the world war which was then already starting; Hitler's antisemitic propaganda made a particular effort to expose and highlight such cases. Hence, in the atmosphere of lawlessness and amorality of 1940–41 there arose a new and unprecedented in Lithuania basis for cruelty and greed, vengeance and fanaticism, for totally unjustified violence toward the Jewish people as a whole, in which, unfortunately, Lithuanians also took part.

In postwar Lithuania, when Stalinism scorned the natural rights of the people to their own existence and development, when human spiritual values and monuments of culture were destroyed, the above-mentioned tragic events of that time also did their work; when the Republic no longer existed, they facilitated the distortion of historical memory and opportunistic propaganda against the former republic and its adherents.

The graves of Jewish victims remained anonymous, with the memory of this people also being blotted out, nor were there any longer Jewish schools or museums, while their old cemeteries were left uncared for. Only now, during the time of the rebirth of a new Lithuania with the common efforts of Jews and Lithuanians is there a desire to repair at least part of the spiritual and cultural losses suffered.

We shall never agree with the antisemitic assertions that claim that the Jews as a people ever wished evil to Lithuania or harmed it; but we also cannot agree with the accusations that allege that the whole Lithuanian people murdered Jews. There were many cases—a portion of them have been published or been recounted in the press—when Lithuanians, despite the risk to their lives, hid and saved Jewish children and even whole families.

Nevertheless, as representatives of the people, feeling a partial guilt for those demoralized Lithuanians who during the war participated in the murder of Jews, we say: in blaming the guilty, do not blame the innocent, and if, for some reason, people have blamed our whole people, reconsider or simply—forgive. The Lithuanian people has also lost many sons and daughters, the victims of the anti-Lithuanian genocide also lie in anonymous graves—from Lithuanian forests to the islands of the Arctic Sea.

May the memory of all the innocent victims help our new generations to foster the sentiment of brotherhood among people, solidarity of sufferers, and of those in danger. Let us extend our hands to each other, those who believe in the future of peoples, let us know and understand each other, let us in a friendly manner start on the path of renewed justice and humanism.

(signature) Vyt. Landsbergis
Chairman of the Council of the Seimas [parliament] of the
LPS [*Lietuvos Persitvarkymo Sajudis*] [Lithuanian Movement for Reform]
Members of the Council of the Seimas of the LPS
(signatures)

4. Pogrom in Kaunas: One Version[28]

[This article appeared in a journal published in 1989 by a Lithuanian association which maintained cultural ties with Lithuanians outside the mother country.]

This article deals with events which took place on June 25, 1941, in the Lietukis garage in Kaunas. Abroad this was referred to as an anti-Jewish pogrom. In 1941 Aleksandras Bendinskas, the author of the article, was a member of the staff (later chief of staff) of the Lithuanian Activist Front (LAF), and during the tragedy he was responsible for the protection of trade, industrial, and transport facilities. He spent many years in Soviet places of incarceration, concentration camps, and deportation. He admits to having been an LAF activist. What we are printing here is Bendinskas's version.[29] *If there are people who know that it happened differently, we shall publish well-based testimonies of theirs.*

Certain security services even today treat in a one-sided way the uprising of June 22–25, i.e., before the entry of the Germans into Kaunas, and the events of June 26–30 (already after the Germans had occupied Lithuania).

The uprising which was prepared and carried out by the LAF and people who joined them, was doomed. The majority paid for their involvement with their lives.

What took place in the Lietukis garage? I hereby testify and assert that there were killed a few more than ten people,[30] or perhaps fewer. The people were murdered cruelly. The very fact that people were killed without sentencing by any court, without accusation, by people who were following only their passions, cannot be justified either legally or morally. The fifth commandment says: "Thou shalt not kill." In regard to how it happened there are no documents on either the one or, apparently, on the other side. Those who prepared the uprising and participated in it can present several facts which explain the prehistory and circumstances of this painful event.

On June 13, 14, and 15, during the deportation of people from Lithuania, trucks were employed from Lietukis and other facilities. People's moaning had not yet ceased when on June 17–18 a rumor began circulating about the preparation of still another deportation of people to Siberia on even a grander scale. We staff members of LAF gathered to consider what to do. At that time, at all enterprises and transport facilities groups of "fives" were organized; their task was not to allow the Red Army to blow up water pipes, the power station, telephone exchange, railway bridge, bread bakery, etc., and not to allow the pillaging of enterprises, stores, or the appropriation of means of transport.

What was to be done if war did not break out and the deportations were repeated? It was decided to resist by force. [. . .] The order was given to the transport "fives" to sabotage as many vehicles as possible.

The fatal day, June 22. The primary evil was Bolshevism, which we already knew. With our own eyes we had seen the mass arrests, the deportation of families without trial or accusation. The secondary evil was war. We had to choose war, i.e., the lesser evil. Although the nucleus of the staff of the LAF consisted of military personnel, in the event of war it did not have strategic plans, maps, and hardly had any weapons. Following orders, the members of the staff who were responsible for enterprises, institutions, and other facilities, acted automatically. Some "fives" were autonomous. From the beginning of the war they acted independently, in accordance with local circumstances and depending on the situation at the moment. [. . .]

What occurred on the "side of the Bolsheviks" I and others did not know. But already on the evening of June 22 in the general commotion the Bolsheviks began to flee *en masse*. But not everyone fled on the first day. Some top security, police, Party and government officials remained to destroy documents which testified to their crimes and their scope, the lists of their agents, the direct involvement of Moscow in provocations of that time. Among these zealous ones were Russians, Lithuanians, and Jews. Toward evening on June 23, security personnel (the majority of whom were investigators) also decided to save themselves. They ran to the Lietukis garage for cars. They were caught by one of the "fives," disarmed and locked up in the garage, since the prison and security departments were not yet fully in our hands. Furthermore, street battles were going on. In some plants and institutions the security departments were broken into and lists were used to find out the names of their heads. Some of these were caught and they also were put into the garage. On June 25, some political prisoners liberated from Soviet jails found out that security personnel were being held in the garage. They came to check this out and recognized some of them. There began something which no one could have foreseen in advance: filled with malice, their backs bloody, driven by revenge, with broken fingers, some had lost their families carried off in train cars to Siberia, the former prisoners killed those held in the garage. They beat them with whatever they found in the garage—with metal bars, with spades, etc. It was a terrible sight! The Lord's commandment "Thou shalt not kill" was broken. There are people still alive who saw this execution. They are known to me. Neither I nor others whom I know find any justification for this bacchanalia of death.

What kind of people were killed in the Lietukis garage? Most authors who wrote about this event have presented it as a pogrom of Jews. Was it that in fact? According to my information, the majority of those killed were investigators of the security organs and heads of the "special departments" of enterprises and institutions; they were killed as officials rather than as representatives of a certain nationality. It turned out that a majority of the victims were Jews (documents found show this).

One is amazed by the manipulations of authors who in describing this crime continually inflate the figures. At the time of the uprising, people spoke of more than ten killed. Later the Soviet press reported thirty, subsequently forty, and recently the respected E. Zilberis[31] already mentioned seventy. Only competent legal organs can establish the number killed, the identity of the victims and the circumstances of this horrible event; if necessary—with the participation of foreign observers. All the spots in this ugly incident of our country—the white ones, the black ones, and the red ones—must be clarified.

5. Pogrom in Kaunas: Another Version[32]

[This letter to the editor appeared in 1989 as a reply to the previous document.]

The author of the article [Aleksandras Bendinskas] in *Gimtasis Krastas*, No. 32, a former member of the organization LAF, and subsequently its chief of staff, after forty-eight years had passed since the terrible murders in the garage in Kaunas, remembered God's fifth commandment "Thou shalt not kill." He attempts to raise the curtain from this bloody bacchanalia, attempts to show the bloody actions of the Activists of the Front, the ugly murders of unarmed, innocent people as an expression of patriotism despite the fact that these groups of fives were conscious accomplices of the occupiers. Something like this could have been done by depraved or bloody sadists. Even a naive person will hardly believe that officials who were specially left behind (the author indicated this) to destroy documents were not provided transportation and on June 23, 1941, went to the garage for transport in order to leave.

From this it follows that the victims supposedly themselves entered the garage and were destroyed as investigators of the security organs and heads of "special departments," i.e., they were killed as officials and not as representatives of a particular people. The claim of the author that in the garage more than ten, perhaps a few more, were killed is an outright lie.

A. Bendinskas's version is contradicted by available archival documents, protocols of investigations, articles published in the press, books . . . and photographs (the Germans photographed this execution).

According to materials at hand, the murders in the garage took place not on the 25th of June 1941, but on the 27th. In Kaunas that day was called "Bloody Friday."

Tomas Venclova, in his article "Jews and Lithuanians"[33] (*Literatura ir menas*,[34] 1989, No. 8), wrote: "Many perished during the first days of the war when the Germans had already entered Lithuania but still had not gained control of it. At that time pogroms took place in Kaunas. It is thought that on June 25–26, 1941, 3,800 Jews were killed in Kaunas. Several hundred of them met their deaths in the garage on Vytautas Prospect."

The slaughter of June 27, 1941, in the garage in Kaunas was described by Y. Damba in his book *V krovavom vikhre*[35] (In the Bloody Whirlwind). It tells of such horrible murders as the shooting of a seven-year-old son along with his father. On page 681 there are two photographs of murders and tortures. The originals are preserved in Yad Vashem in Jerusalem.

Archbishop Metropolitan J. Skvireckas[36] wrote in his diary: "On June 28, 1941, I was visited by Colonel physician Matulionis and the priest Morkunas. They recounted the horrible events, which made me shudder, of the killing of several dozen Jews. All of them who were in the courtyard were battered with sticks until their heads were broken open. When they were all already dying, a new group of captured Jews were brought. A crowd watched this beating."

This is also described in the book *Masines zudynes Lietuvoje* (Mass Murders in Lithuania 1941–1944),[37] 1961, part 1, which adduces eyewitness accounts by J. Vainilavicius and L. Survila. They state that they saw the bodies of fifty tortured Jews lying on the ground while new victims were brought in groups of two and three from the street outside.

In the book by J. Vicas, *Na sluzhbe SS* (In the Service of the SS), published in 1961, the eyewitness N. Goldsteinas stated that approximately one hundred Jews were herded into the Kaunas garage on No. 43 Vytautas Prospect and were cruelly tortured. The bloody orgies of the murder of the Jews in the garage were also described by the writer M. Eglinas in his book *Mirties fortuose* (In the Forts of Death).[38] He described how those beastly cannibals sprayed water with rubber hoses into people's mouths until their intestines burst, how limbs, cut-off fingers, and torn-out tongues floated in pools of blood; how one of the murderers climbed onto a pile of corpses and played a small accordion. Other cutthroats, drunk on vodka and blood, danced around like savages. The book contains a photograph of the killings.

At the locations of the mass murders of Jews there are still no inscriptions memorializing the murdered Jews.[39] Were the more than 200,000 killed (in Paneriai, the Ninth Fort, and elsewhere) simply "Soviet people" or were they killed for their nationality? Unfortunately the Council of Ministers of Lithuania until now has given no attention to this matter, although only the Council of Ministers can do something about it with a resolution on this matter.

I regret that until now there has not yet been translated into Lithuanian the article of A. Terliackas in the newspaper *Soglosie* (1989, no. 3) "*Eshche raz o evreiakh i litovtsakh*" (Once Again about Jews and Lithuanians).[40] This publication would counter those ideas which compromise the Jews on the basis of propaganda from the arsenal of Goebbels. Now you will change nothing, but fifty years after these terrible events there is still no memorial plaque in the wing of the Ninth Fort, in Vilijampole (Slobodka) where the ghetto was, or at the site of the Lietukis garage.

[signature] Haimas Finkelsteinas

From the editor of *Gimtasis krastas*: We wish to clarify only one detail in this striking letter: as we understand it, A. Bendinskas nowhere wrote that the murders in the Lietukis garage were "an expression of patriotism." He categorically condemns this event as lacking in any justification, but only presents a different explanation from the one presented previously and attempts to give the background of these events. *Gimtasis krastas* would never publish an article justifying murder.

6. Were the Jews in 1940 Guilty before Lithuania?[41]

[First published in the newspaper of the Communist Youth League in Lithuania, 1989.]

Political wisdom requires that one end the senseless argument: who was more guilty, the Jews or the Lithuanians? The tasks which have arisen for

Lithuania insistently require that it preserve like the apple of its eye normal relations without conflict between all the peoples living in the Republic: Lithuanians, Jews, Poles, Russians.

> Soviet garrisons enmeshed us with a spider web [in the fall of 1939—L.T.], while the Communists, Red Army men, and Jews openly said that our fate was already decided. . . . Immediately after the arrival of Dekanozov[42] . . . the minorities surrounded him—Jews and a very small number of Communists who succeeded in getting out of jail. They were not interested in the mood, the welfare, the future of the area. They were only hungering to occupy posts, under the protection of tanks and bayonets to serve the provider—"the father, friend and teacher" [Stalin]. This Judaized Georgian Dekanozov and several Party members, especially Jews, want to trade our independence for personal careers. [All emphases mine—L.T.]

These and other phrases, which were reprinted in *Literatura ir menas* from *Zapisi* (Notes) of L. Dovydenas[43] (written in 1943), might make the reader think that the Jews were guilty for the misfortunes which overtook Lithuania in 1940.

Let's begin from the beginning. The mutual aid pact of October 10, 1939, allowed Stalin's Soviet Union to enter Lithuania with one foot, and the ultimatum of June 14, 1940—with the second. However, the pact and ultimatum involved neither Jews nor Communists, but just the Lithuanian government of Smetona[44] and Merkys.[45] The creation of V. Dekanozov—the "people's" government, which disguised the occupation and prepared the farce of the "people's" *seimas* (parliament)—was headed by members of the Lithuanian intelligentsia, Ju. Paleckis,[46] M. Gedvilas,[47] V. Kreve-Mickevicius.[48] It is true that in this government there was one Jew, the Minister of Health, L. Koganas.[49] Of the seventy-nine representatives of the "people's" *seimas*, only four were Jews, despite the fact that they comprised 8 percent of the population of Lithuania. In the delegation of twenty members which traveled to Moscow, "to the sun," two were Jews and five were well-known Lithuanian writers. According to Vydunas,[50] what is inevitable should be accepted with equanimity. It would be good if the elite of the Lithuanian intelligentsia had accepted the summer of 1940 at least with dignity. Alas! Let us listen to an account of how they accepted it:

> The days which we are now living through [June 15 to 17, when the roads of Lithuania were inundated with Red Army troops—L.T.] remain the brightest and best days in the history of the Lithuanian people. About these days the people will create legends and songs.
>
> P. Cvirka[51] (June 19)

> To be a member of the Union of Soviet Socialist Republics—that means to be under the protection of the invincible Red Army. To be in the family of the Union of Soviet Socialist Republics—that means to gain the rights of a person and citizen of the world, that means to be a citizen of that part of the world at whose might and order the rest of the world looks and will look with envy. To be in the family of the Union of Soviet Socialist Republics—that means to create the greatest value of humanity, which every people, every individual constantly desires. . . . May I today be permitted to express the greatest respect . . . to the unforgettable father of nations, who had understood our needs, shown to us such understanding, to [our] best friend and leader Joseph Stalin.
>
> Quoted at the beginning of an article by the writer Liudas Dovydenas (August 24)

Similar dithyrambs one could cite *en masse*. P. Cvirka and L. Gira, S. Neris and A. Venclova, I. Simkus and K Korsakas, K. Boruta and L. Dovydenas,[52] competed in composing paeans to the tyrant and his armies. So should one be upset that many citizens, and not only Jews, but also Lithuanians, Poles, and Russians, with portraits of Stalin and songs like "*Shiroka strana moia rodnaia*" (Broad Is My Native Land, i.e., the USSR) filled the streets and squares of the cities?

In fact, in 1940 the Jews did make up a significant part of the Communist and Soviet activists of Lithuania. However, one should not forget that half of the impoverished towns and villages were also composed of Jews. Nor should one forget that it is not possible to identify Stalin and Dekanozov with all Georgians, NKVD personnel with all Russians, the executioners of Jews with all Lithuanians, just as one cannot identify Todesas[53] and Rozauskas[54] with all Jews of Lithuania. By the way, D. Todesas repented before he died (see "The Truth and Only the Truth," *Gimtasis Krastas* no. 23, [1988]), which one cannot say about his Lithuanian henchmen Pocius and Raslanas.[55]

L. Truska

Notes

This essay was adapted from *Jews and Jewish Topics in the Soviet Union and Eastern Europe*, 1(11) (Spring 1990), 33–66.

1. *Tiesa*, June 30, 1989.
2. *Sovietish heymland* no. 3, 1990, p. 131.
3. This refers to the residents of Lithuania proper, not including 85,000 Jews from the Vilna (Vilnius, Wilno) region, annexed to Lithuania after the Molotov-Ribbentrop Pact, and 15,000 Polish refugees who entered Lithuania after the on-

set of World War II. At the time of the German invasion of the USSR, approximately 250,000 Jews were living in Lithuania; they amounted to 10 percent of the total population of Lithuania.

4. *Yahadut Lita*, vol. 4, Tel Aviv, 1984, pp. 450–51 (Hebrew).
5. Discussion was stimulated, for example, by the letter of T. Venclova (see below); the American television film *Holocaust*; articles of Israeli scholars, for example the report by Sara Neshamit, "Lithuanian Historiography on Jewish-Lithuanian Relations during the Second World War," in the collection *The Holocaust and Historiography: Reports and Discussions at the Fifth International Conference of Holocaust Researchers*, Yad Vashem, 1987, pp. 244, 253 (Hebrew).
6. The Lithuanian researcher Vytautas Zeimantas for many years concerned himself with uncovering the crimes of the German occupiers and their accomplices. He reported on war crimes trials as correspondent for *Tiesa*. His book *Teisingumas reikalavja* (Justice Demands) appeared in Lithuanian in Vilnius in 1984 (Mintis Publishing House, 109 pp.).
7. "Carnival diversions in the Luoke area," *Gimtasis krastas*, 1988, no. 6. Reacting to this publication, the Jewish researcher Emanuelis Zingeris (in ibid. no. 11) attributes these rituals to a lack of spiritual contact between Lithuanians and Jews; I. Kudirka (in ibid. no. 21) views the masks not as insulting to the Jews as a people, but as an expression of the ancient Lithuanian custom of gaily taking leave of winter when everything and everyone but the clergy were made fun of. In issue no. 11 the editors noted that these publications reflect "to some extent the national total isolation of our people at that time."

   In 1968, twenty-six representatives of the Jewish intelligentsia of Lithuania, in a letter to the First Secretary of the SSR of Lithuania, A. Sneckus, stated that they saw in these "amusements" a manifestation of mass antisemitism: see the collection *Petitsii pis'ma i obrashcheniia evreev SSSR* (Petitions, Letters and Appeals of the Jews of the USSR), in the series *Evrei i evreiskii narod* (Jews and the Jewish People), Hebrew University of Jerusalem, Centre for Research and Documentation of East European Jewry, 1973, vol. 1, p. 1.
8. The journal does not indicate source of the publication. The article by Professor Levin, "Arrests and Deportations of Lithuanian Jews to Remote Areas of the Soviet Union, 1940–1941," was published in the journal *Crossroads* (New York, later, Israel), 1984, no. 11, pp. 67–107.
9. Danielius Todesas, "The Truth and Only the Truth" in *Gimtasis Krastas*, 1988, no. 23. D. Todesas (1910–1989), came from a well-off Jewish family; in his youth he joined the Communist movement, for which he was imprisoned in 1934 (he was released in 1940). By profession he was an architectural engineer, and he participated in World War II. He held top administrative posts in the Soviet *nomenklatura* and was known for his translations of political and artistic literature.
10. Stasys Kasauskas, "Rainiai," *Gimtasis Krastas*, 1988, no. 42. These events were also written about by his brother Raimondas Kasauskas (see "The Black Sun of June," *Tiesa*, June 14, 1989).
11. This letter was put at our disposal by Professor Dov Levin.
12. *Ir be ginklo karial* (Fighters without Weapons), compiler Sofija Binkiene (Vilnius: Mintis Publishers, 1967), 295 pp., preface by Chairman of the Presidium of the Supreme Soviet of the Lithuanian SSR, Justas Paleckis. S. Binkiene has been

recognized as a "righteous gentile" for her role in saving refugees from the Kaunas ghetto.

13. Genrikas Zimanas, "People vs. Murderers (Those Who Saved Jews in Hitler-Occupied Lithuania)," *Tiesa*, April 12, 1989. The editor's preface notes that this article was found among the manuscripts left by Zimanas and is to be dated October-November 1984. Genrikas Zimanas (1910–1985)—a well-known public figure, editor-in-chief of *Tiesa*, 1940–41 and 1945–70 and, thereafter, of the journal *Kommunist*. Zimanas was born into the family of a Jewish land renter. In 1932 he graduated from the biology faculty of Kaunas University. He became a member of the Communist Party of Lithuania in 1934. In the 1930s he taught in various Jewish schools and worked for the legal Jewish press. During World War II he was a member of the staff of the Lithuanian partisan movement. His postwar works and articles dealt with issues of ideology, culture, nationality problems, and also opposition to Zionism. His last work was *Di sovetishe Yidn—Patriotn fun zeyer sotsialistish heymland* (Soviet Jews: Patriots of Their Socialist Homeland), (Moscow: Sovetskii pisatel', 1984), p. 64, supplement to *Sovietish heymland*, no. 8 (44).

14. About Yehiel Damba, see n. 35. The same material, with a preface from the editor, appeared in the Belorussian journal *Politicheskii sobesednik*, 1990, no. 5, p. 45.

15. The article "Jews and Lithuanians," by Tomas Venclova, was first published in an unofficial Jewish *samizdat* journal, *Evrei v SSSR* (Jews in the USSR), no. 12, January-March, 1976, Moscow, reprinted in *Evreiskii samizdat* (Jewish *samizdat*) series, *Evrei i evreiskii narod*, Center for Research and Documentation of East European Jewry, Jerusalem, vol. 13, pp. 66–71. The article was published in 1989 in the newspaper of the Writers' Union of Lithuania, *Literatura I menas*. Unfortunately, since this newspaper was not available to us, we could not compare the texts.

16. Tomas Venclova (b. 1937) writer, scholar, and translator, graduated from Vilnius State University in 1960. From 1966 to 1969 he taught European literature and comparative linguistics at his alma mater. In Lithuania he published collections of poetry, articles on literature, and books for the general reader. He left the USSR in the 1970s and was deprived of citizenship on the charge that he did not intend to return. He joined the faculty at Yale University.

17. Paneriai, suburb of Vilnius, site of mass executions of Jews. From July 1941 to July 1944 more than 100,000 people were executed there. In 1948 a memorial was placed there and in 1960 a museum was established. In 1988 the text on the memorial was changed to include the number of Jews killed there.

18. The Ninth Fort—one of the forts of a line built at tsarist command in the late nineteenth and early twentieth centuries. Until World War II it served as a prison. During the Nazi occupation the Ninth Fort was a site of mass murder of Jews. (Before it became a death factory, civilians were executed in the Fourth and Seventh Forts and prisoners of war in the Second, Third, and Sixth Forts.) Approximately 70,000 Jews and 10,000 prisoners of war were killed in the Ninth Fort. In 1959 a museum was established and a memorial placed there. In 1996 it was in part a memorial to the victims of Stalinism. [Since 1989, the museum displays have been revised several times; the depiction of Jewish martyrdom is far more extensive than it was in the Soviet period. Part of the museum complex has been devoted to the Soviet deportees from Lithuania. —ed.]

19. "My father"—Antanas Venclova (1906–1971), a well-known poet, prose writer, and scholar, recognized as a "national writer" of the Lithuanian SSR. He began to publish in 1924 and belonged to a group of progressive writers. He taught in schools, including a Jewish gymnasium, in Kaunas and Klaipeda. In 1940 he served as people's commissar of education of Lithuania; he was evacuated before the Nazis arrived. In 1954–59, he was chairman of the Union of Writers of Lithuania. He joined the Communist Party in 1950, and in 1952–60 he was a member of the Central Committee of the Communist Party of Lithuania. Tomas Venclova's mother was the daughter of the well-known professor of classical philology, M. Rackauskas.
20. "The most famous writer" is Aleksandr Solzhenitsyn.
21. Vladimir Grigor'evich Dekanozov (1889–1953)—political figure from Georgia. In 1939 he was in the Commissariat of Foreign Affairs of the USSR. In 1939–41 he was candidate member of the Central Committee, in 1940–41 Soviet ambassador to Germany, and in 1941–50, a member of the Central Committee of the CPSU. In June 1953 he was relieved of his post as Minister of Foreign Affairs of the Georgian SSR. Together with Beria and others, he was tried on December 18–23 and sentenced to death.
22. The article "Once More about Jews and Lithuanians," by Antanas Terliackas, was written in 1978 but was published only in March 1989, in the newspaper *The League of Free Lithuania.*
23. Antanas Smetona (1874–1944), president of the Lithuanian republic 1919–20, from 1924 leader of the Tautininkai party, from 1926, president of Lithuania. On June 15, 1940, he fled to Germany. Subsequently he lived in the United States.
24. Eusiejus Rozauskas (b. 1907)—participant in the revolutionary movement. From 1926 to 1934 he was a student at Kaunas University. In 1935 he joined the Communist Party of Lithuania. In 1936 he was arrested for revolutionary activity and sentenced to seven years in prison. Under the Soviet regime, he was in the security service. In 1946 he was arrested. But from 1953 he occupied important posts in the Ministry of Culture, in the archives branch of the state library. He was involved in the publication of historical volumes, and was one of the editors of the two-volume *Masines Zudynes Lietuvaye* (Mass Murders in Lithuania 1941–1944).
25. Moisiejus-Leonas Koganas (1894–1956)—prominent physician, specialist in lung diseases. He graduated from Moscow University in 1919 and became a doctor in the Red Army. He worked as a doctor in Lithuania from 1921 and in the 1930s was involved in the Lithuanian Red Cross. For two months (June-July) in 1940 he was Minister of Health and Social Welfare. During World War II he was chief physician in tuberculosis clinics in various cities in the Soviet Union. After the war he served in high posts in the health services and as physician in a tuberculosis sanitarium.
26. This greeting from the Lithuanian Movement for Reform (Sajudis) was preceded by a declaration adopted on May 1, 1989, by Sajudis on Lithuanian-Jewish relations in which, in addition to the greeting, the following was said:

> . . . The murderers can be separated from the people, they can be cursed, but there will remain an irrepressible feeling of guilt due to the fact that in tragic circumstances people did not help another people as was the

custom. Only hundreds of individual Lithuanians, at the risk of their own lives, were saviors of the condemned. This was a noble, desperate attempt which the Jews and their families have not forgotten and will not forget. Even more significant peoples in Europe were able to offer little help to their Jews, but they at least have had the opportunity to repent. The Lithuanians did not. This people, which itself was demoralized by an occupying and totalitarian regime, did not have the chance to find and condemn the murderers.

It has not been able to do this until now because a super-national autocracy has spoken for it and done its judging. We were not allowed to continually remember and to view the sites of the bloody murders. If a ploughman turned up those places, bulldozers were sent to level them. We were not allowed to estimate the number of victims or to refer to the executioners by name. It seemed to us that the bloody massacre of the Jewish people was being implicitly approved. We were not allowed to express our grief; during the years of Brezhnev's rule we were mere voiceless observers when hundreds of Jewish families left Lithuania. In the depths of our souls we felt that they were not leaving us Lithuanians, but that a common woe had affected us.

Our silence increased our guilt. . . .

27. The founding meeting of the Society for Jewish Culture in Lithuania was described by *Tiesa* correspondent Algimantas Budrys in an article titled "Along Steps Paved with Gravestones," *Tiesa,* March 7, 1989:

> Last Sunday there took place in Vilnius the founding meeting of the Jewish Culture Society of Lithuania. No people has suffered so many disasters as the Jews: the Inquisition, pogroms, discrimination, physical annihilation. Thus also in Lithuania, where they settled 800 years ago. In 1940 there lived here 240,000 Jews, but today they number only 13,000; some were destroyed by Hitlerism, others by Stalinism, yet others left to seek happiness in another country.
>
> And yet there are Jews who remained. This is not a miracle. But how have they remained?
>
> A Jewish meeting, but not in a Jewish language? My heart was even more wrung by pity when the writer G. Kanovich recalled: "On the way to this meeting you ascended Mount Tauras along steps paved with stones from a Jewish cemetery. Remember that." Truly this should be remembered not only by Jews, but also by those who paved these steps. It was not without reason that the actor L. Noreika, in the name of the artists' unions of Lithuania, read a kind of manifesto expressing sorrow for the years 1940 to 1944, when some Lithuanians raised their hands against Jews. It has been said that "Murderers may be cursed, but the sense of guilt still remains because in that tragic hour our people did not stand up for another people." However, other sentiments were expressed, and they were expressed by Jews, to the effect that during the years of fascist occupation many honest Lithuanians, at the risk of their lives, saved and hid Jews, and that now, in honor of these noble countrymen of ours, in the capital of Israel, Tel Aviv [*sic*; actually in Jerusalem, at the Yad Vashem Remembrance and Martyrs

Authority] there has been planted a green alley of trees.

One hopes that in the future the relations between our peoples will be embodied in trees and other symbols.

28. *Pergale*—monthly literary and artistic journal, organ of the (Soviet) Union of Writers of Lithuania, no. 3 (1989), pp. 130–31, no. 4, pp. 113–14.
29. Aleksandras Bendinskas, "Death in the Lietukis Garage," *Gimtatis Krastas* (weekly published by the Teviske Association for Cultural Ties with Countrymen Abroad), no. 32, August 10–16, 1989.
30. The word *keliolika* is used in Lithuanian for the numbers 11 to 19. This is the word used by the author of the article.
31. Emanuelis Zilberis—chairman of the Jewish Cultural Society in Kaunas.
32. *Gimtasis krastas* no. 34, Aug. 24–30, 1989, letter to the editor.
33. See the article by T. Venclova (document 1).
34. *Literatura ir menas*, organ of the (Soviet) Union of Writers of Lithuania.
35. Yehiel Damba, *V krovavom vikhre* (In the Bloody Whirlwind), (Israel: Moriya Publishers, 1987), 680 pp., documents and photographs. After the murder of his parents by local police, Damba hid with Lithuanians near Telsiai. After the liberation of Lithuania by the Soviet army, he worked as a translator for the NKVD, fighting against the Forest Brethren. In the 1970s he emigrated to Israel. In this autobiographical work, he describes real people and events of the war and postwar period.
36. During the occupation, Archbishop Metropolitan Juozopas Skvireckas was an active accomplice of the Nazis and justified their crimes. In 1944 he fled abroad and died in Austria in 1955.
37. Collection of documents (Vilnius: Mintis Publishers), part 1 (1965), 347 pp.; part 2 (1973), 422 pp. Testimony of witnesses J. Vainilavicius (p. 231) and L. Survila (p. 232) in the section, "The City of Kaunas, Destruction of Jews, Massacre in Garage Courtyard." The book appeared in three editions (in Lithuanian): 1957, 78 pp., 6,000 copies; 1958, 78 pp., 6,000 copies; and 1966, revised and expanded, 122 pp., 20,000 copies.
38. M. Eglinis (Mejeris Elinas), born 1910—Jewish writer and publicist whose literary activity began when he was still a high school student. In 1938 he graduated from the Technical Faculty of Kaunas University. He worked in the Jewish press. During the Nazi occupation he was incarcerated in the Kaunas ghetto where he was a member of the underground. His brother Chaim Yellin was one of the leaders of the ghetto uprising. In the 1970s, M. Elinas emigrated to Israel.
39. In 1989 words were added to the memorial stone at Paneriai about the nationality of the victims. In November 1989 the Lithuanian press reported that at the Vilnius Jewish cemetery a memorial had been erected to the memory of the Jews who were killed during the German occupation. Present at the dedication ceremony was Rabbi Shlomo Goren, former Ashkenazi Chief Rabbi of Israel. The funds for the memorial were donated by Sh. Epstein, former resident of Vilnius, now a citizen of Israel. [In the 1990s, a dispute broke out between Jews who wanted the monument at Panieriai to mention that the killers of the Jews had been the fascists "and their local helpers," and Lithuanian authorities who rejected this formulation. Apparently, a compromise was reached, because as of 1996, the inscrip-

tions in Hebrew and Yiddish mention the "local helpers" and the Lithuanian does not! —ed.] In Kaunas there was no special memorial, but on June 25, 1989, a memorial gathering took place organized by the Jewish Culture Society of Lithuania and the Organization of Former Ghetto Prisoners and Fighters in Lithuania. [In the 1990s, a number of stone markers, inscribed in Lithuanian, Yiddish, and Hebrew, were placed in several locations in what had been the Viliampolje/Slobodka ghetto. Two buildings that belonged to one of the famed yeshivas of Slobodka were also marked by commemorative plaques. —ed.]

40. Excerpts from the article by A. Terliackas, see document 2.

41. *Komjaunimo tiesa*—organ of the Central Committee of the Leninist Communist Youth League which was published in Lithuanian and Russian. Our text is taken from the Russian version, *Komsomol'skaia pravda* (Vilnius), August 11, 1989.

42. For V. Dekanozov, see document 1.

43. Liudas Dovydenas (1906–?), Lithuanian writer. According to the Lithuanian Soviet Encyclopedia, Dovydenas "worked in the official Lithuanian press." In 1944 he defected to the West and from 1949 lived in the United States.

44. On A. Smetona, see n. 23.

45. Antanas Merkys (1887–1955)—Lithuanian political figure, was minister of security, governor of Klaipeda region, mayor of the city of Kaunas, etc. From November 21, 1939, to June 17, 1940, he was prime minister of Lithuania. In 1940, he was deported from Lithuania.

46. Justas Paleckis (1899–1980)—writer, journalist, he began antifascist activity in 1926. On June 17, 1940, on the recommendation of the Central Committee of the Communist Party of Lithuania, he formed the Peoples' Government of Lithuania. From August 1940 he was a member of the Communist Party of Lithuania and played a role in the incorporation of Lithuania into the Soviet Union. From August 25, 1940, to April 1967 he was Chairman of the Presidium of the Supreme Soviet of the Lithuanian SSR, from 1966 Chairman of the Council of Nationalities of the Supreme Soviet of the USSR, and from 1952 candidate member of the Central Committee of the CPSU.

47. Mecislovas Gedvilas (b. 1901), active in the revolutionary movement, from 1934 a member of the Communist Party of Lithuania and editor of legal publications. In 1940 he was minister of internal affairs of the People's Government. From August 1940 he occupied high government posts. From 1952 to 1956 he was candidate member of the CPSU.

48. Vincas Kreve-Mickevicius (1882–1954)—writer, dramatist, and scholar of folklore who wrote in Lithuanian, Polish, and Russian. From 1920 he was professor at Kaunas University. In the late 1930s he was close to progressive, antifascist circles. In the People's Government of 1940 he served as deputy prime minister and minister of foreign affairs. He was chosen president of the Academy of Sciences of the Lithuanian SSR. During the Nazi occupation he was professor at Vilnius University. In 1942 he made an anti-Soviet declaration. In 1944 he fled to the West and in 1947 settled in the United States.

49. For Koganas, Minister of Health of Lithuania in 1940, see n. 25. In the Lithuanian edition of this issue of the newspaper there is a further remark relating to Koganas: "However, he did not sign the order for arrests and deportations or issue decrees about closing down organizations and newspapers."

50. Vydunas, pseudonym of Vilhelmas Storosta (1868–1953), Lithuanian writer, dramatist, and philosopher, participant in Lithuanian cultural activity in East Prussia; member of the PEN Club from 1925. He was persecuted by the Nazis. From 1945, he lived in Germany.

51. Petras Cvirka (1909–1947)—a well-known Lithuanian writer who was active in the antifascist movement. From 1940 a deputy of the Supreme Soviet of the Lithuanian SSR, member of the Communist Party of Lithuania, secretary of the Union of Writers of Soviet Lithuania. He spent the years 1941–44 in evacuation in the USSR. From 1945, Chairman of the Union of Writers, editor of the journal *Pergale*.

52. Liudas Gira (1884–1946), Lithuanian poet and literary critic; in 1940 he was a member of the delegation of the People's *seimas* which asked the Supreme Soviet of the Soviet Union to incorporate Lithuania into the USSR. In 1940–41 he was deputy people's commissar of education of the Lithuanian Republic. In 1942–44 he fought with the 16th Lithuanian Division of the Red Army.

    Salomeja Neris (1904–1945) was a well-known Lithuanian poetess. Before World War II she was active among progressive antifascist writers. During the war she was evacuated to the USSR.

    On Anastas Venclova, see n. 19.

    Jonas Simkus (1906–1965), Lithuanian poet, prose writer, and literary critic active in the antifascist movement. In 1940, editor-in-chief of several newspapers, evacuated to the USSR during World War II; after the war, editor-in-chief of the newspaper *Literatura ir menas* and the journal *Pergale*. In 1948–54 he was chairman of the Writers' Union of Lithuania.

    Kostas Korsakas (b. 1909), poet, literary historian, and critic; member of the Academy of Sciences of the Lithuanian SSR. Before the war he was involved with antifascist journals. In 1940 he was director of the Lithuanian telegraphic agency and the state press. During the war he was evacuated to the USSR. From 1944 to 1957 he was professor at Vilnius University. He became director of the Institute of Lithuanian Literature of the Lithuanian Academy of Sciences.

    Kozys Boruta (1905–1965) poet, prose writer, and translator. He was arrested as a member of the Social Revolutionary party and deported from Lithuania in 1927. He lived in Riga, Vienna, and Berlin, returning to Lithuania in 1931 when he was arrested, this time for antifascist activity. From 1941 to 1946 he worked at the Academy of Sciences of the Lithuanian SSR. During the war he aided escapees from the Vilnius ghetto and preserved manuscripts at the Library of the Academy of Sciences. In 1946 he was sentenced for anti-Soviet activity. After being rehabilitated, he devoted himself to literature and translation. For Dovydenas, see n. 43.

53. On D. Todesas, see n. 9.

54. On E. Rozauskas, see n. 24.

55. Petras Raslanas (b. 1914)—participant in the revolutionary movement. From 1931 a member of the Komsomol, from 1938 a member of the Communist Party of Lithuania. For his revolutionary activity he was sentenced to five years in jail. From 1940 he worked in state security organs in Kaunas, Telsiai, Vilnius, and Moscow.

THIRTEEN

The Holocaust and the Armed Struggle in Belorussia as Reflected in Soviet Literature and Works by Emigres in the West

Shalom Cholawski

This chapter deals with: (1) Soviet Russian and Belorussian literature; (2) Soviet literature in Yiddish; and (3) Belorussian emigre literature appearing in the West.

At the outset it would be useful to define a unique genre of writing prevalent in the literature published in the Soviet Union—the historical novel. The Soviet historical novel constitutes a certain type of historiography which was particularly popular in the Soviet Union.

The Soviet historical novel is a fable based on documentary fact combined with what could be defined as "freedom of expression" by the author—which includes situations, dialogues, natural landscapes, and different types of personages. We have attempted to sift through the historical novel and glean out the documentary truths. The documentary aspect is not usually based on serious research of the subject, but certain stock elements are constantly repeated in most of the books, at times with some changes and variations. One has the impression that the author who set out to write on the subject of the Jews in World War II in the Soviet Union was given a sort of skeleton outline of facts upon which he constructed his own creative work.

Soviet Russian and Belorussian Literature

In Russian or Belorussian literature, in historiography and the historical novel, in documentary anthologies, encyclopedias, and documented research, there was a permanent and consistent, deliberate disregard or obfuscation of the Jewish aspect of the Holocaust or even the involvement of Jews in the war (apart from a few exceptions to which we will refer below). From the ideological viewpoint this phenomenon was expressed in two ways: (1) in the total negation of the Jewish character and the extent of the unique national aspect of the Holocaust; and (2) by reducing the dimensions of the Holocaust, at times drastically, and restricting it to the dimension of a pogrom—a well-known phenomenon in Russia. This was also the term commonly used in Soviet literature. In the majority of works, no reference at all was made to the Holocaust; the murder of "Soviet citizens" was stressed but the mass murder of Jews was completely ignored.

Following is a typology of treatments of the Holocaust in Russian and Belorussian literatures.

1. Complete Estrangement

In a long list of documentary works about the German atrocities in eastern Belorussia and about the Belorussian partisans, reference is made only to "Soviet citizens"; there is no mention of the word "Jew."

In the book *Heroes of the Underground*,[1] on the German atrocities in Mogilev, it is stated that, during the first months of the conquest, the Germans executed 7,500 "persons." This figure most certainly included several thousand Jews who were murdered in the city, but the term "Jew" is never mentioned throughout this work. In the book *Documents*,[2] the murders carried out in the town of Zhlobin (where thousands of Jews lived) are described, but Jews are never referred to at all. P. Kalinin, the head of the partisan movement, in *The Partisan Republic*,[3] discusses the role of the various peoples in battles fought by the partisan forces, *except for the Jews.*

A. I. Zaleskii, who has carried out research on the partisan movement, completely disregards the existence of the Jewish partisans, as well as the underground organization in the Minsk ghetto, from which thousands of Jews joined the partisan movement, as well as the assistance rendered by Jewish female partisans throughout the area.[4]

These are only a few examples. On the other hand, Soviet historiography presents a comprehensive picture of the murders perpetrated by the Germans in Belorussia. In the village of Khatin (on the fifty-fourth kilometer between Minsk and Vitebsk) on March 22, 1943, the Germans murdered 149 persons and razed twenty-six farms. Much documentation on these atrocities has been published. An impressive memorial has been erected on the site, and Khatin has become a popular tourist attraction. In the village of Borki (between Bobruisk and Mogilev) on June 15, 1942, 1,800 persons were murdered by the unit led by Oskar Dirlewanger. The Mogilev archives contain fifty volumes of testimonies on the Borki murders, and every year a memorial service is held at the site in memory of the victims.[5]

2. Reference by Implication

In the description of the murders in Parichi, reference is made to the "quarter cordoned off by barbed wire" but not to "Jew" or "ghetto."[6]

3. Reference to Jewish Names without Noting Their Jewish Origin

In the works by Lipilo and Bogatyr about the organization of the partisan movement in Belorussia, names such as Boris Poupka, Haim Alexandrowitz, Soshin and Shapiro are mentioned—without stating their Jewish origin.[7]

4. Reference to "Ghetto" or "Prisoners of the Ghetto"

For example, in Mozyr, 306 "prisoners of the ghetto" were executed on January 7, 1942, but they were not referred to as Jews.[8]

5. Mention of the Word "Jew" Once in the Text; Then "Soviet Citizens"

Prudnikov, in his book on Polotsk, states: "The Communists and Jews were killed immediately as usual." Then he goes on to speak of 200,000 "Soviet persons" in the area of Polotsk and describes "non-party, Komsomol members, Communists, old people, women and children, as well as prisoners of war and partisans."[9]

6. "Some of My Best Friends Are Jewish"

Linkov, in his book *The War Behind Enemy Lines*,[10] describes the heroic acts of Abraham Girshfeld, who removed a mine from the railway tracks and blew himself up together with five German officers.

In many Soviet books, the story of a Jewish partisan appears and, in this manner, the authors absolve themselves from describing the overall participation of Jews in the war.

7. Description of a Single Event

Ivan Vetrov, in *Brothers in Arms*[11] describes the role of many other peoples besides the Belorussians in the partisan struggles, e.g., Russians, Ukrainians, Udmurts, Mordovians, Slovaks, Czechs, Poles, Serbs, Romanians, Hungarians, antifascist Germans, Austrians, French, Republican Spanish, Belgians—only Jews are missing from this list.

The description of the "history" of the Jews in the war is summarized on page 86 of this work: "The Jews wore a yellow patch on their chest and the Germans beat them with the butts of their rifles."

8. Diminishing the Dimensions of the Massacre

In certain cases, the author selects a remote village, does not give a description of the Jewish environment, but relates that Jews lived and were murdered there. And thus the story of the Jews in the Holocaust is "done with."

9. Obfuscation through "Balancing"

In certain books there is a definite trend toward "balancing": "The legal situation of the non-Jewish Belorussian population in Minsk was hardly different from the situation of the Jews."[12]

Exceptional Cases

In *These Are My Friends*, Michael Lev tells of a canal (probably near Vitebsk), where 20,000 Jews were massacred. A tank on tracks covered the canal with earth. The book also recalls the murder of Jews in Starobin (they poured gasoline over a certain area and burned 700 Jews to death). Stefina, one of the characters in the book, severely criticizes the non-Jewish population: "With certain people their hearts are so callous as they think: the Jews will be massacred and the Lord be with them, but only do not harm us. And now they ask: How is it better with us? To see how children are dying of starvation?"[13]

In *The Partisans*, Yakovlenko describes the wanton cruelty with which the murderers treated the Jewish population of Bobruisk and the thousands of innocent Soviet citizens of Jewish origin (women, children, and old people) who were massacred within a few days.[14]

In the works of these authors, the desire to convince the reader that the Soviet principle of the "brotherhood of nations" existed also during World War II is pronounced. For example, in *The Swords Fight Obstinately*, Ivan Novikov tells how the underground movement in the Minsk ghetto preceded the establishment of the local underground, how the ghetto assisted the local underground movement, and, on the other hand, how female leaders in the local underground movement helped to bring Jews out of the ghetto. He makes special mention of the terrible isolation of the ghetto: "It would seem that no bird would cross the border between the ghetto and the world outside," but, in the name of the sacrosanct socialist principle of the brotherhood of nations, he states in almost pathetic terms, "not even the barbed-wire fence, guns and automatic weapons were able to cut off one part of the town from the other, despite the fact that the other part was called by the terrible name 'ghetto.' "[15] Did this statement reflect the reality of the relationship between the Jews of the ghetto and the non-Jewish population? Certainly not!

The exception among the Soviet writers is Vladimir Karpov who has devoted his books to the Minsk ghetto. The story "Parting"[16] is a monologue by Sarah Levin, the wife of the Vilna poet and artist Moshe Levin (his pseudonym in the ghetto was Ber Sorin), who died in the Minsk ghetto. He remained in the ghetto with his two daughters, Aliza and Soniaiachka. The story is full of colorful imagery of Vilna meetings on "the green bridge," and is written with more candor than Soviet authors generally exhibit when writing about Jewish subjects. It also makes reference to the rescue operations carried out by the Jewish underground in the ghetto. Moshe Levin says to Sarah, "If the enemy has decreed your annihilation—strive to save life, your life. This is also a way to fight the enemy."

Through Fire and Death by Karpov describes characters from the Minsk ghetto underground, including Sofia Sadovskaya, who grew up and was educated under the Soviet regime (in the story "Sparks in the Night"). Sofia and her seven-year-old son are reading the order put out at the beginning of the Nazi invasion of Minsk, announcing the establishment of a "Jewish Quarter." They stand there, muttering in disbelief: "The right to walk in the streets of my own town denied me? To live behind stone walls? Me, the free citizen of the land of the Soviets?"[17] Among the characters in the book is that of Michael Zorov, head of the welfare section of the *Judenrat*.[18]

The most outstanding among Karpov's works was *The Bloody Shores of Nemiga*.[19] Karpov reveals a certain identification with the Jews of the ghetto, attempts to comprehend the feelings of Jews caged behind the barbed wire, and presents moving descriptions.[20] The story revolves around a young couple, products of the Soviet regime: Dora, the young Jewish woman inside the ghetto, her husband Dimin, and their son Elushka, who are outside the ghetto. There is also a description of a partisan unit that includes Jewish officers—Michael and Yasha Zaritsky—at the time when the question of rescuing the Jews of the Minsk ghetto is raised. Considering the general line of Soviet literature, the extent of Karpov's identification with the Jews of the ghetto is praiseworthy.

The greatest surprise in the Soviet literature on this subject is Anatoli Ribakov's *Heavy Sands*.[21] Its theme is completely Jewish, the author is Jewish, and the work was written in Russian (it appeared in the Soviet periodical *Oktyabr* in 1978, nos. 7–9). The book unfolds before us, skillfully and in an original style, an epic of Jewish life—three generations of a Jewish family in a village on the Belorussian-Ukrainian-Russian border—from the beginning of the century until the end of World War II. The book's motto is a verse from the Book of Genesis (29:20): "And Jacob served seven years for Rachel." The Jewish characters, especially the grandmother Rachlenko and the mother Rachel, are well cast and command respect. This can be considered a literary work, but the latter part, which describes the period of the Holocaust, is written with substantial knowledge of life in the ghetto, of the Nazi policy toward the Jews, and, most especially, with an understanding of the dilemma faced by Jews in a small ghetto.

The problem was of a ghetto in a small village in Belorussia with some 3,000 Jewish inhabitants (4,000 had been executed in the first *Aktion* in the spring of 1942). The central character is the mother, Rachel Ivanovski, forty-nine years old, pretty, clever, and indefatigable. Dina, her beautiful daughter, has been executed; Igor, her grandson, has also been executed on the charge of having had contact with the partisans. Her brother, Grisha, fought with a partisan unit active in the vicinity. Weapons have been smuggled into the ghetto. In September, the second *Aktion* is expected to take place, which would mean the annihilation of all the remaining Jews in the ghetto. Rachel got word to Grisha of the imminent danger. What action should the Jews in the ghetto take? The book describes the situation thus:

> The question was put to Uncle Grisha: What's to be done? If you consider this a serious question, you're far from the truth for this is a question that has no answer. A problem with no solution. Revolt? It was just that in the entire ghetto there were only twenty-three people with arms facing an organized army. Where would they stage the defense? In two streets? In wooden houses? The Germans need only put fire to one house, and the entire ghetto, together with its inhabitants, would be consumed by the fire. To break out into the forest? How? In a mass of 3,000 individuals, a mass of refugees, through armed units closely guarding the open space? And even if we consider it possible that they might succeed in breaking out of the ghetto and in reaching the forest, what then? How would they defend themselves? Autumn was upon them, to be followed by winter. There remained only one way: to submit themselves to their fate, to lie down next to their sons, daughters, even without trying to defend themselves in a manner which was hopeless from the outset, but honorable, although this was the possibility most repulsive of all. All the other possibilities led to loss of life only, but this alternative meant the loss of life as well as retaining their honor. Well—revolt and escape to the forest; this is a non-realistic alternative, but without a goal there is no action; a fanciful, daring, desperate plan, there was no alternative, a plan of death out of despair, but death with honor.[22]

This was the first time in the Soviet literature that the dilemma faced by the Jews was presented: whether to fight the Germans with weapons, and what was the purpose of this struggle ("death out of despair with honor"). As Rachel, the leading figure in the ghetto, says to the Jews: "We will fight, it is our fate to die, but we will die in our homes, and not in a ditch."[23]

The revolt breaks out in the ghetto, some 600 persons, together with Rachel, escape under the protection of Grisha and his partisans. Grisha and his men fall in the ensuing battle.

> Within a few hours it was all over, the ghetto razed to the ground, and nearly 2,000 persons buried in the forest, in a ditch, but they did not go to the forest on their own legs. The Germans were forced to kill the

> inhabitants of the ghetto in their own homes. The ghetto revolted. It struggled and lost with honor.[24]

The survivors succeeded in reaching the forest, joined Sidorov's partisan unit, in whose ranks Grisha had fought. Rachel disappears in the forest in a mysterious manner.

After the war, Boris, Rachel's son, who had been drafted into the Red Army, comes to the village and, together with the non-Jewish partisan commander Sidorov, visits the mass grave in the pine forest. On the grave there is a huge granite stone bearing the legend "A memorial to the victims of the Fascist German conquerors," and underneath there is an inscription in Hebrew. Boris, who had attended *cheder* as a child, was able to read the Hebrew words on the memorial stone: "And I will hold as innocent their blood that I have not held as innocent," and he translated the passage to Sidorov as follows: "Everything will be forgiven, but those who have spilled innocent blood will never be forgiven."[25]

The books *The Bloody Shores of Nemiga* and *Heavy Sands* are exceptions. They do not disprove the rule, but sustain it.

Yiddish Literature in Soviet Belorussia

The desperate situation of Yiddish literary works on the Holocaust and on the fighting in Belorussia can be appreciated only when seen against the background of the Jewish community in this country before the war. An anthology of poetry by Bunim Heller, a refugee from western Poland, which appeared in Minsk on the eve of the Russo-German war, did not include poems on the maltreatment of the Jews of western Poland under the Nazi conquest. An example of poems not included in the anthology is "*Mayn mameh in ghetto.*"[26]

Leizer Katzowitz, a Belorussian Jewish writer very much involved in his Jewish environment, wrote *From House to House*,[27] a book on the withdrawal of Soviet troops at the beginning of the war. The balance was provided by describing two families from among those being evacuated—one Belorussian, that of Makar Sereda, and the other that of Itche Feinstein. The idea of evacuating his home upset Feinstein. He broke down and cried, and thus brought upon him the wrath of Sereda. When the watchmaker and violinist Aharon Kopelewitz appeared in a railway carriage, before it set out, he was greeted by a barrage of questions: "Who needs a watchmaker and violinist in times of war? What contribution can you make to the war effort?" In other words, in the description of the evacuation, there is no specific, direct reference to Jews.

The Jewish and national renaissance, which was greatly emphasized at the time of the war among the Jews of Soviet Russia and the Yiddish writers among them, was, in great part, an expression of the yearning for the Jewish family framework and identification with the Jewish people. This was in complete contradiction to the Soviet policy of disregarding the problem of the Jews as a national entity and of relating to the Jew solely as an individual when dealing with him as a subject for a literary work. The Yiddish writers were greatly perplexed by this problem.

Yosef Rabin describes a character with a "Jewish soul"—but he imports him from western Poland. When the Jewish writer M. Lev describes a Soviet Jewish partisan from East Belorussia, he is careful not to attribute to him any Jewish motivation for his struggle against the Nazis.

The Jewish authors "Der Nister," Itzik Feffer, and Bunim Heller wrote about the ghettos, but they moved their scenes of action to Lvov, Warsaw, etc., i.e., Poland.[28] Peretz Markish dared exclaim: "If one Jew remains alive on this earth—this people will remain forever."[29] He dared—and later paid the price. A. Frumkin, in his story, "In the Hospital,"[30] describes a Jewish soldier from a small village in Polesie (southern Belorussia), David Bogod, who was wounded in battle and is recuperating in the hospital. During the long, dreary days he does some hard thinking.

> Suddenly his eyes were opened: a deep depression of loneliness overtook him: he was as lonely as a stone in the field. It had been a long time since he had heard a word spoken in the Jewish language, since he had seen a Jewish letter.

He looks at his non-Jewish companions: What do they know about his people? For all that, what did he know about them? A few verses, some extracts from "Bar Kochba," "Uriel d'Acosta," the Crusades, the Inquisition, and that was all. He recalls his father, his family. Where are they now? Suddenly he was overcome by the smell of the "Antonovka" apples near his home. In the evening he performed his grandfather's "Brogez" dance before the soldiers, the Habad dance, and the "Kosatshok" his uncle Hayim-Sholem used to dance.

Writer Shmuel Persov was born on the border between Belorussia and Ukraine. He was brought up in a traditional home (his father was a teacher), emigrated to America, and returned to Russia during the October Revolution. He was arrested and became a victim of the Stalin purges in 1952. In his book, *Your Name Is People*,[31] he presents three main motifs: (1) "brotherhood of man" during the war; (2) Jewish partisans; (3) the Jewish aspect of the war period.

The author presented brotherhood as it should have been expressed during the period of the Holocaust, according to his own creative imagination but not in fact as it happened during those years. In one of his stories, the Germans enter a kolkhoz near Lapitshi (eastern Belorussia) and fire at a Russian member of the kolkhoz who tried to defend his Jewish neighbor Berl-Leib. The farmers hide the Jew's daughter, Michal, and spread a rumor in the kolkhoz that "Michal had committed suicide." They even hold a "funeral" for her and, while this is in progress, smuggle her out to a partisan unit. After the Jews of Lapitshi were murdered, the partisan commander decides to attack the village to take vengeance. Luzik, a fourteen-year-old Jewish youth, participates in this attack and burns down his parents' house. The commander commends Luzik for his part in the battle ("The House of Simon, Expert of the Forest"). Participating in the partisan attack on the village are Leib Galov, a Jewish partisan, and Kazatkin, a Russian partisan, who takes his beloved harmonica with him everywhere. Kazatkin is badly wounded, but the harmonica remains undamaged. Leib Galov later takes part in a sabotage mining action and also carries the harmonica with him. He falls in battle, but the harmonica remains intact. The harmonica (the title of the story) symbolizes the harmony among individuals and peoples. That is, every individual, every nation within the Soviet Union, sacrifices something of himself, but harmony lives on forever.

In "Jewish Aspect," Persov presents an assimilated Jewish character ("Pan Michael"), a Polish engineer in a partisan unit. Pan Michael took leave of his son Janek, who had been wounded in a partisan action and who is to be sent to the rear of the Soviet lines. He says, in the form of a testament, "My son, remember who you are, who your parents are, your grandparents, and when you are asked who is your father, reply—a Jew, a partisan!"[32] These are the words of a Jew who had come from Poland, but not of a Soviet Jew.

Sh. Gordon succeeds in introducing the Land of Israel in a positive connotation into his Soviet story "The Winegrower from Tel Aviv."[33] A Jewish youth, Shlomo Tsurman, a winegrower from a settlement near Tel Aviv, comes to visit his family in the town of Chelm in Poland. When the war breaks out, his father tries to persuade him to flee to Russia, saying: "Eretz Israel, my son, is where the murderers of the Jews are annihilated." The young boy from Tel Aviv fights valiantly in the ranks of the Red Army and falls in the battle for Smolensk. His commander eulogizes him at the graveside: "Citizens from Palestine, from Tel Aviv, on whose behalf you fought on our Soviet soil, your people will be proud of you. We are proud of you here." Thus, the author associates in a legitimate manner "our Soviet pride" with the pride of the Jewish people in Palestine.

The motif of vengeance also appears in Yiddish literature with great intensity. In one of his stories, Sh. Gordon writes, "When I meet a Jew today I look at his hands. I want to see in Jewish hands a rifle with which to shoot living Germans. This is the only vocation, the most honorable vocation in the world especially for us Jews."[34] Vengeance is connected with brotherhood. In "Pronina," Sh. Gordon tells about Miriam, daughter of the Greenstein family, the only survivor of a family murdered by the Germans. "Everyone called her Maria—it's easier to pronounce. Who is Miriam—a Jewess or Russian—the inhabitants of the village of Pronina did not give this a thought."[35] Miriam, a doctor by profession, defends a patient before a German officer. Under interrogation, she admits to the officer that she is a Jewess. The Germans are about to hang Miriam, but partisans and villagers attack the Germans on the evening before the hanging is to take place. Miriam is rescued and flees to the forest.

Two books were written in Yiddish by participants in the underground movements in the Minsk ghetto. The book by Smolar, *From the Minsk Ghetto*,[36] is a documentary work written by the person who led the Jewish underground movement in the Minsk ghetto. The "brotherhood of nations" constitutes the underlying theme of the book. Life in the ghetto and the bloody *Aktionen* described in it are minimized, but even so this is a basic work on the history of the Minsk ghetto. In Smolar's second work, *Where are You, Comrade Sidorov*—significantly, it was published in Israel after Smolar immigrated there—which deals with the Jews of Minsk after the liberation, the leaders of the Belorussian Communist Party surprise the Jewish partisans returning from the forests with questions such as "Why is it that only Jews are hated?" and "Who gave you permission to set up a Jewish Underground movement in the ghetto?" These questions led to great disappointment among the Soviet Jewish fighters after the war.

The work of the underground fighter Hirsh Dobbin, *The Strength of Life*,[37] describes the life of the Jewish inhabitants of Minsk during the time of the German invasion up to the first *Aktionen* on November 7, 1941. The book appeared in Moscow in 1969. The main characters are Ida and her father. Ida, the younger daughter, wants to flee when the war breaks out. Her father decides to remain in the city. The author presents extracts from their conversations during the first days of the war: "The Germans are a cultured people." "How is it that the Red Army took such a beating?" "I am unable to imagine that they would take people out and just shoot them." After the Germans arrive, things change; Sasha, the non-Jew who has been friendly with Ida, breaks off relations with her. He attacks her father, and a passerby shouts: "The seven good years have ended for the *Zhids*."

In this work the Minsk *Judenrat* is presented as a body collaborating with the Germans, even though this was not true. In the underground movement, mention is made of the need to force the *Judenrat* to give up part of the property stolen from the Jews for the purpose of purchasing weapons. This is a salient example of an attempt to create a balanced picture between the Belorussian police and the Jewish police, despite the fact that, at that time, the police, under the command of Zama Serebriansky, took their instructions from the underground movement in the ghetto.

Alongside the positive description of the non-Jewish population in its attitude to the Jews of the ghetto, the author interpolates some short quotations which express his true, very distressing, feelings: "From time to time thoughts arise that there are no good people any longer in the world, not to mention anything to do with giving help to Jews. These thoughts demoralize and bring you to the stage where you lose faith in yourself, and, at times, it seems as though you're surrounded by a sealed-off wall."[38] It would seem that in these few phrases the author has revealed the truth about himself, while the other parts of his work cover them up.

Belorussian Emigre Literature

There are various groups of Belorussian emigres: those who fled on the eve of the revolution and immediately after; and those who collaborated with the Nazis and who fled when the Germans retreated in June-July 1944.

Belorussian emigre literature is relatively meagre, but it is an apologetic literature. Some of the books and periodicals that have appeared during the past twenty years will be examined below.

Wiktor Ostrowski, in his *Anti-Semitism in Belorussia and Its Origin*, published by the Belorussian Central Council in London (1960),[39] blames antisemitism on Belorussia's neighbors and conquerors, i.e., the Russians and the Poles. According to him, the Belorussian people have not ruled their own country for over 300 years and are a people conquered by the Russians, on the one hand, and the Poles, on the other. The rulers of a country are responsible for crimes committed in that country. Therefore, it was the Russians, in his opinion, who carried out the pogroms throughout the years, including during the civil war. According to his reckoning, in 1948, 443 Jewish artists, writers, painters, musicians, and actors were executed. Antisemitism is "an authentic Russian invention." On the other hand, the author claims, antisemitism is deeply rooted in the Polish people. Examples of this were the proclamations issued by the Polish government-in-exile in London, which were typically antisemitic. The pogrom that took place in Kielce (July 4, 1946), immediately after the end of the Holocaust, is the most outstanding example of Polish antisemitism.

In the opinion of the author, the Belorussian people should not be accused of antisemitism. As "proof," he submits the facts that the Belorussian poet J. Vitsevitsh wrote the following lines: "God who pitied his chosen people and resurrected Israel—accept our prayer. And build up Belorussia for us." Almost a sort of "joint fate."

After casting the blame at the neighbors' door, and after exonerating the Belorussians of the blame, he closes the circle and reveals his true self in one sentence: "It is possible that in every case of murder and pogrom, the cause is to be found in the victim and not in the murderer. They are guilty through no fault of their own."[40]

Three Years Under Nazi Conquest in Belorussia, by Iliynski, deals with the town of Polotsk.[41] The author claims that all the villainy in Belorussia was perpetrated by the Ukrainians. According to him, large numbers of Ukrainians came to Belorussia at the end of 1941 and the beginning of 1942, were accorded special status, received special food rations, and it was they who carried out the crimes together with the Germans. Iliynski exonerates the Belorussians of any guilt and endeavors to base a more general approach on the good economic relations that always existed between the Jews and the Belorussians. He admits that the Belorussian population willingly welcomed the invading Germans, but, in his opinion, this was the same way they were welcomed throughout Russia. This was not because of hatred of Bolshevism, but rather because the Belorussians knew the Germans from the time of World War I and were not afraid of them. In his opinion, the German military units had no interest in the Jews and showed no animosity toward them, and, according to him, even handed out food to all the inhabitants during the first days of the invasion. "Suddenly," Iliynski explains, like a thunderbolt, a decree was received ordering the establishment of a ghetto, a decree which, he maintained, aroused protest and anger among all sections of the population.

The organ of the Belorussian emigres, *Belorussian Youth*,[42] continues the apologetic campaign on behalf of the Belorussian people. The Belorussians, writes Georg Azarko, did not generally object to the invasion because they saw in the German army a force that would free them from Stalin's clutches. Many inhabitants welcomed the German soldiers with flowers. The Germans regarded Belorussia as a country with no history of its own and not yet mature for any form of political independence. In their opinion, the Belorussians completely lacked political ambition. They also lacked an intellectual class.

According to the author, large numbers of young Belorussians joined the German police for three reasons: (1) to keep watch over the German regime; (2) to protect the Belorussian population against the partisans; (3) to protect the Belorussian population against the Germans. The author denies that the Belorussian police were involved in the murder of Jews. The author places the blame for their murder solely on the Germans and Lithuanians. He bases his argument on a letter from the General Commissar of Belorussia, Kube, to Lohse, written on November 1, 1941, referring to the actions of the Lithuanians of the 11th Battalion during the *Aktion* in Slutsk and the actions of the Lithuanians and Latvians in Minsk.

Among the Belorussian emigres is a group that had been brought from the West by the Germans to serve as the heads of the civil administration following the invasion of Belorussia. Outstanding among them was Professor Radoslav Ostrowski, who, in the course of time, was appointed by the Germans to the position of President of the "*Belorusskaia Tsentralnaia Rada*," which was the highest position bestowed by the Nazis in the "Independent Belorussian Government."

A book about the life of Radoslav Ostrowski and his service to the Germans[43] claims that not only did the local population in Belorussia have no part in the persecution of Jews, but they even dared express their disapproval to the German conquerors. Furthermore, Belorussians had a passively sympathetic attitude toward the Jews and even endangered their lives to help them. Hundreds of Belorussians paid with their lives for the help they rendered the Jews. The author describes the case of the farmers of the village of Osatasha who held a religious procession to pray for mercy for the Jews. According to the author, Ostrowski was instrumental in rescuing the wife of Professor Markow, a Jew from Minsk. (Markow and his wife later fled to the partisans.)

The author asks why it is generally assumed that the majority of the Belorussians collaborated with the Germans and were of so little assistance to the Jews. His reply is that the majority of the material relating to the help extended by the Belorussians to the Jews is in the hands of Jews; Jewish scholars are not particularly interested in revealing the objective truth and do not hesitate to ignore documents that are not in accord with their "theories." Furthermore, the supporters of the German criminals were former Communists and Moscow Russians. The latter wore special tags with Belorussian colors on their shoulders in order to incriminate the Belorussians. The local population refused to carry out crimes against the Jews, and the Germans were forced to bring in Lithuanians. The Germans, according to the author, were concerned over the shock suffered by the Belorussian population who were witness to the horrors perpetrated by the Germans against the Jews.

The author presents Kube, the General Commissar of Belorussia, as a "Righteous German" who wished to prevent the acts of horror, and he asks pathetically, if Kube were unable to prevent these acts of horror, how could Radoslav Ostrowski prevent them? Kalush continues his efforts to exonerate Ostrowski and justifies his actions against the Jews as being carried out under pressure from the Germans.

The periodical *Byeloruss*[44] published a rehabilatory article about four central collaborators who worked with the Nazis: Stanislav Stankewitz, Emanuel Yasyok, Anthony Adamowitz, and Witaut Tomash. This article was published as a reply to John Loftus, an American Department of Justice official who appeared on the "60 Minutes" program on American television. He stated that in America there are over 300 Belorussian Nazis, among them leaders of the Belorussian "Independent Government" that had functioned under the Nazis. The writer of the article quotes Hirsh Smolar's statement that had it not been for the assistance of the Belorussians, no Jews would have survived in that country at all. The Soviets, according to him, had attempted to stir up hatred against Stankewitz, Adamowitz, and Tomash and accuse them of collaboration with the Nazis, because all three were active in the field of Belorussian historiography with an anti-Soviet tendency. The author of this article denies that 750,000 Jews were annihilated in Belorussia, as claimed by Loftus, and sets the number at 400,000 (i.e., half of the 800,000 Jews actually killed in Belorussia).

In conclusion, contrary to the apologetic claims made by the Belorussian emigres, on the basis of Jewish, Belorussian and German documentary sources, it can be stated that:

(1) Large numbers of Ukrainians and Lithuanians and some Poles and Russians were more brutal toward the Jews during the Holocaust than the Belorussians, but this terrible fact in no way exonerates the Belorussians for their actions. On the eve of the war, 75 percent of the population in Belorussia were Belorussians (Poles accounted for 8.7 percent; Russians, 5.6 percent; Ukrainians, 1.5 percent). The Belorussian police, who numbered 60,000 and who took their instructions from the Germans, were recruited from the Belorussian population.

(2) The majority of the non-Jewish population took an attitude of indifference, alienation or hostility toward the Jews in the ghettos throughout Belorussia. There were those who rejoiced in the calamity suffered by the Jews, and others who collaborated with the Nazis by turning in and informing on Jews and being actively involved in the extermination process. Few expressed reser-

vations or remained passive, even fewer gave succor, and only a handful of individuals were prepared to pay with their lives for the assistance they rendered. The greatest disappointment experienced by the Jews in the ghettos was the lack of action on the part of their former neighbors and comrades at work, as well as their unwillingness to stand by them even in situations where their lives were not in danger, such as *not* turning in or informing upon Jews or situations in which there was no external coercion or danger. This attitude on the part of the large majority of the non-Jewish population shocked the Jews of the ghettos and influenced their lives within the ghettos and especially the extent of the rescue operations carried out there.

(3) The majority of Belorussians welcomed the Germans, both because of their hatred of the Bolsheviks and because they believed the Nazi Germans had come to liberate them.

(4) The Belorussian police was established by the Germans not to defend the Belorussians from the Germans, but to strengthen the Nazi German regime in Belorussia, to carry out the extermination of the Jews and to fight the partisans. The argument that the supporters of the Nazis in Belorussia were only "former Communists" or "Moscow Russians" cannot be sustained in light of the facts.

(5) The Belorussian collaborators were not members of the Nazi party, nor was this possible. The murder of Jews, or active involvement in their annihilation did not require membership in the Nazi Party. Active involvement in the murder of Jews could be carried out by administrative measures.

(6) Undoubtedly, there were Belorussians who were shocked by the horrors committed against the Jews, but they remained passive. There were many among the non-Jewish population who feared their turn could come after the Jews' extermination.

(7) Jewish Holocaust scholars have noted in their works the aid given the Jews by the Belorussians and have recorded their respect for the courage of those individuals who risked their lives by these acts.

(8) Witnesses able to testify against the war criminals who were active in Belorussia are Belorussian citizens, or former citizens. The attempt to disqualify their testimony because of their citizenship in a formerly Communist country is a transparent tendency. Claims made by emigre groups that the anti-Soviet approach of those who were accused of these crimes was the source of Soviet charges of collaboration with the Nazis are false. The charge is the perpetration of crimes, and this is in no way to be linked to their attitude toward the USSR.

(9) Loftus's estimate that 750,000 Jews were murdered in eastern and western Belorussia is close to the actual figures.

(10) Hirsh Smolar's evaluation of the role of the Belorussians in the rescue of Jews is exaggerated. His book was written in Moscow in 1945, based on the official Communist Party line and under its supervision. It cannot in any way

be considered an objective evaluation, but it, too, does not relate to those Belorussian groups defended by the Belorussian emigres, but to underground groups which fought against the collaborators.

(11) More comprehensive responses to the claims of the Belorussian emigres can be found in research papers that have been published on Belorussia.

In the Soviet literature in Yiddish there is a tendency—mainly veiled, albeit resolute—to give expression to the unique Jewish aspect of the Holocaust and to a sense of the increasing Jewish awareness of these authors. However, the non-Jewish Soviet literature, with the very few exceptions we have noted, had much in common—absurd as this may be—with the emigre literature, despite the extreme differences between them, in their general approach to the main subject. This includes repudiation of the Holocaust and reference to the Jewish victims of the Nazis under the general term "Soviet citizens."

Notes

An earlier version of this essay was published in Yisrael Gutman and Gideon Greif, eds., *The Historiography of the Holocaust Period* (Proceedings of the Fifth Yad Vashem International Historical Conference [Jerusalem: Yad Vashem, 1988]), 315–58.

1. *Geroi podpolia* (Moscow, 1966).
2. *Dokumenty (zverstva nemetsko-fashistskikh zakhavatchikov)* (Moscow, 1945).
3. P. Kalinin, *Partizanskaia respublika* (Minsk, 1968).
4. A. I. Zaleski, *Geroicheskii podvig* (Minsk, 1970); *V partizanskikh kraiakh i zonakh*, (Moscow, 1962); *V tylu vraga* (Minsk, 1969); V. E. Lobanok, *V boiakh za rodinu* (Minsk, 1964); V. K. Iakovlenko, *Partizanskoe mezhdurechie* (Moscow, 1976).
5. *Khatyn* (Minsk, 1978); G. Pralow, "A reizeh kayn Veisrussland," *Sovietish heymland*, 1978, no. 12.
6. *Dokumenty*.
7. P. U. Lipilo, *Organizatsiia partizanskogo dvizheniia BSSR* (Minsk, 1979), p. 90; Z. A. Bogatyr, *Bor'ba v tylu vraga* (Moscow, 1969).
8. *Znamia iunosti*, August 29, 1975.
9. M. S. Prudnikov, *Neulovimie deistvuiut* (Moscow, 1965).
10. G. M. Linkov, *Voina v tylu vraga* (Moscow, 1951); Noah Gris, "Di teme fun Yiddisher gvureh un umkum in der Sovietisher-Russisher literatur," *Parizer tsaytshrift*, 1953, no. 1.
11. Ivan Vetrov, *Brat'ia po oruzhiiu* (Minsk, 1965), p. 86.
12. *Nemetsko-fashistskii okkupatsionnyi rezhim, 1941–1945* (Moscow, 1965), p. 54.
13. Mikhail Lev, *Esli by druzia moi* (Moscow, 1968), p. 279.
14. V. K. Iakovlenko, *Partizanki* (Moscow, 1980).
15. Ivan Novykov, *Ruiny streliaiut v upor* (Minsk, 1965), p. 309.
16. Vladimir Karpov, *Priznanie v nenavisti i liubvi* (Moscow, 1978).
17. V. Karpov, *Skvoz ogon' i smert* (Minsk, 1970).

18. Ibid., p. 78.
19. V. Karpov, *Nemigi krovavie berega* (Moscow, 1963).
20. Ibid., p. 21.
21. Anatolii Rybakov, *Chol Kaved* (Tel Aviv, 1980).
22. Ibid., p. 240.
23. Ibid., p. 242.
24. Ibid., p. 244.
25. Ibid., p. 250.
26. Yitzhak Lan, *Hishtakfut ha-Shoah veHitnagdut shel Yehudei Brit Hamoatzot ve-Polin ve-Pirsumim ha-Yidim be-Brit Hamoatzot bein haShanim 1941–1948* (The Holocaust and the Resistance of Soviet and Polish Jewry as Reflected in Yiddish Publications in the Soviet Union 1941–1948), M.A. Thesis, Jerusalem, 1973.
27. Leizer Katzowitz, *Fun haym zu haym* (Moscow: Emes, 1946).
28. Y. Rabin, *Mayne eygene* (Moscow, 1947); M. Lev, *Partizanisher vegn* (Moscow, 1948); "Der Nister," *Oifshtand fun di farurteilte* (Lvov); Itzik Feffer, *Shotens fun Varshaver geto—Shein un aufshein* (Moscow: 1946); Bunim Heller, *Di erd hot getzitert* (Moscow: Emes, 1946).
29. *Tsum zig—literarischer zamelbuch* (Moscow: Emes, 1944), p. 230. See Lan, *Hishtakfut ha-Shoah.*
30. *Tsum zig.*
31. S. Persov, *Dayn nomen iz Folk* (Moscow: Emes, 1944).
32. *"Pan Michael" un zein zun Janek*, in ibid., pp. 46–52.
33. Sh. Gordon, *Milchome tsayt* (Moscow: Emes, 1946).
34. Ibid., pp. 22–24.
35. Ibid., p. 155.
36. H. Smolar, *Fun Minsker geto* (Moscow: Emes, 1946).
37. Hirsh Dobin, *Der koach fun lebn* (Moscow: Sovietskii pisatel'), 1969.
38. Ibid., pp. 307–308.
39. Wiktor Ostrowski, *Anti-Semitism in Byelorussia and Its Origins* (London: Byelorussian Central Council, 1960).
40. Ibid., p. 60.
41. Iliinskii, *Tri goda pod nemetskoi okkupatsii v Belorusi* (Frankfurt-am-Main: Gran, n.d.).
42. Georg Azarko, "The German Occupation in Byelorussia," *Byelorussian Youth*, vol. 3, no 1 (fall, 1974).
43. V. Kalush, *In the Service of the People for a Free Byelorussia, Biographical Notes on Professor Radoslav Ostrowski* (London, 1964).
44. *Byeloruss Monthly*, May 1982.

FOURTEEN

Soviet Jews under Nazi Occupation in Northeastern Belarus and Western Russia

Daniel Romanovsky

Of the six million Jews who perished in the Holocaust at least one in four died within the territory of the USSR. If this area is limited to the regions which constituted the USSR before September 1, 1939, the number of victims comes to somewhere between one-eighth and a quarter of the total number of Jews killed during World War II, according to various estimates.

In spite of these figures, the Holocaust in the occupied territories of the USSR is probably the most obscure and least examined aspect of the history of the Jewish catastrophe. Thus, one of the first and still foremost examinations of the history of the Holocaust, Raul Hilberg's *The Destruction of the European Jews*, devotes only seventy of the first edition's 700 pages to the tragic events on Soviet soil, the events themselves being viewed from the German perspective. In Nora Levin's *The Holocaust*, no more than eighty out of 700 pages even touch upon the Soviet events (along with events in Poland and other countries), and *The War against the Jews* by Lucy Dawidowicz does not even include a chapter on the events in the USSR.

The exact number of Jews who perished in the war is not yet firmly established. Existing estimates of the number of victims of the genocide, covering the whole of occupied Europe and its separate parts, vary precisely because of differing figures for the number of Jews killed in the USSR. The estimates for the Soviet Union (using 1938 borders) range from 700,000 Jews killed (Reitlinger) to 1,500,000 (Lestchinsky).[1]

There is nothing surprising about this situation. Soviet historiography was largely silent on the Jewish tragedy for over forty years. The rather scarce official documents concerning the annihilation of civilians were drawn up by various official Soviet bodies; almost nowhere are they concerned with Jews specifically. Soviet Jewry was unique inasmuch as an officially acknowledged Jewish community did not exist for over half a century. Nowhere, either in rural or urban areas, did the Jews constitute a legal or religious entity, nor did they have communal and cultural institutions, for reasons elucidated in Chapter One. This means that for more than half a century Jewish records were not kept, except insofar as Jews were included in the censuses, records of passport registrations, and the records of the KGB and its predecessors. Therefore, there were no independently maintained Jewish institutions to keep historical and demographic records, and the very habit of keeping such records vanished, except among a few amateurs. The sources available to a Western historian—community documents, archives, journalistic accounts, etc.—were unavailable in the USSR and are only now being unearthed from often-neglected and in some cases partially destroyed, libraries and archives.

The proceedings of the war crimes trials of the Nazis and their collaborators (the first wave of which swept the USSR immediately after the war—the best known being the Minsk trial of 1946—followed by the second wave under Khrushchev in 1957–63, along with the Eichmann trial in Jerusalem and the Frankfurt trial of 1963) are potentially good sources of information regarding the Holocaust. Unfortunately, the materials of these proceedings were mostly in the archives of the KGB and were therefore unavailable to the researcher, so that they remained a largely unexploited resource. Another possible source are German official documents—Hilberg based his work almost exclusively on these. However, even leaving aside the fact that these are the documents of the executioners with all of their inherent shortcomings, it should be noted that these documents were also mostly held as spoils of war in Soviet archives, which were closed to the majority of historians. In the 1990s, however, researchers from Israel, the United States, and Russia itself have gained access to these documents, and many have been microfilmed for deposit and analysis at the Yad Vashem Institute in Jerusalem.

Other currently available sources of information are the living witnesses of the catastrophe—Jews and non-Jews who saw the terrible events of 1941–42 with their own eyes. Obviously, this is a diminishing resource, but despite the presence of many survivors from the USSR now in Israel and the United States, and despite the creation of survivors' groups in many cities of the former Soviet Union, to my knowledge there has been no systematic, large-scale effort to interview them, and most attempts to do so have been sporadic and amateurish. This chapter uses no archival documents and almost no published data—only eyewitness accounts—and is the fruit of perhaps the first attempt (1985–87) to interview survivors within the former Soviet Union itself.[2] The focus is on events in eastern Belarus (then Soviet Belorussia) and adjacent regions of Russia.

The German Occupation of Eastern Belorussia

The German advance through Belorussia was more rapid than on any other front in the Soviet Union. Belorussia lay on the path to Moscow, and the best forces of the Wehrmacht were therefore thrown into that fray. Minsk was seized by the Germans on June 28, 1941; by July 5 they had advanced to the Dnieper; Vitebsk was occupied on July 11. The swiftness of the German advance caught the civilian population, Jews included, by surprise.

Generally, before the Germans seized a town or city, about half the Jews would have managed to leave. There were, of course, departures from this pattern, but on average, according to numerous accounts, no more than half of the Jewish population of eastern Belorussia/western Russia succeeded in escaping inevitable death at this stage. Viewing these events from the peaceful perspective of the postwar period and armed with the knowledge of what was to come, one wonders why so few attempted to leave. Everyone seemed to know that the Germans hated Jews more than any other group, so it would have been sensible for them to abandon their homes and flee to the interior of the USSR. Moreover, it seems that it would have been easy to do so, because eastern Belorussia was sufficiently far from the western border, from which the Germans had entered, and several main highways and railroads passed through it.

The reality, as usual, was much more complex, and could not be addressed by the simple plan "arise and go." Withdrawal of local populations in the face of an enemy advance can be successful only when it is organized, and organized in advance, while the enemy is still far away. To flee from the front-line area on one's own was a very difficult and risky undertaking. The roads were crowded, and few people owned adequate vehicles. Bicycles were a luxury, and a bicycle was hardly adequate for carrying an entire family's possessions; few people had horses with carts. Most of the refugees were townspeople with little knowledge of the countryside or the roads. They could easily become disoriented, and fall into the hands of the Germans or of thieves. Columns of refugees often became targets for German airplanes. Groups without an experienced leader often panicked and suffered losses.

There was, however, an even more significant factor which kept the people from leaving a front-line town on their own: martial law. According to laws introduced not long before the war (in 1940), a worker in a Soviet state enterprise could not leave work or be dismissed without permission from rather high authorities; to leave work without permission was a serious crime. Workers were effectively chained to their positions at least up to the moment when universal chaos began or while the enterprise itself still existed.

Another equally forceful imperative was also connected with one's place of employment. Moral imperatives kept even those who did not have jobs with the state from leaving. The civilian population in the rear was helping out the front, and in a sense, the rear actually was a second front. Fortifications were being built; schoolchildren and high school students went on night air defense duties. Even in peacetime, it was difficult to leave one's home, and many times more difficult when each person leaving (before the officially announced evacuation) was regarded both officially and by public opinion as a deserter. Factory and office workers stayed, as did doctors and nurses. Men and women who were sent to dig trenches, shop assistants in closed shops, and watchmen in already useless stores stayed in their places, convinced that they were doing their duty to the Motherland.

The only sources of initiative in the Soviet rear were the Party and state authorities and the military. For them, it was not saving civilians but repulsing the enemy that mattered. To announce the evacuation of a town any time sooner than immediately before a German attack was unthinkable, for to do so meant to acknowledge the inadequacy of the measures taken for defense and lack of confidence in the Red Army. (The latter in particular could cost not only one's post but one's head.) In order to remain innocent of these two sins, the authorities had to display tireless activity in support of the front even after the front line had been broken, and any defense measures taken were utterly futile.

In Gorki, Mogilev region, two or three days before the Germans attacked, the leadership sent youngsters born in 1924–25 (that is, fifteen- and sixteen-year-olds), mostly Jews, to dig trenches near Shklov. They perished at the hands of the Germans. Similar instances of Jewish townspeople being seized by the Germans after being sent by Soviet authorities to defense works were described by inhabitants of Gorodok, Vitebsk region, and others.

When an evacuation was finally organized by the authorities, the entire civilian population was not included. The Soviet authorities, both military and civilian, had their own "hierarchy of values" that dictated who was to be saved from the enemy. The leadership was responsible not for the lives of the people—who were probably in mortal danger—but first and foremost for state property and military inventory. When an evacuation convoy was formed, the priority was as follows: first the wounded from hospitals or directly from the front, then the equipment of the most important plants and factories, then the pedigree cattle, and so on. In other words, anything was more important than the civilian population. The rescue of equipment, though, saved many thousands of Jewish lives—those of factory workers and others who accompanied them.

The only big enterprise in Shklov, Mogilev region, was the paper factory. Its evacuation started two or three days before the announcement of an organized evacuation of the population. Many factory workers managed to leave along with machine tools and other equipment. Workers with their families were put in carriages together with machine tools, sometimes on top of them. (The family of one informant, "J," traveled in the one-meter-high space between a rolling press and the ceiling of the carriage. J's mother—at considerable personal risk—took with her several illegal passengers, refugee Jews from Vileika. In other carriages were other "illegals" from Bialystok and Minsk.) In this way, the refugees came to Krasnokamsk in the Urals, where the factory was reassembled.

When at last the local authorities summoned up the courage (or were instructed) to start evacuation of the population, the first (and often the only) train would be filled by those categories of people who were, as the authorities understood it, in the greatest danger from a German occupation. Jews as such did not fall into any of these categories. From the official point of view, those in the greatest danger were the state and Party officials, the staff of Internal Affairs Boards (including the police and NKVD) and families of Red Army officers. Whenever possible, they were provided with the swiftest, most reliable, and most comfortable means of evacuation—an automobile, a seat in a passenger train, etc. Others could hope for a cart at best—either their own or one provided by the authorities, but more often they had to rely on their own legs and shoulders.

Despite these obstacles, spontaneous evacuation (usually little more than a panicked rout) did take place. In many towns where the leadership was either disorganized or had itself fled, leaving the people to their fate, this was the only kind of evacuation. Usually the stampede was started by an aerial bombardment, but by then flight was usually futile, and many of the refugees could not escape the German offensive.

In addition to the "objective" physical and social barriers to evacuation, the Jewish population faced "subjective" psychological barriers; alongside those who could not leave were those who did not wish to go. The psychology of a peaceful period was still at work. Few Jews really understood how serious the situation was. Prewar Soviet propaganda had led the nation to believe that the coming war would be "with little blood and on foreign soil." This conviction, combined with the absence of truthful information about the course of military events, nourished all sorts of exaggerated hopes. The common belief was that the Soviet retreat before the Germans was a temporary phenomenon and would end with a major Soviet offensive. Throughout Belorussia, people pinned their hopes on various means to beat back the German advance. Those living in the northern areas, the Vitebsk and Nevel regions, set their hopes on the fortifications near Polotsk; those living in central Belorussia looked to the fortifications near Minsk. They had no idea at all that the fortifications along the old (pre-1939) border had been dismantled.

In general, the local population did not fear the Germans. They were more afraid of military operations than of actual occupation. Initially, the townspeople believed that the best thing to do would be to sit out the war in their villages. Later, as the threat of German occupation became more of a reality, people reassured themselves by saying that any occupation could not last for long, since the war itself would be over quickly.

One of the most important issues is to what extent the Jews themselves were aware of the danger that awaited them as Jews. They undoubtedly knew that the Nazis would persecute them, but what form did they imagine this persecution would take? Young Jews, especially Komsomol members, saw a possible German invasion as a serious threat. In the 1930s there had been a good deal of discussion of Nazi antisemitism. The anti-Nazi films *The Family Oppenheim* and *Professor Mamlock* were shown widely, and had a great impact on public opinion. In 1939–41, with the coming of the Soviet-German Nonaggression Pact, the antifascist propaganda lost much of its urgency. There was little information about the Nazis' potential anti-Jewish measures. Even the term "the Final Solution" lost much of its ominous tone in the interpretation offered by the Soviet mass media. "Who knows what 'Final Solution' means? Maybe the Jews won't lose too much to it." When, at the beginning of the war, the mass media renewed attacks on German antisemitism, many Jews consequently believed it a mere propaganda ploy.

According to the official Soviet version of reality, it was not Jews who faced the greatest danger from the Germans, but Communists. Everyone, Jews included, believed this to be true. Most of the Jews who left the front areas were either Communists or Komsomol members; other Jews were less troubled by the thought of German occupation. Many earnestly believed that former tradesmen, "NEPmen," and others would enjoy a good life under the Germans, because "the fascists are for capitalism, you know, and will be good towards former bourgeois."

Memories of the German occupation during World War I contributed the most to Jewish complacency in the face of German invasion. Of all the armies which passed through Belorussia between 1915 and 1921, the Germans treated the population, including Jews, best. For some towns, the German occupation was also the first contact with modern civilization. For example, in Borisov (near Minsk) electrical lighting was introduced for the first time under German occupation. Many other towns had similar experiences. If a town had not been occupied during World War I, a Jew who had been to Germany before Nazism's rise might be living there and might dissuade the others from leaving.

On the other hand, many refugee Jews came to eastern Belorussia from Poland. These refugees had seen the "new, improved" Germans with their own eyes and could have a greater impact than any newspaper. There was at least one such refugee family in every city, town, or shtetl in eastern Belorussia. Mostly, however, they were inconspicuous people, and the locals did not place much faith in their stories. In some places, however, the Polish refugees were in the public eye and greatly influenced public opinion. (Thus, "T" from Minsk maintained that he left the city only because of his steady contacts with Polish Jews.)

In an atmosphere of contradictory rumors, missing information, and a public consciousness dominated by collective fantasies, the question "to leave or not to leave" was answered on basis of what now seem like trivial considerations. Many people were reluctant to leave their houses, land, and cattle. At the time, of course, this may not have seemed like such a trivial motive. Once the

Communists stopped their economic experimentation around the end of the 1930s, the standard of living began to rise. The first signs of this material well-being were generally quite simple things—basic furniture like a table or bed, a sewing machine, or even a warm hat. The greatest luxury of all was a bicycle or a radio (a tunable radio, that is; radio transmitters that were preset to receive only Moscow and the official stations were quite plentiful). After two decades of a hungry, poor life, it was not easy to part with these possessions, move to an unfamiliar place, and start all over from nothing. For those Jews whose shtetls were turned into kolkhozes (collective farms, like those of Sirotino, in the Vitebsk region), and for thousands of Jewish *yishuvniki* (Jews living in rural areas in non-Jewish surroundings), who had become peasants, these belongings might also include a plot of land, a cow, and farm implements. Peasants were even more reluctant to part with their *khadobe* (livestock) than were townspeople, and it is therefore not surprising that almost all Jewish peasants were exterminated during the war.

Jews and Their Neighbors under Nazi Rule

The situation in which the Soviet Jews under Nazi rule found themselves was unique in many respects; it differed from the situation of the rest of the European Jewry under Nazi occupation. In order to understand this specificity, one must take into account two circumstances. First, according to the Nazi myth, Bolshevik Russia was the main headquarters for world Jewry, the nexus of the world Jewish plot. (The other headquarters, that of the Jewish plutocracy, was in America, but America was far away—and what were the financiers compared to the Judaeo-Bolsheviks?) The struggle against world Jewry had to begin with its decapitation; it was no accident that the "Final Solution" assumed its most violent form—that of total annihilation of all Jews—on Soviet soil. The extermination of Jews in the USSR was carried out not according to any special decree, but in fulfillment of the widely known *Komissarbefehl*, the Commissar Order of June 6, 1941. Nazi dogma declared all Jews, including women, children, and the aged, to be "commissars." Surprising as it may seem, the German authorities—ranging from Nazi Party propagandists to the Wehrmacht High Command—believed in earnest that the Soviet state, its policies, and even the resistance to the German invasion were controlled by Jews. Field Marshal von Reichenau's notorious order of October 10, 1941, and Keitel's directive of September 12, 1941, concerning "Jews in the newly occupied eastern territories" vividly illustrate how strongly the Wehrmacht leadership believed the Nazi myth.

The second unique factor in the situation of Soviet Jews was the Soviet environment itself. The Jewish situation in the USSR was unique inasmuch as Soviet society was unique; it has already been noted that Jews of the USSR were the only Jewish group in the world that did not have its own community. No less unique, however, were the other ethnic groups of the USSR—Ukrainian, Russian, etc. Every member of Soviet society had been deeply affected by twenty years of Soviet socialization. One could say that in 1941 Soviet society was as different from the rest of Europe as was China.

"The Final Solution of the Jewish question" and the doctrine of eliminating Judaeo-Bolshevism had, in this context, additional value to the Germans in their dealings with the non-Jewish population of the USSR. It gave them the chance to portray their invasion as a war of liberation in which the Germans came not to seize the land and exploit the people, but to liberate the peasants from the Bolsheviks. However, the idea that foreign soldiers were liberating the Russians from a regime which, whether good or bad, was the native, Russian rule, seemed somewhat unnatural. The Nazis had to find a way to overcome this. Their propagandists handled this task masterfully by declaring that it was not the new, German rule which was alien, but the old Soviet one. This was made plausible by identifying the Jews with Communists. The words "Communist," "Bolshevik," "Jew," and "Yid" were virtually synonymous in German propaganda. Everything that had aroused the peasants' and townspeoples' resentments—collectivization, liquidation of the kulaks (rich peasants), the daily grind of work on kolkhozes and in factories, the pay, the poor supply of foodstuffs and consumer goods—everything was attributed to the Jews, both collectively and as individuals. Moreover, Jews were accused of having unleashed the war; in this way, the Germans were able to transfer their own, perfectly evident, blame for the calamitous invasion. An image of the Jewish exploiter, sucking the blood from the masses, was instilled into popular consciousness. Jews were accused of everything from serving as commissars of the hated and feared NKVD to using Russian women as domestic servants. The mission of the German army was portrayed, using words and images that were first introduced into the Soviet population's vocabulary by Soviet propaganda and which were understood by all, as causing a "national-socialist revolution" and the downfall of a class of Jewish exploiters. The new rule was called *die neue Ordnung*, which could be translated either as "the new order" or as "the new social system," the latter having been applied to socialism in Soviet rhetoric. At the same time, the new order was a resurrection of the old, pre-Bolshevik, Russian order. Under Nazi occupation, the population began to resurrect traditional Russian forms of local government.

The Soviet arrangement of regional government was preserved under the Nazi occupation. Administrative districts were headed by a Russian or Belorussian director and an entirely Russian or Belorussian staff. A village (known as a *selsoviet* under the Soviet regime and as a *volost'* under the Nazis) would be headed by a Burgermeister. Subordinate to him was the *uprava*, a kind of local governing board organized into several departments—for land-use planning, public health, etc.—and a police force staffed by locals. A village elder would be elected by a peasants' gathering, although occasionally one would be appointed by military authorities; subordinate to him would be one or two (or more) policemen. The local populations managed to organize all these governing bodies, including a numerous police force which frequently had less-than-benign functions, in an astonishingly short period of time—generally a matter of a few days.

The majority of Russians and Belorussians at first accepted the doctrine of "liberation from Bolshevism." There is nothing surprising in this; the memories of the horrors of collectivization and the collapse of the agricultural system were still vivid. The Germans were often awaited as liberators; not only Jews but also Ukrainians and Belorussians of older generations remembered the German occupation of World War I. The Soviet reality of 1940 did not compare favorably with the remembered German occupation of 1918. The belief that German occupation would bring freedom from the kolkhoz was held not only by Belorussians who had suffered during the collectivization and the liquidation of the kulaks, but also by Jews who were often only indirectly connected with the kolkhozes. There were even some—albeit extremely rare—instances when Jews, together with Ukrainians and Belorussians, met the German invaders with "bread and salt" ("K," from Gorodok, Vitebsk region, reported one such incident).

The seeds of German propaganda were therefore planted in uncommonly fertile soil. Ukrainians and Belorussians of the older generation remembered the time of "Yid-commissars," when Jews played a disproportionately large role, as they saw it, in the revolution and civil war. The numerous Jews in the new Party and state governing bodies of the 1920s also confirmed the thesis of "Judeaocratia." Many Jewish activists took part in collectivization—some among the "twenty-five-thousanders," others as NKVD staff. By the end of the 1930s, however, the time of the "Yid-commisars" was long past; Jews no longer played leading roles in the Party and state organizations, and the NKVD had begun to purge its apparatus of Jews. But it was not the distant and untouchable Party leadership or the mysterious and terrible NKVD that were the bosses in the eyes of Ukrainian and Belorussian peasants and townspeople. A much more real authority would be the chairman of an official body in charge of procurements, the chairman of the district financial department, or even a financial inspector or official of the district department of public education—in other words, the officials seen and dealt with on a daily basis. Here, in the 1940s, Jews were still numerous. This is not surprising since during the course of the nineteenth century Jews had regulated exchange between town and village in the western areas of the Russian Empire, as traders, cattle dealers, wholesale buyers, etc. In the 1920s and 1930s, drawing on their pre-Soviet experiences and family traditions, they occupied analogous positions as Soviet officials.

The widespread popular notion that Jews had suffered less than non-Jews from Soviet power played a significant part in public acceptance of the Nazi myth. Collectivization was not as painful for Jews as for non-Jews. For many Jews, it was more of a blessing—it gave thousands of jobless *luftmentshn* a chance to make a living, and to poor Jewish agricultural communes it gave a chance to gain economic success (albeit at the expense of the dispossessed). "B," a former member of a Jewish agricultural community in Sirotino, Vitebsk region, which was transformed into a kolkhoz in 1930, observes: "Jews wanted to go to the kolkhoz; Russians didn't—they ran away, they shot at the authorities, and so on." It is therefore not surprising that in the minds of Sirotino Belorussians, Jews were associated with collectivization.

The cessation of the NEP in 1928, which ruined thousands of people and deprived them of various civil and political rights, came as a severe blow for Jews, but this reversal of fortunes was not as visible to Russians and Belorussians as Jewish prosperity during collectivization; deprived of means of existence and of rights, Jews moved to Minsk, Leningrad, Moscow, Kharkov, and other urban centers, vanishing from the peasants' view. Even firmly established Jewish peasants, when hit by collectivization, gave up their newly obtained land and moved to towns and cities. Moreover, every Jew, even if he or she had suffered in 1928 and 1931, was in some degree grateful to the Soviet government for delivering him or her from the Pale of Jewish Settlement and pogroms. (Technically, of course, it was the Provisional Government of March-October 1917 that delivered Jews from the Pale, but this fact was easily forgotten.) Russians had far fewer reasons to feel grateful to the Soviets, under whom they had made a good start, but a bad finish. It would be wrong, however, to conclude that the reaction of the non-Jewish population to the Nazi occupation in general and to the extermination of the Jews in particular should be described as deriving only from acceptance of the "liberation from Bolsheviks" doctrine. Their reaction was certainly more complicated, and only after having examined it in detail can one pose the potentially damning question of complicity of the local non-Jews with the Nazis. Did Belorussians and Russians help the Jews in this terrible time? With whom did they sympathize more—the executioners or the victims? Does the burden of guilt lie, at least in part, on the shoulders of the population among whom the Jews were living?

The strongest motive determining the conduct of non-Jews who witnessed the mass murder of the Jews was fear. It was fear that made the majority of the population abandon the Jews to their fate, it was fear that most frequently made non-Jews close their doors to Jews seeking refuge, and it was fear that made them drive the Jews from villages or give up refugees from the ghettos. Let us not, therefore, blame the Russians and Belorussians too severely. A non-Jew who hid a Jew risked being shot. To give refuge to someone who was a stranger in every respect while at the same time placing one's own life and family at risk required heroism, and heroism was a commodity in desperately short supply.

Traditional antisemitism did, however, exist, and it played a role. Forbidden and suppressed, driven underground by the Soviets, it emerged again under the Germans, manifesting itself in the attitude of the non-Jewish population toward the genocide of the Jews. The same people who refused to give refuge to Jews gave it freely to escaped prisoners of war and *okruzhentsy* (literally, "the surrounded," soldiers who had been surrounded by enemy troops, cut off from the front and were forced to live illegally in the occupied territories), although the punishment for this was no less severe than that for harboring Jews. This was because in the eyes of the local population the *okruzhentsy* were "our boys" even when their homes were hundreds of kilometers away, while Jews, even neighbors, were aliens. When a Jew was given refuge, he or she was expected to reward his benefactor materially (in accordance with the popular stereotype of Jews as richer than most), while Russians were saved "for nothing." A Russian *okruzhenets*, after settling in a village and passing for a local, could usually rely upon the villagers' silence (sometimes even policemen and Germans pretended not to notice these peaceful "surrounded ones"), while a Jew who tried to pass for a villager was at risk of being turned in every day. Deeply embedded in the consciousness of Belorussians, Ukrainians, and Russians was the notion that Jews were aliens, second-class citizens who could not be relied on to have the same attitudes as "our folks."

Fear and traditional antisemitism are obvious motives of the non-Jewish population's behavior, but these were present in all the occupied countries. There were also motives unique to the Soviet Union. First of all, what happened to the Jews in the USSR in 1941–42 was hardly unique in the Soviet context. The twenty-four years between the 1917 revolution and the German invasion were an exceptionally brutal period in Russian history. There had always been officially designated enemies of Soviet power to be struggled against, often in a cruel and bloody fashion. In 1917–18, this enemy was the old "class of exploiters," the elite of prerevolutionary society; in 1921, it was the remnants of the White Army and peasants who were discontented with the War Communism policy; in 1928, the enemies were urban NEPmen; in 1930–31, village kulaks; all through the 1930s the enemies were the Trotskyites and Bukharinites, that is, the "left" and "right" deviationists. All of these were portrayed by the authorities as life-and-death struggles which required the active participation of every citizen—deviationists had to be condemned publicly, kulaks had to be expelled, etc.

Then came the Germans, who brought with them a new list of official enemies, which included the Jews. The designation of Jews as enemies was no more absurd than, for example, the designation of Bukharinites as enemies, and the struggle against them was only a little more cruel in its methods than the struggle against the kulaks. As in the past, every citizen was expected to take part in the struggle. The new bosses may have had new enemies, but the general idea was the same—Jews, like the kulaks, NEPmen and "Whites" who came before them, were oppressors and exploiters of the workers, and the struggle against them was a class struggle. Everything was quite familiar to the New Soviet Man. How could peasants in 1941 feel empathy for Jews if in the 1930s they had felt no empathy for the expelled? How could they abstain from taking part in the anti-Jewish actions of the Nazis if in 1931 they drove their kulak neighbors from their houses? Soviet rule had produced a type of citizen well suited to life under a totalitarian regime, especially one such as the Nazis established.

The last and perhaps most horrible factor affecting the fate of Soviet Jews of the occupied territories was the inherent indifference of the surrounding population, the indifference due to which, in the words of Bruno Jasienski, "murder and betrayal exist on the Earth."

In the town of Sebezh, Pskov region, in the first days of the occupation two Jews were accused of arson and shot. The police did a poor job of burying them and left their legs sticking out of the ground. This served as a source of jokes for the Russian population of the part of the town where the shootings had taken place. A mass final shooting of Sebezh Jews in March 1942 (including ninety-six people, mostly the elderly, women, and children) was also seen as entertainment by the townsfolk, a way of relieving the monotony of their lives. The policemen, apparently having no shame whatsoever, told the townspeople about the shootings, and to this day the older residents laugh when they retell jokes about this terrible event: how the "crazy Yid" Hanna cried "Great Stalin, look how they torture us!"; how Buss, the chief of police, tore a three- or four-month old baby from the hands of one of the women, tossed it into the air with the words "Let Jewish blood not defile Russian soil!" and shot the child so that the blast knocked the infant's body into the pit that had been dug as a mass grave.

Was this mere antisemitism? It was something more. It was a general ethical backwardness, a lack of cultivation of the spirit. The inhabitants of many other towns and shtetls of Belorussia, Russia, and Ukraine did not hate Jews—they were simply indifferent to them. The life and death of a stranger, especially a member of a different ethnic group, was of no consequence to them. ("How were the Jews shot? Well, what's there to tell about? They were shot, that's all."—from a conversation with an elderly Sebezh woman, who had witnessed the events.) In the Russian popular consciousness, the notion of the intrinsic value of human life was absent. For an average Russian, there was nothing extraordinary about the act of murder.

In this way, the unique conditions of Soviet society determined the fate of the Jews who lived within it. The Jews who had worked peacefully alongside Belorussians and Ukrainians had to pay with their own blood for the crimes of People's Commissar Lazar Kaganovich and the notorious "Yid-commissars," and there was no way to escape. Everyone, old and young alike, had to pay to those who could not and would not distinguish between guilty and innocent, who simply did not give a damn about human life, and who had been prepared to take part in any action organized by a remorseless totalitarian power, no matter how ruthless.

German Techniques of Mass Murder

How was the extermination of the Jewish population of eastern Belorussia actually carried out? The first thing the Germans did upon capturing a town was to form a Russian governing body; they appointed a Burgermeister and a town council, or had them elected, and began to set out policies. They then usually liquidated the former political elite (if they had not been able to escape) with the cooperation of the newly created collaborators. The first people shot were Communists, Soviet activists, and the most prominent Komsomol leaders. These could range in number from one or two to several dozen people. The next step was to deal with the Jews. If there were many Jews in the town, a special Jewish elder would be appointed (in Chashniki, Vitebsk region, it was the former local hospital assistant manager Chereisky; in Yanovichi, Doctor Lifshits; in Senno, the former school principal Svoisky). In smaller villages there were no elders. The elder was usually appointed at the recommendation of the Russian or Belorussian Burgermeister out of that group of Jews who were believed to be easiest to work with, most respected in their communities, and who spoke German. The elder had no real power; his duties generally included compiling lists for the Germans, informing Jews of the occupiers' orders, and distributing work. In small towns in the area under investigation, as in the smaller Polish ghettos, there were practically no Jewish police. I know of only one case where there were police in a ghetto—in Velizh, Smolensk region, where there were no less than 1,400 Jews in the ghetto, which existed until January 30, 1942.

The Germans, in keeping with Nazi doctrine, had to determine who was and was not a Jew. In order to do so, they would arrange a "Jewish census"—a registration of the Jewish population. Jews were forced to wear identification badges to distinguish them from the non-Jewish population. Sometimes this was a six-pointed star of yellow cloth, but usually it consisted simply of two yellow circles on the right shoulder, one in front and one in back. The locals ironically referred to these as "the Order of Lenin—the Order of Stalin." Later, in many locations, special "Jewish camps"—that is, ghettos—were set up. These were often extremely primitive in structure. In Gorodok, Vitebsk region, the ghetto was arranged in August 1941 on the hill slope running down to the river Gorozhanka. It included a big wooden building (formerly a school) and a few other houses. The ghetto was enclosed with barbed wire on three sides, the fourth being the river, and at the highest point on the ghetto border was a watchtower on which a German submachine gunner stood guard. There were about 500 Jews in the ghetto, living in terribly crowded conditions. In Velizh, Smolensk region, the ghetto had twenty-seven houses in Zhgutovskaya Street, and a big pigsty, where 500 Jews lived, at the end of the street.[3] The pigsty was furnished with plank beds in two or three "stories" and a stove; the windows of the pigsty were boarded up, and the entire ghetto was guarded. In other places the ghetto was arranged in simpler fashion. In Yanovichi and Ushachi, both of the Vitebsk region, and in Usvyaty, Pskov region, the ghetto was a district of the town fenced in with barbed wire, from which all non-Jews had been evicted before the Jews were moved in. The ghetto was guarded by one policeman. In Sirotino, Vitebsk region, Sebezh, Pskov region, and Toropets, Kalinin region, ghettos of the same kind were not even fenced. In

Nevel, Pskov region, Jews were driven out of town to an area referred to as "the Blue Dacha," where no less than 700 people were crammed into a few country-type houses. The Blue Dacha was not fenced in, and it was guarded by a single sentry. In Chashniki and Beshenkovichi, Vitebsk region, there were no ghettos at all—Jews were simply driven from numerous houses on the outskirts of town and crammed together in the center. The Jewish district was not even fenced or walled, neither was it guarded; Jews were not even officially forbidden to leave this area. In Senno, Vitebsk region, a similar expulsion of Jews from the outskirts of town and the west side of the lake to the east one (a district known as Golynka) took place in several stages. After the first expulsion, the Jews were "compressed"—that is, the territory of the Jewish sector was diminished. In Yezerishche, Vitebsk region, and Opochka, Pskov region, not long before they were to be shot, all the Jews were gathered in one big house (in Yezerishche, it was a former inn, and in Opochka, the ground floor and basement of a burnt-out four-story house), but up until that moment, they were formally free.

So not everywhere and not always immediately were ghettos set up. In many places there was not even a formal order prohibiting contacts between Jews and non-Jews. Nevertheless, residents of these places almost always remember ghettos. Almost all old residents of the town of Gorki maintain that there was a ghetto in Gorki, on Mstislavskaya Hill, when in fact there was never any ghetto there! The Mstislavka district was neither fenced nor guarded. However, Jews rarely ventured to districts other than those assigned specifically to them; residents of the "Russian" sections of town almost never saw Jews walking on "their turf" without escort, because almost immediately following the German arrival, it became dangerous for Jews to enter the "Russian" parts of town. Any Jew could be assaulted or abused there, and not only at official instigation. In Chashniki, Jews preferred to get to the few water taps located within the Jewish central district in groups of up to ten people, because a person who went to get water alone could have his bucket turned upside down or have worse things done to him. In Yanovichi the ghetto was set up relatively late (in August 1941), and there were no decrees prohibiting contacts between Belorussians and Jews, but many Belorussians stopped greeting their Jewish neighbors in the street at once. Belorussian boys stopped playing with their Jewish schoolmates.

Whether the source of this conduct was fear, antisemitism, or acceptance of the Nazi myth, it had a devastating impact on the Jews, giving them the impression that the world had turned against them. This so demoralized the population of the ghettos, half-ghettos, and special districts that they lost any desire to flee from the towns to the countryside or to seek help from their non-Jewish neighbors. This is one answer to the question of why the Jews did not simply run away from the poorly guarded ghettos.

Organization of ghettos or Jewish camps in eastern Belorussia served no economic purpose, and unlike those in Poland and Lithuania, was unconnected with the occupiers' needs for a labor force. Jews were very seldom sent to any work of real importance, either for the town's economy or for the German army. In Chashniki, young Jews were sent out to cut peat; in other ghettos they were from time to time sent to do construction or perform repairs. Mostly, however, Jews were used for auxiliary, service, or odd jobs—to chop firewood, to clean out cesspits. "G" from Beshenkovichi has clear recollections of what Jews did there: "What kind of jobs did we do? We loaded corn or repaired roads with picks, but mostly we demolished brick buildings, crushed the bricks and used them to cover roads. Besides that, we cut up trees in the forest and in the park for timber." Sometimes Jews were given jobs meant to be humiliating—carrying water on carts without a horse, or perhaps catching flies in the commandant's office. In small towns and villages, most Jews were not subjected to any forced labor. The main purpose of the concentration of Jews was to bring them "safely" to total liquidation in the form of mass shootings.

Ghettos and half-ghettos in eastern Belorussia were ephemeral structures. Most Jews in them were exterminated in the autumn of 1941, although a smaller part survived until the spring of 1942. The exact procedure followed in liquidating the Jewish population varied in different parts of Belorussia and Russia. Contrary to the common perception of most contemporary Russians (and many Jews), the annihilation of the entire—frequently very large—Jewish population of a town or shtetl was in no way an easy operation for Germans. Such operations were very carefully planned and directed by specialists from the SS.

For the areas to the north of Vitebsk, a two-stage liquidation was characteristic. Let us take an operation of this kind in Gorodok as an example. The first shooting of Jews took place in August of 1941, less than a month after the town was occupied by Germans. The victims were mostly young, strong men, along with some older but healthy men and a few women. One morning in August they were assigned to work, which is why they all gathered at the appointed time and place with the shovels that were to be used to dig their own graves. They were put in trucks and taken to the village of Beryozovka, 1.5 kilometers from the town along the Vitebsk highway. From the village they were taken to a narrow gully, well hidden from any chance passersby, and told to dig a pit. On the hillocks around the gully, machine guns had already been placed. There was no hope of escape—when the pit was finished, all the Jews were shot.

Immediately after the first shooting, a ghetto was set up for old people, women, and children. An epidemic broke out in the ghetto, and some of the prisoners died. The last 450 inhabitants of the town ghetto were escorted beyond the barbed wire early on the morning of October 14, 1941, marched through the whole town to an area known as the Volkov Posad and shot in the forest there. The column was escorted by only five Germans with machine guns and some policemen.

What was the purpose of such a two-stage operation? The first stage was intended to eliminate the "backbone" of the Jewish community, that segment of the population most capable of offering resistance to the Germans. This group, the Germans believed, consisted of former Party, Komsomol, and Soviet activists, young men of draft age and other healthy, strong men, and sometimes women. This active group was not large; most young men were in the army, and moreover, in provincial Jewish communities older people predominated, since the younger people had moved to the big cities in the 1920s and 1930s. The elimination of the active segment of the Jews was usually carried out by large forces of Germans, by experienced executioners, and with all possible precautions. The number of executioners in relation to the numbers of victims was relatively large at this stage (for example, according to "E" 's testimony, in Yanovichi during the August 1941 shooting there were about 150 to 200 Jews and sixty-four SS men plus a number of policemen).

The remaining Jews, demoralized, depressed, lacking even the will to live, and consisting mostly of women, the elderly, and children younger than thirteen or fourteen, could be eliminated virtually with bare hands. Some time after the first shooting they would be taken out of the ghetto without much resistance and with minimal escort, driven to the execution site, and exterminated. It was this kind of action that gave birth to the popular myth of thousands of Jews obediently going to their deaths guarded by only two Germans. This job was mostly carried out by the Russian/Belorussian police.

In those areas where the liquidation of the Jewish population took place early on in the occupation (such as Yanovichi, Gorodok, and Sirotino), the element of surprise helped everything to go smoothly. In places where the liquidation took place later in the course of the occupation, however, things went less smoothly. The Jewish population had to be rounded up. For example, in Chashniki, the liquidation took place on February 12, 1942. That morning, about 100 young Jews were sent out to clear out snow. In the afternoon, the German executioners entered the shtetl. The Belorussian police, mobilized from throughout the district, cordoned off all of the roads leading from Chashniki, flooded the Jewish quarter, and led the Jews out to the former Polish Roman Catholic church. The scene resembled a military operation; people were running up and down the streets, and shots and bursts of machine gun fire could be heard. By evening, however, all the Jews were gathered in the church. At the same time, the police intercepted the column of young people coming back from clearing snow and drove them to the church as well. By morning, all of the Jews had been shot. About ten people escaped death, mostly from the group of young people who had been clearing snow.

Something of the same kind happened on February 11, 1942, in Beshenkovichi. About 100 to 150 fit men were gathered in the town park, then taken to a stable in which they were locked. Simultaneously, the Germans started a round-up of Jews in the town, similar to that of Chashniki. The Beshenkovichi men were killed separately, after the women, the elderly, and children.

In some places the occupiers drove Jews to utter demoralization with hunger and unbearable living conditions. In the shtetl of Lyady, which had about 900

Jews before the war, all those remaining were driven in to the former school building a month before their liquidation. There they were kept for a month without food, medical care (there was a violent outbreak of typhus), or heating. The school was guarded by police. It is no wonder that when, on April 2, 1942, the Lyady Jews were led to their deaths, none offered any resistance. In some places, where due to the migration of the young to the cities during the 1920s and 1930s, the Jewish community was on the verge of disappearing (such as in Toropets, Kalinin region, or Pustoshka and Sebezh, Pskov region), the Germans did not even need to hide their motives.

Why didn't the Belorussian Jews take any measures to save themselves? Why didn't they flee the ghettos and half-ghettos during the comparatively quiet period between occupation and liquidation? Why did they not simply run away when they knew beyond any shadow of a doubt that they were being led to death?

Some of the answers to these questions have already been given. The whole atmosphere of the occupied regions was hostile to Jews. The non-Jewish majority was, at best, afraid of them, or hated them outright as the people responsible for collectivization and other crimes of Soviet power, or simply saw them as enemies since the Germans considered them enemies. To seek refuge among the peasants was dangerous, and there was nobody in the forests to whom one could run. In 1941 and early 1942, there were practically no partisans, despite rumors to the contrary. The first detachments which began to form in the autumn of 1941 were so weak that they could not even consider helping the relatively unimportant Jews. Besides, the partisans felt about as much sympathy for the Jews as the non-combatant Russian/Belorussian populations did; that is, they were at best indifferent to them. As the partisan movement got stronger toward the end of 1942, Jews were only reluctantly accepted into detachments, for they were believed to be incapable of fighting. Jewish women and children were, as a rule, not accepted into partisan detachments at all. Partisan detachments were fighting units performing tasks from one directing center; saving civilian populations—especially Jews, the aliens—could in no way be included in their tasks.

Other factors prevented the Jews from leaving the doomed towns and villages. Only the young and healthy could go—the life of a refugee was, after all, very hard. To go meant to leave one's family—one's parents and young children—without any support. Even if they were not shot by the Germans as a way of punishing the fugitive, they would be left quite helpless in a hostile world. Such an action was unthinkable to most of the ghetto inhabitants, who held the traditional Jewish attitude toward family, children, and parents. In general, families of partisans were the first mass victims from among the Belorussian people in 1941–42. A Belorussian might find it easier than a Jew to "get over it."

To resist the actual murder—to try to escape, to attack the executioners—was almost hopeless. The Germans did their best to prevent such attempts from succeeding. Escape was prevented by holding the executions far from the forests; the Germans even carried out executions in plain sight of the population. Even if a Jew could escape shooting, it would be extremely difficult to save oneself by hiding unobtrusively among the Belorussians; all Jews realized this to some extent. Attempts on the part of Jews to resist the executioners were therefore rare. Jews of the shtetl of Kamen, Vitebsk region, were warned that on September 16 (1941) there would be a shooting. That morning, all Jews were driven to a hollow near the Russian cemetery; the site was surrounded by police, and on the hill above, there was a machine gun. Men aged thirty to thirty-five were ordered to dig pits. One of the adult men, Meishe A., shouted "Run away!" threw himself on a guard, and hit him with a shovel. Some time passed before the policemen recovered their wits. Nevertheless, all the Jews but Meishe were shot, while he managed to escape and died only after the war. On that day, his wife and four children were shot. The Jews of the village of Kublichi also attempted to offer resistance. On the night before the shooting they set the ghetto on fire. Out of the 200 Kublichi Jews, only two youngsters escaped.

Although Belorussians, Russians, and Poles also rarely offered resistance, they did so more frequently than Jews. Not only could a Slav hide himself more easily among other Slavs, but by the time the mass executions of Belorussians started, there was a powerful partisan movement. Also, the Jewish model of dignified behavior at death's door differed from that of their neighbors. The persecutions encountered by Jews during the centuries of the Diaspora accustomed them to the thought of violent death. Death is always possible, and must be met with calm and dignity. However great the distance between a Soviet Jew and the ancient Jewish tradition might have been, the significance of this tradition for the Jews of Belorussia and Ukraine cannot be ignored.

"K," a Belorussian woman from Gorodok, offered to supply a Jewish girl, Tanya, a blonde, with the identification documents of her daughter, who had left the town. "K" relates that Tanya declined the offer, saying "No, I will die a Jewess." Had she taken the papers she might well have survived the war. Russian witnesses of mass shootings in Nevel recall with respect how Jewish men met death from Nazi executioners without a single sound or plea for mercy, standing straight and looking their murderers in the eye. But was such stoicism what was needed under the circumstances? Wasn't it more important for somebody to try to survive, not to let the Nazis realize their monstrous plan, to show the murderers that their victims would not yield to them easily, if nothing else? In this regard, the Russian attitude toward death was, in some regard, more constructive. The Jews of the Soviet Union were poorly served by their traditional attitude toward death.

After the Jews Were Gone

As soon as Jews were led away to be shot, their neighbors would stream into their empty houses, searching for "Jewish things." "Jewish property" became an additional, smoldering conflict between the Russian/Belorussian and Jewish communities, a conflict which persists until this day. Both real and imagined "Jewish riches" have been an object of envy among Gentiles, nourishing antisemitism worldwide for centuries. In fact, even in the late nineteenth and early twentieth centuries, the average Jew in Russia lived better than the average Russian, inasmuch as the average town-dweller lived better than the average peasant. Naturally, under the Nazis, the Jewish property issue came once again to the fore. The looting of Jewish property generally started in the first few days of occupation. If some time passed between the retreat of the Red Army and the arrival of the Germans, looting could begin before the actual occupation as looters entered the houses of Jewish evacuees who had already left. Sometimes Jews who had failed to escape from the Germans would return to their houses only to find them completely devastated.

The impetus for mass looting was provided by the occupiers. As a result of military operations, a considerable number of houses were demolished or burned. Many people, both Jews and non-Jews, were left homeless. The Germans solved this problem in typical Nazi style—that is, at the expense of the Jews. Jews would generally be evicted from the better parts of the town that they lived in, or they were driven from the suburbs, if the Germans wished to concentrate them in the center of town. The remaining houses would be given to non-Jews; first in line among these, naturally, were collaborators. Displaced Jews would be resettled in special districts. Thus, the Nazi solution to the housing problem was the first step toward ghettoization. Meanwhile, the non-Jews quickly realized that the Jews had been relegated to a kind of outlaw status that prevented them from complaining to the authorities. The relocated Russians and Belorussians took over not just Jewish houses, but all the furniture, household utensils, and even livestock that had belonged to the former inhabitants. Only a few of the new settlers ever allowed the Jews to take their possessions to their new homes. The authorities generally turned a blind eye to the robbery of the Jewish population. Moreover, they actually encouraged it through their propaganda, saying in effect, "Jews are exploiters of your labor; everything that Jews took from you is yours; go and take it back." The looting of Jewish households was a kind of "expropriation of the expropriators" which neatly dovetailed with the image of "national socialist revolution" that Nazi propaganda sought to create. Allowing the local population to loot at will was a way for the occupiers to buy their sympathy and gratitude at no cost to themselves. Thus, Jewish livestock, stores of foodstuffs, household furnishings, and even bicycles quickly passed into the hands of the more unscrupulous segments of the non-Jewish population.

It was during the mass shootings that the looting degenerated into a virtual orgy. Whereas only the most unscrupulous took part in the "expropriations," theft from the doomed often involved the majority. In many places, the authorities forbade the locals to enter abandoned Jewish houses, but this ban was not always enforced. If the occupiers were able to keep the property more or less untouched, they usually sold it to the Russians and Belorussians in exchange for food—potatoes, eggs, poultry, etc. In larger towns, the authorities sometimes set up shops where property taken from the dead was sold. There was such a shop in the village of Kublichi, Vitebsk region, and probably in Chashniki as well. In smaller villages a one-time public sale occurred. For example, in the village of Ostrovno, Vitebsk region, the Germans simply piled all the possessions of the executed Jews in a public square and assigned a soldier to be an auctioneer. The soldier would pick a sheet or pillow out of the heap and call out, "Who wants it?" The peasants would try to shout each other down, shouting, "Me, sir, me, sir!"

The chief motive of Russians or Belorussians who entered Jewish houses was the mythic "Jewish gold." Any gold the Jews may have had would have been either confiscated by the NKVD at the beginning of the 1930s, traded for food during the occupation, or taken by the Germans before the executions. In the village of Ushachi the looters were shameless enough to climb down into the mass grave where the bodies of the Jews lay after the shooting (the shooting took place on January 14, 1942, but the pit remained open for some time thereafter). The most striking aspect of all this is that even today some witnesses remember how much gold the Germans took from their Jewish neighbors far better than they remember the details of their neighbors' deaths. The quantities that they describe are quite fantastic. The myth of Jewish gold continues to disturb the minds of some inhabitants of eastern Belarus even to this day.

Was it moral for Russians and Belorussians to take things from the dead? Given the circumstances, this is not a simple question. In general, relatively simple things were taken from Jewish households—sheets, pillows, kitchen utensils, and so forth. The life of non-Jews under the Germans was extremely difficult, and every additional plate or spool of thread—regardless of where it came from—helped. It should be noted that many felt it beneath their dignity to take possessions from the dead and would not touch Jewish property. Many others saw "Jewish goods and chattels" as their rightful booty. Most non-Jews, however, rationalized their actions by maintaining that if they didn't take the property, it would be lost for good.

Whether or not theft from the dead is a sin is debatable; however the same cannot be said about theft from the living, no matter how close they are to death. Nevertheless, sometimes locals broke into Jewish houses as the Jews were being gathered for execution—that is, while they were still alive. Sometimes, attempts were made even earlier. For example, after the son of one Jew, Nakhmanson, was shot in the Usvyaty ghetto, his former neighbor approached him and said, "Zalman Itskovich, give me your cow—they're going to shoot you anyway and the Germans will get your cow." Such an attempt to beg possessions from the living was hardly unique.

Finally, some Jewish property passed to Russians and Belorussians not as a result of looting, but in exchange for food. In rare instances some non-Jews helped feed Jews confined to the ghettos, who were not given food even in exchange for forced labor, even while working. Non-Jews usually helped out "their" Jews. Jews who were married to Gentiles could get help from their Gentile relatives, village Jews (*yishuvniki*) could get help from their fellow villagers, and so forth. Only a small percentage of Jews fell into the category of "our" Jews; the majority could not rely on such help. They could rely only on exchange—on the principle of "you scratch my back and I'll scratch yours." Even such an exchange could be daring when carried out under the watchful eyes of the police, but the bread and potatoes brought to Soviet prisoners of war—often at considerable risk to the bearer—stand in stark contrast. No matter how cordial interethnic relations had been before the war, the Jews remained strangers to the Russians and Belorussians. In this paradox lies the key to why the Jews' neighbors effectively abandoned the Jews to their fate.

Survivors

Naturally, there were some Jewish survivors. Who survived and how were they able to do so?

On escaping execution or the ghetto, a Jew had a number of options. The first was to go to a village and try to pass for a Russian. This was possible only for those who did not look Jewish. Villagers could often identify local Jews facially; a runaway Jew could often be recognized even in a far away village. The police knew that many Jews were hiding in the villages and trying to pass as Russians or Belorussians, and they hunted for them actively. Many peasants cooperated, since this was an easy way to gain the occupiers' favor. Many Jewish refugees could not hide their accents, and circumcision provided an additional means of identification.

If a Jew looked Jewish and not Russian or Belorussian, he had no hope of making himself inconspicuous in a village. He could try to link up with a band of partisans—many tried to do so, but in 1941, there were practically no partisans. By 1942 when there were partisans, they were often reluctant to accept Jews, and actually saving Jews was something they did even less willingly. For example, in 1942, one of the partisan detachments was assigned the task of bringing a group of Jews across the front line. The commander of the detachment ordered a Spanish partisan (the only Spaniard in the detachment, he had emigrated to the USSR in 1938) to perform the rescue. The commander knew that a Russian or Belorussian fighter might simply shoot all of the Jews and then report that he had fulfilled his task.

A more reliable means of escape for a Jew was to go through the forests, avoiding villages or main roads, and cross the front lines. "S" from Chashniki walked for thirty-five days through snow and temperatures of minus twenty degrees centigrade, finally crossing the front line near Velikie Luki. "G" from Beshenkovichi wandered for several months in the Vitebsk region, was identified by the Germans as a Jew, escaped, and also managed to cross the front lines near Velikie Luki. Although there are numerous similar examples, there were also many Jews who could not get to the front lines, find the partisans, or find a safe village, but who were captured and identified as Jews, betrayed to the Germans, or killed on the way.

The main problem for a Jewish refugee was getting food. This meant going into the villages. It took a very finely developed intuition to guess which houses it was safe to approach in order to ask for bread. By 1941, there were few villagers who preserved the notion of Soviet patriotism, and even fewer who included helping Jews in that notion. Moreover, a friend of Soviet power might be no friend of Jews. When Jews found help in the form of food (and perhaps lodging for the night in the house or family bath house), it was usually from people who themselves held a kind of "outsider" status—poor peasants living on the outskirts of town, childless old couples, singles, and so forth. The peasants who had been socialized into the Nazi new order turned away from Jews.

There were some unique cases of survival. In Chashniki, the head of the investigations department of the local police force, a man named Pakhomov, who was otherwise known for his atrocities toward Jews, hid an entire Jewish family at his relatives' house. "N" from Yanovichi went not to the east—toward the front lines—but to the west, and lived through the occupation in Germany, passing himself off as a Belorussian who had been conscripted for work. "G" from Sirotino worked for a long time in a German kitchen in a railroad station.

An entire book could be written about Jews who escaped the occupation, but here I have said only a few words about them. This chapter, in sum, is based on perhaps the very first attempt to interview people who were involved in the Holocaust in the Soviet Union. In the 1990s, in Russia, Belarus, and Ukraine, groups of local activists and amateur scholars, as well as a few sociologists and historians, began to interview people in their localities, almost all of them Jews, who had experienced the German occupation. Perhaps in a few years these scattered efforts will be mined and synthesized so that our knowledge of the Holocaust in the Soviet Union will be enriched by the contributions of a rapidly diminishing resource: those who actually witnessed the terrible events of 1941–44.

Notes

1. Gerald Reitlinger, *The Final Solution: The Attempt to Exterminate the Jews of Europe* (New York, 1967 or London, 1953). Jacob Lestschinsky, *Balance Sheet of Extermination* (New York: *American Jewish Congress*, 1976); see also L. Poliakov, *Das Dritte Reich und die Juden* (Berlin, 1955), or see, e.g., Nora Levin, *The Holocaust: The Destruction of European Jewry, 1933–1945* (New York, 1968), p. 718.
2. The interviews are now deposited in the Yad Vashem Archive, Jerusaelm, Israel, in

collection 03, numbers 03/4596 to 03/4740. In the case of Velizh, documentary sources were used in addition to the eyewitness accounts.

3. *Zverstva nemetsko-fashistskikh zahkvatchikov*, no. 3 (1942), pp. 61–62; P. Kurbatova, *O zlodeyaniyakh nemetsko-fashistkikh zakhvatchikov na Smolenshchine* (Smolensk: n.p., 1944), p. 29.

DOCUMENTS

FIFTEEN

Nazi Directives

"The soldier must be deeply aware of the necessity . . . of punishing the Jews."

From the order of the Commander in Chief of the 6th Army, Von Reichenau. October 10, 1941.

Top Secret

Headquarters of the 6th Army

The Conduct of Troops on the Eastern Territories

. . . The question of the attitude of our military toward the Bolshevik system remains unclear in many cases. The main goal of the campaign against the Judaeo-Bolshevik system is the complete defeat and annihilation of Asian influence on European culture. Thus, the armed forces are facing tasks that do not belong to the domain of the usual tasks of the military. A serviceman on the eastern territories is not just a soldier, fighting by the rules of combat, but the carrier of the national idea and an avenger for all the calamities inflicted upon the Germans and the peoples related to them.

That is why a soldier should be deeply aware of the necessity of the stern but justified punishment of the Jews. Another goal is to nip in the bud rebellions in the rear of the German Armed Forces. These rebellions are always inspired, as our experience shows, by the Jews.

Source: Nuremberg Documents D-411, as cited in Yitzhak Arad, ed., *Unichtozhenie Evreev SSSR v gody nemetskoi okkupatsii* (1941–1944) (Jerusalem: Yad Vashem, 1991), p. 52.

The Annihilation of the Judaeo-Bolshevik System

Order of Commander in Chief of the Eleventh Army, von Manstein, November 20, 1941

Top Secret

Beginning with June 22, the German people have been in a holy battle with the Bolshevik system. This battle is not based on the European rules of combat (it would if we were fighting only the Soviet Army). The struggle continues behind the front line: guerrillas, snipers, dressed as civilians, attack separate individuals and small groups of soldiers. By terrorism, using mines and explosive devices, they try to destroy our communication lines. Remaining Bolsheviks terrorize the population which has been liberated from Bolshevism. Thus, they try to prevent the political and economic emancipation of the country. They destroy provisions and industrial sites, forcing the population, especially the urban one, to starve. Jews provide communication between the enemy in our rear and the remnants of the Red Army that are still fighting, as well as the Red administration. They hold firmly, more so than in Europe, all key positions in political administration, trade, and crafts. They are the instigators of all disorders and misconduct. The Judaeo-Bolshevik system should be destroyed once and for all, so that it never threatens our European vital space.

That is why the German soldier is faced, not only with the task of destroying the armed forces of that system, but also should be the carrier of the national idea, an avenger for all the cruelty suffered by the German people. . . . The soldier should understand the necessity of the punishment of Jewry—the carrier of the very spirit of the Bolshevik terror. This is also needed to nip in the bud all disorders that are mainly inspired by the Jews.

Source: Nuremberg Documents PS-4064, as cited in Yitzhak Arad, ed., *Unichtozhenie Evreev SSSR v gody nemetskoi okkupatsii* (1941–1944) (Jerusalem: Yad Vashem, 1991), p. 54.

Provisional Directives by Lohse, *Reichskommissar* for *Ostland*, Concerning the Treatment of Jews, August 13, 1941

The *Reichskommissar* for *Ostland*
IIa 4
Secret!
Provisional Directives for the treatment of Jews in the area of the *Reichskommissariat Ostland.*

The final solution of the Jewish question in the area of the *Reichskommissariat Ostland* will be in accordance with the instructions in my address of July 27, 1941, in Kovno.

Insofar as further measures are taken, particularly by the Security Police, to carry out my verbal instructions, they will not be affected by the following *provisional directives*. The purpose of these provisional directives is merely to assure that where, and as long as, further measures for the final solution are not possible, minimum measures will be taken by the *Generalkommissare* or *Gebietskommissare*.

257

I.a. For the time being only such Jews who are citizens of the German Reich, the Protectorate of Bohemia and Moravia, of the former Republics of Poland, Lithuania, Latvia, Estonia, of the USSR or of its component states, or stateless Jews, will be subject to these directives.

I.b. Other Jews of foreign citizenship, *Mischlinge*, and spouses of Jews who do not wish to share the fate of their Jewish spouses, will be denied permission to leave the area of R.K. [*Reichskommissariat*] Ostland as it is a military area. They are to be kept under surveillance. In addition they may be subjected to the following [measures] among others: Obligation to report daily, a ban on moving [from their place of residence], assignment to a specific dwelling, a ban on leaving the city area, limitations on moving about. If necessary they may be taken into police custody until a further decision is made.

II. A Jew is a person descended from at least three grandparents who are fully Jewish by race.

In addition, a Jew is a person descended from one or two grandparents Jewish by race, if he:

a) belongs or belonged to the Jewish religious community, or
b) on June 20, 1941, or subsequently, was married to, or living in common-law marriage with, a person who is Jewish within the definition of these directives, or who now or in the future enters into such a relationship.

III. In case of doubt, the *Gebietskommissar* or *Stadtskommissar* will decide who is a Jew in accordance with his best judgment and within the definition of these directives.

IV. The *Generalkommissar* in whose areas a civil administration has been introduced will provide immediately for the following:

a) Jews are to be registered by means of an order to report by name, sex, age, and address. The records of the Jewish communities can be used as a further basis for the registration, as well as the statements of reliable local residents.
b) It will be decreed that Jews identify themselves by the wearing of constantly visible yellow six-cornered stars, at least ten centimeters across, on the left side of the chest and in the center of the back.
c) The following is forbidden to Jews:
    1. To move from their locality or change their place of residence without the permission of the *Gebietskommissar* or *Stadtskommissar*.
    2. The use of sidewalks, public transportation . . . and automobiles.
    3. The use of recreational facilities and institutions serving the public (resort areas and bathing facilities, parks and open spaces, playgrounds and athletic fields).
    4. To attend theaters or movie houses, libraries, or museums.
    5. To attend schools of any type.
    6. To possess automobiles or radios.
    7. [Kosher] slaughtering.

d) Jewish doctors and dentists may treat or advise Jewish patients only. Where ghettos or camps are set up they will be distributed through them for the care of the inmates.
Jewish druggists are permitted to practice their profession only in ghettos and camps, according to need. Drug stores previously managed by Jews are to be transferred, under trusteeship, to Aryan druggists.
Jewish veterinarians are forbidden to practice their profession.

e) Jews are forbidden to engage in the professions and occupations listed below:
   1. Attorney-at-Law. . . .
   2. Banking, money-changing, and pawnbroking.
   3. Middlemen and agents.
   4. Trade in real estate.
   5. Traveling peddlers.

f) The following is decreed for the handling of Jewish property:

1. *General*:
The property of the Jewish population is to be confiscated and placed in safekeeping. . . .

2. *Compulsory Registration*:
All Jewish property is to be registered. . . .

3. *Compulsory Surrender*:
Jewish property is to be surrendered on special demand. The demand may be made by general proclamation or by order to certain individuals.
The *Generalkommissare* will order the immediate surrender of the following by proclamation:
   a) Local and foreign currency.
   b) Securities. . . .
   c) Valuables of all kinds (coins and gold and silver bullion, other precious metals, jewelry, precious stones, etc.).

4. For their subsistence, the Jewish population may retain:
   a) Household items needed for minimum requirements (furniture, clothing, linens).
   b) A daily sum of money amounting to 0.20 RM (2 Rubles) for every Jewish member of the household, the money to be released one month in advance.

V. The following further measures are to be strived for vigorously, with due consideration for local, and particularly economic, conditions.
   a) The countryside is to be cleansed of Jews.
   b) Jews are to be removed from all trade, and especially from trade in agricultural products and other foodstuffs.
   c) Jews are to be forbidden residence in localities that are of economic, military, or ideological importance, and also in resorts and spas.
   d) As far as possible, Jews are to be concentrated in cities or in sections of large cities where the population is already predominantly Jewish.

There, ghettos are to be established, and the Jews are to be prohibited from leaving these ghettos. In the ghettos the Jews are to receive only as much food as the rest of the population can spare, but not more than is required for their bare subsistence. The same applies to the allocation of other essential goods.

The inmates of the ghettos will regulate their internal affairs by an administration of their own, which will be supervised by the *Gebietskommissar* or *Stadtskommissar* or a person appointed by him. Jews can be assigned as police for internal order. They may be equipped at most with rubber truncheons and sticks, and are to be identified by wearing white armbands with a yellow Jewish star on the right upper arm. The external hermetic sealing of the ghetto is to be carried out by auxiliary police drawn from the local population.

Permission must be obtained from the *Gebietskommissar* before any person may enter the ghetto.

e) Jews fit for work will be drafted for forced labor as required. The economic interests of deserving members of the local population should not be harmed by the use of Jewish forced labor. Forced labor can be performed by working parties outside the ghettos, or in the ghettos, or, where a ghetto has not yet been established, by single persons outside (for instance, in the workshop of the Jew).

Payment for the work need not be based on performance, but should cover only the bare subsistence of the forced laborer and members of his family not capable of working, taking into account other monies at his disposal. The private establishments and persons on whose behalf the forced labor is being carried out will pay an appropriate sum into the payments office of the *Gebietskommissar*, which, in turn, will pay the forced laborers. Special orders will be issued regarding the accounting for these monies.

VI. The *Generalkommissare* will decide whether to order the measures under Para. V. for the entire districts at one time, or whether to leave their introduction to be carried out separately by the *Gebietskommissare*. The *Generalkommissare* are also authorized to issue more detailed instructions within the framework of these directives or to instruct their *Gebietskommissare* to do so.

Distribution:
Reichskommissariat
Higher SS and Police Leader [*Hoherer SS-und Polizeiführer*]
Generalkommissar:

Estonia
Lithuania
Latvia
Belorussia

Source: Nuremberg Documents PS-1138, as cited in Yitzhak Arad, ed., *Unichtozhenie Evreev SSSR v gody nemetskoi okkupatsii* (1941–1944) (Jerusalem: Yad Vashem, 1991), pp. 378–82 (Document 172), 46.

Rosenberg's Order on Forced Labor for Jews in the Occupied Territories, August 16, 1941, Regulation on the Introduction of Forced Labor for the Jewish Population, August 16, 1941

Pursuant to Article 8 of the Führer's Edict on the Administration of the newly occupied Eastern Territories of July 17, 1941, I order the following:

Article 1

Male and female Jews aged from their completed 14th to completed 60th year, residing in the newly occupied Eastern Territories, are liable for Forced Labor. The Jews will be collected in Forced Labor groups for this purpose.

Article 2

1) Any person evading Forced Labor will be sent to prison with hard labor.
2) In the event of several persons conspiring to avoid Forced Labor, or in other especially grave cases, the death penalty may be imposed.
3) Cases will be judged by the Special Courts.

Article 3

The orders required for the implementation of this regulation will be published by the *Reichskommissare*.

Berlin, August 16, 1941
The Reich Minister for the Occupied Eastern Territories
[signed] Rosenberg

Source: Yitzhak Arad, Yisrael Gutman, and Abraham Margaliot, eds., *Documents on the Holocaust* (Jerusalem and Oxford: Yad Vashem and Pergamon Press, 1987), p. 383 (Document 173).

Exchange of Letters between *Reichskommissar* Lohse and the Ministry for the Eastern Territories, Concerning the "Final Solution"

Riga, November 15, 1941

Reichskommissar for *Ostland*
IIa 4 M.219/4lg
Secret

To: Reich Minister for the Occupied Eastern Territories
Re: Execution of Jews
In reply to letter I/259141 of October 31, 1941

Report from: Government Counselor Trampedach

I have forbidden the unauthorized ["wild"] executions of Jews in Libau because the manner in which they were carried out was irresponsible.

Will you please inform me whether your Inquiry of October 31 should be interpreted as a directive to liquidate all the Jews in *Ostland*? Is this to be done regardless of age, sex, and economic requirements (for instance, the Wehrmacht's demand for skilled workers in the armament industry)? Of course, the cleansing of *Ostland* of Jews is a most important task; its solution, however, must be in accord with the requirements of war production.

So far I have not been able to find such a directive either in the regulations concerning the Jewish question in the "Brown Portfolio" [*Braune Mappe*] or in any other decree.
L[ohse]

Source: Nuremberg Documents PS-3663, as cited in Yitzhak Arad, Yisrael Gutman, and Abraham Margaliot, eds., *Documents on the Holocaust* (Jerusalem and Oxford: Yad Vashem and Pergamon Press, 1987).

Berlin, December 18, 1941

Reich Minister for the Occupied Eastern Territories
Nr. I/1/157/41
To: *Reichskommissar for Ostland*, Riga
Re: Jewish question

In reply to your letter of November 15, 1941:
The Jewish question has presumably been clarified meanwhile by means of verbal discussion. In principle, economic considerations are not to be taken into account in the settlement of the problem. It is further requested that any questions that arise be settled directly with the Higher SS and Police Leader [*Hoherer SS und Polizeiführer*].

f/ Brautigam.

Source: Nuremberg Documents PS-3666, as cited in Yitzhak Arad, Yisrael Gutman, and Abraham Margaliot, eds., *Documents on the Holocaust* (Jerusalem and Oxford: Yad Vashem and Pergamon Press, 1987), pp. 394–95 (Document 178).

Order by Keitel Banning Wehrmacht Contacts with Jews in the Occupied Territories in the East, September 12, 1941

High Command of the Wehrmacht
WFST [Armed Forces Operational Staff] Div. L (IV/Qu)
No. 02041/41 Secret

Führer Headquarters, September 12, 1941
Re: Jews in the Occupied Eastern Territories

. . . The struggle against Bolshevism demands ruthless and energetic action, and first of all against the Jews as well, as the main bearers of Bolshevism. There will, therefore, be no cooperation whatever between the Wehrmacht and the Jewish population, whose attitude is openly or secretly anti-German, and no use is to be made of individual Jews, for any preferential auxiliary services for the Wehrmacht. Under no circumstances are papers to be issued by Military Offices to Jews confirming that they are employed for purposes of the Wehrmacht.

The only exception to be made is the use of Jews in specially organized labor columns, which are only to be employed under German supervision.

It is requested to make this order known to the troops.

Chief of the High Command of the Wehrmacht

[signed] Keitel

Source: Nuremberg Documents NOKW-3292, as cited in Yitzhak Arad, Yisrael Gutman and Abraham Margaliot, eds., *Documents on the Holocaust* (Jerusalem and Oxford: Yad Vashem and Pergamon Press, 1987), p. 387 (Document 175).

Order by Himmler for the Liquidation of the Ghettos of *Ostland*, June 21, 1943

Field Command, June 21, 1943

Reichsführer SS

Secret

To:

1. The Higher SS and Police Leader [*Hoherer SS- und Polizeiführer*] *Ostland*
2. Chief of the SS Economic and Administrative Main Office [*Chef des SS-Wirtschafts-Verwaltungshauptamtes*]

1) I order that all Jews still remaining in ghettos in the *Ostland* area be collected in concentration camps.
2) I prohibit the withdrawal of Jews from concentration camps for [outside] work from August 1, 1943.
3) A concentration camp is to be built near Riga to which will be transferred the entire manufacture of clothing and equipment now operated by the Wehrmacht outside. All private firms will be eliminated. The workshops are to be solely concentration camp workshops. The Chief of the SS Economic and Administrative Main Office is to see to it that there will be no shortfall in the production required by the Wehrmacht as the result of this reorganization.
4) Inmates of the Jewish ghettos who are not required are to be evacuated to the East.

5) As many male Jews as possible are to be taken to the concentration camp in the oil-shale area for the mining of oil-shale.
6) The date set for the reorganization of the concentration camps is August 1, 1943.

[signed] H. Himmler

Source: Yitzhak Arad, Yisrael Gutman, and Abraham Margaliot, eds., *Documents on the Holocaust* (Jerusalem and Oxford Yad Vashem and Pergamon Press, 1987), p. 456 (Document 207).

SIXTEEN

Nazi Actions

The Wehrmacht and the *Einsatzgruppen Aktionen*, September 1941

High Command
Army Group South
Ic/AO (Abw. III)

H.Q., September 24, 1941

Re: The Struggle Against Elements Hostile to the Reich

The investigation of and struggle against tendencies and elements hostile to the Reich (Communists, Jews, etc.), insofar as they are not a part of a hostile military force is, in the occupied areas, *exclusively* the task of the *Sonderkommando* [Special Unit] of the Security Police and the SD, which will take the necessary measures on their own responsibility and carry them out.

Individual actions by members of the Wehrmacht or participation by members of the Wehrmacht in excesses by the Ukrainian population against the Jews is forbidden; they are also forbidden to watch or take photographs of measures taken by the *Sonderkommando*.

This prohibition is to be made known to the members of all units. [Commanders] in charge of discipline at all levels are responsible for the implementation of this prohibition. In the event of breaches it is to be investigated in every case whether the commander failed to carry out his duty of supervision, and when necessary he is to be severely punished.

[signed] von Rundstedt

Distribution:
AOK [Intelligence Command, PzGr tank Group]
Bef rückw H [Rear Command]

Befehlsstelle Süd [Southern Command]
Abt. des Stabes u. Wach-Kp. [Staff Dept. and Guard Companies]
Nachr.: Luftflotte [info: Air Force]

Source: Nuremberg Documents NOKW-541, as cited in Yitzhak Arad, Yisrael Gutman, and Abraham Margaliot, eds., *Documents on the Holocaust* (Jerusalem and Oxford: Yad Vashem and Pergamon Press, 1987), p. 388 (Document 176).

Extracts from a Report by *Einsatzgruppe A* in the Baltic Countries, 1941

Reich, Secret Document

Einsatzgruppe A

General Report up to October 15, 1941

II *Cleansing [of Jews] and securing the area of operation.*

1) *Encouragement of Self-cleansing* Aktionen (*Selbstreinigungsaktionen*).[1]

Basing [oneself] on the consideration that the population of the Baltic countries had suffered most severely under the rule of Bolshevism and Jewry while they were incorporated into the USSR, it was to be expected that after liberation from this foreign rule they would themselves to a large extent eliminate those of the enemy left behind after the retreat of the Red Army. It was the task of the Security Police to set these self-cleansing movements going and to direct them into the right channels in order to achieve the aim of this cleansing as rapidly as possible. It was no less important to establish as unshakable and provable facts for the future that it was the liberated population itself which took the most severe measures, on its own initiative, against the Bolshevik and Jewish enemy, without any German instruction being evident.

In Lithuania this was achieved for the first time by activating the partisans in Kovno.[2] To our surprise it was not easy at first to set any large-scale anti-Jewish pogrom in motion there. Klimaitis, the leader of the partisan group referred to above, who was the first to be recruited for this purpose, succeeded in starting a pogrom with the aid of instructions given him by a small advance detachment operating in Kovno, in such a way that no German orders or instructions could be observed by outsiders. In the course of the first pogrom during the night of June 25/26, the Lithuanian partisans eliminated more than 1,500 Jews, set fire to several synagogues or destroyed them by other means, and burned down an area consisting of about sixty houses inhabited by Jews. During the nights that followed, 2,300 Jews were eliminated in the same way. In other parts of Lithuania similar *Aktionen* followed the example set in Kovno, but on a smaller scale, and including some Communists who had been left behind.

These self-cleansing *Aktionen* ran smoothly because the Wehrmacht authorities who had been informed showed understanding for this procedure.

At the same time it was obvious from the beginning that only the first days after the occupation would offer the opportunity for carrying out pogroms. After the disarmament of the partisans the self-cleansing *Aktionen* necessarily ceased.

It proved to be considerably more difficult to set in motion similar cleansing *Aktionen* and pogroms in Latvia. The main reason was that the entire national leadership, especially in Riga, had been killed or deported by the Soviets. Even in Riga it proved possible by means of appropriate suggestions to the Latvian auxiliary police to get an anti-Jewish pogrom going, in the course of which all the synagogues were destroyed and about 400 Jews killed. As the population on the whole quieted down very quickly in Riga, it was not possible to arrange further pogroms.

Both in Kovno and in Riga evidence was taken on film and by photographs to establish, as far as possible, that the first spontaneous executions of Jews and Communists were carried out by Lithuanians and Latvians.

In Estonia there was no opportunity of instigating pogroms owing to the relatively small number of Jews. The Estonian self-defense units eliminated only some individual Communists, who were particularly hated, but in general limited themselves to carrying out arrests. . . .

3) *The Fight against Jewry*

It was to be expected from the beginning that the Jewish problem in the *Ostland* could not be solved by pogroms alone. At the same time, the Security Police had basic, general orders for cleansing operations aimed at a maximum elimination of the Jews. Large-scale executions were therefore carried out in the cities and the countryside by *Sonderkommandos* [Special Units], which were assisted by selected units of partisan groups in Lithuania, and parties of the Latvian Auxiliary Police in Latvia. The work of the execution units was carried out smoothly. Where Lithuanian and Latvian forces were attached to the execution units, the first to be chosen were those who had had members of their families and relatives killed or deported by the Russians.

Particularly severe and extensive measures became necessary in Lithuania. In some places—especially in Kovno—the Jews had armed themselves and took an active part in sniping and arson. In addition, the Jews of Lithuania cooperated most closely with the Soviets.

The total number of Jews liquidated in Lithuania is 71,105.

During the pogrom 3,800 Jews were eliminated in Kovno and about 1,200 in the smaller cities.

In Latvia, too, Jews took part in acts of sabotage and arson after the entry of the German Wehrmacht. In Dünaburg [Dvinsk, Daugavpils] so many fires were started by Jews that a large part of the city was destroyed. The electric power station was burned out completely. Streets inhabited mainly by Jews remained untouched. Up to now 30,000 Jews have been executed in Latvia. The pogrom in Riga eliminated 500.

Most of the 4,500 Jews living in Estonia at the start of the Eastern campaign fled with the retreating Red Army. About 2,000 stayed behind. In Reval [Tallinn] alone there were about 1,000 Jews.

The arrest of all male Jews over the age of sixteen is almost completed. With the exception of the doctors and the Jewish Elders appointed by the *Sonderkommando* they [the remaining Jews] are being executed by the Estonian Self-Defense under the supervision of *Sonderkommando* 1a. Jewesses between the ages of sixteen through sixty in Reval and Pernau, who are fit for work, were arrested and used to cut peat and for other work.

At present a camp is being built at Harku in which all the Jews in Estonia will be sent, so that in a short time Estonia will be cleared of Jews.

After carrying out the first large-scale executions in Lithuania and Latvia it became clear that the total elimination of the Jews is not possible there, at least not at the present time. As a large part of the skilled trades is in Jewish hands in Lithuania and Latvia, and some (glaziers, plumbers, stove-builders, shoemakers) are almost entirely Jewish, a large proportion of the Jewish craftsmen are indispensable at present for the repair of essential installations, for the reconstruction of destroyed cities, and for work of military importance. Although the employers aim at replacing Jewish labor with Lithuanian or Latvian workers, it is not yet possible to replace all the Jews presently employed, particularly in the larger cities. In cooperation with the labor exchange offices, however, Jews who are no longer fit for work are picked up and will be executed shortly in small *Aktionen*.

It must be also noted in this connection that in some places there has been considerable resistance by offices of the Civil Administration against large-scale executions. This [resistance] was confronted in every case by pointing out that it was a matter of carrying out orders [involving] a basic principle.

Apart from organizing and carrying out the executions, preparations were begun from the first days of the operation for the establishment of ghettos in the larger cities. This was particularly urgent in Kovno, where there were 30,000 Jews in a total population of 152,400. At the end of the early pogroms, therefore, a Jewish Committee was summoned and informed that the German authorities had so far seen no reason to interfere in the conflicts between the Lithuanians and the Jews. A condition for the creation of a normal situation would be, first of all, the creation of a Jewish ghetto. When the Jewish Committee remonstrated, it was explained that there was no other possibility of preventing further pogroms. At this the Jews at once declared that they were ready to do everything to transfer their co-racials as quickly as possible to the Viliampole Quarter [Slobodka], where it was planned to establish the Jewish ghetto. This area is situated in the triangle between the River Memel and a branch of the river, and is linked with Kovno by only one bridge, and therefore easily sealed off.

In Riga the so-called Moscow Suburb was designated as the ghetto. This is the worst residential quarter of Riga, which is already inhabited mainly by

Jews. The transfer of Jews into the ghetto area proved rather difficult because the Latvians living in that district had to be evacuated and residential space in Riga is very crowded. Of about 28,000 Jews remaining in Riga, 24,000 are now housed in the ghetto. The Security Police carried out only police duties in the establishment of the ghetto, while the arrangements and administration of the ghetto, as well as the regulation of the food supply for the inmates of the ghetto, were left to the Civil Administration; the Labor Office was left in charge of Jewish labor.

Ghettos are also being set up in other cities in which there are a large number of Jews. . . .

1. The reference is to *Aktionen* against Jews carried out by the local population.

2. A nationalist organization in Lithuania which rose against Soviet rule on the day the Germans moved in.

Source: Nuremberg Documents L-180, as cited in Yitzhak Arad, Yisrael Gutman, and Abraham Margaliot, eds., *Documents on the Holocaust* (Jerusalem and Oxford: Yad Vashem and Pergamon Press, 1987), pp. 389–93 (Document 177).

Extract from a Report by Karl Jager, Commander of *Einsatzkommando 3*, on the Extermination of Lithuanian Jews, 1941

Commander of the Security Police and the SD
Einsatzkommando 3

Kovno, December 1, 1941

Reich Secret Document
Final Summary of Executions carried out in the operating area of EK [Einsatzkommando] 3 up to December 1, 1941.

. . . I can confirm today that *Einsatzkommando 3* has achieved the goal of solving the Jewish problem in Lithuania: There are no more Jews in Lithuania, apart from working Jews and their families.

These number:
in Shavli, about 4,500
in Kovno, about 15,000
in Vilna, about 15,000

I wanted to eliminate the working Jews and their families as well, but the Civil Administration [*Reichskommissar*] and the Wehrmacht attacked me most sharply and issued a prohibition against having these Jews and their families shot.

The goal of clearing Lithuania of Jews could be achieved only through the establishment of a specially selected Mobile Commando under the command of SS *Obersturmführer* Hamann, who adopted my aims fully and who was able to ensure the cooperation of the Lithuanian Partisans and the Civil Authorities concerned.

The carrying-out of such *Aktionen* is first of all an organizational problem.

The decision to clear each subdistrict systematically of Jews called for a thorough preparation for each *Aktion* and the study of local conditions. The Jews had to be concentrated in one or more localities and, in accordance with their numbers, a site had to be selected and pits dug. The marching distance from the concentration points to the pits averaged four to five kilometers. . . . All the officers and men of my command in Kovno took active part in the *Grossaktionen* in Kovno. Only one official of the intelligence corps was released on account of illness.

I consider the *Aktionen* . . . to be virtually completed. The remaining working Jews and Jewesses are urgently needed. . . . I am of the opinion that the male working Jews should be sterilized immediately to prevent reproduction. Should any Jewess nevertheless become pregnant, she is to be liquidated. . . .

Jager

SS *Standartenfuher*

Source: Yad Vashem Archives, 0-18-245, as cited in Yitzhak Arad, Yisrael Gutman, Abraham Margaliot, eds., *Documents on the Holocaust* (Jerusalem and Oxford: Yad Vashem and Pergamon Press, 1987), pp. 398–400 (Document 180).

Application by Kube, *Generalkommissar* of Belorussia, to Lohse Concerning the Condition of Jews in Minsk, December 16, 1941

Minsk, December 16, 1941

Generalkommissar for Belorussia
to *Reichskommissar* for *Ostland*
Gauleiter Hinrich Lohse
Riga

Reich Secret Document

My Dear Hinrich,
I wish to ask you personally for an official directive for the conduct of the civilian administration toward the Jews deported from Germany to Belorussia. Among these Jews are men who fought at the front [during World War I] and have the Iron Cross, First and Second Class, war invalids, half-Aryans, even three-quarter Aryans. Up to now only 6,000 to 7,000 Jews have arrived, of the 25,000 who were expected. I am not aware what has become of the others. In the course of several official visits to the ghetto I noted that among these Jews, who also differ from the Russian Jews in their personal cleanliness, there are also skilled workers capable of doing five times as much in a day as the Russian Jews.

These Jews will probably freeze or starve to death in the coming weeks. They present a terrible threat of disease for us, as they are naturally just as much exposed to the twenty-two epidemics prevalent in Belorussia as we Reich-Germans [*Reichsdeutsche*]. Serum is not available for them.

On my own responsibility I will not give the SD any instructions with regard to the treatment of these people, although certain units of the Wehrmacht and the police already have an eye on the possessions of the Jews from the Reich. Without asking, the SD has already simply taken away 400 mattresses from the Jews from the Reich, and has also confiscated various other things. I am certainly a hard [man] and willing to help solve the Jewish question, but people who come from our own cultural sphere just are not the same as the brutish hordes in this place. Is the slaughter to be carried out by the Lithuanians and Letts, who are themselves rejected by the population here? I couldn't do it. I beg you to give clear directives [in this matter], with due consideration for the good name of our Reich and our Party, in order that the necessary action can be taken in the most humane manner.

With heartfelt greetings
Heil Hitler!

Yours
Wilhelm Kube

Source: Nuremberg Documents PS-3665, as cited in Yitzhak Arad, Yisrael Gutman, Abraham Margaliot, eds., *Documents on the Holocaust* (Jerusalem and Oxford: Yad Vashem and Pergamon Press, 1987), p. 408 (Document 185).

Report by Waffen SS on Killing of Jews in the Pripet Marshes

Regt. st. Qtrs., Aug. 12, 1941

2nd SS-Cavalry Regiment
Mounted Unit

Report

On the Course of the *Aktion* in the Pripet [Marshes] from July 27 to August 11, 1941.

Impressions of the battle: None
Population: Mainly Ukrainian; Belorussians in second place; in third place Poles and Russians; only a very few of the latter. The Jews are mainly in the larger places, where they make up a high percentage of the population, in some cases from 50 to 80 percent, but in others as little as 25 percent.

In many cases when the troops moved in we found that, according to a Ukrainian practice, a table with a white cloth had been prepared with bread and salt that was offered to the commanders. In one case there was even a small band of musicians to welcome the troops. . . .

Type of land: The whole area consists of large marshes interspersed with patches of sand, so that the ground is not very fertile. There are some better places, but others were all the poorer. . . .

. . . Jewish doctors were preferred. In the towns and villages it was also noticeable that only Jewish artisans were found. There was a large number of Jewish emigres from the *Altreich* [Germany before 1938] and the *Ostmark* [Austria]. . . .

Pacification: Pacification was carried out through the commanders of units or companies who contacted the local mayors and discussed all matters concerning the population. On these occasions the numbers and composition of the population, i.e., Ukrainians, Belorussians, etc., were checked. Further, whether there were still Communists in the locality or secret members of the Red Army, or others who had been active Bolsheviks. In most cases local residents also reported that they had seen gangs or other suspicious persons. Where such individuals were still in the locality, they were detained and, after a brief interrogation, they were either released or shot.

Jewish looters were shot. Only a few skilled workers employed in the Wehrmacht repair workshops were permitted to remain.

The driving of women and children into the marshes did not have the expected success, because the marshes were not so deep that one could sink. After a depth of about a meter there was in most cases solid ground (probably sand) preventing complete sinking. . . .

. . . The Ukrainian clergy were very cooperative and made themselves available for every *Aktion*. It was also conspicuous that, in general, the population was on good terms with the Jewish sector of the population. Nevertheless they helped energetically in rounding up the Jews. The locally recruited guards, who consisted in part of Polish police and former Polish soldiers, made a good impression. They operated energetically and took part in the fight against looters. . . .

The total number of looters, etc., shot by the Mounted Units was 6,526. . . .

[signed] Magill

SS *Sturmbannführer*

Source: *Kriegstagebuch des Kommandostabes Reichsführer SS* ("War Diary" of the *Kommandostaff Reichsführer* SS), Vienna, 1965, pp. 217–20, as cited in Yitzhak Arad, Yisrael Gutman, Abraham Margaliot, eds., *Documents on the Holocaust* (Jerusalem and Oxford: Yad Vashem and Pergamon Press, 1987), p. 414 (Document 188).

From a Report by *Einsatzgruppen* on the Extermination of the Jews in Ukraine, October 1941

Operations and Situation Report No. 6 by the *Einsatzgruppen* of the Security Police and SD in the USSR (for the period October 1–31, 1941)

. . . c) Jews
The bitter hostility of the Ukrainian population against the Jews is extremely great, because it is thought that they were responsible for the explosions in Kiev. They are also seen as NKVD informers and agents, who unleashed the terror against the Ukrainian people. All Jews were arrested in retaliation for the arson in Kiev, and altogether 33,771 Jews were executed on September 29th and 30th. Gold, valuables, and clothing were collected and put at the disposal of the National-Socialist Welfare Association (NSV), for the equipment of the *Volksdeutsche*, and part given to the appointed city administration for distribution to the needy population.

Schitomir [Zhitomir]
In Schitomir 3,145 Jews had to be shot, because experience showed they must be considered as bearers of Bolshevist propaganda and saboteurs.

Cherson [Kherson]
In Cherson 410 Jews were executed in retaliation for acts of sabotage.

The solution of the Jewish question in the area east of the Dniepr in particular has been firmly attacked by the *Einsatzgruppen* of the Security Police and the SD. The areas newly occupied by the commandos were cleared of Jews. In the course of this action 4,891 Jews were liquidated. In other localities the Jews were marked and registered. This made it possible to put at the disposal of Wehrmacht offices Jewish worker groups of up to 1,000 persons for urgent work. . . .

Source: Nuremberg Documents R-102, as cited in Yitzhak Arad, Yisrael Gutman, Abraham Margaliot, eds., *Documents on the Holocaust* (Jerusalem and Oxford: Yad Vashem and Pergamon Press, 1987), p. 416 (Document 189).

From a Wehrmacht Report on the Extermination of Jews in Ukraine

December 2, 1941

Armament in the Ukraine
Inspector

Secret

To: The Office of Wi Rü [Industrial Armament Department]
O K W [High Command of the Wehrmacht]
General of the Infantry Thomas
Berlin

. . . c. The Jewish Question
Settling of the Jewish Question in Ukraine has been made more difficult be-

cause in the cities the Jews constituted a major part of the population. What we have here is therefore—just as in the Government-General—a massive population policy problem. Many cities had more than 50 percent Jews. Only the rich Jews fled before the German troops. The great majority of the Jewish masses remained under the German Administration. The entire situation was complicated by the fact that *these Jews carried out almost all the work in the skilled trades and even provided part of the labor for small- and medium-sized industries;* apart from trade, some of which had become superfluous as the result of the direct or indirect effects of the war. *[Their] elimination was therefore bound to have profound economic consequences,* including even direct effects on the military economy (supplies for troops).

From the outset the attitude of the Jewish population was anxious-willing. They tried to avoid anything that might displease the German Administration. That they hated the German Administration and the Army in their hearts is obvious and not surprising. However, there is no evidence that the Jews, either as a body, or even in any considerable numbers, have taken part in sabotage, etc. Without doubt there have been some terrorists or saboteurs among them, just as there have been among the Ukrainians. But it cannot be claimed that the Jews as such present any kind of danger for the German Wehrmacht. The troops and the German Administration have been satisfied with the work output of the Jews, who are of course motivated by no emotion except fear.

Immediately following the military operations, the Jewish population remained undisturbed at first. It was only weeks, in some cases months, later that systematic shooting of the Jews was carried out by units of the Order Police specially set up for this purpose. This *Aktion* moved in the main from east to west. It was carried out entirely in public, with the assistance of Ukrainian militia; in many cases, regrettably, also with the voluntary participation of members of the Wehrmacht. These *Aktionen* included aged men, women, and children of all ages, and the manner in which they were carried out was appalling. The gigantic number of executions involved in this *Aktion* is far greater than any similar measure undertaken in the Soviet Union up to now. Altogether about 150,000 to 200,000 Jews may have been executed in the section of Ukraine belonging to the RK [*Reichskommissariat*]; up to now no consideration was given to the interests of the economy.

To sum up it could be said that the solution of the Jewish Question as carried out in Ukraine, evidently motivated by ideological principles, has had the following consequences:

a) Elimination of some, in part superfluous, eaters in the cities.
b) Elimination of a part of the population which undoubtedly hated us.
c) Elimination of urgently needed craftsmen, who were in many cases indispensable for the requirements of the Wehrmacht.
d) Consequences in connection with foreign propaganda that are obvious.

e) Adverse effects on troops which in any case have indirect contact with executions.
f) Brutalizing effects on the units (Order Police) which carry out the executions. . . .

Source: Nuremberg Documents PS-3257, as cited in Yitzhak Arad, Yisrael Gutman, Abraham Margaliot, eds., *Documents on the Holocaust* (Jerusalem and Oxford: Yad Vashem and Pergamon Press, 1987), p. 417 (Document 190).

SEVENTEEN

Eyewitness Accounts

A Live Message of Greetings from Hell

My name is Dina. Dina Mironovna Vasserman. I grew up in a poor Jewish family. I was brought up under the Soviet regime in the spirit of internationalism. Thus, it is not surprising that I fell in love with a Russian guy, Nikolai Pronichev, married him and lived with him in love and happiness. That is how I became Dina Mikhailovna Pronicheva. My passport said I was Russian.

We had two children: a boy and a girl. Before the war I worked as an actress at the Kiev Children's Theater. On the second day of the war my husband joined the Soviet Army, and I was left with two children and my old sick mother.

Hitler's troops seized Kiev on September 19, 1941, and from the very first day they started plundering and killing Jews. Terrible stories about the treatment of Jews were circulating in the city. We lived in terror. When I saw announcements posted in the streets, ordering "all the Jews of the city of Kiev to gather at Babi Yar" (a place we had no idea about), I felt trouble was coming. I started shivering. I saw that nothing good was awaiting us there. That is why I dressed my children, three and five years old, packed their stuff in a small bag and took them to my Russian mother-in-law. Then, following the order, my sick mother and I went along the road to Babi Yar.

Jews were walking in hundreds and thousands. Beside me there was an old Jew with a long white beard. He had on a *tallis* [prayer shawl] and *tfilin* [phylacteries]. He was mumbling. He prayed exactly as my father did when I was a child. A woman was walking ahead of me. She was carrying two children and a third one was walking alongside, holding her skirt. Sick women and elderly were riding in carts among piled up bags and suitcases. Small children were crying. Old people, having trouble walking, sighed and trudged on in their mournful journey.

Russian husbands were walking with their Jewish wives. Russian wives were walking with their Jewish husbands. When we approached Babi Yar I heard shooting and inhuman shouting. I started to grasp what was going on but did not say anything to my mother.

When we entered through the gates we were ordered to turn in our papers and valuables and undress. A German came over to my mother and tore a gold ring off her finger. Only then mother said: "Dinochka, you are Pronicheva, you are Russian. You should survive. Rush to your children. You should live for them."

But I could not flee. We were surrounded by fascists with submachine guns, Ukrainian policemen, and ferocious dogs who were ready to tear a human being to pieces. And then, I could not leave my mother alone. I embraced her, burst into tears but was unable to leave her. Mother pushed me away and yelled: "Hurry!"

I went to a table at which a fat officer was seated, showed him my passport and said quietly, "I am Russian." He was contemplating my passport when a policeman came over and barked, "Don't believe her, she's a Kike. We know her. . . . " The German told me to step aside and wait.

I saw groups of men, women, children, and elderly undress. Then they were taken to an open pit and shot by soldiers. Then another group would come. I saw this horror with my own eyes. Even though I was not standing close to the pit, I could hear awful shrieks of terrified people, weak voices of children, crying, "Mother, mother. . . . " I saw all that and was unable to understand how people could kill others because they are Jewish. And I concluded that the fascists were not humans, they were—beasts.

I saw a young completely naked woman feed her naked baby with the breast when a policeman came to her, took the baby, and thrust it into the pit. The mother rushed after the child. A fascist shot her dead, and she fell into the pit. Had someone told me this, I would not believe it. It is impossible to believe.

The German who had ordered me to wait took me to his superior, gave him my passport and said, "This woman says she is Russian, but a policeman says she is Jewish." The officer studied my passport for a while and then said, "Dina is not a Russian name. You are Jewish. Take her!"

A policeman told me to undress and pushed me to the edge of the pit where another group was waiting for its fate. But before the shooting started, I, driven by terror, fell into the pit. I fell on dead bodies. At first, I could not understand anything: where was I? How did I get there?

I thought I had gone mad. But when people started falling on me, I came to my senses and understood everything. I started checking my arms, legs, abdomen, head. It turned out I was not even wounded. I pretended to be dead. Under me and above me there lay the killed and wounded. Some of them breathed, others moaned. Suddenly, I heard a child cry, "Mommy!" It seemed like it was my little daughter. I burst into tears.

The execution went on, and people kept falling. I was pushing corpses away in fear of being buried alive. But I did this in a way so that the policemen would not notice.

All of a sudden everything was quiet. It was getting dark. Germans with submachine guns were killing those who had been wounded. I felt someone was standing above me, but pretended to be dead, no matter how hard it was. Then I felt we were covered with earth. I closed my eyes to protect them. When it became completely dark and quiet—deadly quiet in literal sense—I opened my eyes and, having made sure no one was around and watching me, I dug myself out of sand that was covering me. I saw the ditch filling with thousands of killed. I got scared. Here and there earth was moving—half-alive people were breathing.

I looked at myself and got scared. The undershirt that was covering my body was all bloody. I tried to get up and could not. Then I said to myself: "Dina, get up, leave, run from here, your children are waiting for you." I got up and ran. Suddenly, I heard a shot and understood that they noticed me. I fell on the ground and waited. All was quiet. Without getting up, I started moving toward the high hill that surrounded the pit. Suddenly, I felt something was stirring behind me. First I got scared and decided to wait for a while. I turned quietly and asked, "Who are you?"

A delicate, scared child's voice answered, "Don't be afraid. It's me. My first name is Fima. My last name is Shneiderman. I am eleven years old. Take me with you. I am very afraid of the dark." I moved closer to the boy, embraced him and started crying. The boy said, "Don't cry."

We both started to move quietly. We reached the edge of the pit, got some rest and continued climbing, helping each other. We had already reached the top of the pit, stood up to run away when a shot was fired. We fell on the ground instinctively. For some time we were quiet, being afraid to speak. Having calmed down, I moved closer to Fimochka, touched him and asked in a whisper, "How are you doing, Fimochka?"

There was no answer. In the dark I could feel his legs and arms. He did not stir. No signs of life. I got up a bit and looked in his face. He was lying with his eyes closed. I tried to open them but understood that the boy was dead. Probably, the shot we heard had taken his life.

I caressed his cold face, said good bye to him, got on my feet and ran. Having made sure that I was far from that terrible place called Babi Yar, I decided to approach a house that could just about be seen in the dark. Shivering, I came to a window and knocked. In a few minutes a sleepy woman lifted up a curtain and asked, "Who is it? What do you want?" I answered her, "I escaped from Babi Yar." And then I heard her angry voice: "Go away. I don't have anything to do with you."

I left. I ran, because day was breaking and I knew that they should not see me there. But there was no place to go, so I approached a second house and knocked. The door opened, and an elderly woman appeared on the porch. When she saw me in the undershirt she crossed herself and recoiled. "Who are you? Where have you come from?" she asked. I replied, "Don't be afraid, dear. I'm not a devil. I'm human." And then I lied for the first time in my life. "I'm Ukrainian. I saw my friend to Babi Yar and barely escaped."

The old lady took my hand and let me in. Then she told me to wash myself, gave me a clean shirt, a blouse, a skirt, and old shoes. I looked at myself and got a shock: a real Ukrainian! My hostess gave me a glass of hot milk with homemade bread and told me to get some rest. I ate with gusto, went over to the old lady, embraced her, kissed her, and burst into tears. My savior also cried. But having wiped her tears with an apron, she said, "Daughter, I know who you really are. But we are all alike for God. We have one God. Because I have helped you, my two sons will come back from the war alive. But my place is not safe for you. Police hounds search here every day. They are looking for Jews. These beasts pay money for Jews. Now, go get some sleep. I'll give you some provisions and try to get to our people. May God help you."

I felt relieved because there were good people on earth who were ready to help others. The old lady made my bed and left. I slept for a while but could not sleep long. The images of the previous day were passing in front of my eyes. I believed I heard shots, shouting, and children crying somewhere. . . .

Who knows where my children are? Did my mother-in-law manage to save them? I did not have time to think. I was aware that the old lady could suffer because of me. And I decided to go. I looked in a mirror and was terrified to see my hair gray. "This is from last night," I thought. I put some soot on the face to seem older, wrapped my head in a kerchief, as was done by old Ukrainian women, and said good-bye to my dear hostess and set out for Daritsa. My friend Natalia, with whom I had played in the theater, lived there.

At first glance Natasha did not recognize me. When she did, she got scared. She told me to take off my clothes and get some rest. But I felt something unnatural in her attitude toward me. There was some alienation.

Once we had eaten, she said to me, "Dina, I should tell you the truth. You can't stay here for a long time. My husband Andrei deserted from the Red Army. He hates the Soviet power and the Jews who invented it. I'm afraid he'll inform on you. You'd better leave."

And I left.

Source: I. Vinokurov, Sh. Kipnis, N. Levin, *Kniga pamiati* (New York, 1983), reprinted in Yitzhak Arad, ed., *Unichtozhenie Evreev SSSR v gody nemetskoi okkupatsii* (1941–1944) (Jerusalem: Yad Vashem, 1991), pp. 107–112.

"The devil's game began": On the Massacre of Jews in Lvov during the First Days of the Occupation

At the time Lvov was occupied by the Germans, 135,000 Jews resided in the city. Among them there were refugees from Poland, who managed to flee in

September 1939. Besides that, many Jews moved to Lvov from small towns in western Ukraine after Soviet rule had been established there. Lvov had never had so many Jews before.

It began on Tuesday, July 2, in the morning, when the Soviet troops left Lvov. The city had three prisons stuffed with inmates. Inmates were of different sorts, but most of them were either criminals or political prisoners. Many of them were sentenced to death, and their corpses were buried in the prison courtyard. The Germans opened the prison gates and released most of the inmates.

The Gestapo decided to make use of what had happened in the prisons under the Soviet rule for the purposes of propaganda. In presence of special commissions, Jews were made to dig out the corpses of prison inmates. The action was shot by film operators to be shown later as evidence of the execution of innocent people by the "Jewish Bolsheviks."

The devil's game started. The Germans were seizing Jews in the streets or at home and forcing them to work in prison. The arrests of Jews were also conducted by the newly created Ukrainian police. The Ukrainians and Poles were ready to help the Germans. The operation was over in three to four days. Every morning about a thousand Jews were brought and distributed among the three prisons. Some were ordered to break concrete and dig out corpses. Others were shot in the small inner courtyards of the prisons. But even those "lucky ones" who were working often did not come home. Some fainted because of the stench of open graves. These people were dragged away and also shot. Guards in gas masks were German soldiers and officers. From time to time they would cheer themselves by yelling, "Revenge is sweet!" The "Aryan" residents of Lvov participated in this brutal show. Their crowds wandered along prison corridors and courtyards, observing with satisfaction the suffering of Jews. There could be heard hysterical outcries, "Shoot them! Shoot the murderers!" Here and there volunteers could be found to help the Germans in the beating of Jews. During the first days of the occupation of Lvov more than 3,000 Jews were killed in the Lvov prisons. Among them one of the best-known and popular rabbis of Lvov—Doctor Yehezkel Levin and his brother, the rabbi of the town of Zheshkov, Aaron Levin.

The story of the death of the rabbi, Doctor Levin, deserves attention. Immediately after the seizure of Lvov by the Germans, the city was filled by rampaging Ukrainians. Information about pogroms conducted by Ukrainians started coming in to Lvov from surrounding towns. Rabbi Yehezkel Levin decided to address a complaint to the archbishop of Ukraine, Sheptyts'kyi, known for his sympathy toward Jews.[1] Accompanied by two representatives of the Jewish community, the rabbi went to the residence of the archbishop on the Iura Hill on the morning of July 2. The archbishop talked to the delegation immediately upon its arrival and promised to send a pastoral letter to his parish, in which he would warn the Ukrainians against murders and plundering. Yet, he admitted his inability to influence any matters concerning the

Germans. At the end, the archbishop suggested that Levin stay with him, since the streets were dangerous. At this time the rabbi of the town of Podhaitsy, Lilienfeld, a close acquaintance of the Sheptyts'kyi family, was staying at Sheptyts'kyi's house. The rabbi expressed his gratitude but rejected the offer. At the gates he was awaited by a priest, who was supposed to see him home. On Kollontai Street he sent the priest back. He walked into his house and went up the stairs. At the door to his apartment he was met by two policemen. They arrested him. He never came home.

1. Archbishop Andrii Sheptyts'kyi (1865–1944)—the head of the Greek-Catholic (Uniate) church in the western Ukraine. One of the most significant leaders of the Ukrainian national movement in prewar Poland and during the German occupation. See the chapter by Shimon Redlich in this volume. For a corollary account, see notes made by Professor Maurycy Allerhand before his death in the Lvov ghetto, in Bella Guterman, ed., "Lvov takhat hakibush haNazi," *Masuah*, vol. 13, 1985.

Source: D. Kahane, *Yoman geto Lvov* (Jerusalem: Yad Vashem, 1978), pp. 27–29, reprinted in Yitzhak Arad, ed., *Unichtozhenie Evreev SSSR v gody nemetskoi okkupatsii* (1941–1944) (Jerusalem: Yad Vashem, 1991), pp. 75–77. For an English edition of the diary see David Kahane, *Lvov Ghetto Diary* (Amherst: University of Massachusetts Press, 1990).

"Jews were shot by policemen while Germans observed."

[From the testimony of a witness, former guerrilla soldier, V. Burnosova, on the execution of Jews in the town of Sebezh, Pskov district (Russian Republic), in the spring of 1942.]

Jews survived in Sebezh for a long time in spite of the fact that the Germans used them for the hardest labor: digging trenches, repairing a railroad dismantled during the retreat of the Red Army. In the beginning, the commandant of the town was Austrian. Jews bribed him (gold, valuables) and he made various concessions. These were bribes in the proper sense, not some sort of official requisitions.

By the spring of 1942, a new commandant came and executed Jews after all. Jews were taken to be shot.[1] Ditches were ready in spite of it being winter time. Probably, they had been dug by POWs. Jews were shot by policemen, headed by their Chief, Buss. They say that during the execution Buss took a three-to-four-month-old baby from a woman, thrust it in the air and shot from a hand gun, saying, "So that Kike blood does not pollute Russian soil." The child fell right into a pit.

Russians were made to bury corpses. One of them said that some of the executed were only wounded, some slightly scratched. But they all were buried. In the next half hour one could hear moaning from under the ground (it was ten to fifteen degrees below zero).

The Jewish population of Sebezh at this time consisted mostly of women, children, elderly, and adolescent girls. One boy of twelve, following his mother's advice, hid in the chimney and then left. He reached the house of the head of the village of Presni, having crossed a frozen lake. The boy begged the man, "Take me, I'll be your helper and you will not have to feed me. I'll pick mushrooms and berries. Just don't take me back to Sebezh." The village chief's wife fed the boy. The chief harnessed his horse, placed the boy in a cart and took him to Sebezh to turn him in to the Germans. He could have saved him.

One Jewish woman worked as an interpreter for the Germans. She was from Leningrad, a Hertzen Institute graduate. First she worked in Sebezh. Then she was transferred to Idrits. Someone informed on her, and the commandant sent a car to bring her to Sebezh. A witness saw her in a car with Germans. The Jewish lady said, "Valia, I will not be back. Someone denounced me." She was so eager to live.

There were people in Sebezh who greeted the arrival of the Germans. Jews were killed in March only by [local] policemen. The Germans were merely looking on. Later the Germans could argue, "No, we are not cruel. Your people are."

There were a few policemen who joined the partisans. The police force in the area was very large. After the war policemen were sentenced to twenty-five years but were amnestied and rehabilitated soon.

(The language and style of the original are preserved for publication.)

1. There were ninety-seven Jews shot in Sebezh.

Source: Yad Vashem Archives, D-3/4655, as cited in Yitzhak Arad, ed., *Unichtozhenie Evreev SSSR v gody nemetskoi okkupatsii* (1941–1944) (Jerusalem: Yad Vashem, 1991), pp. 214–15.

"They made Jews lie down on both sides of the ditch."

[From the testimony of Heinrich, a serviceman in the 307 police battalion, concerning the massacre of the Brest-Litovsk Jews on July 10, 1941.]

That day we were awakened at three. The day of the execution was probably July 10, 1941. At first we were ordered to line up, armed with "98" rifles and ammunition. The task was to take all the males in the Jewish neighborhood out in the streets. They could get dressed and take as much luggage as they could carry. We were told that Jews were being sent to work in Germany. . . .

The gathering of Jews and their arrangement in the streets inside the Jewish neighborhood went on until six in the morning. Part of our battalion was sent to the site of the execution in trucks. The rest guarded Jews on their way there.

The site was located to the south of Brest-Litovsk, outside the forts, and looked like dunes. A ride to this place from the downtown would take fifteen minutes.

When we arrived, i.e., at 6:30, we were met by an SS unit, obviously a company. The SS soldiers, armed with sub-machine guns surrounded an area (a circle) 600 meters in diameter. Besides the SS, there were SD soldiers in gray uniforms. Judging by what I heard later, these units, after the execution of the men, took care of the women and children who were brought by SS units to the site of the execution after noon. These soldiers were also armed with automatic weapons.

There were twelve ditches: ten meters in length, 2.5 meters in width, and three to four meters deep. I think one could fit 600 corpses in such a pit. To avoid a mistake concerning the number of Jews that were shot that day (since I gave the figure of 10,000 before), I want to emphasize that during the described action about 6,000 male Jews were shot. From later discussions I learned that the figure was 10,000.

We did not have chloride or lime or any other disinfectants. Shortly after we had arrived, a big column of Jews came from the town. It was stopped about 300 meters from the ditches. While the Jews were turning in their luggage, platoon commanders designated shooting soldiers. After this we were given instructions on how the execution should be conducted. . . .

According to the instructions, groups of fifty people were taken to the ditches and laid down on both sides of them, face to the ground, so that their heads stuck out above the pits. Behind each Jew there was a designated soldier with a "98" rifle, bayonet attached. A shot was made as following: the tip of the bayonet was put to the back of a victim's head. After this, a rifle was to be moved to an angle of forty-five degrees, and a shot was to be fired. It often happened that a skull was torn off along a bullet path. From time to time, if an angle was too wide or a victim was holding his head too high during a shot, a bullet would go through the neck. In such cases an officer or a platoon commander would finish off victims, shooting them from hand guns.

We soldiers had to throw corpses into the ditches. No one was putting the corpses into stacks. In such fashion the execution went on until the afternoon. In the beginning, one of the long sides of a ditch would be approached by ten to twelve men to be shot. But later it became impossible to maintain such a uniform rate, and the shooting became sporadic.

The Jews were dressed when approaching the pits. They did not need to undress in advance. This action ended by 4 p.m. After it ended we were taken back to barracks in trucks. Our service for the day was over.

As far as I remember, we did not get any food and, this is for sure, alcoholic beverages during the day. There were no festivities.

We were not to keep the action secret. There were no discussions among us servicemen after the action. And if there were, then only condemning it.

Almost all of the Jews that I am describing accepted their fate with stoicism and heroic self-control. I personally lived through this in a state of trance and could not help being amazed by the Jews.

Source: Yitzhak Arad, ed., *Unichtozhenie Evreev SSSR v gody nemetskoi okkupatsii* (1941–1944) (Jerusalem: Yad Vashem, 1991), p. 80.

"Thousands of Jews have already been shot."

[From the report of the Chief of the SS and SD on the annihilation of Jews in Kaunas. June 30, 1941.]

Top Secret

Operations Report, the USSR, #8

Einsatzgruppe A:
Einsatzkommando 1-b

The advance command arrived at Kaunas on June 28 and started its activities. The buildings of the former Trade Unions, NKVD, and two more houses were occupied. At night there was heavy fire between Lithuanian volunteers, Jews, and irregular military units. . . .[1]

During the last three days Lithuanian guerrilla groups[2] have already shot thousands of Jews.

1. Retreating Red Army units.
2. Lithuanians who collaborated with the Germans.

Source: Nuremberg Documents NO-4543, as cited in Yitzhak Arad, ed., *Unichtozhenie Evreev SSSR v gody nemetskoi okkupatsii* (1941–1944) (Jerusalem: Yad Vashem, 1991), p. 73.

"Activists[1] comprised half of the groups that were conducting executions. The rest were Gestapo officers."

[From the testimony of Vilunas,[2] given on December 20 and January 12, 1946, to Soviet investigators.]

On June 23, 1941, once the Soviet troops had left Lithuania, I decided to take over the position of the Chief of the Kaunas prison. I considered myself competent for the job since I was a former officer of the Lithuanian army. Besides, I thought the Germans would trust a man who had been persecuted by the Soviet regime.

Mass executions started from the very first day of the German occupation, at first in the Fourth Fort, on the outskirts of Panemut, and in the Seventh Fort, five kilometers from Kaunas, in the vicinity of the village of Kalrechai.

These mass massacres were conducted under the supervision of activists who had taken power in Lithuania immediately after the retreat of the Red

Army. They were headed by former officers of the Lithuanian army: Lieutenant Papulionis, Captain Matsiliokas, and Major Ferentsas. . . .

In November 1941 (I cannot recall now the exact date), following Gestapo instructions, some space for new inmates was created in the Ninth Fort in Kaunas. Previously, prisoners had been transferred to the central Kaunas jail. On the next day, Gestapo officers and a larger number of activists, headed by Kazis Simkus, drove hundreds of women, children, and elderly to the already overcrowded prison.

In a couple of days, in November 1941, more than 10,000 people were gathered in the courtyard of the Ninth Fort. The inmates were not given any bread. Instead, once a day they ate rotten potatoes. It was then that I was ordered by chief of the prison, Bronus Ausrotas, to come to the Ninth Fort to guard the prisoners and maintain order during mass executions that would go on for a few days.

According to the order of Chief Ausrotas, I was responsible for the mass execution of the prisoners. The garrison of the Ninth Fort and its commander, Iudras Shlezoraitis, were at my disposal. Upon my arrival at the Ninth Fort, I first of all, made sure the inmates were properly guarded. I ordered some additional sentry posts and doubled the number of sentinels on the watch towers. They did not register the names of inmates. The latter would be just taken out of the prison and shot without being counted.

A couple of days before the beginning of the execution, 200 Red Army prisoners of war had been brought to dig vast ditches on the territory of the Fort, approximately 300 meters south of the prison building. These ditches were fifty meters long, two meters deep, and two meters wide. Their bottom was filled with about twenty to thirty centimeters of water.

On November 25, 1941, when everything was ready, eighty Gestapo officers, headed by Jaeger, and fifty Lithuanian partisans, headed by Simkus Barzda, arrived in the Ninth Fort. Gestapo Chief Jaeger ordered his soldiers to get ready. It should be noted that activists comprised half of the groups that were conducting executions. The rest were Gestapo officers. Gestapo officers guarded prisoners, who were taken to the sites of execution right out of the fort. Activists who were not involved in the operation were put on the prison's outposts.

The mass execution started at seven in the morning, November 25, 1941. Groups of ten Gestapo officers each were coming to the prison courtyard to take one hundred inmates who were mostly women, children, and elderly. No one cared to ask their names. Prisoners were put into columns of four, approximately 150 meters from the prison gates, directed toward the ditches, ordered to reach the bottom and lie down. There they were shot. The first rows would lie in water. Those who tried to stand up would be beaten by clubs and rifle butts, and were thus forced to lie down.

In all, more than 10,000 people were shot on November 25, 1941.[3] It is impossible to describe the atrocious site of the mass execution. Guards were beating people with sticks and rifle butts on their way to the ditches when their orders were not obeyed. The cries of mothers and children could be heard from the Fort all day long.

1. Lithuanians who collaborated with the Germans.

2. Ionas Vilunas—former captain of the Lithuanian army, a member of a profascist organization. Served the Germans from the first days of the occupation and participated in the mass executions of Jews in Kaunas.

3. Obviously, the witness is mistaken. He is talking about the so call[ed] "Big Action" that was carried out at the end of October and the beginning of November, 1941, during which 10,000 Jews were killed.

Source: *Tiesa* (Vilnius), May 25, 1959, as cited in Yitzhak Arad, ed., *Unichtozhenie Evreev SSSR v gody nemetskoi okkupatsii* (1941–1944) (Jerusalem: Yad Vashem, 1991), pp. 73–75.

EIGHTEEN

Collaboration and Resistance

The Election of Elkes as Head of the *Judenrat* in Kovno

. . . In the first days of August, Kaminsky informed the Jewish Committee that the ghetto in Slobodka would be headed by an *Eltestenrat* [Council of Elders] which would be elected by the Jews themselves. But first of all they would have to elect a "Head of the Jews"—that was the demand of *Hauptsturmführer* Jordan, who was responsible for Jewish affairs in Kovno. This created a very grave problem for the Kovno Jews: whom to elect to this position of exceptionally great responsibility, which was at the same time difficult and dangerous. For this purpose the Council called an expanded meeting of all those who had been active in public affairs of any kind and had remained in the city. The meeting was held on August 5 in the offices of the Council in Daukshos Street, and about thirty persons attended.

This Jewish meeting, the last in the city of Kovno itself before it was left by its Jewish residents, was unusually dramatic. Everybody was deeply aware that a solution must be found for a problem which literally involved their lives. It was not easy to find a suitable candidate for this unusual position. The candidate would have to know how to find a common language with the Germans, and know also how to appear before them as the representative of the ghetto. Even if it was understood from the outset that the man elected would be only "Head of the Jews," that is, the lowly representative of the "accursed Jews"—in the defiled vocabulary of the Germans—nevertheless it was also understood that everything possible must be done that the man elected would, despite everything, have a certain authority in the eyes of the Germans and that they would take into consideration what he said. Everybody understood that the man elected must have qualities that enabled him to influence the Germans to a certain degree. It was also necessary that the man who would stand at the head of the ghetto must have a clean public record, be a good Jew and a good man, discerning and clever, courageous and of strong character, so that he would not be easily discouraged and would not bend his knees when he had to stand before the Germans as the tragic messenger of an unhappy Jewish community, without salvation and surrounded by ravaging beasts.

Several candidates were proposed at the meeting. However, none of them could unite those taking part in the meeting around himself. In addition, the candidates proposed all refused to accept this task. A great feeling of depression spread through the meeting. After lengthy discussions Dr. Z. Wolf, the chairman of the meeting, proposed the candidacy of Dr. E. Elkes, a loyal and Zionist Jew, and a famous doctor in the city of Kovno. The proposal was accepted immediately by the whole assembly, and with great enthusiasm. But Dr. Elkes refused to accept this appointment. Again there was great confusion of spirit. Rabbi Schmukler then rose from his place and made a speech that was moving and full of pain, and shook everyone deeply. "How terrible is our position"—he said in a trembling voice—"that we are not offering the revered Dr. Elkes the respected position of head of the Jewish Community of Kovno, but the shameful and humiliating one of 'Head of the Jews,' who is to represent us before the Germans. But please understand, dear and beloved Dr. Elkes, that only to the Nazi murderers will you be 'Head of the Jews,' in our eyes you will be the head of our Community, elected in our most tragic hour, when blood runs from all of us and the murderer's sword is suspended over our heads. It has fallen to your part to accept duties of unequaled difficulty, but at the same time it is also a great privilege and a deed of charity, and you do not have the right to escape from it; stand at our head, defend us, you shall be with us and we will all be with you, until we arrive at the great day of salvation!" When Rabbi Schmukler had finished speaking he wept, and all the assembly wept bitter tears with him. Dr. Elkes stood pale and silent. All could see what was happening in the depth of his soul and all felt that in these tragic moments Dr. Elkes understood that it was his duty to make this great sacrifice that a cruel fate had imposed upon him. A feeling of relief descended on all, and a ray of secret hope shone into the broken hearts of all those present. . . .

Source: L. Garfunkel, *Kovna ha-Yehudit b'-Hurbana* (The Destruction of Jewish Kovno), Jerusalem, 1959, pp. 47–48. Translated in Yitzhak Arad, Yisrael Gutman, and Abraham Margaliot, eds., *Documents on the Holocaust* (Jerusalem and Oxford: Yad Vashem and Pergamon Press, 1987), pp. 384–86 (Document 174).

Proclamation by Jewish Pioneer Youth Group in Vilna, Calling for Resistance, January 1, 1942: They Shall Not Take Us Like Sheep to the Slaughter!

Jewish youth, do not be led astray. Of the 80,000 Jews in the "Jerusalem of Lithuania" [Vilna] only 20,000 have remained: before our eyes they tore from us our parents, our brothers and sisters. Where are the hundreds of men who were taken away for work by the Lithuanian "snatchers"? Where are the naked women and children who were taken from us in the night of terror of the *provokatzia*? Where are the Jews [who were taken away on] the Day of Atonement? Where are our brothers from the second ghetto? All those who were taken away from the ghetto never came back. All the roads of the Gestapo lead to Ponary [Ponar, Panierai: the woods near Vilnius where Jews were massacred].

And Ponary is death!

Doubters! Cast off all illusions. Your children, your husbands, and your wives are no longer alive. Ponary is not a camp—all are shot there. Hitler aims to destroy all the Jews of Europe. The Jews of Lithuania are fated to be the first in line.

Let us not go as sheep to the slaughter! It is true that we are weak and defenseless, but resistance is the only reply to the enemy! Brothers! It is better to fall as free fighters than to live by the grace of the murderers,

Resist! To the last breath.

January 1, 1942, Vilna Ghetto.

Source: Moreshet Archives, D.1.4630, as cited in Yitzhak Arad, Yisrael Gutman, and Abraham Margaliot, eds., *Documents on the Holocaust* (Jerusalem and Oxford: Yad Vashem and Pergamon Press, 1987), p. 434 (Document 196).

Gens Reports to the Jewish Leadership in Vilna on the *Aktion* in Oszmiany,[1] October 1942: Protocol of the meeting on the *Aktion* in Oszmiany

October 27, 1942

Present: The head of the ghetto, Mr. J. Gens; Commissar Dessler; the head of the Health Department, Milkonovicki; the deputy head of the ghetto, Fried; Mr. Fishman; Mr. Braude, liaison; Rabbi Jakobson; Z. Kalmanovitch; the Commander of the Gate Guards, Levas; the Commander of the Work Police, Toubin; the Commander of Police District No. 1, Ring; P. Natanson; and M. Ganionska.

Gens: Gentlemen, I asked you to come here today in order to relate to you one of the most terrible tragedies in the life of Jews—when Jews led Jews to their death. Once more I have to speak openly to you.

A week ago Weiss of the SD came to us in the name of the SD with an order that we were to travel to Oszmiany. There were about 4,000 Jews in the Oszmiany ghetto and it was not possible to keep so many persons there. For that reason the ghetto would have to be made smaller by picking out the people who did not suit the Germans, to take them away and shoot them. The first to go should be children and women whose husbands were taken away last year by the "snatchers." The next to be taken would be women and aged among the Jews, forgive us. They were a sacrifice for our future.

I don't want to talk about what our Jews from Vilna have gone through in Oszmiany. Today I only regret that there were no Jews [i.e., Jewish Police] when the *Aktion* was carried out in Kiemieliszki and in Bystrzyca. Last week all the Jews were shot out there, without any distinction. Today two Jews from Swieciany (Old-Swieciany) came to me and asked me to save them. The Jews from Swieciany, Widze, and other small places in the neighborhood were [collected] there. And today I ask myself what is to happen if we have once more to carry out a selection. It is my duty to tell them: my good Jews, away with you; it is not my wish to soil my hands and send my police to do the dirty work. Today I will say that it is my duty to soil my hands, because terrible times have come over the Jewish people. If five million people have already gone it is our duty to save the strong and the young, not in years only, but in spirit, and not to indulge in sentimentality. When the Rabbi in Oszmiany was told that the number of persons required was not complete and that five elderly Jews were hiding in a *maline* [hiding place], he said that the *maline* should be opened. That is a man with a young and unshaken spirit.

I don't know whether everybody will understand this and defend it, and whether they will defend it after we have left the ghetto, but the attitude of our police is this—rescue what you can, do not consider your own good name or what you must live through.

All these things that I have told you do not sound sweetly to our souls nor yet for our lives. These are things one should not have to know. I have told you a shocking secret which must remain locked in our hearts. I want to tell you what the policemen did who carried out the terrible task, who segregated people and ordered "left" or "right." . . . This is no court of law. I want men of public affairs, men of *Gemara* [Talmud] to know what is a ghetto, and, on the other hand, what is police and what were the roads that other Jews had to tread.

From you, gentlemen, I want moral support. We all want to live to leave the ghetto. Today, as we work, it may be that not many of the Jews fully comprehend the danger in which we operate. None of us can know how many times every day he could get to Ponary. . . . I myself, as it happens, was on the battlefield. I was not afraid then, only later when I remembered it. It is the same for us now. We will think about it well later, after the ghetto. Today we must just be strong. Those who have faith will say the Almighty will aid us. Those who have no faith must ask the aid of the spirit of Jewish patriotism and public feeling. To survive it all and to remain, after the ghetto, a human being fit for the great Jewish future. Rosenberg said recently that it is the task of the Germans to exterminate the Jewish people in Europe. I don't know what he means. If he were to come here to us in the ghetto he might well be frightened by us—people who have been driven into *malines*, to Ponary, torn from their families—and in the course of a year we have built up a new life, we have built up much more than the Aryans. That is the Jewish people: a strong spirit and faith that we shall live. So that Rosenberg's words do not come true, we must fight today. In every fight the aim justifies the means, and sometimes the means are terrible. Unfortunately we must use all means in order to fight our enemy.

The Jewish people saw no blood in the whole of the 2,000 years. They saw fire, but blood they did not see. But now the ghetto has seen it. Jews have come from Ponary with bullets through their feet and hands. Once there were five women and a child in the hospital, all returned from Ponary. The Jewish people has become familiar with blood, and then one loses one's sentimentality.

I want to draw you into today's life a little and to let you understand the naked facts of this life, the naked fight. That is why I called you here, you, who are people far from police [affairs]. . . .

1. Spelled "Oszmiana" in the original, changed to conform with the Polish spelling used in the rest of the document. —ed.

Source: Moreshet Archives, D.1.357, as cited in Yitzhak Arad, Yisrael Gutman, and Abraham Margaliot, eds., *Documents on the Holocaust* (Jerusalem and Oxford: Yad Vashem and Pergamon Press, 1987), p. 440 (Document 199).

From a Diary by Zelig Kalmanovitch following the Report by Gens

October 27 [1942]
This evening at the Commander's the men were relating things that had happened to them. The scroll of agony. How they handed over 400 souls to the murderers. An order came together with a threat. They went there, and a thousand and more were demanded. They demanded women and large families. Till they agreed on 600, and gave 400. Ring saved women who were already on the carts. They were assembled in the square. The children were left in the houses; it was not known in advance what their task would be. They only guessed in their hearts. Slowly, it became clear. The Jews themselves agreed when they realized that it was possible to save the rest. The rabbi ruled that the old ones should be handed over. There was one woman who was a hundred. They asked for police, sons of servants, soldiers of the Mistress [Germany]. They paid no heed. They offered their lives in ransom, it was not accepted. The possessions remained. The food remained. If outsiders had done the job—there would have been more victims and all the property would have been stolen. In the synagogue some read Psalms. The women wept in front of the Holy Ark.

Sunday, November [1942]

Hard and bitter days once more. The [Jewish] Police has again been called on to "fix" affairs in the city of Swieciany. They were afraid that it would be done without them, and then the number of victims would have been greater. But apparently their fear was unnecessary. But it is here that the difficulty starts. The Commander began to demand that he and his assistants should not be the only ones employed in this operation; he does not want others to say "our hands are clean." At first sight he seemed to express the view that all the responsibility was his and that he alone would have to be judged by his Maker. But in fact he is not willing to be satisfied with spiritual cooperation, and he demands practical cooperation. The man who was his former assistant[1] was arrested yesterday because he refused to obey the order to go out to S[wieciany] with a group of policemen for this operation. The ghetto is boiling; gatherings, meetings, consultations. Apparently he demands that others take part. In truth we are in any case not innocent in [among the people of] Israel; we have bought our lives and our future with the death of tens of thousands. If we have decided that we must continue with this life despite everything, then we must go on to the end. May the merciful Lord forgive us. The old rabbi can show us the way. One must have what one can. That is the situation and it is not in our hands to change it. Of course, delicate souls cannot bear such acts, but the protest of the soul has no more than psychological value, and there is no moral value to it. Everybody is guilty or, more correctly, all are innocent and holy, and most of all those who take real action, who must overcome their spirit, who must overcome the torture of the soul, who free the others of this task, and save their souls from pain. . . .

1. The reference is to Josef Glazman, Deputy Commander of the Ghetto Police and member of the F.P.O. staff in Vilna.

Source: Z. Kalmanovitch, *Yoman be-Getto Vilna u-Ketavim me-ha-Izavon she-Nimze'u ba-Harisot* (A Diary from the Ghetto in Nazi Vilna), Tel Aviv, 1977, pp. 85–87, as cited in Yitzhak Arad, Yisrael Gutman, and Abraham Margaliot, eds., *Documents on the Holocaust* (Jerusalem and Oxford: Yad Vashem and Pergamon Press, 1987), p. 445 (Document 200).

Proclamation by the F.P.O. Calling for the Revolt in Vilna, September 1, 1943: Jews, Prepare for Armed Resistance!

The German and Lithuanian hangmen have reached the gates of the ghetto. They will murder us all. They will take us, group by group, through the gates. That is how they took them in their hundreds on the Day of Atonement. That is how they took them at the time of the White, Yellow, and the Pink papers.[1] That is how they took our brothers, sisters, fathers, mothers, our children. That is how they took tens of thousands away to their death.

But we will not go!

We will not let them take us like animals to slaughter.

Jews, prepare for armed resistance!

Do not believe the false assurances of the murderers, do not believe the words of traitors. Whoever is taken through the gate of the ghetto has only one road ahead—Ponary. *And Ponary is death.*

Jews, we have nothing to lose.

Death is certain. Who can still believe that he will survive when the murderers kill systematically? The hand of the hangman will reach out to each of us. Neither hiding nor cowardice will save lives.

Only armed resistance can save our lives and honor.

Brothers, it is better to fall in battle in the ghetto than to be led like sheep to Ponary.

Know that in the ghetto there is an organized Jewish force which will rise up with arms in its hands.

Rise up for the armed resistance!

Don't hide in the *malines*. You will fall there like mice in the hands of the murderers.

Jewish masses—*Out into the streets!* Those who have no arms get hold of an axe. Those who haven't an axe take hold of an iron bar or a cudgel!

For our murdered children,
For our parents,
For Ponary
Strike the murderers!

In every street, in every yard, in every room, within the ghetto and outside the ghetto.

Strike the dogs!

Jews, we have nothing to lose. *We can save our lives only if we kill the murderers.* Long live liberty! Long live armed resistance! Death to the murderers!

Command Staff
United Partisans Organization—F.P.O. [*Fareinikte Partizaner Organizatsie*]
Vilna Ghetto
September 1, 1943

1. Documents of various types that were distributed in the ghetto.

Source: Moreshet Archives, D.1.382, as cited in Yitzhak Arad, Yisrael Gutman, and Abraham Margaliot, eds., *Documents on the Holocaust* (Jerusalem and Oxford: Yad Vashem and Pergamon Press, 1987), p. 459 (Document 209).

NINETEEN

Rescue

The Rescue of Jews in the Town of Zbarazh, Ukraine

We survived due to an accidental meeting with our savior. Stefan Dragan visited our ghetto Zbarazh. My late husband Yakov invited him. They talked, and my husband prepared some provisions for him. Stefan said he wanted to come back tomorrow to pay for the provisions. But my husband said: "It's out of the question. We are living in a hard time. Today I'm helping you. Maybe tomorrow I'll need your help."

Since then we stayed in contact and even came to be friends. Stefan felt responsible for us. After each action he would come all scared and was glad to see us alive. After a fifth action in the ghetto, Stefan came with the elaborate plan of our rescue. . . . It was in the winter of 1942–1943.

Four of us left the ghetto. Before that Stefan had led out of the ghetto two of my sisters, Mira and Zhenia. We left after midnight, after a snowstorm. Dogs were barking. We felt uneasy. When we came to Stefan's place, he was shivering with anxiety. It turned out that the cave he had prepared for us was too small and dangerous. The men started digging a bunker under the house at night. To avoid any suspicion we spread earth in the attic.

In a few months, when the ghetto was liquidated in summer 1943, my sister-in-law with her husband and her small daughter fled and hid in an abandoned house that was close to Stefan's. After three days in the attic, feeling completely exhausted, my brother-in-law came to Stefan's house during the day and asked for bread and water. Stefan recognized him, but in order to show his neighbors his attitude toward Jews, he drove him away and slammed the door after him. At night Stefan opened the bunker and asked us, "What am I to do? Can you forgive me, Yakov, that I drove away your brother-in-law? If you agree to let them live in the bunker, I'll take them here tonight." This he did.

From then on, there were nine of us in the bunker. We lived through days of hope and despair. Time dragged on. We were afraid we would not be able to bear it any more. Besides, we feared that our saviors would have a hard time feeding nine people. Certainly, Stefan's wife, Olga, also participated in our rescue. Without her it would have been impossible. She helped him from the beginning to the end.

We gave them all money we had to make up for their expenses, at least partially. Sure, they were under constant danger. We stayed in the bunker until the liberation [on] March 5, 1944.

It is a pity that Stefan is no longer. He was a simple and nice man with a noble and great soul.

Source: Yitzhak Arad, ed., *Unichtozhenie Evreev SSSR v gody nemetskoi okkupatsii (1941–1944)* (Jerusalem: Yad Vashem Institute, 1991), pp. 331–33.

"He made his goal the rescue of professionals."

[From the testimony of Tania Ipp about the rescue of a group of Kaunas Jews by Ionas Paulavichius.]

It happened in the beginning of 1944 in the Kaunas ghetto where we had been living since 1941. A man named Shames came to my husband, Doctor Ipp, and asked if he wanted to flee. He said that a Lithuanian called Ionas Paulavichius wanted to save a group of Jews. By that time Mr. Paulavichius had already been hiding Shames's four-year-old son, but there were difficulties, because the child was taken away from his mother. They decided that the mother should join the boy. The Lithuanian was ready to give asylum to Shames himself and to his mother-in-law on condition that Shames would find some Jews who were educated and professional. Ionas was an idealist and saw that after the war there would be a need for physicians, engineers, architects, and other professionals. He made his goal to save as many professionals as possible. Having heard of us from Shames, Paulavichius wanted to meet my husband, who was a physician. Shames arranged the meeting outside of the ghetto. At first my husband was skeptical, because he could not offer Ionas any money. They had taken everything we had. And my husband could not believe that a Lithuanian would risk his life to save Jews. But Ionas Paulavichius proved to be an extraordinary person, a rare breed: an extremely pure, honest, and fearless man. He conscientiously jeopardized himself and his family. For us he was a real father and a personality to admire. He was a carpenter by occupation.

We agreed and in April 1944 left the ghetto. Our escape deserves a separate narrative.

Ionas lived in the suburb of Kaunas, Panemun. He arranged a hideout for us close to the basement. He and his son risked their lives, digging a huge pit and hiding ground so that neither his neighbors nor the Germans saw them. He fixed wooden beds for eight people and a table. He even managed to get a short-wave radio with ear-phones. One more problem was the ventilation of the pit. But he made a vent canal with an outlet in his garden. Another problem was the supply of food. Buying provisions for eight people without attracting neighbors' attention was difficult.

Ionas ran all that risk and jeopardized his family, saving nine of us and two Russian POWs. Besides, he had a Jewish boy hidden in some other place.

At last, in August 1944 we were freed by the Russians.

Unfortunately, this extraordinary man, who risked his life for the sake of others and many times escaped the fascists by the skin of his teeth, was killed by Lithuanian nationalists. We hope his good deeds will never be forgotten.

Source: Yitzhak Arad, ed., *Unichtozhenie Evreev SSSR v gody nemetskoi okkupatsii (1941–1944)* (Jerusalem: Yad Vashem Institute, 1991), p. 333.

" 'Who!? She, a Kike?!'—she yelled.—'She is my sister!' "

[From the testimony of Basia Ganeles (Pikman) about her rescue by Elena Tseluiko.]

I, Ganeles (Pikman) Basia Tsurielevna, born in 1916, testify that I owe my rescue during World War II to Gelena Slizhevska (also known as Elena Vasilievna Tseluiko), now a citizen of Poland. The rescue was carried out in the following circumstances.

I am a native of Mozyr in Belorussia. From 1933 I lived and worked in Minsk. After Minsk had been occupied by the fascists on June 27, 1941, I, along with all Jews, was put in a ghetto. I fled and reached Mozyr on foot. All my relatives were gone, the house was looted. I was in despair, but pulled myself together and decided to go east to the front line. It was in early autumn. I have a good memory for all important dates in my life. So, I remember that on September 6 a Belorussian girl came to me and said: "I learned that you were going to ours. Take me with you." Obviously, she learned about it from a woman at whose place I was staying overnight. The girl was sixteen. Along with her mother and two baby sisters she left the town of Baranovichi, occupied by the Germans, and came to Mozyr. They settled at their relatives', in a village that was close to the town. That was Lena Tseluiko.

I answered Lena: "I am older than you are and cannot take you with me without your mother's permission. Besides, I am Jewish, and it is dangerous for you to come along with me." Lena said: "I don't mind your nationality. And you don't look Jewish. Everything will be OK. The main thing is to get to the front line and start fighting the fascists." Nevertheless, I refused. But subsequent events proved the necessity of a fast decision.

On September 8, 1941, a punitive expedition came to Mozyr. Later during the war I described fascist atrocities in Mozyr to the writer Ilya Ehrenburg, and he published my story in the "Black Book."

I fled to the village of Bobry, close to Mozyr, and stayed there overnight. In a coincidence that happened on September 11 Lena saved my life for the first time. Peasants suspected that I was Jewish. They surrounded me, armed with pitchforks and pokers. Someone ran to inform the punitive expedition. Suddenly, Lena rushed into the crowd.

"Who!? She, a Kike?! [*kakaya ona zhidovka*!?]"—she yelled.—"She is my sister!"

Lena took me by the hand and led me out of the crowd. Astonished by her force, the peasants stood speechless. Lena hurriedly took me away. When we left the village and got on a road, Lena said: "From now on you are my sister." Then she scrutinized me and said: "We don't look alike. Let's be cousins."

Lena's mother lived seven kilometers from Mozyr in the village of Berezovka. She was reluctant to let Lena go with me. But when I said that I was Jewish and would perish unless I left, she said: "I have had many Jewish friends. They helped me more than my relatives. Let my daughter join you." She gave Lena her passport, we said good bye in a wood and parted.

Next day we were in Kalinkovichi, ten kilometers from Mozyr. Punitive expeditions had not reached them yet. Lena and I started walking in the streets and telling Jews to flee to the woods. We told them what had happened three days ago in Mozyr but, unfortunately, they did not believe us. Only two young Jews left with us.

Four of us set out to Gomel. We walked along railroad tracks, spending nights at desolate and broken cabins of railroad workers. When we were approaching Gomel, our companions stayed in a wood while we saw Germans in villages. Lena and I entered Gomel on September 24. We were inexperienced, easily confided in local residents, but soon we realized, that we were surrounded by enemies. In Gomel, for example, we asked a woman for a place to stay overnight but she denounced us to a patrol, said I was Jewish. Fortunately, the patrol was Austrian [*sic*] and helped us leave the city.

We were very imprudent, because we were young and eager to fight. We made a lot of mistakes. I have to admit that Lena, though eight years my junior, proved to be wiser. She knew people better, could react faster in difficult circumstances. She had a keener sense of danger, was more inventive in critical situations.

We were surrounded by hostility. The further the front line moved, the smaller the number of people who wanted to help the Jews, the more people were ready to denounce anyone who could be suspected of being Jewish. The police, formed from local residents, were especially active.

We decided to go back to Minsk, where we had many acquaintances in the ghetto. We thought they were not aware of the danger they were facing. We wanted to warn them, help them run away to the woods. We reached Minsk, saw tens of thousands of people, gathered on a strip of city land and understood how unrealistic our goal was. When I left the ghetto for the second time (and that time Lena accompanied me) it was October 1941. . . .

Lena and I went back to Gomel. We went on foot. We stayed in Bobruisk for a while. There was no ghetto in Bobruisk yet. We stayed with Jewish families, and Lena became very close with them: she consoled people, gave them hope, did her best. In Bobruisk we were noticed by the police. Since no one could show us the way to guerrilla unit locations, we left the town. We reached Zhlobin and turned to Rogachev, passed by Mogilev and reached Orsha.

In Orsha they already had a ghetto, but it was not fenced. We were shocked by the sight of starved, cold, suffering, sick, constantly humiliated, mocked, and beaten people. I saw how much Lena suffered from all that. She was less afraid of walking in the town streets than I. She would procure bread from somewhere and bring it to the ghetto. Often, she would enter the territory of the ghetto a few times a day. Once, in a very dangerous situation, she helped a Jewish woman with two children to hide. That woman pretended to be Polish, but her younger boy was very Jewish looking, and she was denounced.

I almost perished in Orsha: a small girl of five or six called me a "Kike" in public. Only due to Lena's inventiveness was the crowd distracted. I hid. We had to flee from Orsha and ended up in Smolensk.

In Smolensk I got into trouble that confined me to bed for a long time: on November 4, 1941, I was run over by a German car and broke my leg. Germans took me to a hospital, and that saved me, because I did not have any papers. Lena's inventiveness came handy again. She said that I lost a purse with my passport in the accident. It was she who made them give me a duplicate of this passport. I was saved. Lena claimed me to be her cousin, named Natasha. Thus I became Tseluiko, Natalia Matveevna.

To get me a passport Lena had to schedule an appointment with the Russian Commandant of Smolensk, Menshagin. The latter conducted a real interrogation. Having learned that she was from Baranovichi, he said, "If you are from Baranovichi, your father must have been a Communist. I'm going to arrest you." Lena answered, "So what? They say you also were a Communist before the war." It must have been a good shot, because the Commandant got confused and ordered that a passport be issued.

During those few months that I spent in bed, hosted by a wonderful woman, Lena did everything to help me recover. We were starving, but Lena would bring potato peelings, fix a soup from them, and give it to me. She suffered from her knowledge of what was going on in the Smolensk ghetto.

Once she brought with her a seven-year-old boy, Ruva, whom she picked up in the street. The boy left the ghetto to get some food for his mother and small sisters. Starting with that day, Ruva visited us often. Lena would always spare some soup from potato peelings for him. She would say: "It's OK, we'll get by. And this soup and potato we'll leave for Ruva."

Ruva looked very Jewish, and on his way to our place he was frequently beaten up. He would often come with a blood-stained and swollen face. He would always take to the ghetto the bigger share of what Lena was giving him. Then he would appear in a couple of days all covered with blood again.

In the spring of 1942 I was already able to move. Lena and I often visited the Smolensk ghetto, bringing some food. The ghetto was not fenced, but we ran a great risk. I often said to Lena: "I am Jewish, but what are your reasons to run such a risk?" She would not even listen. She would have risked her head, without regretting it.

There was one more woman with us, a Russian, Niura Odnokrylova. Three of us formed a small group of resistance: we helped the prisoners of the ghetto, gathered leaflets that were dropped from aircraft, and spread them among the population. We also gave special tear-off surrender passes to the German soldiers who, we knew, would not turn us in to the Gestapo. But one day we had to flee from Smolensk. A neighbor informed on our helping a Jewish boy. Besides, she suspected that I was Jewish. Germans from a patrol company, whom we knew, warned us, and Niura Odnokrylova helped us leave Smolensk. It was on May 30, 1942.

After long wandering and adventures we came to the town of Pochinok, Smolensk district. We settled down in the village of Priverzhenka, close to Pochinok. Our hostess was a very poor but kind woman, Nastia Tsybarikova, who gave asylum to many escaped POWs and soldiers whose units were cut off from the main Soviet troops by German offensives. We found a local underground resistance group and were accepted. Of the people who were in it, I knew only two last names—Nadia Ryzhikova from Kolomna and Sergei Liubimov from Moscow. The rest were known only by their first names. At the same time we worked on a farm, gathering mushrooms and herbs. Then, as many times before in various places, I was denounced as being Jewish. A town shoemaker, to whom I went to fix a pair of shoes (I was barefoot), informed on me.

When I was arrested, Lena came to the Gestapo herself, and they arrested her as well. We were put into different cells of the Pochinok prison. They beat us up terribly. Especially me. There was only one question: "Nationality?" They beat Lena too, but she kept saying: "Natasha is not Jewish. She is my sister." Then I underwent an anthropological test and a professor from Berlin "established" that I was a product of the blend of Slavic and Mongol blood.

Lena and I were released in August 1942. We were prohibited from leaving the village of Priverzhenka. I was trying to talk Lena into going west: "Go back to your mother! It would be OK if we were killed as members of resistance. But if you perish because of my being Jewish, I'll never forgive myself." "Don't say that!" Lena yelled at me. "I can't leave you! Who do you think I am?!" Lena's generosity was amazing. In February 1943 she found somewhere a Jewish girl named Basia who crawled out of a pit full of corpses in Dorogobuzh. The girl passed herself off as an Uzbek. She lived with us for several weeks, but fell sick. Lena took her to a hospital. I do not know what happened to her afterwards.

In March 1943 tension around us was growing. And we fled from Priverzhenka. We reached the front line in the vicinity of Orel but failed to cross it. I was arrested on April 19 and survived by accident. On August 5, 1943, the Red Army entered Orel. I was ignorant of Lena's fate. I looked for my savior for twenty-six years.

Only on June 22, 1969, did I get a phone call and hear Lena's voice. The call was from Poland.

It turned out that in 1943 Lena was taken to a concentration camp in Germany. She survived. In the camp she fell in love with someone. He was Polish. She did not return to the USSR after the war.

I think Gelena Slizhevska (it is now Lena's name) deserves the high award given by the Jewish people to those who during the tragic years risked their lives, helping our humiliated, rejected, trampled, but unsubdued people. It is a great heroic deed.

Ganeles (Pikman) Basia Tsurielevna
City of Minsk

(The language and style of the original are preserved for publication.)

Source: Yad Vashem Archives, 0-33/2672, as cited in Yitzhak Arad, ed., *Unichtozhenie Evreev SSSR v gody nemetskoi okkupatsii (1941–1944)* (Jerusalem: Yad Vashem Institute, 1991), pp. 313–19.

TWENTY

Bitter Legacy

Memorandum of the Head of the Secret Service in Ukraine* (September 13, 1944)

Strictly Secret

Central Committee of the Communist Party (Bolsheviks) of Ukraine
to Comrade N. S. Khrushchev
Kiev

Special Report on Antisemitic Manifestations in Ukraine

With the liberation of the territory of Ukraine, the organs of the NKGB of the Ukrainian Soviet Socialist Republic have reported incidents of severe antisemitic manifestations on the part of the local population in almost all cities. Recently in a number of localities in the UkSSR, our organs have noted an increase in antisemitic manifestations, in specific cases tending toward overt acts of a pogromist nature.

In analyzing the cause of antisemitism and its extensive spread at the present time, one must say that it first of all derives from remnants of German fascist propaganda and propaganda of Ukrainian nationalists which they spread in regard to the Jews during the [Nazi] occupation.

At the present time, in connection with the return home of citizens (including part of the Jewish population) who formerly lived in Kiev and other cities of Ukraine, antisemitic manifestations have been noted which basically originated with people who lived in territories occupied by the Germans.

It has been established that the heads of some institutions and enterprises sometimes assume antisemitic positions because they fail to comprehend and [hence] distort the matter of the selection and training of ethnic Ukrainian cadres and their use in staffing the government bureaucracy of the UkSSR. Often for no reason whatsoever some leaders of institutions and enterprises refuse to employ people of Jewish nationality in ordinary work positions.

The very low percentage of Jews in the ranks of the Red Army in comparison with the numbers of people of other nationalities [*sic*] is being used by anti-Soviet elements to reach various conclusions which ultimately lead to antisemitic manifestations.

At the same time it should be pointed out that recently there has been an increase in incidents of a provocative nature caused by certain elements of the Jewish population which engender antisemitic manifestations. These cases of provocation are manifested by spreading rumors to the effect that top posts in the government bureaucracy of the Ukrainian Soviet Socialist Republic (UkSSR) are supposedly, in the near future, to be occupied by Jews while Ukrainians are to be driven out and punished for alleged manifestations of antisemitism.

Moreover . . . certain members of the Jewish population . . . have begun to spread various provocative accounts about the allegedly antisemitic policy of the government of the UkSSR and of Comrade Khrushchev[1] personally; hence, supposedly the near future will see changes in the composition of the government of the UkSSR, etc.

Such ideas, when they penetrate the unorganized population, lead to an increase in and incitement of antisemitic manifestations and to overtly hostile acts regarding Jews.

Furthermore, in the city of Chernovtsy,[2] and other cities . . . elements of the Jewish population engage in commercial speculation and in various ways avoid serving in the Red Army and work assignments in the Donbas; by such actions they arouse anger on the part of non-Jews, which often assumes the form of antisemitic manifestations.

Some influential members of the Jewish intelligentsia are defending those Jews who avoid being called up to the Red Army and labor assignments; their remarks are clearly anti-Soviet.

We consider it necessary to focus on the following selected cases of overt manifestations of antisemitism:

On June 22 of this year in . . . Kiev in the Galitskii market (popularly referred to as the "Jewish market," *Evreiskii bazar*, or *Evbaz*) the stall-tradeswoman Dar'ia Platonovna Kobylianskaia (born in Kiev in 1892 and a resident of Kiev . . .) who works as a guard in a special construction and assembly department, hit Ivan Stepanovich Kartavyi, an invalid of the Patriotic War and Party member, after the latter had mistaken her for a Jewess and cursed her in an antisemitic vein.

Kartavyi was taken unconscious to a clinic from which he was sent home after receiving medical treatment.

This incident attracted a large crowd from which serious pogromist cries were directed at the Jews. Soon rumors were circulating in the city that at the market a Jewess had killed a Red Army officer, that a Jewess had killed a Hero of the Soviet Union, etc.[3]

On June 27 of this year Ekaterina Ivanovna Babenko (without any definite occupation), Matrena Nikitichna Artamonova (who is engaged in commerce), and Olga Stepanovna Nedoshkovskaia (a cleaning woman at the Podolsk district hospital) entered a cafeteria located at 16 Verkhnii Val St. Two sailors of the Red Fleet Dniepr flotilla entered the cafeteria with them.

While drinking alcoholic beverages, the aforementioned people got into a fight during which one of the sailors pushed Artamonova into the street; she fell on the pavement and banged her head. Elizaveta Borisovna Spivak (a Jew), who was then passing by in the street tried to help Artamonova, but Nedoshkovskaia came out of the cafe and attacked Spivak. While beating her, she [Nedoshkovskaia] began to shout, "Jews are killing Russians." At her screams, a crowd gathered. Efim Ivanovich Kolevorov emerged from the crowd and also began to beat Spivak. Artamonova, Nedoshkovskaia, and Kolevorov have been detained while an investigation is being carried out.

On August 25 of this year, in . . . Dnepropetrovsk, according to a decision of the prosecutor's office, by administrative order, Iuzef Markovich Petelevich, born in 1922, Jewish, dental technician at the Dnepropetrovsk artillery school, was settled into one of the apartments in the house at 29 Ispolkomovskaya Street. In these quarters were already living Pelageia Tikhonovna Orlova, (born in 1907; the wife of a Red Army soldier called up in September 1943; engaged in private commerce), her two children, and invalid sister. Orlova was to be resettled in another apartment, which in fact was not suitable for habitation.

Orlova resisted being moved. Her cries were answered by a crowd of up to 200 and the following shouts were heard: "Beat the kikes and save Russia," "Death to the kikes," "37,000 kikes have already been slaughtered, we'll finish off the rest," etc. Out of those in the crowd the most active were the policewoman Kosiak, a certain Sekhraiants, Sergeant Golovin, and Orlova's sister, who by their shouts and actions urged the crowd on to take care of the Jew Petelevich. Sekhraiants grabbed a rock and hit Petelevich in the face. Another woman (whose identity has not been determined) hit him in the back with a rock. Further, Sekhraiants, Kosiak, and Golovin, accompanied by a group of people, attempted to break into the neighboring apartment which was occupied by the Jew, Ulanovskii. Since the apartment was locked, the group brought an axe, broke down the door, forced its way into the apartment, and dancing to the tune of antisemitic cries, began to smash the furniture. The crowd was dispersed. . . .

In . . . Kiev a Red Army sergeant (family name undetermined) of Jewish nationality came to citizen Dmitrii Mikhailovich Khomenchuk, residing at 22 Mezhigorskaia St., and asked that some things in the apartment be returned to him since he had lived there before the war. Khomenchuk refused to return the items and shouted that Jews were beating him. Neighbors, including Vera Krupko and Ul'iana Khomenchuk, came running when they heard his cries and attacked the sergeant with knives and forks. The police rushed to the rescue, detaining Krupko and Khomenchuk and dispersing the crowd.

In . . . Kiev, Bukhover, a Jew who was head of the housing and consumer department of the . . . Corrective Labor Camp and Colony Administration of the NKVD of the UkSSR, appeared at apartment 102 at 7 Saksaganskii St. with documents authorizing the resettlement of a certain Gromova, who was living in this apartment, elsewhere. Not wishing to vacate the apartment, Gromova raised a cry. Residents of the house and passersby who gathered began to shout in regard to Bukhover, "Jews and members of the NKVD are beating people!" Chairman of the district soviet Gikalo and the district prosecutor, who arrived on the scene, did not realize the legality of Bukhover's actions and forbade Bukhover to resettle Gromova.

The following deserve to be singled out among antisemitic manifestations in certain government institutions.

Evgenii Konstantinovich Sezonenko, deputy head of the manpower registration and distribution office of the Soviet of People's Commissars (*Soviet narodnykh komissarov*—SNK) of the UkSSR systematically has expressed antisemitic views. In the presence of Comrades Litvinov, deputy people's commissar of the coal industry, and Maksimov, deputy head of the manpower registration and distribution office of the SNK UkSSR, Sezonenko made fun of people of Jewish nationality, stating that "the Jews have never worked, they seek the easy life, they are useless for labor."

On another occasion, in the presence of the same people and of Spivak, secretary of the Zhitomir obkom of the Ukrainian Communist Party (Bolsheviks),[4] Sezonenko made the following antisemitic comment: "If one defends people in Ukraine, then it should be only Ukrainians, and perhaps Russians, but not Jews."[5] Spivak pointed out to Sezonenko the incorrectness of his views.

Gaidamachenko, deputy people's commissar of the local fuel industry expressed similar antisemitic views, asserting "that not a single Jew would work in the people's commissariat cafeteria."

Basenko, head of the Glav URS of this commissariat [i.e., of the fuel industry] banned the hiring of Jews as waiters and cooks.[6] At the People's Commissariat of Trade of the UkSSR many rumors are circulating among the staff about government restrictions on the number of Jews in the people's commissariats and in the city's trade network. The Commissariat of Trade and other civilian . . . commissariats might have on the staffs not more than 5 percent Jews, the NKGB 10 percent, and the city trade network up to 25 percent, but not in top positions.

The management of Footware Factory No. 8 in Kiev received plots for individual vegetable gardens for top workers of the factory. When the list was compiled with four Jews in top positions, the director of the factory, Kireev, crossed out three of them, and substituted for them people who were not employed at the factory itself but had work in other parts of the enterprise.[7]

Anatolii Iakovlevich Kryzhanovskii, an engineer of the Dnieper River Steamship Line, stated in the presence of his fellow workers:

> The policy toward Jews has now changed sharply. I heard that there is a decision to set quotas for them in educational institutions because the Jews have been getting all the places in the institutes of higher educations. In the future this will also be carried out for other institutions.

Among incidents of a provocative nature the following should be noted:

In . . . Kiev . . . a certain Valentina Petrova Marinenko (born in 1917), Ukrainian, a member of the Komsomol from 1933 who lived in Kiev under the Germans, did not work, was arrested three times by the Gestapo and was subsequently released after being recruited as a secret agent for them. After the liberation of Kiev, Marinenko began working at the Podol'skii district Komsomol of Kiev and then at the Podol'skii district executive committee where she engaged in arousing hostility among Russians, Ukrainians, and Jews. Marinenko openly stated that "Soon all of us Ukrainians will be driven out now that the Jews have begun to move in." Once, when she was working as head of the manpower department of the Podol'skii district industrial plant, under false pretenses Marinenko managed to get fourteen employees of the district industrial plant to sign a provocative and slanderous letter she wrote to Comrade Khrushchev. After she was fired, Marinenko began to spread provocative antisemitic rumors far and wide to the effect that "Jews had gotten in everywhere and corrupted top Party and government functionaries, and NKGB, NKVD, and other officials. . . . " Inciting ethnic hostility, Marinenko spread a provocative story about speaking personally with Comrade Khrushchev, who supposedly responded to her information about the situation in the Podol'skii district industrial plant, by saying: "That is why things in the Podol'skii district are bad since the bosses there are various Fishers and other Jews."

Preparations are now under way to arrest Marinenko. Vladimir Mikhailovich Nagachevskii, a resident of the city of Kiev who is currently unemployed, said, among other things:

> A secret order has been received from the center that the percentage of Jewish workers not exceed the percentage of the Jews in the total population. This order is currently being implemented.

Particular attention should be paid to incidents of nationalistic manifestations on the part of certain representatives of the Jewish population and their spreading of provocative rumors. Thus:

Khaim Tokar',[8] a journalist and member of the Communist Party who lives in Kiev and before the war was editor of a Kiev newspaper, complained about his failure to find appropriate work. He said:

I am certain that Litvin, a member of the central committee of the Communist Party of Ukraine, cannot stand our people, while Bazhan[9] is happy to act in accordance with this attitude of Litvin. These two people are doing all they can so that I find no work here, while each blames the other [for this situation].

Comparing the situation of Jews in the USSR and America, Tokar' referred to a recent conversation with the Yiddish poet Fefer,[10] who came to Kiev for a plenum of Soviet writers and is now living in Moscow.[11] He [Tokar'] said: "After returning from America,[12] the writer Fefer related that Jews in America lived far better than in the USSR, and that there are real democratic freedoms there."

According to Tokar', Fefer spoke in sympathetic tones and at length about the Zionist movement in America. Fefer characterized the Zionist party in America as one that enjoys considerable support and authority among the Jewish population and with America's ruling circles. Fefer spoke about his meetings in America with leading representatives of the Zionist party.[13]

Fefer allegedly told Tokar', "We Jews must have our own state; otherwise, nothing will come of us."[14] Citing Fefer, Tokar' spread rumors in Kiev to the effect that in a recent conversation with Comrade Molotov,[15] Fefer and the actor Mikhoels[16] raised the question "of antisemitism in the USSR." Tokar' said:

After many requests, Fefer and Mikhoels gained an audience with Molotov. Among other issues, Fefer and Mikhoels raised the question of antisemitism in the USSR and, particularly, in Ukraine. Molotov replied that this is known, that some orders had been given to Ukraine, that now was not the time to deal with this, but that it would be taken up after the war.[17]

During Fefer's stay in Kiev, he said that many Jews appealed to him with various "complaints." In particular, Fefer was addressed by the doctoral student, Tokman, the Jewish writer from the front, Shkarovskii,[18] and many others. Fefer promised to help them all, stating that he would speak with Comrade Shcherbakov[19] and the writer I. Ehrenburg[20] in Moscow.

The Yiddish writer Hofshtein[21] evaluated this situation and reacted in his own way. He said, "What the Jews are now undergoing is good. This will revive their national consciousness which had been lost."

Professor Podgaets and the writer Shkarovskii expressed similar ideas. Iakub Davidovich Sherf[22] (who writes under the pseudonym Kon), a member of the [Jewish] Antifascist Committee and of the Union of Writers, who arrived in . . . Chernovtsy from Moscow, turned to the Chernovtsy *obkom* of the Communist Party, stating that he considers the mobilization of Jewish youth for work in Donbas and the Urals incorrect, provocatively pointing out that Jewish girls were being used as prostitutes in the [hinterland] of the Soviet Union. At the same time Sherf attempted to compile lists of Jews in Chernovtsy who wish to emigrate from the USSR to America and Palestine.

Genia Izrailevna Brand (born in . . . Kiev in 1901 and before the war a shop seamstress) arrived in Kiev from the hinterland of the USSR. She turned up at the apartment which she had lived in before the occupation, 22 Korolenko St., and demanded that Kornieva, who was living there, vacate it. When the latter refused, Brand threatened to get even with Kornieva; she spread provocative ideas among the residents of her house: "The entire population which lived on occupied territory will be resettled and Ukraine will be settled with Jews." In a queue in front of a store Brand said, "Thirty Russians will be destroyed for every Jew killed. If the Russians touch a Jew, there will be such a massacre of Russians that they will never forget it."

Brand was arrested by the Ukrainian NKGB of Kiev *oblast'*.[23]

Petr Mikhailovich Kovtun (born in . . . Kiev in 1908), Jew, senior lieutenant of the Red Army, assistant commander of the 191st guard aviation regiment, who served in the Red Army since 1941 and who was in Kiev on assignment, entered the premises of the district department of the NKGB of the Zheleznodorozhnyi district of Kiev in a drunken state. Having brought a woman named Chemikhova with him to the NKGB, in the presence of NKGB personnel, Kovtun got into an argument with her and tried to shoot her. After being disarmed, Kovtun made an uproar, calling the NKGB staff members "fascists and antisemites. . . . " Kovtun said: "I have come from the front to defend the Jewish people and will deal with the Union of the Russian People[24] which killed Jews." Kovtun was detained, an investigation is being carried out by the military prosecutor of the Kiev garrison. . . . [25]

Recently in Kiev and some other cities provocative rumors have been circulating widely to the effect that Comrade Khrushchev is, allegedly, being called back to Moscow and Comrade Zhdanov[26] is coming to take his place. Rumors about the departure of Comrade Khrushchev have been circulated among a literary circle by the writers Ianovskii[27] and Panch[28] and the dramatist Sukhodol'skii.[29] All of them have "attributed" the supposedly imminent departure of Comrade Khrushchev to the "alleged displeasure of the Central Committee of the Communist Party . . . with Khrushchev for showing indulgence toward the spread of antisemitism in Ukraine."

According to Ianovskii,[30] who revealed himself to be an antisemite, these rumors "are being spread by Jews in order to . . . regain control of leadership positions."

Senior lieutenant of the Red Army and photo-correspondent of TASS [Telegraphic Agency of the Soviet Union] Iakov L'vovich Povolotskii, a resident of Kiev, said that:

> Khrushchev is being transferred from Ukraine and Zhdanov will be named to replace him. Khrushchev is being transferred for distorting

nationality policy, especially in regard to the Jews. Since this has not yet been officially publicized, no one should speak about it.

Stage actor Astakhov, who recently arrived in Kiev from the Third Ukrainian front, said in a conversation:

I know well that Moscow is displeased by the policy being carried out in Ukraine by Khrushchev. He will be soon recalled and Zhdanov will be sent from Leningrad to replace him. A person close to Khrushchev told me about this.

The rumors about the allegedly imminent departure of Comrade Khrushchev from Ukraine are circulating not only in private conversations. In mid-August . . . rumors were circulated among the hierarchy of the UKOOPINSOVET [Ukrainian Council of Cooperative Workshops of Invalids] about the "replacement of the Ukrainian government" by members of the Ukrainian Communist Party Sara Iakovlevna Blomberg[31] and Karpman, an economist at UKOOPINSOVET.

According to her own testimony, Blomberg passed rumors about the removal of Khrushchev and Korneits[32] to Davydov, secretary of the Party organization of UKOOPINSOVET who, instead of putting a halt to the circulating of such provocative ideas, said, "There's no smoke without fire."[33] The local Party organization expelled Blomberg and Karpman from the Party.[34]

On July 29 of this year Ol'ga Nikolaevna Litvak, head of the sewing shop of the people's commissariat of municipal economy (*narkomkhoz*), entered the shop and said aloud that "Khrushchev had been removed from his post."

We are investigating Litvak.

We have undertaken measures to root out enemy agents among people who have encouraged antisemitic actions and circulated provocative rumors with this purpose. At the same time we are attempting to uncover nationalistic, Zionist elements among the Jewish population and their anti-Soviet activity.

People's Commissar of State Security of the UkSSR
Savchenko

Source: *Jews in Eastern Europe* 3(22), Winter 1993.

Report of the Investigating Commission

[November] 1944
No. 1773/s[ecret]
Kiev
EXTREMELY CONFIDENTIAL
To Secretary of the Central Committee of the Communist Party (Bolsheviks)

of Ukraine,
Comrade D. S. Korotchenko

In accordance with your order we have carried out an investigation of the materials set out in the special report of the People's Commissariat of State Security of the Ukrainian SSR of Comrade Savchenko of September 13 of this year, "On Antisemitic Manifestations in Ukraine."

The report discusses three questions:

1. The alleged increase in antisemitic manifestations in Ukraine;
2. Nationalistic manifestations on the part of certain representatives of the Jewish population;
3. The spreading of provocative rumors about the allegedly antisemitic policy of the government of the UkSSR and, connected with this, imminent changes in the composition of the government.

Investigation of the matter has revealed:

1. On the Question of Antisemitic Manifestations

The report said: "Recently in a number of localities in the UkSSR our organs have noted an increase in antisemitic manifestations in specific cases tending toward overt acts of a pogromist nature."

Investigation of the incidents mentioned in the report indicates:

a. Five incidents involved cases of hooliganism during which provocative elements among the crowd (in the majority of cases not identified) were responsible for antisemitic shouts. After these incidents of hooliganism, provocative rumors of an antisemitic nature circulated among some of the residents of the city of Kiev.

b. Incidents of antisemitic manifestations on the part of deputy people's commissar of the fuel industry of the UkSSR Gaidamachenko, of the worker of the same commissariat Basenko, and of director of the Footware Factory No. 1 Kireev—were not confirmed by the investigation.[35]

c. The antisemitic activity of former engineer Krzhanovskii[36] of the Dnieper Steamship Line and of former worker of the Podol'skii district industrial plant Marinenko was confirmed. For active work on behalf of the Germans during the occupation Krzhanovskii was sentenced to twenty years. During investigation Marinenko admitted that she was a Gestapo agent.

d. Secretary Spivak of the Zhitomir *obkom* of the CP confirmed the antisemitic remarks of E. K. Sezonenko, deputy head of the manpower registration and distribution office of the SNK of the UkSSR.

Thus, it has been established that a number of antisemitic manifestations have occurred during the past five to six months. These incidents are of a random nature and occurred, as a rule, on the basis of hooliganism or domestic matters involving apartments or other such problems.

It should be noted that these antisemitic manifestations arose primarily due to remnants of German-fascist propaganda (or provocation by German agents) and propaganda of Ukrainian nationalists, which they directed against the Jews during the occupation.

At the same time the examples cited in the report do not reflect the real political and moral attitudes of the population and cannot serve as grounds for generalizing about their manifestations, especially about [allegedly] increasing manifestations of antisemitism on the part of the local population in Ukraine.

2. On Nationalistic Manifestations on the Part of Certain Representatives of the Jewish Population

The report stated: "Particular attention should be paid to incidents of nationalistic manifestations on the part of certain representatives of the Jewish population and their spreading of provocative rumors."

. . . Cases are cited of the manifestation of Jewish nationalism on the part of journalist Khaim Tokar', the Yiddish writers Hofshtein and Sherf, citizen Brand, and senior lieutenant of the Red Army Kovtun.

Checking of these incidents established the following: In relation to the journalist Khaim Tokar', the report stated that Tokar' said:

> I am certain that Litvin, a member of the central committee of the Communist Party of Ukraine, cannot stand our people, while Bazhan is happy to act in accordance with this attitude of Litvin. These two people are doing all they can so that I find no work here, while each blames the other [for this situation].

Referring to his conversation with the Jewish poet Fefer, who had arrived in Kiev for the plenum of the Union of Writers, Tokar' said: "After returning from America, the writer Fefer related that Jews in America lived far better than in the USSR, and that there are real democratic freedoms there." According to Tokar', Fefer spoke in sympathetic tones about the Zionist movement in America. Fefer allegedly told Tokar': "We Jews must have our own state; otherwise, nothing will come of us." Citing Fefer, Tokar' spread rumors in Kiev about a recent conversation of Fefer and the actor Mikhoels with Comrade Molotov. Tokar' said:

> After many requests, Fefer and Mikhoels gained an audience with Molotov. Among other issues, Fefer and Mikhoels raised the question of antisemitism in the USSR and, particularly, in Ukraine. Molotov replied that this is known, that some orders had been given to Ukraine, that now was not the time to deal with this, but that it would be taken up after the war.

Checking information regarding Tokar' established that Khaim Tokar', journalist, member of the All-Union Communist Party (Bolsheviks), was a member of the Bund until 1919. In conversation with us in regard to the accusations, he stated that he never said that Litvin and Bazhan could not stand Jews but that it seemed to him that Litvin was preventing him from getting a job. Tokar' also denied that Fefer had said that the Jews in the USSR lived worse than those in America but confirmed that at a meeting of Fefer with the leadership of Zionist organizations in America, the latter had expressed his sympathy for Jews living in the USSR. In conversation [with us] Tokar' confirmed that he believed that the Zionist party in America was progressive and that the existence of such a party in the USSR was permissible. Further, Tokar' confirmed that Fefer told him about his visit with Comrade Molotov and also about the supposed agreement of Comrade Molotov regarding the allocation of . . . Crimea for Jewish settlement.

. . . Tokar' insisted on including in his explanation the following idea: "If the Party changes its attitude toward the Jews by one iota I will commit suicide."[37]

On the Yiddish writer Hofshtein[38]

The report stated: "The Yiddish writer Hofshtein evaluated the situation and reacted in his own way. He said: 'What the Jews are now undergoing is good. This will revive their national consciousness which had been lost.' "

It was not possible to confirm this due to the fact that Hofshtein was sent on an assignment to Moscow. However, in relation to his personality it was established that D. N. Hofshtein [is] a Yiddish writer, member of the CP from 1940, formerly a Zionist activist. In 1918 he worked in the Jewish department of the Central Rada.[39] In 1920–1921 he worked for an anti-Soviet newspaper in Vilna.[40] He was one of the organizers of the Jewish nationalist organization *Shtrom*.[41] In 1924 he traveled to Palestine where he wrote anti-Soviet articles and satires.[42] After returning from Palestine he wrote and published a number of anti-Soviet works; for example, until 1931 he published poems idealizing Trotsky.

According to NKGB information, Hofshtein left for Moscow with some anti-Soviet letters which he was going to hand over to the British Embassy. There are grounds for asserting that Hofshtein is still continuing his active nationalistic activity. In particular, it has been established that during the current year Hofshtein attempted to organize in the city of Kiev a mass demonstration of the Jewish population on the anniversary of the German massacre at Babi Yar.

On the Yiddish writer Ia. D. Sherf

The report stated that "Iakub Davidovich Sherf (who writes under the pseudonym Kon), a member of the [Jewish] Antifascist Committee and of the Union of Writers, who arrived in the city of Chernovtsy from Moscow, turned to the Chernovtsy *obkom* of the Communist Party, stating that he considers the mobilization of Jewish youth for work in Donbas and the Urals incorrect, provocatively pointing out that Jewish girls were being used as prostitutes in the hinterland of the Soviet Union. At the same time Sherf attempted to compile lists of Jews in Chernovtsy who wish to emigrate from the USSR to America and Palestine."

Checking this information confirmed the anti-Soviet behavior of Sherf. It was also established that Sherf-Kon was not a member of the [Jewish] Antifascist Committee as the report had stated. Sherf-Kon arrived in the Soviet Union in 1932 from Poland. In 1938 Sherf was sentenced . . . to three years in a labor-correction camp on the charge of anti-Soviet activity.

Checking did not confirm information in the report about manifestations of Jewish nationalism on the part of citizen Brand and of serviceman Kovtun. Citizen Brand was found innocent by the military tribunal. Serviceman Kovtun was sentenced to five years for hooliganism and sent to the front.

Thus, of the report's information on nationalistic activity of individual representatives of the Jewish population, only three cases of nationalistic activity, those of the journalist Tokar' and the Yiddish writers Hofshtein and Sherf, were confirmed.

3. *On the Spreading of Provocative Rumors*

The report stated that recently in Kiev and some other cities of Ukraine provocative rumors have been circulating about the allegedly antisemitic policy of the government of the UkSSR and in this connection about imminent changes in the composition of the government. The report cited as purveyors of such rumors the writers Panch Ianovskii and Sukhodol'skii, TASS correspondent Povolotskii, the actor Astakhov, the white-collar workers of the UKOOPINSOVET Blomberg and Karpman, and worker . . . Litvak. Checking the statements established that:

(a) Writer Panch confirmed that in August of the present year the writer Ianovskii visited him and spoke about supposedly imminent changes in the composition of the government of the UkSSR in connection with the incorrect nationality policy in regard to the Jews, and that Ianovskii had heard this from the writer Sukhodol'skii.

(b) Writer Ianovskii did not deny the conversation with Panch but softened its content. He did confirm that the writer Sukhodol'skii had reported this conversation to him.

(c) Writer Sukhodol'skii in private conversation [with us], in the presence of Ianovskii, categorically denied a conversation on this topic with Ianovskii.

(d) Incidents of spreading provocative rumors by . . . Blomberg were confirmed. In conversation [with us] Blomberg stated that this conversation was reported to her by UKOOPINSOVET worker and former Communist Party member Karpman, who denied this incident. Blomberg and Karpman were

expelled from the Party and arrested by organs of the NKGB. Their case is being investigated.
(e) The actor Astakhov and the worker . . . Litvak denied spreading provocative rumors on this topic to anyone. There is no one else who might confirm these incidents.
(f) It was not possible to verify the information regarding TASS correspondent Povolotskii, who has been dispatched to the front. Thus, it has been established that provocative rumors about alleged imminent changes in the composition of the government of the UkSSR were heard by certain people and have been circulating since July of the current year, i.e., approximately from the time of the plenum of the Writers' Union in Kiev.

These rumors did not circulate widely and soon ceased. On the basis of the people and incidents mentioned in the NKGB report, we were not able to establish the sources of . . . these provocative rumors.

It should be noted that the NKGB did not react in time to the incidents of spreading provocative rumors and did not deal with uncovering their sources, but rather limited itself only to recording such rumors.

Conclusions

1. The special report sent to the central committee of the Communist Party (Bolsheviks) of Ukraine about the question of "antisemitic manifestations in Ukraine" based on random facts collected is basically incorrect and distorts the real attitudes of the population in Ukraine.
2. The materials of the NKGB which baselessly assert the existence of antisemitic manifestations in Ukraine and, moreover, their increase, basically reflect the attitudes of Zionist elements which have been circulating rumors about the existence of antisemitism in Ukraine as a political tendency, and even about the allegedly antisemitic policy of the government of the UkSSR.
3. The NKGB is not performing as required in uncovering German agents and organizations of Ukrainian nationalists who are attempting to sow ethnic strife and is also doing an unsatisfactory job of uncovering Zionist elements which have recently become active and even attempted to carry on organizational work.

In connection with the weakness of work in this regard, the NKGB turned out to have been ignorant of such incidents as the attempt of Zionist elements to organize a mass demonstration of the Jewish population in the city of Kiev on the anniversary of the massacre by the Germans in Babi Yar.
4. All these serious failures in the work of the NKGB are a result of the fact that the person who heads . . . operative intelligence-gathering on the intelligentsia, deputy head of the Second Department of the NKGB of the UkSSR Gersonskii (he was the author of the special report), insufficiently understands the political significance of the work entrusted to him and, going to extremes, has allowed political mistakes in his work.

5. Due to a lack of the required supervision over the work of the Second Department of the NKGB, People's Commissar of State Security Comrade Savchenko did not correct these defects in time but displayed too much confidence in Gersonskii and sent to the central committee of the Communist Party of Ukraine information which did not reflect the real situation.
6. Individual cases of antisemitic manifestations confirmed in the process of verification, as well as individual cases of nationalistic activity by members of the Jewish population, are random phenomena and do not characterize a mass phenomenon of this kind in Ukraine.
In order to put a decisive end to these incidents, the NKGB should not collect information on these questions but rather react as they arise and inform the central committee of the Communist Party of Ukraine about them in time.

Proposals

As a result of our investigation we believe it is necessary to:
1. Require the NKGB (Comrade Savchenko) to improve its work in uncovering and isolating German agents and organizations of Ukrainian nationalists who are attempting to stir up ethnic strife.
2. Require the NKGB (Comrade Savchenko) to improve its work in uncovering the activity of Zionist elements and putting a decisive halt to their organizational work. . . .
3. Order Comrade Savchenko to carry out an urgent investigation of the Zionist activity of the Yiddish writers Hofshtein and Sherf and of the journalist Tokar' and, in the event that organizational connections are proved, to isolate them.
4. Order the appropriate Party organization to discuss the question of manifestations of antisemitism on the part of E. K. Sezonenko, deputy director of the manpower registration and distribution office of the SICK UkSSR.
5. Require Comrade Savchenko:
(a) To remove from his post deputy director of the Second Department of the NKGB of the UkSSR Gersonskii. . . .
(b) Select and present for confirmation of the CC CPUk an appropriate candidate for the post of deputy director of the Second Department of the NKGB of the UkSSR for operative intelligence gathering on the intelligentsia.
6. Make clear to Comrade Savchenko that as a result of the lack of required supervision over the work of the 2nd administration and too great trust in its workers he presented to the CC CPUk information which did not conform to reality.
7. Order the Agitprop department of the CC CPUk to elaborate measures to strengthen the fight against remnants of German-fascist propaganda and propaganda of Ukrainian nationalists regarding the ethnic question in Ukraine.

[date illegible] November, 1944

Deputy director,
Department for Organization and Instruction,
Central Committee of the Communist Party of Ukraine
Alidin

Deputy director,
Personnel Department,
Central Committee of the Communist Party of Ukraine
Zhukovoskii

Deputy director,
Agitprop Department,
Central Committee of the Communist Party of Ukraine
Zolotaverkhii

Source: *Jews in Eastern Europe* 3(22), Winter 1993.

Appendix A

The Jews of Chernovtsy: Zelen'iuk's Report to Central Committee Secretary Khrushchev (April 30, 1944)

Excerpt: The Jewish Population

According to all types of investigation [among the Jews] there remained [alive] mainly those who curried favor with the Romanian authorities; the rest were craftsmen and professionals. The progressive part of the Jewish population was either killed off or exiled from Romanian territory. It is typical that all the Jews who previously worked in our Soviet institutions remained alive and unharmed, while this was absolutely not the case with other nationalities.

Zelen'iuk's Report to Khrushchev and Korotchenko (July 16, 1944)

Excerpt
Together with the actions of Ukrainian and German nationalists, there are manifestations of Zionist trends among the Jewish population, which are particularly pronounced in the city of Chernovtsy, where they comprise over half the total population.

In addition to the political awakening of the Jewish population, there are fairly clear manifestations of religious sentiments. Thus, the Chernovtsy Jewish community has been making strenuous efforts to open . . . a school for training rabbis, for 150 people, [specifically] for boys of thirteen to fourteen.

On the day when Chernovtsy *oblast'* was liberated from the Romanian and German occupiers, the Jewish population in the province was considerably smaller. Their number has increased by the addition of those who have come from the so-called Transnistria (to which the Germans and Romanians had exiled Jews from the cities and villages of Bukovina). During the second half of April and May they arrived in an unorganized manner, without permission, with the majority settling in the city of Chernovtsy, as well as in the Khotin and Storozhinetsk regions and other parts of the province.

Manifestations of Zionist trends among the Jewish population result from the fact that during the occupation of Chernovtsy *oblast'* (1941–1944) by the German and Romanian occupiers there was a significant increase in the activity of the Jewish nationalistic profascist youth organization Betar. This organization, headed by a Bucharest center of Zionist-revisionists, had as its goal the accumulation of means and cadres to establish their own Jewish national state, "Transjordan," [*sic*] headed by a dictatorship on the model of Italian fascism and the establishment . . . of its own . . . army, and preparations to settle in Transjordan all fourteen million Jews of the world.

During the occupation this organization waged the fiercest and particularly rabid anti-Soviet propaganda, openly aided the Romanian intelligence services, compiled lists of those who were unhappy with Romanian rule, of pro-Soviet people and Communists, and submitted them to the security police [*sekurantsa*] so that they would be liquidated.

The Romanian security police, who made considerable use of them, made it possible for this organization to exist and expand its influence among Jewish youth.

With the restoration of Soviet rule this year, the vast majority of the Jewish population which survived the Romanian occupation was engaged in private business, speculation, rifling and pillaging of abandoned apartments and houses, in every way possible avoiding socially useful labor. The Jews also, like citizens of other nationalities, [eventually] began to engage in socially useful labor, be mobilized into the Red Army, and also took part in the implementation of Soviet rule.

All this and, in particular, the engagement of Jews in labor activity and their mobilization into the Red Army, was viewed by many of them as "antisemitism" and "insult" on the part of the Soviet regime against an oppressed national minority. They allege that the Soviet government has altered its attitudes toward the Jews and that today's Soviets are not the same as those in 1940–41.

In this regard many Jews have started on the path of a direct fight against the Soviet regime, of spreading vile anti-Soviet slander, directing their efforts toward disruption of measures undertaken by the Soviet regime, calling upon Jews to go over to the side of the German and Romanian occupiers.

The following are several statements by individual Jews:

Dr. B. S Reznik, in a conversation with other Jews, stated:

> In connection with the mobilization of Jewish men into the Red Army and women into the work force. . . . People arriving from Transnistria thought that when they returned home they would be met warmly by the Soviet government, but on their arrival in Chernovtsy, they were immediately mobilized into the army.

Railway depot inspector of the Chernovtsy station Rugendorf said to his subordinates:

> I am struck by the actions of the Soviet government. Why are they acting so roughly with the population, mobilizing and sending them off without justification? It seems to me that there is an antisemite among our leaders and that he is responsible for such outrages. When the Germans were here, we were condemned to death, while at the present time when Soviet rule has come, we are administratively sentenced to long suffering.

There are statements about people leaving for Romania in order to avoid mobilization into the Red Army. A fire-brigade member named Feier [*sic*!] stated:

> In order to avoid being drafted into the Red Army and Soviet rule in general, I and my two acquaintances . . . intend to leave for Romania . . . change our names for Romanian ones since we know the Romanian language well. Life there is very good. They don't draft you into the Red Army, the draft affects only those who lived within the 1940 borders. . . .

In addition to the anti-Soviet slanderous provocative agitation, there are many cases when the Jewish population of draft age go[es] underground, prepare[s] false documents in order to disrupt measures of the Soviet authorities, and also engage[s] in profiteering and speculation by forging and selling false documents to the Jewish population. . . . There were cases of individuals attempting to give large bribes to representatives of Soviet organizations in order to avoid being drafted into the Red Army. . . . During the mobilization into the Red Army in . . . Chernovtsy, 1,853 Jews avoided the draft; 528 of those were arrested. The rest emigrated to Romania. . . .

Notes

*Originally published, in somewhat different form, in *Jews in Eastern Europe* 3(22), Winter 1993, pp. 40–81.

1. Here and elsewhere, words enclosed in angle brackets were added to the document.
2. Chernovtsy was under Romanian rule and more Jews were saved from the Holo-

caust there than in other areas of Ukraine. A report dated April 30,1944, from I. Zelen'iuk, the CP secretary of Chernovtsy *oblast'*, to Khrushchev stated that 17,341 (41.8 percent) of the residents of the city of Chernovtsy were Jews. In his report of July 16, 1944, Zelen'iuk wrote that 52,570 (7.7 percent) of the residents of the *oblast'* were Jewish. TDAGOU, T 1, op. 23, spr. 817, p. 4, and spr. 1057, p. 117. For Zelen'iuk's suspicious and hostile attitude toward Jewish war survivors, see passages from his reports in Appendix A.

3. The various testimonies about these incidents do not coincide. A Jew from Kharkov, who left the city in March, 1944 and reached Palestine in January, 1945, reported that in Kiev, "16 Jews were killed in the course of a pogrom which took place after the murder of a Russian officer by a Christian woman who was believed to be a Jew" (Joint Rescue Committee, Bulletin, March 1945, p. 2). Leon Leneman, without citing his source, tells of a pogrom in Kiev, in the spring of 1944 that began with a quarrel between a Jewish officer and a drunken Ukrainian officer who attacked the former with remarks like: "Where did you get all your medals and decorations? I bet you bought them in the market." When the Ukrainian attempted to rip off the Jew's decorations, the Jew shot him dead. The Jew then went straight to the militia, reported the incident, and was arrested. At once rumors spread through the city and assumed a vicious antisemitic character. The dead officer was given a splendid funeral attended by senior officials, with Khrushchev at their head. The pogrom began immediately after the funeral. Among its victims were the wife and baby of the arrested Jewish officer. Giorgii Malenkov was urgently dispatched to Kiev from Moscow to deal with the situation and restore order (L. Leneman, *La Tragedie des Juifs en URSS* [Paris, 1959], pp. 80–81). This description of events in Kiev seems unreliable, for the following reasons: 1) given Khrushchev's response to the memorandum from the head of the security services, it is unlikely that he would participate in a funeral of this nature; 2) if Malenkov really did come from Moscow to deal with the situation, the head of the security services would probably have mentioned this fact in his memorandum; 3) had the wife and child of the Jewish officer been killed, this would certainly have been mentioned in the memorandum; 4) the pogrom is attributed explicitly to Ukrainians, but there is no proof that Ukrainians constituted the only violent element against the Jews.

   The correspondent of the (London) *Jewish Chronicle* (Dec. 10, 1948, p. 11) wrote that immediately after the German evacuation, a pogrom took place in Kiev in which sixteen Jews were murdered. A Jewish member of a Polish farmers' delegation in 1949 reported that a Jewish tailor told him that "immediately after . . . the liberation [of Kiev] by the Red Army, . . . one Jew was killed by hooligans. . . . The incident was immediately investigated by Lazar Kaganovich, who was visiting the area at the time, and there have been no further attacks on Jews since" (*The Jewish Chronicle*, July 29, 1949). Given the pogrom climate that prevailed at the time, many rumors circulated and must be treated with utmost caution.

4. Moisei Spivak served as Communist Party secretary in the Zhitomir district at least until the beginning of 1948, when he was awarded the Order of Lenin (*Izvestiia*, Jan. 21, 1948).

5. At the request of the inquiry committee, E. Sezonenko submitted a signed deposition.

6. Responding to the charge that he did not hire Jews as waiters and chefs, Petr Basenko submitted to Zhukovskii, a member of the inquiry commission, a deposition that ignores the exclusion of Jews from these positions.
7. At the request of the inquiry commission, Kireev submitted a deposition.
8. The following was written about Khaim Tokar' at the time of anticosmopolitan struggle: "Khaim Tokar' belongs to the group of stooges of the UTO [Ukrainian Theater Association]. In his day, this rootless cosmopolitan sang praises to bourgeois nationalists who were enemies of the Soviet people, i.e., Kurbas and Meyerhold. Tokar' has still not changed his positions." A. L. Dmiterko, "Sostoianie i zadachi teatral'noi i literaturnoi kritiki na Ukraine" (The State and Tasks of Theater and Literary Criticism in Ukraine), *Literaturnaia gazeta*, March 9, 1949.
9. Mikola Bazhan (1904–1983), Soviet Ukrainian poet. From 1943 to 1949 he served as deputy prime minister of Ukraine.
10. Itzik Fefer (1900–1952), Soviet Yiddish poet. During the civil war he volunteered for the Red Army, and during the Denikin regime he was active in the underground in Ukraine. In 1919 he began publishing poems sympathetic to the Communist Party, of which he was a member. . . . He was arrested (in 1948) and executed (in 1952) along with the other leading lights of the Jewish Anti-Fascist Committee.
11. Fefer was in Kiev in June 1944, during the plenary session of the Writers' Union of Ukraine, which both he and David Hofshtein addressed. (See *Einikayt*, July 6, 1944.)
12. In mid-1943, Itzik Fefer and Shlomo Mikhoels visited the United States on behalf of the Jewish Anti-Fascist Committee.
13. Clearly, we may doubt the accuracy of the remarks Fefer is supposed to have made about the United States. Praising the United States as superior to the Soviet Union would have been an extremely parlous venture; it is not likely that Fefer, with his acute political sense, would express opinions of this sort, especially in the presence of someone not known as his close friend. Particularly doubtful are the remarks attributed to Fefer about Zionism, which was considered a reactionary movement to be vigorously opposed. It may be that we have here the incipient traces of the plot woven by the security services, or some of its members, against the Yiddish authors in the Soviet Union. In any case, the inclusion of Fefer's name and the attribution of such injudicious statements to him warrants further study.
14. There is some likelihood that Fefer might have made remarks in this vein, although not necessarily as presented here. At the time, the Jewish Anti-Fascist Committee and Itzik Fefer personally were associated with the proposal to allocate the Crimean Peninsula to Jewish settlement and the establishment of a Soviet Jewish republic. For more on this, see S. Redlich, "The Crimean Affair," *Jews and Jewish Topics in the Soviet Union and Eastern Europe* 2(12) (1990), pp. 55–65.
15. Vyacheslav Molotov (1890–1986), a member of the Communist Party from 1906, one of the secretaries of its Central Committee in 1921–30, prime minister of the Soviet Union, 1930–41. In 1941–47, he served as first deputy premier and, in parallel, in 1941–45 as deputy chairman of the State Defense Committee.

16. Shlomo Mikhoels (1890–1948), the outstanding actor of the Moscow Jewish Theater and its director from 1929. During the war he headed the Jewish Anti-Fascist Committee. He was murdered by the Soviet security services in Minsk.
17. Although we have no direct evidence, a meeting of this sort may have taken place. Molotov's response sounds plausible in the context of Soviet policy at the end of the war. After meeting with the director of the Agitprop Department, who was a member of the inquiry commission, Khaim Tokar' submitted a written deposition.
18. Isaiah Shkaravoskii (1891–1945) began his journalistic career in the Russian press in 1909. From 1915 he also published in the Yiddish press. He wrote stories, novels, and critical articles.
19. Alexander Shcherbakov (1901–1945), first secretary of the Moscow Party *gorkom* (city committee) and *obkom* (provincial committee) from 1938, secretary of the Central Committee candidate member of the Politburo (from 1941). He was head of the Main Political Administration (GPU) of the Red Army from 1942.
20. Ilya Ehrenburg (1891–1967), Soviet Russian author of Jewish origin, whose prolific output included much on Jewish themes. During World War II he was active in gathering testimonies about the Holocaust and fought against manifestations of antisemitism in the Soviet Union.
21. David Hofshtein. See below, n. 38.
22. Naftali Hertz Kon (1910–1971) was born in Bukovina. He published his first Yiddish poems in the newspaper *Tshernovitser bleter* in 1929. On account of his Communist activities he fled to Poland, only to be arrested there. In 1932 he was expelled to the Soviet Union as part of an exchange of Communist activists. In that country he published works in Yiddish anthologies. In 1937 he was arrested and was not freed until the beginning of the Soviet-German war. In 1948 he was again arrested and sentenced to twenty-five years. He was released from the gulag in 1956. In 1959 he emigrated to Poland. Due to a lack of caution on his part, he was arrested there, too, and sent to prison for several years. In 1965 he arrived in Israel and died in Jerusalem. Because of his various wanderings and arrests, he went by a number of different family names; the name Sherf (which sometimes appears in the documents as Sher) mentioned here is apparently one of these.
23. Brand was court-martialed but acquitted.
24. *Soiuz russkogo naroda* (Union of the Russian People) was a stridently antisemitic political organization established at the end of 1905. Its newspaper, *Russkoe znamia*, called for pogroms against the Jews.
25. Kovtun was sentenced to five years in prison, commuted to combat duty at the front.
26. Andrei Zhdanov (1896–1948), first secretary of the Leningrad Party *obkom* (1934–1944), candidate member of the Politburo of the Central Committee (from 1935), Party ideologist on questions of culture, and at one time considered to be Stalin's heir apparent.
27. Iurii Ianovskii (1902–1954), Ukrainian poet and author, published his first poems in Russian in 1922. In 1924 he began writing prose in Ukrainian, and later wrote poetry, stories, novels, and plays in both languages. During the war he served as a military correspondent and was present at the Nuremberg Trials. A collection

of his articles on the trials was published in 1946. He was condemned in the 1946 Communist Party resolutions against the literary journal *Znamia*. He was a member of the executive of the Union of Writers in Ukraine.

28. Because Panch's name had been linked with the rumor of Khrushchev's replacement, the inquiry commission asked him about the opinions he had expressed concerning Jews. In this context he submitted two handwritten depositions on the same day.

29. Vladimir Sukhodol'skii (1889–1962), Soviet-Ukrainian playwright, whose first play was published in 1930. During the war, he wrote short one-acters. A number of his plays were made into movies.

30. On September 25, 1944, at the request of Alidin, the deputy director of the Organization Department of the Central Committee of the Ukrainian Communist Party and a member of the inquiry commission on antisemitism, Ianovskii submitted a deposition.

31. After Sarah Blomberg was interrogated by the inquiry commission, she drafted two statements on the same day, evidently at the behest of the investigators, which differ in both phrasing and some particulars. Despite these depositions, Blomberg was arrested and interrogated by the security services.

32. Leonid Korniets (1901–1969) was chairman of the Presidium of the Supreme Soviet of the Soviet Union from 1938, and from 1939 was prime minister of Ukraine. During the war he helped organize the partisan movement in Ukraine. In 1943, he received the rank of lieutenant general. When Khrushchev was appointed prime minister of Ukraine, in addition to his post as secretary of the Communist Party in that republic, Korniets was appointed first deputy prime minister of Ukraine.

33. For Davydov's statement, see Appendix 8 (in the original source).

34. After Rakhel Karpman was expelled from the Party, she appealed to the Kiev Party *gorkom* as well as to the Central Committee of the Communist Party of Ukraine.

35. In Document 1, "Footware Factory No. 8." (in original).

36. In Document 1, "Kryzhanovskii."

37. See Appendix B 4 (in original).

38. David Hofshtein (1889–1952) received a traditional Jewish education and studied Hebrew and Russian with private tutors. At an early age he began writing poems in Hebrew and later switched to Yiddish. His poems were first published in 1917. In 1924 he emigrated to Berlin and from there proceeded to Palestine in early 1925, before returning to the Soviet Union in 1926. In the Soviet Union he belonged for a while to the Union of Proletarian Writers, but left it in 1929. His many volumes of Yiddish poetry garnered critical praise. During the war he was evacuated to Ufa and returned to Kiev in 1944. Arrested on September 18,1948, he was executed following the trial of the leaders of the Jewish Anti-Fascist Committee, on August 12, 1952.

39. We have failed to locate any information on Hofshtein's work in the Jewish Department of the Rada. But he was active at that time in the Kultur Lige, that department's executive arm for culture.

40. It is not clear which Vilna newspaper is being referred to.
41. In 1922–24, five issues of the literary journal *Shtrom*, of which Hofshtein was one of the editors, appeared in Moscow. The periodical supported the October revolution, but its unwillingness to place literature at the service of the Communist Party was attacked by the newspaper *Der Emes*.
42. During Hofshtein's stay in Palestine (1925–26), he published in the Hebrew press.

Contributors

Mordechai Altshuler is Professor of Contemporary Jewish Studies and director of the Centre for Research and Documentation of East European Jewry, Hebrew University of Jerusalem.

Shalom Cholawski received his doctorate from Hebrew University. He is the author of several books on the Holocaust in Belarus and a member of Kibbutz Ein Hashofet. He participated in the uprising in the Nesvizh (Nieswiez) ghetto, Poland/Belarus.

Zvi Gitelman is Professor of Political Science, Preston R. Tisch Professor of Judaic Studies, and director of the Frankel Center for Judaic Studies at the University of Michigan, Ann Arbor. His publications include *A Century of Ambivalence: The Jews in Russia and the Soviet Union, 1881 to the Present.*

Mykhailo I. Koval is a Senior Member, Institute of History, Ukrainian Academy of Sciences, and a member of the editorial board of the *Ukrainian Historical Journal*, Kiev.

Yosef Litvak received a doctorate from Hebrew University. Now retired, he was formerly research associate of the Institute of Contemporary Jewry, Hebrew University of Jerusalem.

Michael MacQueen is a research associate at the Office of Special Investigations, United States Department of Justice, Washington, D.C.

Shimon Redlich is Solly Yelin Professor of Lithuanian and East European Jewish History, Ben Gurion University, Beer Sheva, Israel. He is editor of *War, Holocaust, and Stalinism.*

Daniel Romanovsky, a native of the USSR, is a research associate at Yad Vashem Institute, Jerusalem.

Sara Shner-Neshamit is a member of Kibbutz Bet Lokhamei Hagetaot. She conducts research on the Holocaust.

Shmuel Spector is a former senior researcher at Yad Vashem Institute, Jerusalem. He is author of many works on the Holocaust in Ukraine.

Hans-Heinrich Wilhelm, Berlin, has published several books on the military history of World War II and on the role of the Wehrmacht in the Holocaust.

Sima Ycikas is a research associate of the Centre for Research and Documentation of East European Jewry, Hebrew University, Jerusalem.

Index